Ralph Martin served as consultant for the ABC Television series on Winston Churchill. He has written several books, including *Man of the Century: Churchill*.

LADY RANDOLPH CHURCHILL

A Biography

Volume Two: 1895–1921

Ralph G. Martin

CARDINAL edition published in 1974
by Sphere Books Ltd
30/32 Gray's Inn Road, London WC1X 8JL

First published in Great Britain by
Cassell & Company Ltd in 1972
Copyright © Ralph G. Martin 1971

Set in Lectura

Printed in Great Britain by
Hazell Watson & Viney Ltd
Aylesbury, Bucks

ISBN 0 351 17327 7

This book is dedicated with love to my wife Marjorie Jean. She was part of this work, from the very inception of the idea. She spent countless hours deciphering the almost-illegible handwriting of hundreds of Jennie's letters, collected from dozens of sources. She spent uncounted weeks in the library of the British Museum searching out varied references in magazines, books, manuscripts. She accompanied me on many of my interviews, remembering things that my tape recorder had not caught and my eyes had overlooked. She examined each draft of the manuscripts of both volumes, commenting on them in great detail with excellent criticism and expert editing. She is therefore truly a deep part of both volumes. Were it not for her, the work would have taken much more than seven years. But, above all, these books are buoyed with her spirit, as I am.

CONTENTS

LIST OF ILLUSTRATIONS

ACKNOWLEDGEMENTS

I am deeply indebted to a great many people, a large number of whom were similarly helpful with the first volume of this biography: William Heinemann Ltd for their kindness in granting permission to quote from letters in the various volumes of the biography of Winston S. Churchill by Randolph S. Churchill, as well as the Companion Volumes. I further appreciate the generous help of their staff in the correction of dates and text; British historian Martin Gilbert, who has succeeded Randolph S. Churchill as the author of this distinguished biography – his advice and help have been most important to me.

Also Peregrine Churchill, who very generously allowed me to quote from Jennie's published and unpublished letters – as well as his father's letters – whose copyright he controls. He also made available to me his large collection of his grandmother's letters, some photographs, and – most important – revealed his own memories and anecdotes; the Duke of Marlborough, who graciously permitted me to examine and copy a trunkful of letters and documents written by Jennie, in the Muniments Room of Blenheim Palace; Mrs Oswald Frewen, who so kindly permitted me to examine the private diary of her husband, who was Jennie's nephew; C & T Publications Ltd, for permission to quote from the letter written by Winston Churchill about his mother's death; Lady Altrincham, for a most pleasant afternoon of reminiscence about Jennie, and the photograph she gave me; Baroness Cedestrom, Jennie's niece, and Lady Betty Cartwright, also for sharing with me their vivid memories; Prince Clary of Venice and Countess Kinsky in London, who helped so much in making Charles Kinsky come alive for me; British historian and author John Grigg, for helping me with advice, and finding an important letter; the Executors of the late Sir Allen Lane, who so generously made available to me the full file of John Lane's correspondence with Jennie concerning the *Anglo-Saxon Review*; Michael Rhodes, British historian at University College, who pinpointed the material for me and amplified it with his own broad research in the area; the Marquess of Bath, who freely permitted me to examine his vast Churchill library and make copies of various letters and documents; Mrs Hadley Hucker in Glastonbury, who talked to me at length about her dear friend, Montagu Porch, Jennie's third husband; Allen Andrews, the distinguished British author and historian, for helping me in so many ways with advice and contacts, even to the extent of enlisting his wife Joyce to write inquiries for me in Italian; Jo and Michael Wybrow who helped me canvass their own Churchill library – one of the best private Churchill libraries in England – and who also found for me some magazine articles by Jennie which were otherwise unavailable; C. H. N. Hamilton-Miller Esq. of Austin & Bath, Montagu Porch's solicitors in Glastonbury, who gave me much background and many contacts; Porch's physician, Dr Tom A. Pinniger, in Bath; the Viscountess de Soveral in Lisbon, for permitting free access to and use of the papers of the Marquis de Soveral, and even making available some photographs; Doctor J. M. Villas Boas and Doctor Deixeira da Motta of the Portuguese Embassy in London; Lady Kinnaird, who has written so well of this period and who gave me so graciously of her time; the Marquis Henri-François de Breteuil in Paris, who opened up his family archives to provide his grandfather's papers for my use; Thomas R. Campbell, Secretary of the United States Lines, who became intrigued with this project and searched and found the minutes and records of the transaction providing for the gift of the *Maine* as a hospital ship; Jean-Hervé Donnard, Cultural Consul at the French Embassy in New York, who was most helpful in many ways; Miss C. M. Wyatt and Miss Doris Rush of the British Red Cross Society; the staff of the General Nursing Council in London; the Croix Rouge Française in Paris; Dr Rebecca Rainsbury of *The British Medical Journal*; Wayne C. Grover of the National Archives in Washington, D.C.; Miss Hallett, of Frederick Warne & Co., who spent much time in finding the one copy of the privately printed booklet about the Shakespeare Ball, for which I am indeed grateful; Miss A. J. Fraser, who was especially patient with me in my searches at the Public Record Office in London; my friend Kenneth Parker at Cassell & Co., who was most important in locating people and in offering suggestions and needed criticisms; and Miss Laura James, who took time and trouble with my questions at the British Information Service in New York.

My gratitude to a number of people in different countries who followed up my research: Mrs Ann Ebner in England; Mme Barbara Wollak,

Mrs Louise Spicehandler, and Aline Mosby in France; Robert Neville, Al Hine and Grace Donini, in Italy; D. A. Kirkby in Lisbon. A special note of thanks to Henry Ebner for researching some important legal documents in England.

My appreciation also to the staffs of a number of libraries: particularly the Manuscript Room and Library of the British Museum and its Newspaper Library at Colindale; the New York Public Library, especially to John Philip Baker for providing me with the marvellous facilities of the Frederick Lewis Allen Room; the New York Public Library Berg Collection, and to the curator, Dr Lola Szladits, who gave me the benefit of her vast knowledge of their large collection of letters of Pearl Craigie and Edward Marsh; the Manuscript Room of the New York Public Library, which has the papers of Bourke Cockran so invaluable to this book; and the New York Public Library Picture Collection, especially Mrs Lenore Cowan, Mrs Mildred Prause, Miss Marion Weithorn, Mrs Sylvia Kronish, and Romana Javitz, its past Director; Raffaele Vacca of the Archivio Principe Colonna in Rome; the Maritime Museum Library in Greenwich, England; Lt-Colonel H. N. Ingles, acting librarian at Longleat, England; Jennifer Aylmer at the British Theatre Museum Library; Mrs Mollie Travis, archivist at the Broadlands Library in England; G. Acloque, archivist of the Duke of Westminster's library; Anthony Latham of the Gabrielle Enthoven Collection at the Victoria & Albert Museum; Timothy Beard of the Genealogical Room at the New York Public Library who helped in this volume, as he did in the previous one, by making clear to me complicated genealogies; Mrs Mary Hirth, Librarian at the University of Texas; the staff of the University College Library in London; T. H. Kelly, Librarian at the London *Daily News*; the staff of the National Register of Archives in London; and the Westminster Library — all deserve my thanks. So does Mrs Carol Cronkhite, head of the Microfilm Section of the Photographic Service at the New York Public Library for providing me with access to special material. My thanks too, to Mason Tolman, Associate Librarian, and Ida M. Cohen, Senior Librarian of the New York State Library.

As always, I am grateful and indebted to the staff of the Oyster Bay Public Library, and its Director, Richard N. Powdrell. My special appreciation goes to Mrs Christine Lane, who not only makes sure that I get the books and materials I need, but also quietly offers her own valuable suggestions. My gratitude, too, to Mrs Carmine F. Mecedonio, Mrs Dorothea C. Hosom, John F. Moak and Mrs Laura Lucchesi.

To Mrs Mari Walker, I owe much, because she is the one who had the unwelcome job of translating my cluttered changes and corrections, my tape recordings, my varied notes into clean manuscript copy. My thanks, too, to her husband Dick for his help, in so many ways. For emergency typing, I am grateful to Mrs Harriet Carlin, Lucia Saccente, and Maria Makroulakis.

For the photographs in this book, I give appreciative credit to the British Museum, the Picture Collection of the New York Public Library, the Library of Congress. Mrs Shirley Green in Washington, D.C., is one of the best picture historians and researchers I know and was invaluable to me. Her background knowledge is immense and her taste is perfect. Milton Kaplan at the Library of Congress also deserves my thanks for his help. In London, Mrs Zena Fry was instrumental in finding pictures I needed, and my good friend John Byrne assisted ably in this.

I particularly want to thank Mr and Mrs Bert Vail, two very dear people, who were kind enough to let me have the portrait of Jennie, shown on the book cover. It was drawn by Mrs Vail's uncle, George Tobin.

For a variety of help and information, my thanks to: Russell Bryant, Mrs Vineta Colby, Stan Swinton, Andrew A. Rooney, Ed Antrobus, Miriam Stern, Ed Plaut, David Dilks, the Reverend James Richards, David Karr, Edward D. McDougal, Sir Archibald James, Violet Pym, Ed Hoyt, Arthur Leonard Ross, Madeleine Clarke, Elizabeth Collins, Capt. George Brodrick, David Lewin, John Ryder, Douglas Plummer, Penny Redmond, Mrs Nina Wallace, Herman Cohen, Alan Dent, Sir Christopher Armstrong Cowan, Kay Halle, Jack Fawcett of the London *Daily Express*, Mrs Hope Roberts and the LuJon Beauty Salon which provided her with some important magazines for my use. My gratitude also to Dr Harvey Pastel and his wife Jane, and Dr Robert Pastel and his wife Bea.

I thank my good friends who were always available for any help I needed, particularly Paul and Shirley Green, Lionel and Pearlie Bernier, John and Harriet Weaver, Howard Byrne, head of the Mayflower Studios in London who provided me with space and staff and facilities during my long stays in London. My dear sister Naomi arrived with her husband Stanley Van Clair and my niece Joyce to help at a critical time in the proof-reading. So did my dear friends and neighbours: Irma Remsen; the Moonelis family, Jerry, Goldie, Judy, and Carol; my niece Mary

Pastel; and Richard Christian Scapicchio; and Mrs Betty Copithorne, a most talented editor. My special thanks to my tried and true friends Ruth and Larry Hall, who gave up part of their vacation to help with the final corrections on the page proofs of this book. My three children, Maury, Betsy, and Tina, helped in a variety of ways.

These two volumes might never have been published had it not been for the initial decision and aggressive determination of Eugene Rachlis, then Editor-in-Chief at Prentice-Hall. He accepted the idea of two volumes after many editors had refused to consider it. I thank publisher Bill Eastman for believing in the idea and for supporting Gene in the project, and I will always be grateful to my friend Knox Burger for suggesting that I present this project to Gene Rachlis.

My working editor on both volumes was Cecile Grossman, and she deserves considerable credit for helping to give the final shape to the books. She is an editor of taste and wisdom, great perception, and even greater patience. It was a pleasure to work with her. And to Phil Rosenberg, the copy-editor on both books, who caught and corrected so many necessary things, my appreciation. I am also grateful to Barbara Palumbo and especially to Dorothy Lachmann, who was so helpful and patient during the last round of editing changes.

I am especially grateful to Eileen Quelch for allowing me to make generous use of material from *Edwardian Hey-Days*, by George Cornwallis-West, the copyright of which she owns. Miss Quelch has written the biography of George Cornwallis-West, which is published by Cecil & Amelia Woolf under the title *Perfect Darling*.

A final word of gratitude must go to Sterling Lord, who is not only my literary agent – and one of the best in the business – but, more importantly, my friend.

I

For Jennie, the year 1895 began bitter and bleak. After a lingering illness, her husband had died of syphilis, raving mad. Only weeks before, her lover, unwilling to wait any longer, had married.[1] Her sons Winston and Jack both had problems that required her full attention.

Physically and emotionally, she felt drained.

Was it any wonder? She had taken a maniacal husband on a year-long world tour to keep him out of trouble at home, and his final illness had been prolonged and excruciatingly painful. 'You would have thought it was some wild animal,' Jennie's elder sister Clara wrote to her husband, describing Lord Randolph Churchill's terrible groans.[2]

The deathbed scene took place at the London home of Randolph's mother, the Dowager Duchess of Marlborough. She and her daughters never left Jennie alone with Randolph for a moment, '. . . all of them criticizing every word she says, everything she does . . . it is positive torture. . . . I sometimes think that if it isn't soon over she will soon go mad herself.'

When Jennie's younger sister Leonie reported to her that the doctors did not think Randolph would live through the day, Jennie herself had reached the point of near hysteria and 'burst out *laughing*'.

'. . . Poor, poor little Jane,' Clara wrote to her husband, 'when I think of the future, I shudder for her. . . .'[3]

'Man is justified by the greatness of his acts,' it is written in the Koran, 'but woman, through the magnitude of her illusions.' What were Jennie's illusions?

She had none about her husband's death. It was a relief and a blessing. She had done all her mourning and paid her penance many years before.

Nor did she have illusions about her financial security. Lord Randolph Henry Spencer Churchill left an estate whose gross value was £75,971, but much of it was needed to pay off his debts. Of the remaining portion,

17

most of it was in trust funds for their two sons. Lord Randolph's last will and testament allowed Jennie a slim legacy of £500 plus all their 'horses, carriages, plate, linen, china, glass, books, pictures, prints, furniture and other household effects'.[4]

To make matters worse, as Clara explained to her husband, the fact that Randolph had died before his mother meant that the Duchess was free to leave the family money to whomsoever she pleased, 'and she isn't likely to befriend Jennie, whom she doesn't like, or the boys, whom she never liked either'.[5]

But nothing had shattered Jennie's illusions and darkened her future more than the sudden marriage of the man she had loved most, Charles Rudolf Andreas Kinsky. Jennie had once written that Count Kinsky was 'like opium' for her. A young Austrian diplomat of noble lineage, he was extraordinarily handsome, with the kind of good looks that won a woman without his making any effort. A brilliant young man, he wrote books about international diplomacy; musically talented, he played the piano excellently. He was charming, with old-world manners but a modern wit. Above all, he was a spectacular horseman and a national hero in Great Britain, the first foreigner to have won the Grand National on his own horse. And he was in love with Jennie, desperately so.

Theirs was a fiery, intense love, lasting as long as they lived. Kinsky had begged Jennie to leave her husband and marry him, but she felt she could not abandon Randolph when he needed her most. Long afterwards, Jennie's nephew noted what a marvellous stepfather Kinsky would have been to Winston and how close and warm the relationship between young Winston and his mother's lover had been.[6] Winston so admired Kinsky that only two weeks after his own father's death he wrote to his brother Jack at Harrow: 'I should very much like that picture of Count Kinsky on Zoedone [his Grand National winner] – very much. . . . If you send it down here, I will pay you a sovereign for it. . . .'[7]

Kinsky might have waited for Jennie, but he was subject to enormous pressure from his father, Prince Kinsky. The Prince was one of Austria's great landowners of aristocratic stock that traced back through hundreds of years. He objected strenuously to Jennie because she was not of noble lineage, because she was not Catholic, but, most of all, because she was then forty years old and therefore unlikely to produce an heir. The Prince's candidate for his son was the young Countess Elizabeth Wolff-Metternich, who had all of the required qualifications.

The Prince also had powerful leverage: he was the source of his son's lavish allowance, which was always quickly spent. And so, out of combined despair and pressure, Kinsky agreed to marry the Countess Elizabeth.

'I hate it!' Jennie wrote to her sister Clara upon hearing the announcement. As for Count Kinsky, although his marriage put a great gulf between himself and Jennie, it never dampened his love for her. At his death many years later, the one picture found hanging over his desk was a portrait of Jennie.[8]

So here was Jennie, with the man who had loved her most now married to someone else, little money and not even a home of her own. She had once said in a note to Clara, 'Your life is not couleur de rose. Whose is?'

And yet, such was the inner resource and resilience of this woman that her life soon took on an excitement and vitality such as she had never dreamed of. As her friend Lady Curzon said in a letter to her: 'You are the only person who lives on the crest of a wave.'[9]

That she lived on the crest of a wave was certainly true, and to do so she had to rely upon two of her most fundamental traits: her courage and her drive. The result was a vital force that was seldom smothered. It could be blunted or stalled, but never obliterated.

She seemed to have, deep within her, a feeling of exhilaration for all the unknown things to come, a sense of adventure. Her determination was strengthened whenever she faced crises in her life – and they often came in succession. These were qualities she passed on to her son Winston. 'Never give in,' Winston later told the boys at Harrow, 'never, never, never, never, in nothing great or small, large or petty – never give in except to the convictions of honour and good sense.'[10] That could have been Jennie speaking.

Certainly it would take more than a lack of funds to stop her. She still had the annual $10,000 (almost £4,000) from the rental of her family's home on Madison Square in New York City.[11] For a woman in upper-class British society with two young sons, however, that was very little income. But she had somehow managed before, and she would manage again.

She was a woman of superb taste who appreciated the best and recognized it when she saw it – whether it was in clothes or books or furniture or men. She was a woman of such high style that one felt that she was meant to have money. And yet she never really did. The amazing thing was that essentially this did not matter.

What else could Jennie's future lack besides money? Friends? Never. Tolstoi had written in his diary in 1853: 'The means to gain happiness is to throw out from oneself like a spider in all directions an adhesive web of love, and to catch in it all that comes.' An adhesive web of love was Jennie's great gift. It was instinctive in everything she did, and it drew women as well as men to her. This was part of the reason for her effectiveness in political campaigns, in fund-raising, in organizing. She had more than charisma; there was a kind of radiation from within her so full of warmth and sincerity that it reached almost everyone she met. Two generations after her death, a woman whose life she had touched only tangentially would say with a glisten in her eyes, 'I *loved* her.' [12]

Shortly after her death a British magazine tried to describe all of Jennie's qualities:

Beauty and brains, wealth and social position are admirable things, but they would not of themselves have won for Lady Randolph Churchill her pre-eminence among the women of her time. . . . To be greater than one's peers is not possible without personality of the outstanding type. . . . It may be magnetism, it may be charm, it may be strength of will, it may be vitality, it may be arrogance of temper, it may be supreme sweetness of disposition, it may be the ability to smile or to frown at the right time or in the right place. Tact may have something to do with it, foresight may be a help, belief in oneself counts for something, a certain ruthlessness comes in useful, perhaps. . . . [13]

In 1895 a new era was beginning which called for all these qualities. Queen Victoria was in her last years, and much of the old magnificence that had been associated with her reign was now in decline. Aristocrats no longer commanded sweeping social power. Dynamic wealth was creating its own aristocracy, capturing Park Lane. The new aristocracy was described by some as 'a religion of gold'.[14] Even in the days of James I, in the early seventeenth century, £10,000 could buy a barony.[15] Benjamin Disraeli described how the younger Pitt, in the eighteenth century, 'created a plebeian aristocracy and blended it with the patrician oligarchy. He made peers of second-rate squires and fat graziers. He caught them in the alleys of Lombard Street, and clutched them from the counting-houses of Cornhill.' [16]

'There is no country where so much absolute homage is paid to wealth,' wrote Ralph Waldo Emerson about England.[17]

'It is not fair to say that they were wholly wrapped up in materialism, and the pursuit of wealth,' countered Herbert Asquith. 'But it took a great deal to make them realize that they might be paying too high a price for capturing the markets of the world in a system of production which crippled and stunted and decimated the women and children of the country.' [18]

The British Empire extended over twelve million square miles around the world and was by far the strongest power.[19] Yet a scullery maid in London would earn about twenty-three pounds a year,[20] and the law allowed women factory workers to add three nights to their six-day week. What is more, with the average working woman expected to experience ten pregnancies, child labour was considered necessary to help support large families. For children under five, the death rate in industrial Birmingham was 95·6 per thousand.[21] Even years later, over twelve million people in the country were living on the verge of constant hunger and 'in the grip of perpetual poverty'.[22] Human beings were still cheap.

It was the Golden Age, though, for the rapidly-growing moneyed middle class, and it was no longer easy to answer the question: Who rules Britain? It was certainly not the 150 great families. Tory gentility could no longer hand down an undiminished tradition, and along with their power went some of the British pomp and plush. Gone, too, were the carriage flunkeys whose overcoats swept to their feet, and the boyish grooms with cockaded hats and white breeches. And going rapidly were more and more of the magnificent mansions.

The Victorian age had made its mark. It had created or nurtured many British institutions – public schools, the professional civil service, military regiments, political parties, universities – and it had given the British a sense of stability and supremacy. British constitutional government was a model for the world. But the world was changing.

The new era also brought a new Prime Minister. At the age of eighty-five, the distinguished William Gladstone had resigned after sixty-one historic years in politics and government. His successor could scarcely have been more of a contrast. Lord Rosebery was the Prince Charming of politics. Everything came easily to him, perhaps too easily. 'I think

Lord Rosebery would have had a better nervous system and been a happier man if he had not been so rich', wrote his friend Margot Asquith. 'Riches are overestimated in the Old Testament: the good and successful man received too many animals, wives, apes, she-goats and peacocks.' [23]

It was a pertinent point. Rosebery had reputedly told a friend at Eton that he had three great ambitions: to marry an heiress, to win the Derby, and to become Prime Minister. He married not only an heiress, but a Rothschild; his horse won the Derby not once but three times; and he became Prime Minister without having to fight for it – the Queen personally chose him for the post. 'Only Heaven left', telegraphed his American friend, the railroad magnate Chauncey Depew.[24]

But the nineties were a pleasure-loving time, and Rosebery was a pleasure-loving man. The Prime Minister's job required too much work to suit his taste – he likened it to 'riding a horse without reins'.

'There are two supreme pleasures in life,' Rosebery said, 'the one ideal, the other real. The ideal is when a man receives the seals of office from his Sovereign. The real pleasure comes when he hands them back.' [25] Jennie understood all this about Rosebery because they had known each other well for many years. They shared a love of politics, horses, literature and new ideas.

'Ideas were in the air', wrote Richard Le Gallienne in his study of this exciting decade. 'People . . . were convinced that they were passing not only from one social system to another, from one morality to another, and from one religion to a dozen or none. . . . Our new-found freedom seemed to find just the expression it needed in the abandoned nonsense-chorus of "Ta-ra-ra-boom-de-ay. . . ." '[26]

The 'Elegant Eighties' had become the 'Naughty Nineties'. It was a time of growing contempt for old ideas, of willingness to challenge tradition and taboos, of a rather upstart arrogance. People were more fun-seeking, more emotional, more gregarious. It was a testing time for power in every area of society, from business and politics to social relations. It was a time when people thought anything could happen, that convention was a cage you broke out of in order to live your own life in your own way.

'Not to be new in these days is to be nothing', wrote H. D. Traill in an essay on 'The New Fiction'. Magazines were filled with articles on everything new: The New Realism, The New Voluptuousness, The New Spirit, The New Woman.[27]

Jennie had been the new woman long before it became fashionable.

She had little interest in such fads as microbe farming, which involved the bizarre practice of displaying such exotic germs as 'a lovely purple cholera' in test tubes at afternoon teas.[28] But she had been one of the first to free herself from the armour-like corset, and her house had been the first in London to use electric lighting.[29]

But, even more significantly, Jennie believed in the kind of new woman recommended by George Bernard Shaw:

> ... unless you do something in the world, you can have no real business to transact with men; and unless you love and are loved, you can have no intimate relations with them. And you must transact business, wire-pull politics, discuss religion, give and receive hate, love and friendship with all sorts of people before you can acquire the sense of humanity. . . .[30]

As a 'new woman', Jennie would have been 'as unsuitable as possible for a bishop's wife or the president of the YWCA', her nephew noted. 'She saw no need for Victorian humility or modesty.'[31]

Or hypocrisy, either. English society had been well aware of the romance between Jennie and the Prince of Wales. Its peak had passed, but some of the emotion was still alive, ready to be stirred. Of course, for the Prince there had always been others, many others. He was deservedly well publicized as 'a professional lovemaker'.[32] The Prince usually disassociated himself from his mistresses when his affairs with them ended, but with Jennie it was different. Unlike the women who told him only what he wanted to hear, Jennie always spoke her own mind, whatever the subject. The Prince was not a man of profound intellect, but he respected those who had it, particularly women. They intrigued and stimulated him.

In 1895, Albert Edward, the Prince of Wales, was fifty-four years old and portly, the picture of opulence. A heavy-lidded man, with protruding eyes, a sensual mouth, and an elegant beard, he was usually seen smoking an enormous cigar. Rudyard Kipling called him 'a corpulent voluptuary'. But his overfed body was always superbly attired, and he was still a vigorous man with an air of geniality and a certain charm and flair.

He liked the lavish show, the morning hunt, the good joke, the pretty ankle and the uses of power. Jennie had a significant and lasting influence on him because he respected her judgment. He also knew he could

23

rely on her. If he wanted a small private party arranged, he often asked her to organize the guest list and to decide on the menu. Jennie knew his particular friends as well as his favourite foods. She knew what kind of music he liked. She knew the level of his impatience and boredom, the danger point of his anger, and how to cope with them. In return, he was lavish in his gifts and in his open affection for her.

Certainly nobody could have been more solicitous than the Prince during her husband's last days and after his death. He sent her a steady flow of notes: 'Should you wish to see me, I could call at five tomorrow.' And he often turned up to spend a consoling hour with her.

During the previous years the tone of their correspondence had been circumspect. He was, after all, the future King of England, and in the early days she had been the wife of a man who might have become his Prime Minister. The Prince had to be particularly careful after his involvement in a widely publicized adultery suit, a matter over which he and Jennie's husband had almost fought a duel and which had forced the social exile of the Randolph Churchills to Ireland. But after Randolph's death, the Prince's letters began to address Jennie as '*Ma chère Amie*', and they were signed '*Tout à vous*, Albert Edward' or simply 'A.E.'

Alexandra, the Princess of Wales, was hard-of-hearing, but she was not blind. She knew all about her husband's many extramarital affairs. She probably even knew of his favourite London restaurants that thoughtfully equipped a private dining room with a settee as well as a panel button for a disappearing bed. Kettner's, in Soho, proudly named a room on the second floor 'The Edward Room'. Frances, Countess of Warwick, a close friend of Jennie's and the Prince's mistress for a prolonged period, wrote of the Princess: 'Beneath her placid exterior there was shrewd judgment that expressed itself now and again in no uncertain terms.' [33]

Whether out of shrewdness or resignation or for some other reason, the Princess maintained cordial relations with some of her husband's women. With Jennie especially Alexandra had a remarkably close friendship. After parties the Princess frequently invited Jennie to her room for a *tête-à-tête*, and Jennie was often a guest at the Princess's private soirées. The two women liked and trusted each other. 'She was always such a tried dear friend of mine,' Alexandra would write of Jennie.[34] They shared a fine sense of humour, and both had generous and impulsive instincts, as well as a dislike of pretence and arrogance. Princess

Alexandra, after all, had been brought up in the simplicity of the Danish Court where she had even been taught to darn her own stockings.

Alexandra and Jennie were both affectionate mothers. There was a similarity in their sons; with the two older boys tempestuous, and the younger ones quiet and placid.[35]

Winston was then twenty years old but still a 'mother's boy'. For many years to come, almost until his marriage, his letters to his mother would be gushingly affectionate, almost romantic outpourings. The boy's closeness to his mother is understandable, as his father had been a remote figure to him. 'If ever I began to show the slightest idea of comradeship, he was immediately offended,' Winston wrote in *My Early Life,* 'and when once I suggested that I might help his private secretary to write some of his letters, he froze me into stone.'[36]

Winston had known his father best as one of the important men of his time. But he was also a man who had died in political disfavour. What brave young man would not have dreamed of vindicating his father's memory, and therefore himself as well? What ambitious young man would not have hoped to emulate and perhaps even surpass the reputation his father had had at the height of his career?

Winston's feeling for his father revealed admiration, envy, and strong filial respect. He memorized some of his father's speeches, imitated his gesture of resting his hand on his hip while giving a speech, and ultimately wrote a two-volume biography of him.

Winston was now at Sandhurst, and more than anything else, he wanted to be able to join a cavalry regiment after passing out.

'Horses were the greatest of my pleasures at Sandhurst,' he later wrote. 'No hour of life is lost that is spent in the saddle. Young men have often been ruined through owning horses, or through backing horses, but never through riding them; unless, of course, they break their necks which, taken at a gallop, is a very good death to die.'[37]

One of his mother's ardent admirers, Colonel John Palmer Brabazon, commanded the 4th Hussars, which was stationed at Aldershot near Sandhurst. Winston had dined with him several times at the regimental mess, where he was overwhelmed by the 'glitter, affluence, ceremony and veiled discipline'.[38]

'After some months, my mother told me that Colonel Brabazon was anxious that I should go into his regiment but that my father had said "No". . . .'[39] Lord Randolph decided long before that Winston should enter an infantry regiment. After his father's death, however, Winston lost little time in asking his mother to contact Brabazon.

Brabazon was everything a man or a woman might admire. Jennie liked him not only because he was a magnificent figure of a man – six feet tall, with a strong jaw, symmetrical features, an elaborate moustache, and bright grey eyes – but also because he was genial, thoroughly good-natured, and adept at repartee. The Prince of Wales liked him because he was knowledgeable at the race course, good in the hunting field, and brave on the battlefield. Moreover, the Prince was a faultless dandy about his clothes, and *Vanity Fair* had called Brabazon, 'The Beau Brummel of the day . . . equally exquisite in dress and manner.'[40]

Women called him 'Beautiful Bwab' because of his good looks and his inability to pronounce 'r'. One of the best-known stories about 'Bwab' concerned the time he was drawing heavy fire during a battle and refused to take cover, saying that he believed certain people had cast aspersions 'on my personal couwage and so I wish to show you all that my personal couwage is as good as ever it was.'[41]

The love affair between Jennie and Brabazon had been brief, but they maintained a solid and reliable friendship, and Brabazon was devoted to her. Within a week after her husband's death Jennie sent him a telegram and Brabazon replied:

Now this is what I want you to do *at once*. I have seen Sir Reginald Gipps, & have written to Fitzgeorge the Duke's private secretary – You must write to the Duke [of Cambridge] & at once. His address is

Hotel Prince de Galles

Cannes.

. . . What I should say was that the boy had always been anxious to go into the Cavalry, but for certain reasons Randolph put his name down for Infantry. That latterly he completely came round to Winston & Your wishes & was anxious he should join my regiment. . . . You can say there is *now* a vacancy in the 4th Hussars, that you are very anxious he should not be idling about London & that I personally knew the boy, liked him, & was very anxious to have him. I should add – which is the case – that Winston passed very much higher than any of the candidates for Cavalry & hope that the Duke will allow him to be appointed to the 4th Hussars, and thus fulfil one of Randolph's last wishes.

The fact is, there are more men passed for Cavalry than there are vacancies, and that's the hitch, but I feel certain that if you write to the Duke, he will make a personal matter of it and that all will be arranged. . . .[42]

Jennie did as Brabazon suggested, and several days later there was a letter from the Duke of Cambridge: 'I will write home at once to the Military Secretary, and if it can be arranged, it shall be carried out. . . .' [43]

In less than two weeks, Winston was posted to the 4th Hussars at Aldershot, and on February 20 he received his commission. Several years later, he wrote, 'Solitary trees, if they grow at all, grow strong; and a boy deprived of a father's care often develops, if he escapes the perils of youth, an independence and vigour of thought which may restore in after life the heavy loss of early days.' [44]

But Winston was not a solitary tree. Just as he had relied on his mother to know a Brabazon or a Duke of Cambridge at this turning point in his life, so would he turn to her again and again, confident that she would know whom to call upon and what move to make. As Winston himself acknowledged, her range and her resources seemed limitless:

My mother was always on hand to help and advise. . . . She soon became my ardent ally, furthering my plans and guarding my interests with all her influence and boundless energy. . . . We worked together on even terms, more like brother and sister than mother and son. At least so it seemed to me. And so it continued to the end.[45]

As Winston noted, she was more than his mother and ally. For a long time, she was his only confidante, the only one to whom he could pour out his loneliness, the only one he loved, the only one who really believed in him. And when sternness was necessary, she also had to be his taskmaster.

In Victorian England the conventions of mourning were strictly observed. The mourning period was supposed to last two years, during the first of which the dress was to be completely covered with black woven crepe. During the second year the crepe could be used just for trimming. Only after two years could the widow accept social invitations.[46] Queen Victoria set an extreme example by still wearing black in mourning for her Prince Consort, even though he had died nearly

27

thirty-five years before. But widow's weeds were not for Jennie – not for long, at any rate. In February 1895 she would go to Paris, where it was perfectly permissible for a beautiful young widow wearing long black bloomers to bicycle in the Bois de Boulogne.

The weather in London that month was so cold that the Thames froze solid enough for an ox roast to be held on it. It had been a month of howling gales, heavy blizzards, and violent thunderstorms.[47] But Jennie was counting on the weather to be better in Paris.

2

Paris was almost as familiar as home to Jennie.

Her birthplace was American, her manners British, but part of her was French. It was more than the family coat-of-arms that her French Huguenot ancestors had registered in Paris in 1699; it was her own memories of excitement in this city that had been so large a part of her life.

Here she had grown up in the fairyland court of Louis Napoleon and Empress Eugénie. The tall graceful Empress, who had many American friends, had often been more of a mother to her than Jennie's own mother. At only sixteen Jennie had already bloomed and was being ogled and chased by men. Then in 1870 came the Franco-Prussian War, and Jennie and her mother and sisters barely caught the last train out of Paris before the enemy surrounded the city.[1]

Paris was also where she and Lord Randolph had played the final scene of their courtship. Here, too, they were married in a hurried, brief ceremony at the British Embassy. And several times during their long, unhappy marriage Jennie had come here alone. Paris was always the place where she could find the fullest freedom.

Much of this surely must have been in her mind as she rode in a carriage down the Champs Elysées. The scene along this broad avenue had long had both a reminiscent and an invigorating effect on her.

'If you look from the Arc de Triomphe to the Tuileries, you see a broken mass of glittering carriage tops and lace parasols, and what looks like the flashing of thousands of mirrors as the setting sun strikes on the glass of the lamps and windows and on the lacquered harness and polished mountings.' [2]

The Champs Elysées was a boulevard of vivid vignettes: the young men on the upper deck of the horse-drawn omnibuses stooping to have a better look at the young women in the open carriages below; a young marquess in a dog-cart proudly flaunting his coquettish passenger; a fashionably dressed, middle-aged woman, driving a victoria, flourishing her whip while her pug-dog sat placidly alongside her on a cushion; and not too far away, a heavy and red-faced woman driving a wagon piled high with bright carrots – she, too, with a dog, this one big and threatening and chained beside her; and on the spacious tree-lined sidewalks fashionable women showing off their tightly corseted figures, their long dresses almost sweeping the ground as they sauntered among Indian maharajahs, New York millionaires, Turkish pashas, Haitian nabobs, and English tourists dressed in flannel shirts, deer-stalkers, and knickerbockers 'exactly as though they were penetrating the mountains of Afghanistan or the deserts of Syria'. The Champs Elysées was still the best show in town.

As she rode by, Jennie knew that this was not yet Paris at its peak. A few more weeks would make the difference for the city. For Paris, which looked like a vast ice-skating rink in winter, February was still the season of artificial flowers. Almost timed with Jennie's arrival, was the famous annual lace sale at *Bon Marché*, and the great store was accented with exquisite but artificial Parma violets. Within a few weeks, *Printemps* would give away thousands of bouquets of real violets to shoppers, and the old chestnut tree in the Tuileries would fulfil its tradition of being the first to put forth a spring bloom. For both Paris and herself, Jennie was looking forward to the first sign of a fresh spring.

'Americans go to London for social triumph, or to float railroad shares; to Rome, for art's sake; and to Berlin to study music and to economize; but they go to Paris to enjoy themselves.'[3] Richard Harding Davis, the man who made that comment, was a handsome, adventurous war correspondent. He was then thirty-one years old, living in Paris, and writing a book about the city. Davis later wrote of Jennie and her son: 'I do not remember Winston ever seeming young enough to be his mother's son, just as I do not remember Lady Randolph ever seeming old enough to be his mother.'

Davis and Jennie were part of a large American colony in Paris. Americans had a firm social tradition in the city. An American had been one of the founders of the Jockey Club, which was, after the *Cercle de L'Union*, the most exclusive club in Paris; two of Empress Eugénie's ladies-in-waiting had been American and some of the most exclusive salons in Paris had been and still were run by Americans.[4]

Shortly after Jennie's arrival, a story appeared in the Paris edition of the New York *Herald* about a dinner given by Sir Clare Ford in honour of the Duchess of Manchester. The *Herald* quoted a conversation between a German Baron and the Duchess:

'At last I am able to leave those Americans,' the Baron asserted, 'really, they haunt one, they are ubiquitous, it is impossible to get away from them. You cannot imagine what a relief it is to speak to you, there is such a contrast between the English and the American manner.'

The Duchess of Manchester smiled and answered, 'You may be right, Baron, but, being an American, I naturally cannot see it.' [5]

The Duchess was the former Consuelo Iznaga of New York, one of Jennie's closest friends, and the two women delighted in that story.

American expatriates were a special breed. Jennie knew a sampling of many of them. There were those who quickly became part of the French scene, such as Loie Fuller, a short, plump woman from Illinois who became a Paris celebrity after discovering that a certain combination of colour and light lent an air of mystery to the serpentine wriggle of her dancing. Miss Fuller lived above the Folies Bergères in an apartment so small that she saved space by painting the chairs on the walls. During the early spring of 1895, she became a theatrical manager, producing a French-American version of *Salomé* in pantomime. The show flopped and Miss Fuller went back to her serpentine wriggle. Later that year, her French and American friends threw a gala party for her, the kind which most of the Americans in Paris would have attended.

Jennie's family friends, the William Kissam Vanderbilts, were also in town, but, having just been divorced, they stayed well away from each other. Commodore Vanderbilt, who had founded the family fortune, had been a friend and business partner of Jennie's father, the fabulous Leonard Jerome, and the two families had been close ever since. William Vanderbilt settled on the Champs Elysées in a plush apartment, complete with billiard room. Mrs Vanderbilt arrived with her tall, charming, nineteen-year-old daughter Consuelo, whose future husband Mrs Vanderbilt had already selected. He was Jennie's nephew, 'Sunny', the twenty-one-year-old Duke of Marlborough.

'I forced my daughter to marry the Duke,' Mrs Vanderbilt admitted many years later. 'I have always had absolute power over my daughter. When I issued an order, nobody discussed it. I therefore did not beg, but ordered her to marry the Duke.' [6] Mother and daughter did not linger long in Paris, as they were being hard-pressed by an American suitor, Winthrop Rutherford. 'Winty was outclassed,' one magazine remarked. 'Six-foot-two in his golf stockings, he was no match for five-foot-six and a coronet.'[7] The Duke's hand in marriage cost the Vanderbilts $2·5 million in Battle Creek Railway Company stock, plus $100,000 a year for life: a dowry totalling $15 million (nearly £6 million).[8]

It was said by some that Jennie had played an important part in the matchmaking, but a letter to her son Jack indicates that at the time she was surprised by the engagement. Besides, it turned out to be a miserable, loveless marriage, and if Jennie had engineered it, Consuelo would not have remained her close friend.

The current society news in Paris, when Jennie arrived, concerned the Count Castellane and his young, newly arrived American bride. Jennie knew the whole clan of Count Boni de Castellane, particularly his uncle, the handsome Prince de Sagan, who had been a trusted friend of Jennie's father and the first mature man who had stirred any romantic feelings in her.[9] The Count's bride was Anna Gould, the daughter of the late celebrated international financier, Jay Gould, and the wedding had been appropriately lavish. Fifty florists had worked all through the night before the ceremony arranging wagonloads of orchids, roses, and lilies. Each guest received a solid silver, heart-shaped box lined with gold and containing a piece of wedding cake. However, the wedding was not as ostentatious as a birthday party that Count Castellane afterwards gave for his wife in Paris, featuring eighty thousand Venetian lamps, an illuminated ballet by a cast of eighty on the banks of a lake, fifteen kilometres of carpet laid on the grass so the 250 guests representing 'the bluest blood in France' would not get their feet wet from the dew. There were also an orchestra of 200 musicians, eighty footmen in scarlet costume, and spectacular fireworks.[10]

That same spring, two of Jennie's other men friends, George Curzon and Sir Bache Cunard, were going to the United States to meet their American brides. An American newspaper complained that $161,653,000 had travelled to Europe in the form of American brides.[11] A magazine further suggested that it might not be a bad idea to establish a protective export duty on American heiresses.[12]

The Paris *Herald* noted a growing resistance to the American invasion[13] and reported that a set of prominent European matrons were forming a social boycott of unmarried American ladies, no matter how laudatory their letters of introduction. The newspaper, however, was always filled with notices offering a variety of liaisons:

> Young Literary Gentleman is Starving in Paris. Money gone, his wife has deserted him; lives luxuriously at leading hotel. Deep gratitude for temporory help.

> Young English Gentleman, through disappointments, temporarily dependent on wife's income, would act as confidential secretary or travelling companion; would arrange business or financial matters for lady who finds them irksome.

> Platonic friendship — A lady holding the doctrine of Plato on the above subject, wishes to form a friendship, on purely platonic principles, with a gentleman. He must be of good position and appearance, tall, dashing, of the type one calls chic. Lady is handsome (sparkling brunette), an accomplished linguist and musician.

Jennie did not have to advertise for companionship, even though she was alone at a hotel. She was still a great beauty and now in her prime. Her son Winston later wrote of his mother that 'She was still, at forty, young, beautiful, fascinating', and her nephew Shane Leslie was still more descriptive:

> I remember visiting her the week after Randolph died. She was haggard, but her beauty was never more apparent. I remember her so well, lying in bed, her face absolutely white, her black hair hanging, a marvel. It was the first time I realized how beautiful women could be.[14]

Hers was the kind of dark, full-figured beauty for which Parisians particularly had a passionate appreciation. That appreciation sometimes showed itself in direct, but unorthodox ways. For example, Jennie awoke early one morning in her hotel room to see a very corpulent French gentleman slowly approaching her bed. The man had managed to get the room adjoining hers, which had a connecting door. Then he had very quietly removed the lock from the door and entered Jennie's room. Now he was slowly approaching his intended pleasure. Jennie watched him, waiting until he was almost upon her. Then she hit him as hard as she could in his overstuffed midsection. The man gasped and doubled over. Then he disappeared through the connecting door much more quickly than he had entered. When Jennie later told the story, she explained that she did not believe in screaming, either in a hotel or in a foreign country.[15]

Jennie was planning a lengthy stay in Paris and soon found a more permanent place to live than this hotel, with its limited privacy. Her new home was the kind of place one would expect her to find, on a quiet, fashionable, tree-lined boulevard in a lively part of the city. Avenue Kléber radiated from the Arc de Triomphe at the end of the busy Champs Elysées. The Arc de Triomphe could be seen from her street, as could the six-year-old Eiffel Tower. (There was talk in Paris at this time about tearing down the Eiffel Tower, as it seemed to have a magnetic attraction for would-be suicides.) The winding Seine was only a short distance away from Jennie's house and, fittingly enough, the Place des Etats-Unis was just around the corner. The sculptor Bartholdi, who had recently finished the Statue of Liberty, was completing a bronze of George Washington and Lafayette for the area.

The large grey mansions in Avenue Kléber were all homes with distinctive heavy doors and inner courts, in careful keeping with the *cachet*. The exiled Queen of Spain had lived on this street for more than thirty years. Number 34 was a handsome seven-storey house, with gargoyles decorating the windows. Most of the windows had small balconies. But it was the interior that Jennie soon made her own. She had a passion and a gift for decorating, following no style but her own taste. She liked bright colours for curtains, hated heavy furniture, and loved to fill walls with paintings. She could move into a cold, formal house and very quickly convert it into a warm comfortable home.

Jennie's younger sister Leonie Leslie and her three sons were the first house guests to arrive. Their older sister Clara was in Tunbridge Wells, taking care of their mother, who was ill. Clara, or Clarinette, as the sisters often called her, striking in her blonde beauty, was married to Moreton Frewen (who came to be called 'Mortal Ruin' by his unfortunate financial partners). Never was there a more brilliant, eloquent man who failed so magnificently in so many schemes in so many places, from Kenya to Canada. Moreton was so often away that his marriage seemed more one of correspondence than contact. Clara's letters to him were full of loneliness and longing.

Leonie, the youngest sister, whom Jennie called 'Sniffy', was dark, not as pretty as Clara, but twice as clever and talented. Her husband was John Leslie, who like Frewen also found it necessary to spend considerable time away from his family, but was more often at the race course than in remote corners of the world. His three sons seldom saw him, and he was especially a stranger to the youngest boy, Seymour. Jennie often told of the first time John Leslie visited her Avenue Kléber home and spent the night. The seven-year-old Seymour opened the door of his mother's bedroom in the morning and was so surprised to see John Leslie in bed beside her that he asked, '*Qui est ce Monsieur, Maman?*' Seymour Leslie would later write of his father, 'He had never domineered or been unkind, which would be forgivable; only completely indifferent, which is not.' [16]

The three sisters were so close that they were a kind of spiritual unity. Each not only knew what the others thought and felt, but what they *would* think, what they *would* feel. They told one another their innermost secrets, shared their limited funds, and acted more like mothers than aunts over their various nieces and nephews. It was a mutual love and tenderness. And when outside trouble threatened any one of them, their compact formed a fortress against the world.

If Jennie unburdened herself somewhat more to Leonie, it was not only because Leonie was the wiser one, but also because the two were somehow more closely attuned, had more of the same interests, even preferred the same kind of men. 'I do hope, my dearest mama,' her son Winston had written, 'that you will keep well and not give way to depression. I am sure Aunt Leonie will look after you and make the time pass pleasantly.' [17]

Jennie, of course, had her periods of depression. What soon made Paris much brighter for her was that the city was filled with so many of her friends, as well as some of her lovers. Among them was Albert Edward, the Prince of Wales, who had come somewhat earlier aboard his own yacht, *Britannia,* which he was preparing to race in the Mediterranean Regatta.

Our nurse was shaking in a paroxysm of loyalty when she woke my brother and myself, soaked us in eau de cologne, and led us into the drawing room. . . . [wrote Shane Leslie] We were told to shake hands with an enormous gentleman with a beard and a guttural voice. We did not know whether he came out of pantomime or Grimm's Fairy Tales.

35

The Prince was kind enough to enquire what we intended to be when we grew up. I was tongue-tied, but my brother had the presence of mind to answer: 'Please, one of your soldiers,' I suspect under the prompting from my mother. The Prince immediately felt in his pockets and gave him a Queen's shilling in the form of a gold piece. The sovereign was confiscated, and we were both returned to bed. In future years, my brother made good his word, for he was one of the first officers killed in October, 1914.[18]

While he was in Paris, the Prince of Wales unexpectedly visited the British Embassy. The Ambassador was having his tea, and when the groom burst in announcing, 'His Royal Highness, the Prince of Wales,' the startled Ambassador let his teacup fall as he jumped up exclaiming, 'Good God!' The Prince, who was a marvellous mimic, later re-enacted the whole scene, coming in and announcing himself, then jumping up, dropping his cup and saying, 'Good God!'[19]

Princess Alexandra had been left in London. This was not unusual. In Paris the Prince preferred his freedom, and he had become very adept at eluding his equerry.

Two other men in Paris who assuredly left their wives at home when they visited Jennie were Paul Bourget and the Marquis de Breteuil. Jennie had known both men before they were married, and had she been free, each would willingly have married her. It must have seemed to Jennie as if life went round in concentric circles. It would always be that way for her. Those who had loved her never wanted to let her go.

Henri Charles Joseph le Tonnelier de Breteuil, a member of the French Chamber of Deputies and a distinguished diplomat, would have been Foreign Minister of France if the monarchy had been restored. An ancestor of his had been French Ambassador to the Imperial Court of the Empress Catherine of Russia, which was one of the excuses Breteuil had used to accompany Jennie and her husband on their trip to Russia in 1887.[20] But their romance had begun before that trip. Jennie was caustic about his marriage to Marcelite Garner, an American girl,[21] and temporarily terminated their relationship. The Marquis wrote to Jennie, 'What I miss most is not seeing you any more.'

Jennie and Breteuil shared many things. They were both extraordinary equestrians, both were dynamic speakers, and he was as handsome as she was beautiful. Both also most enjoyed creative people. Marcel Proust later used Breteuil as a model for Bréauté in *Remembrance of Things*

Past: '. . . A snob! But, my dear, you must be mad, it's just the opposite. He loathes smart people, he won't let himself be introduced to anyone. Even in my house! If I ask him to meet someone he doesn't know, he swears at me all the time.' [22]

Proust added that Bréauté visited only those who had a certain reputation for intellect, 'with the result that from his presence, were it at all regular, in a woman's house, one could tell that she had a "salon".'

It was obvious why Breteuil clung to Jennie. In addition to everything else, she was a fresh breeze in his formal world. The Prince of Wales, a good friend of Breteuil's, delighted in calling him 'Braces'. Jennie had the same unstuffy spirit.

Paul Bourget was of a different cut, but equally distinguished and equally in love with Jennie. She had met him years before at the Paris literary salon of a fellow American, Mrs Ferdinand Bischoffsheim. As Jennie discreetly put it in her memoirs, he was 'then unmarried'.

Just slightly older than Jennie, Bourget was one of France's most celebrated novelists. In June of that year he would be elected to the French Academy, taking the seat once held by Voltaire. Critics called Bourget a poet of delicate fancy, a writer of subtle psychological observation, a critic capable of 'the finest shades of appreciation and discrimination.' His novels, of which there would be fifty before he died, hinted rather than thundered, and always in elegant style. Women, particularly, admired his genteel analyses of their emotions and the delicate way he sought the secrets of their inner selves.

He had just returned from a long visit to the United States, where he and Mark Twain – whom Jennie also knew – had tilted literary swords in the *North American Review*. Bourget referred to American women as 'the real Romans of decadence' and mocked the ladies of Baltimore and Philadelphia who wanted to cover up their cities' naked public statues. His American stories must have amused Jennie.

Bourget was a handsome, shaggy-haired man with an impressive moustache and an elegant manner. The celebrated American novelist Henry James noted in his diary at the time that Bourget's marriage was not going well and was unlikely to survive in the Paris scene.[23] His elaborate apartment was only ten minutes' walk from Avenue Kléber.

Bourget's correspondence with Jennie through the years was long and prolific. He had once written to her, 'Arrived at a certain point in life, one knows too much about it, wishes to do too much, and is not able to express what one has to say. Do you know that Turgenev has summed it all up when he said, "Life is a brutal affair"?' [24]

The brutality of life reached Jennie that spring in Paris when she picked up the Paris *Herald* and noted two new arrivals at the Hotel Bristol: Count Charles Kinsky and his bride, fresh from their honeymoon. [25]

If Jennie was anguished, Kinsky was certainly as much so when he heard of her presence in Paris. There was no love in his marriage, but his heritage, his religion, and his father made divorce inconceivable. The disintegration of his marriage soon became publicly obvious.

As for Kinsky and Jennie, what would these two frustrated lovers do? Would he try to see her? Probably. And would Jennie see him? She was a unique woman. Her pride had not been merely damaged; it had been battered. As much as she loved this man – and she would love him until she died – she was stubborn enough then to refuse for years to see him. But that, too, would change.

3

It was Jennie who was the most influential factor in the development of her son Winston. Besides the courage, spirit and drive she instilled in him, besides shaping his mind through their constant discussions and correspondence, besides introducing him to the people who helped determine his future, besides her own manœuvring in every area in which she could protect his interests and further his ambition – besides all these things, at a crucial stage in his life Jennie provided Winston with the only real father figure he ever had, the one man who was most vital in helping him develop the greatest of all his gifts.

Several generations later, Democratic presidential candidate Adlai E. Stevenson, himself a speaker of sparkling wit and elegance, asked Winston Churchill whose example had helped fashion the famous Churchill oratorical style. 'It was an American statesman who inspired me . . . and taught me how to use every note of the human voice like an organ,' Churchill answered. And then, to Stevenson's amazement, Churchill quoted long excerpts from speeches made by Bourke Cockran some sixty years before. 'He was my model,' Churchill said.[1]

In March 1895, Bourke Cockran was just a man who came to dinner one night at 34 Avenue Kléber. Leonie had invited him to Jennie's home because he was a good friend of their brother-in-law Moreton Frewen. Romanticists might say that Jennie and Bourke Cockran were fated for each other. Wasn't it more than strange, they might ask, that these two remarkable people, who had never met before, just happened to be in Paris at the same time for the same reason? Jennie had become a widow only a month before Cockran became a widower. His wife, like Jennie's husband, had died after a long illness. Cockran and Jennie had both come to Paris for a change of scene and mood. Both believed that their lives had reached an ebb. Both had lived so long with the dying and the dead that they were ripe for the freshness of loving and living. Seldom were two people more open and ready for each other.

'Live intensely and die suddenly', was Bourke Cockran's motto,[2] and no motto could have suited Jennie better.

The passport issued earlier that month to William Bourke Cockran noted simply: 'Age, 41 years. Stature, 5 ft. 11 inches. Forehead, high. Eyes, grey. Nose, straight. Mouth, moustache. Chin, round. Hair, dark brown. Complexion, dark. Face, round.'[3]

'Leonine' was the best word to describe him. Particularly when he was speaking, he truly looked like a lion ready to spring. The single most striking physical characteristic about him was his magnificent head, with its long dark hair that tossed like a flowing mane. A big, broad-shouldered man, he was a commanding figure with deep-set, widely spaced eyes, a strong jaw and thoughtful brows that slanted upward and inward. He was not handsome, and Alice Roosevelt Longworth, Theodore Roosevelt's daughter, affectionately described him as 'an enormous ogre'.[4] But he moved with grace and energy, and his presence radiated charm and power. 'When he entered a room, it was like somebody turning on the electric light', observed the Irish statesman, Sir Horace Plunkett.[5]

Cockran and Jennie were so much of the same cut. They had the same sparkling wit, never barbed for injuring, and they were both generous givers of themselves – their time, their money, their strength, and most of all, their spirit. They both had penetrating intelligence, inner fire, and titanic vigour.

Cockran's voice was almost magical, 'a low rumble of thunder that has the sweetness of the lute in it.' It had the lilt of Irish laughter and vibrated with vitality. Despite his talents as a talker, he never tried to dominate conversation, although he was always ready to reply with a witty riposte. And when he chose, he could be a swift, dangerous thruster in repartee.

'When I was a young man, we used to regard Carlyle as the greatest conversationalist of his time,' wrote the Marquess of Ripon, a former Viceroy of India. 'Then, later on, we spoke of Gladstone as the greatest conversationalist since Caryle. Well, I heard Carlyle and Gladstone many times, and I am quite convinced, in wit, wisdom, and elegance of expression, neither of them approached the American statesman Bourke Cockran.'[6]

Jennie, too, knew the great conversationalists of her time. They had come to her parties and crowded her dinner table, the Prime Minister, Gladstone, among them. Having been trained in that art herself, she was never simply the polite hostess who quietly poured the tea; she injected her opinions forcefully, and yet in a way which nobody could really find objectionable.

There was much to discuss in the current news: Japan at war with China over Korea; Cubans rebelling against Spanish rule; 3,000 troops called in to quell violence caused by a trolley-car strike in Brooklyn; an abortive attempt by partisans of ex-Queen Liliuokalani to restore the monarchy in Hawaii; the anticipated United States Supreme Court decision declaring the income tax unconstitutional; and the strange, controversial case of Captain Alfred Dreyfus. As a lawyer, Cockran was particularly interested in the Dreyfus case. Having been convicted of treason in a secret court martial, Captain Dreyfus had been publicly degraded, stripped of his rank in front of 5,000 soldiers, and imprisoned in solitary confinement on Devil's Island. Proving Dreyfus's innocence had already become a cause, and the case would confound several French governments before Dreyfus would be exonerated.[7]

There were lighter items for table talk: a scheduled race of horseless carriages (at a predicted speed of sixteen miles an hour); an old-fashioned duel between a composer and a noted clubman caused by comments made during the dress rehearsal of a Paris play; Lady Wolseley's ball at which guests wore costumes copied from eighteenth-century paintings; and the opening match of the Ladies' Football Club, organized by a Miss Honeyball at the Nightingale Lane Football Grounds.

Jennie and Cockran might also have talked about Ireland. She had lived there for more than three years, when Randolph had served as secretary to his father who was then Viceroy of Ireland. Jennie had loved Ireland. Her second son Jack was born there.

Bourke Cockran had been born in Ireland, in County Sligo which he called 'the most Irish part of Ireland . . . the weird and solitary grandeur of Knocknarea, the music of the waterfall at Ballysodare, the moonlight on Lough Hill, and the perfumed breath of the Tyreragh meadows where we saw the swaying of the cowslips and daisies, not the movements of the senseless winds, but the capers of the dancing fairies. . . .'[8] He had emigrated from Ireland alone at seventeen, worked as a clerk in a New York department store, taught French and Latin, become principal of a school, worked briefly as a foreign correspondent,[9] and got his law degree by studying at night. His first wife had died in childbirth and his second wife had been the daughter of a millionaire merchant. He himself was now a very successful lawyer.[10]

Jennie and Cockran shared a common love of horses, too. Both of them were born to it. As a boy, Bourke had lived on a farm and had virtually moved from his cradle into the saddle. His father had had a similar love, and when young Bourke was only five years old had died of a broken neck in a steeplechase.[11] Jennie, too, came to her love of horses through her father, for Leonard Jerome was 'the father of the American turf' and the man largely responsible for making horse-racing respectable in the United States.[12] In fact, Cockran had often attended the races at Jerome Park.

They also shared memories of New York City. Jennie had vivid memories of her father's luxurious home in Madison Avenue with its own private theatre where Jerome personally auditioned young singers, and where she had strutted on the stage, pretending to be an actress. New York to Jennie also meant elegant balls where as a child she had daydreamed of dancing with the Prince of Wales.

Bourke Cockran, too, had had a home in Madison Avenue, near where Jennie had lived, and he could tell her about the changes in the neighbourhood – the end of the trolley-car barn, new hotels replacing old mansions, the move of elegance northward.

And they could spend a whole series of evenings talking about Jennie's brother-in-law, Moreton Frewen, 'the splendid pauper'.[13] A friend of Presidents and Princes, Frewen had an unbroken record of fiscal failure, but he remained an indomitable optimist, a man of a thousand ideas, a visionary who forecast the Panama Canal and the St Lawrence Seaway. Jennie and Bourke had both lost money in some of his schemes. Shane Leslie remembered sitting with Frewen and Cockran, who

> could endlessly debate the Silver Question, the Irish Question and Tariff Question together, and when each was fought to exasperation, they would laugh and turn to one another. Often I was deafened between their rival torrentades. And, afterwards, Moreton would confide to me, 'Poor Bourke, such a windbag, but such a good fellow!' And Bourke would mutter, 'Was ever so much intelligence so sublimely misdirected!'[14]

Politics was another field in which Jennie and Bourke could meet as equals. Not only did Jennie understand the intricacy of back-room dealings, but she had conducted single-handed several of her husband's political campaigns at a time when other upper-class women didn't even go out into the street unescorted. An American newspaper had referred to Jennie as one of three women in England 'who were intelligent politicians'.[15]

She had considerable knowledge of American politics, particularly that of New York. In his capacity as assistant district attorney, her favourite cousin, William Travers Jerome, had served on the Lexnow Commission investigating New York City's political corruption.[16] His detailed revelations had helped destroy some of the power held by Tammany Hall, New York's Democratic organization, and in 1895 Jerome helped elect a reform Mayor. He himself would later become the state's Attorney General, a prominently mentioned candidate for Governor, and even a much-discussed possibility as a presidential nominee.

Cockran's connection with Tammany had been double-edged. He had fought them, joined them, and was now again against them. He had fought them during the corrupt Boss Tweed days, when everything was for sale and the price high. In the early 1870s a big, broad ex-soapstone cutter and amateur actor named 'Honest John' Kelly succeeded Tweed and reorganized Tammany Hall. Kelly decided to recruit unimpeachable candidates and to work more subtly behind the scenes. 'Honest John' even lectured on Jesuit Missionaries in North America, and it was he who persuaded Cockran to join the new Tammany team.[17]

West Side Tammany leader George Washington Plunkitt had remained sceptical of Cockran's convictions: 'I'll admit he's a grand gentleman and the greatest orator in the land, but take it from me, he's not a dependable politician. He calls himself a Democrat but his heart was never in Tammany Hall. . . . While he was in Congress, he never darkened the door of a Tammany clubhouse.'[18]

Cockran's connection with Tammany grew weaker when Richard Croker succeeded 'Honest John' as Tammany leader. Boss Croker was a mild-mannered, soft-spoken, sad-faced, small chunk of a man who believed that 'To the victors belong the spoils.' Within a short time, Boss Croker owned a Fifth Avenue mansion, a vast estate in England, a stock farm for race-horses worth £100,000, and a well-bred bulldog which cost £4,000.[19]

Croker helped elect Cockran to Congress for several terms but then decided he was too independent and refused to endorse him for United

States Senator in 1895. Charles Emory Smith, editor of the Philadelphia *Press*, guessed at the reason: 'Bourke Cockran has never been able to make his principles elastic. That is something that Boss Croker does not appreciate or even understand.' [20]

Cockran had been an effective Congressman during his three terms in office, but he made the politically unforgivable mistake of voting on the basis of principles and issues, rather than political party. He later explained his independence by telling of the wandering Indian who refused to admit he was lost: 'Me here; tepee lost!'

Boss Croker was vehement in his denunciation of Cockran, calling him the most objectionable man he had ever met in his political career. Pressed for a reply, Cockran said, 'Croker never said anything that was worth replying to.' Then he paused and added, 'Except on a few occasions. That was up to a few years ago when I wrote what he was to say in advance.' [21]

Nothing Bourke said as he sat next to her at dinner that night at 34 Avenue Kléber could have stirred Jennie as much as she might have been had she been able to hear him speak from a public platform. Perhaps the best speech of his career was at the Democratic National Convention in Chicago in 1892. 'Not until the last delegate to the convention sleeps in his grave will the famous oration cease to be discussed with wonderment and ecstasy,' one reporter wrote.[22]

The convention had been in continuous session for more than ten hours and it was then long past midnight. The more than fifteen thousand delegates in the enormous tent were hot and tired and hungry. The great majority of them clearly wanted Grover Cleveland as their presidential nominee. The song they had sung was:

> Grover, Grover,
> Four more years of Grover;
> Out they go
> In we go;
> Then we'll be in clover.[23]

In fact, everybody there wanted Grover Cleveland except Tammany Hall.

His audience seemed to him then like a wall of darkness, punctured with white spots. 'The only person I recognized was Governor Flower [24] of New York. The rain was constantly coming through the roof, and he sat on the back of the chair to keep his feet from the wet floor, with an umbrella over his head. I remember that I thought he looked like a huge turtle.' [25]

At first Cockran felt like a swimmer in a stormy sea. He started out with tender, mellow tones, with sorrow and pathos rather than anger. A reporter described it as 'the tongue of gentleness, whose words ripple as flowing water. . . .' [26] Then, with his eyes half closed, his eloquence came with a rush. The delegates sat on their hard, cramped seats 'as silent as death'. From outside could be heard the thunder of a storm and the whistle of a passing train.

The notes of his two-octave voice now picked up added purpose and passion, 'the blood suffusing his great neck and his fiery Irish soul leaping from his wonderful eyes. . . .' [27]

'I have said that I believe that Mr Cleveland is a popular man,' he intoned. The crowd broke into enthusiastic applause. Cockran stood still, a small smile on his mobile face. When the cheers subsided, he continued, 'Let me say, a man of extraordinary popularity.' Again, the audience cheered. A moment later, after taking a sip of water, Cockran completed his point, 'A very popular man on every day of the year except one, and that . . .' (he paused dramatically) '. . . and that is Election Day.' [28]

He had caught the delegates' complete attention. From then on, the vast audience alternated between agitation and stillness 'as a field of summer barley is swept by gusts of summer wind.' They were carried along 'upon the melodious current of his speech, unconscious, and when he was done, they turned to one another like men who have awakened from a vivid dream.' [29]

'The severest test of oratory is to compel applause from a hostile audience,' said Senator Champ Clark. 'I have nearly blistered my hands applauding William Bourke Cockran when I dissented from everything he said.' [30]

Only after their thunderous applause did the delegates remember that they were tired, hungry, thirsty, and still pledged to Grover Cleveland, whom they afterward nominated.

There is no knowing how much of his background Bourke revealed to Jennie that evening at dinner at 34 Avenue Kléber in March 1895. But that evening was just the first of many. The attraction was quick and mutual. The timing was perfect and the formula was right. They were free enough to do as they pleased, adult enough to know what they wanted in this summer of their lives.

Years before, when Jennie had rented an apartment in Paris on the Rue Marbœuf, she found an enormous snake drawn over the head of the bed, with the words, *J'enlace et jamais l'en lasse* (Entwine yourself with me, and never lazy shall I be).[31]

Filed away among Cockran's papers is a bit of doggerel he had copied. The original title was 'The Rhyme on the Hungry Husband', but he had changed it to 'Any Husband to Any Wife':

> Feed me on victuals
> For I'm sick of bran.
> Feed me on bacon, eggs and coffee, too.
> Feed me on beefsteak, if you can't get ham.
> Feed me on beans and peas and Irish stew.
> Feed me on custard,
> And when at length the festive board is spread,
> Just shut the door and hurry off to bed.[32]

In the language of the gypsies, a 'jennie' is a merry-go-round, which is what life must have seemed like to her then. For Jennie and Bourke, part of the pleasure of being together in Paris that spring was that it was a natural habitat for both of them. They had spent their young days there, both spoke French as fluently as English, and they knew all the best places to go together. They knew where to walk for quiet conversation: the tree-lined quays on the Ile Saint-Louis, down the still streets near the Jesuit Church at the Place Saint-Sulpice. They knew what it was to walk the gas-lit streets all night and greet the dawn, the Seine almost motionless in the sunrise, and the drifting mist lending a softness even to the skeletal steel of the Eiffel Tower.

They went riding and cycling in the Bois de Boulogne. Jennie loved cycling and everybody was learning it, even the portly Prince of Wales. Women wore *bicyclettes* – divided skirts [33] of which each leg was composed of alternating strips of lace and fabric. Even Queen Victoria was entertained by a group of women who performed a bicycle ballet set to music.

Jennie wrote to her sons that she was 'very busy', that Paris was 'charming', and that, in her ice skating at the Palais de Glace, 'I find I have not forgotten my various figures – Sea Breeze, etc. . . . ' [34]

There was the theatre, which she and Bourke both loved. Jennie was a frustrated playwright, and Bourke a frustrated actor. As a young man he had played bit roles, and his first speech, at sixteen, concerned the moral influence of drama.

Every new Paris play was a social event, and intermissions were noisy with comments. Everybody seemed to have some point to make and there was hardly time to savour the *glacé* sweetmeats from Boissier's, which the women ate using a pair of tongs so as not to soil their suede gloves.

One of the popular plays in Paris at the time was called *L'Age difficile*, about the extramarital affairs of a woman named Jeanne. A critic said, 'It is suggestive, but with dainty skill, cutting almost to blood flow, but yielding immediately a bit of pretty batiste to bind the wound.' Another less successful play called *Mademoiselle Eve* was by 'Gyp' (pseudonym of the Comtesse de Partel) and dealt with the several love affairs of a society lady and her unsuspecting husband.[35]

The most popular play in Paris at the moment was *La Princesse lointaine*, a sad, sumptuous, dreamy fantasy by a young playwright named Edmond Rostand. The play was considered slight, but Sarah Bernhardt was its star. The gossip was that 'the divine Sarah', then fifty-one years old, had invested her own money in the play because the twenty-seven-year-old playwright, whom she called '*mon poète*', 'hung from one of her rays'.[36] Bernhardt was still the actress with the golden voice that could move any audience to tears, and yet such was her perfect control of emotion that she could always wink at a stagehand.[37]

Paris was full of concerts, and Jennie and Bourke both loved music. Paderewski had just returned from a highly successful American tour and reported all the details to Jennie. Paderewski was indebted to Jennie. It was she who had arranged his première performance in London when he was yet little known. She called him 'Paddy' and they played duets together.[38] Even then, he wore his hair long and flowing and reported, 'How I hate my damned hair! But I have to wear it like this because the public have grown to expect it from my portraits.' [39]

At the end of his Paris concert there was such cheering that the Paris *Herald* reported, 'Not even Liszt received the ovations which were accorded to M. Paderewski.' [40]

There was a different kind of music at the Ambassadeurs where Yvette sang her ballads. Yvette Guilbert was the rage of Paris, and Toulouse-Lautrec later immortalized her on canvas. Her songs were highly suggestive and more scoffing than subtle. Some people listened to them with a sense of outraged propriety, but they listened and loved her, because she had grace and audacity and style.[41] In one of her ballads she sang of a son who had killed his mother at the request of his sweetheart. As he held his mother's heart in his hand, he slipped suddenly and the heart said, 'Don't fall, dear son, and hurt yourself. . . .'[42]

The Ambassadeurs was decorated like a roof garden, complete with gravel, lined benches, and gas jets. People dined and listened from boxes at the back. 'The Dead Rat' and 'The Black Cat' were places with a different mood. 'The Black Cat' had massive rafters, heavy broad tables, an immense fireplace, and black cats everywhere – stuffed in their natural skin, carved in wood, cut out of wrought iron with gas jets flaming from their mouths, and depicted in illustrations as waltzing in the woods, running over red tiled roofs, racing over the ocean. In an informal theatre upstairs local poets recited their verses in the dark. It was very romantic.

Aristide Bruant, another Paris personality, recited a different kind of poetry at his tiny café on the Boulevard Rochechouart. Bruant liked to refer to himself as a modern François Villon, a poet of the people. He always dressed in brown velvet, a red shirt, a broad sombrero, and high boots. There were only three long tables in his tiny place and guests needed to know the special knock to gain entry. Bruant sang in a swaggering style, his hands deep in his pockets, his long hair shaking. He also insisted on kissing the women – the pretty ones – goodbye when they left.[43]

Spring in Paris was carnival time, and that meant clowns, confetti, coloured balloons, and a parade with mounted trumpeters and the Queen of Queens, robed in white, her hair powdered, wearing a diadem and holding a sceptre. It was a time when the students, singing and marching arm in arm, made the boulevards impassable. But one newspaper reporter described an argument between an angry *agent de police* and an equally angry student that was 'hysterically funny' because they were both 'so animated and at the same time so exquisitely polite.'[44]

Jennie and Bourke were lovers of good food, and they never stinted. Then, as now, the speciality at the Tour d'Argent was pressed duck – the meat carefully carved off the skeleton, and the skeleton then put into a great silver press and crushed before the diners' eyes. The juice of the bones gave the sauce a particularly delicious flavour.

There were also the receptions given by Madame Emile Straus. She was better known as Geneviève, the widow of composer Georges Bizet. Geneviève's salons featured sparkling conversation by the most eminent and fascinating people in Paris. Geneviève herself once said of a beautiful woman who had spread with age, 'She is no longer a statue; she is a group.' And when somebody said to her, 'Madame, you may say what you like about *my* friends,' Geneviève answered, 'I didn't know you had any.' But her most repeated remark, made to a woman whose name appeared on the Honours list, was, 'The feminine chest was not made for hanging orders on.' [45]

It is also possible that Jennie pulled Bourke along to the Fourteenth Annual Exhibition of Lady Painters. She herself had started to paint more often and more seriously. She was also often asked to pose for other artists and would tell of the strange incident when she had posed for the French artist Hébert. They were at Hébert's studio and suddenly were almost overcome by a compelling odour. Hébert broke into the studio below to find the corpse of a fellow artist, 'who had been lying dead for two weeks!' [46]

The weather in Paris had been lovely during the onset of spring, but in London the cold had helped spread an influenza epidemic. Jennie wrote to her son Jack, 'Go to bed early and take care of yourself . . . I don't like hearing of a cough. . . . I hope you won't get influenza. . . .' [47] Newspapers reported thirty-four dead, and 1,200 London policemen and many members of Parliament, including Lord Rosebery, had been incapacitated. A newspaper even blamed the influenza for causing a fit of temporary insanity in a respectable workman; he had murdered his wife and six children by cutting their throats with a razor and then committed suicide.

Jennie's mother was ill, but Clara was still there to take care of her. Winston had visited her and wrote to his mother that grandmama 'looked very pale and worn. . . . She carped a little at your apartment in "the gayest parts of Champs Elysées" but was otherwise very amiable – or rather was not particularly malevolent.' He also wrote that he hoped to get a few days' holiday and come to Paris at Easter, 'so you must keep a fatted calf for the occasion. . . .' [48] He told her that he was sending her three boxes of her favourite cigarettes, Royal Beauties. Jack was also planning to visit his mother for Easter, and she wrote to him, '. . . Mind you bring a knickerbocker . . . for you will want to bicycle . . . and a pair of low shoes. . . . I will send an order for your coat. . . .' [49]

At the end of March 1895, Jennie's mother's health suddenly worsened, and the two sisters made preparations to hurrry to her side. Jennie was to go first, and Leonie wrote to Clara asking her to tell their mother that Jennie was coming on business. 'It will be everything for you having Jennie,' Leonie wrote, observing that Jennie was 'practical and helpful'.

Winston wrote immediately to his mother. 'What sad times you are having, my darling Mummy. I trust you may have strength to go through them. . . . I can come at an hour's notice if you feel you want to see me – so don't hesitate to wire. . . .'[50]

The weather also had changed, and a vicious gale was blowing over the English Channel. But their mother's condition was critical, and the two sisters rushed to leave. Several days later, the Paris *Herald* social column noted that Bourke Cockran, too, had left for England.

4

Jennie's father had passed on to her his drive, his imagination, his love
of life, and she had adored him. But her mother was a cold, strait-laced
woman. 'Poor darling, she has had so little pleasure these last years,'
wrote Clara, the eldest daughter, the one who had been named after
her and the one who had loved her most.

'She had grown very old and we had to be very quiet, for fear of dis-
turbing her,' recalled Clara's daughter Clare Sheridan, who became a
noted sculptress. 'At the end of her days, she became superbly squaw-
like, and would sit impassively for hours, staring into the fire, her head
shrouded in a shawl. A figure of great moral fortitude and self-oblation
was gradually fading out. She had lived a selfless life.' [1]

But it had not really been selfless. Leonard Jerome had been a man
of many women because his wife could not give him the love and the
life he wanted. Since divorce at that time was unthinkable, Clara moved
with her daughters to Europe, while Leonard remained in New York.

Clara Jerome's goal in life was social prominence. She would have
bought it if she had more money, or married it if she had been widowed.
Her last hope, therefore, was to push her daughters into outstanding
marriages and bask in their social success. But that, too, failed. She was
bitterly unhappy with all three of her sons-in-law: Randolph terrified
her; Moreton Frewen had wasted her family jewels on his ill-conceived
ventures; and John Leslie and his family always treated her with disdain.
Was it any wonder then that she sat grimly over her teacups in a cheap
boarding-house in Tunbridge Wells, surrounded by the dregs of her life,
pinching pennies until the end came?

'Poor Grandmama is to be buried tomorrow, Friday,' Jennie wrote to
Jack on April 4, 1895.

You must meet us at Charing Cross at *eleven o'clock*. Please ask Mr.
Welldon [Headmaster of Harrow] to allow you to come. Aunt Leonie
returns to Paris Saturday and I will come, if possible, and take you

over Tuesday. If you have no black gloves, get some at Harrow. I have ordered a wreath for you. Don't be late – *eleven o'clock*. The train is very punctual. Winston is here.

Jennie could not pretend an emotion she did not feel. She and her mother had long lived in separate worlds, and there had been no bridge between them. They had had different values, different insights, different dreams.

Clara Jerome's will declared that two-thirds of her estate was to go to Clara and one-third to Leonie. This meant an income of £1,600 a year for Clara and £800 for Leonie.[2] 'What breaks my heart, Moreton,' Clara wrote to her husband, 'is that she sacrificed so much these last years of her life in economizing and saving just to leave me in comfort.'[3]

Moreton was just then involved in another disastrous venture called Electrozone, and welcomed the chance to get at some more funds.[4] He urged his wife to go to America to try to raise some money on her share of the American estate, and he promised to come from Australia and meet her there in June.

The three sisters had already decided to take their mother's body back to America for burial in the elaborate family vault in Greenwood Cemetery, Brooklyn, where their father lay. They now agreed to postpone the trip until June, when Clara could meet Moreton.

London newspapers gave scant attention to the death of Clara Jerome. The front-page news was the sensational Oscar Wilde affair. The scandal sprang from Oscar Wilde's libel action against the Marquess of Queensberry for intimating that Wilde had persuaded Queensberry's son into a homosexual act.

Jennie found herself in the awkward position of being good friends with both Oscar Wilde and the Marquess's attorney, Edward Carson. Carson was a brilliant, fiery M.P. from Dublin. At Jennie's suggestion, he had once journeyed to Harrow to lunch with Winston and talk to him about his future. He also invited Winston to watch Parliament in action 'and dine with me then to view the scramble of a House of Commons dinner.' Carson was probably one of the first men to talk with Winston about politics.

Edward Carson had a reputation for extraordinary courage and determination. An admirer of Carson remarked when discussing him and another great lawyer, 'I should be ready to hunt tigers with Carson; I wouldn't hunt cats with the other.'[5] Another comment often repeated was 'I would rather be defended by Carson when I was wrong than by any other man when I was right.' [6]

Oscar Wilde, the plaintiff in this celebrated case, had been a frequent guest at Jennie's parties and dinners. In fact, there were few great London houses where he had not dominated the dinner table. He was, after all, famous, rich, flooded by commissions from theatrical managers, courted by the intelligentsia, constantly interviewed by the press, and aggressively imitated by a whole generation. Even captains of football teams were seen with the long Wilde hair-style.[7] 'I was a man who stood in symbolic relation to the Art and Literature of my age,' Wilde wrote. 'Few ever hold such a position in their own lifetimes and have it so acknowledged.' [8]

He enjoyed Jennie's dinners because he had spent a year in the United States and genuinely liked American women. He thought they were 'pretty and charming – little cases of unreasonableness in a vast desert of practical sense.' [9]

Jennie did not fit easily into that generalization about American women, and Wilde had great respect for her. When she wrote and asked him to settle a bet she had made on the accuracy of a quotation from one of his plays, he promptly answered:

'The only difference between the saint and a sinner is that every saint has a past and that every sinner has a future!' That, of course, is the quotation. How dull men are! They should listen to brilliant women, and look at beautiful ones – and, when, as in the present case, a woman is both beautiful and brilliant, they might have the ordinary common sense to admit that she is verbally inspired.[10]

Wilde once said, 'The first duty in life is to be as artificial as possible. What the second duty is, no one has yet discovered.' [11] And he lived by this rule. At his trial, he was 'as artificial as possible'. Describing the first day in court, a New York *Herald* correspondent wrote that it was the first time in the history of the Old Bailey that the dock of that court was occupied by a peer of the realm. 'Yet, though it was the Marquis who was technically in the dock, it was quite evident that before the day's proceedings finished, it was his accuser, the heavily-jowled, broad-shouldered person, lounging ungracefully over the front of the witness box, who really stood on his defense before the world.' [12]

'He made one think of an enormous doll, a preposterously exaggerated puppet, a rather heavy dandy of the Regency period,' wrote Richard Le Gallienne.[13] Wilde had a large, loose face, thick sensuous lips, and his curly hair was modelled to his face, almost like a wig. 'All his bad qualities began to show in his face,' another reporter wrote.[14] His eyes, however, were haughty and humorous, and he modulated his strong voice with elaborate self-consciousness.

When asked whether iced champagne was a favourite drink of his, Wilde said that it was, though strictly against the doctor's orders. And when Carson rapped out, 'Never mind the doctor, Mr Wilde,' he replied, 'I don't mind the doctor.'[15] 'It was all very amusing, and there were roars of laughter,' wrote E. F. Benson, 'but the entertainment was madly out of place, and most prejudicial to him, for these answers were given to questions which clearly had a very ugly significance, and a more unsuitable occasion for jests could not be imagined.'[16]

Carson cut into Wilde's witty quibbles 'with his bitter, shameless questionings, like an apple corer plunging down into the heart.'[17] The questioning revealed that Wilde's father had been an alcoholic oculist in Dublin, his mother a poetess who wanted a daughter and consoled herself by dressing and treating Oscar as if he were a girl.[18]

This was Carson's first *cause célèbre* at the English Bar and 'it fitted him as closely as an executioner's mask.'[19] One of Wilde's letters to Queensberry's twenty-year-old son, Lord Alfred Douglas, was read aloud in court:

My own dear boy – Your sonnet is quite lovely and it is a marvel that those red roseleaf lips of yours should be made no less for the music of song than for the madness of kissing. Your slim gilt soul walks between passion and poetry. I know that Hyacinthus, whom Apollo loved so madly, was you in Greek days. Why are you alone in London, and when do you go to Salisbury? Do go there and cool your hands in the grey twilight of Gothic things, and come here whenever you like. It is a lovely place; it only lacks you, but go to Salisbury first. Always with undying love,

Yours,
Oscar.[20]

In the witness box Wilde stood 'in a clumsy posture, clasping his hands nervously in front of him, over a pair of doeskin gloves he held, and occasionally wiping his forehead with his hand or with his handkerchief.'[21]

The jury's verdict was in favour of the Marquess of Queensberry as 'having proved justification for the libel'. Oscar Wilde was arrested and charged under Section II of the Criminal Law Amendment Act for acts of gross indecency between males. No charges were brought against Lord Alfred Douglas, the young man who held Wilde's affections. Similarly, no charges had been brought six years before when a police raid found Lord Arthur Somerset, a friend of the Prince of Wales, in a homosexual brothel.[22] The difference was that Wilde had forced public notice of an ugly side of society, instead of keeping it discreetly quiet.

'The two great turning points of my life,' Wilde said, 'were when my father sent me to Oxford, and when society sent me to prison.'[23] Two of his plays were then playing in London, and the management quickly covered his name on the bill-boards. The plays were soon suppressed, however, and his books were withdrawn from library lists. The ultimate insult came from Wilde's brother who told George Bernard Shaw, 'Oscar was not a man of bad character; you could trust him with a woman anywhere.'[24]

It was a trial of fascination and horror for Jennie, as it was for all England. But for Jennie the trial would have a meaning far beyond her imagination. At that very same time, her own son Winston was enmeshed in a situation which would result in a charge that he had engaged in 'acts of gross immorality of the Oscar Wilde type'.

The scandal concerning Winston would not become public until a year later, in the spring of 1896. But the alleged incident on which the scandal was based was said to have taken place just before the Wilde affair.

The charge against Winston came from Alan Cameron Bruce-Pryce, a graduate of Oxford and a member of the Bar. His son, Alan George Cameron Bruce, had been a classmate of Winston's at Sandhurst and had gone into Winston's cavalry regiment, the 4th Hussars. Early in March 1895, six subalterns of the 4th Hussars invited Bruce to dine with them at the Nimrod Club. Winston Churchill apparently acted as the spokesman for the junior officers and 'informed Mr Bruce, almost in so many words, that he had been invited to the dinner in order to let him know that he was not wanted in the regiment.' The primary reason given was that Bruce's allowance of £500 a year was not sufficient to 'go the pace' of the regiment. Oddly enough, Winston's own allowance was less than £300 a year.

According to one account, the young men intimated that 'they had got rid of Hodge [Bruce's predecessor] and they would get rid of Bruce, too, adding that if the latter gentleman did not choose to make a graceful exit now, he would probably make a disgraceful one before very long.' [25]

Hodge, whose allowance had also apparently been 'inadequate', had been hauled from his bed to a horse trough, pushed under the bars, 'dragged to the other end, and then hauled out, wet through, bruised and bleeding, and carried back to his room, his night clothing torn to shreds.' They repeated the same action the next night, and shortly afterward Hodge resigned from the regiment.[26]

Despite all this, Bruce was determined to remain in the regiment, so a general social boycott against him was put into effect. Within a short time Bruce was called up on charges of forcing his way into the Sergeants' Mess, and he was asked to resign.

Bruce vehemently denied the allegation, but he did resign and nothing else was heard of the matter until almost a year later. At that time his father was negotiating with the new subaltern taking his son's place for the sale of some of Bruce's equipment. It was in a letter to this subaltern, Ian Hogg, in February 1896, that Bruce's father made the charge that led to the scandal.

Winston and his mother consulted their friends and solicitors and issued a writ:

STATEMENT OF CLAIM
In the High Court of Justice
QUEEN'S BENCH DIVISION
Writ issued 15 February 1896
Between WINSTON SPENCER CHURCHILL...
Plaintiff
AND
A. C. BRUCE-PRYCE ... Defendant

1. – The Plaintiff is a lieutenant holding Her Majesty's commission in the 4th (Queen's Own) Hussars.
2. – On or about the 11th February 1896 the Defendant falsely and maliciously wrote and published to 2nd Lieutenant Hogg of the said regiment of and concerning the Plaintiff and of and concerning the Plaintiff in his said profession the words following that is to say: –
'His real offence however was that he was at Sandhurst with Mr

Churchill and that they had been rivals in shooting, fencing and riding throughout their career and incidentally that he knew too much about Mr Churchill.

'There was for instance one man whose initial is C, flogged publicly by a subaltern court-martial for acts of gross immorality of the Oscar Wilde type with Mr Churchill.

'I have not as yet ascertained what was done by the E Company to Mr Churchill, but as soon as I do I shall lay the statement before the War Office.'

3. – The Defendant meant and was understood to mean by the said words that the Plaintiff was a person of vile and disreputable character unworthy of associating with the officers of his regiment or any honourable men and unfit to hold Her Majesty's commission. That he had been guilty of gross acts of indecency with male persons and in particular had been detected and exposed in one flagrant case. That by reason of the premises the Plaintiff had been guilty of criminal offences and was liable to be indicted under the Criminal Law Amendment Act 1885.

4. – By reason of the premises the Plaintiff has been grievously injured in his credit and reputation and in his said profession and in his position as officer in Her Majesty's Army and has been held up to hatred and contempt.

The Plaintiff claims 20,000 pounds damage.

W. Temple Franks.

Delivered the 21st day of February 1896 by Messieurs LEWIS and LEWIS Ely Place, Holborn E.C. Solicitors for the Plaintiff.

The case was settled within a month for £500 and the withdrawal of the charges by Bruce-Pryce: 'I unreservedly withdraw all and every imputation against your character complained of by you . . . and I hereby express my regret at having made the same.'

Colonel Brabazon promptly wrote Winston a letter expressing his 'intense pleasure' at the outcome and his delight that the case had not come to trial:

For altho you would have come out of it with flying colours & there could have been but one issue to the case, yet it is a thousand fold better that it should have terminated as it has, for one cannot touch pitch without soiling one's hands however clean they may have originally been, and the world is so ill natured & suspicious that there would always have been found some ill natured sneak or perhaps some d——d good natured friend to hem and ha! and wink over it – perhaps in years to come, when everyone even yourself had forgotten all about the disagreeable incident.[27]

The following week Brabazon wrote to Winston that he had discussed the affair with Sir Redvers Buller, who was perfectly satisfied, 'so we will consider the incident as closed for ever. Oddly enough Buller told me that he had on his table a letter from Lansdowne [Secretary of State for War] to Mr B. P. [Bruce-Pryce] declining to reopen the racing case or to have anything more to do with him. He threatens to bring it before Parliament.'[28]

The racing case was still another scandal in which Winston was involved, and this, too, occurred in March 1895.

Shortly before Jennie's mother died, Winston rode in a steeplechase for the 4th Hussars' Subalterns' Challenge Cup. He used the pseudonym of 'Mr Spencer', probably because he had promised his mother he would not ride in steeplechase races. The winning horse, at 6–1 odds, was 'Surefoot'. A year later, at the time the Bruce scandal broke, the National Hunt Committee reported irregularities in the race. After an investigation, the race was declared null and void, and the horses which had taken part in it were disqualified from all future races run under National Hunt rules.

When Colonel Brabazon told Winston that the incident was 'closed for ever', he was being hopeful but not realistic. *Truth*, a weekly magazine owned and edited by Henry Labouchere, had taken up the Bruce case as a cause. Labouchere, who was also Member of Parliament for Northampton, demanded a full investigation by the Army and personally brought the matter up for debate in the House of Commons. In addition to raking up all the details of the Bruce case, Labouchere now combined it with the race scandal, observing that some of the same subalterns were involved in both affairs.

Labouchere asserted that the subalterns in the steeplechase race had substituted a superior horse for Surefoot as a last-minute 'ringer' to collect on the heavy odds.[29]

The Army investigated the Bruce case and placed the fault on Bruce for not being proper regimental material. It also refused to reopen the racing case. Labouchere increased the pressure in his magazine and in

Parliament, and Winston was worried. He urged his mother, '. . . what you do must be done from my point of view alone and not with reference to the regiment – who have no ideas beyond soldiering and care nothing for the opinion of those who are not their friends. I leave matters in your hands – but in my absence my dearest Mamma – you must be the guardian of my young reputation.'[30] In his next letter, a week later, Winston again referred to the damage being done by the Labouchere articles, and added, 'Therefore do muzzle him if you can.'[31]

Jennie had already been busy making the necessary contacts. Brabazon was her confidant and strongest ally. The man who would make the final decision was Viscount Wolseley, Commander in Chief of the Army. He had often dined at Jennie's home, as had the Marquess of Lansdowne. Sir Redvers Buller, the Commander at Aldershot, was an even closer friend of both Jennie and Brabazon. The Under Secretary of State for War, William St John Brodrick, who defended the Army position in the House of Commons, was an old Churchill family friend. Jennie must certainly have been in touch with all of them, either personally or through Brabazon. Perhaps she also called on Labouchere himself, reminding him that he had once been a friend of her husband.

Labouchere described the growing pressure to drop the case:

> . . . The public must bear in mind that the young officer who assumed the part of ringleader in the conspiracy to eject Mr Bruce from the 4th Hussars belongs to an influential family, and that all the influence at his back has been used to prevent a reopening of the case, as I can testify from my own experience.[32]

Soon afterwards, however, Labouchere finally dropped his attack.

In his letters to his mother Winston had seemed more concerned about the racing scandal than about the homosexual charges. It is likely, however, that Jennie had been more deeply troubled about the intimation of homosexuality.

When her own marriage disintegrated with the discovery of her husband's syphilis, Jennie sought other men. Lord Randolph, however, did not seek other women. It was as if he blamed all women for the syphilis which destroyed his brilliant political career. He increasingly took long trips with men friends, and there was some talk of his growing effeminacy.

Winston and Jack had never had the sort of close relationship with their father that is so important in encouraging the development of manliness in young boys. It was said of Jennie that she had invaded more of the man's world than any other woman of her time, but no woman can be a father to her sons. Jennie had toughness, but her sons' needs went beyond toughness, beyond strength, beyond love.

The relationship between father and son is an irreplaceable relationship, almost a spiritual kind of transference. It is a reaching and a giving of a unique kind. The mother–son feeling is usually soft, gentle, perhaps enveloping; but the father–son feeling is firmer and fuller. Winston and John had never had this.

This absence of a father–son relationship was not unusual in upper-class England during the nineteenth century, and it was probably part of the reason that homosexuality and sadism were so rampant in public schools. All older public-school boys were catered to by younger 'fags', who were often brutalized if they failed to give quick and proper service. Jennie's nephew, Shane Leslie, remembered one boy so brutalized that he attempted suicide one night by chewing on the green copper of a pipe in the lavatory, believing it to be a deadly poison.[33]

Jennie might have been concerned that even though he was almost twenty-one, Winston showed little interest in women. Perhaps the knowledge of his father's syphilis deterred him. 'Ambitions I still have: I have always had them,' said the hero in Winston's novel Savrola, 'but love I am not to know, or to know it only to my vexation and despair.'[34]

The only real love Winston had shown was for his mother. Filling his faithful flow of letters to her – at least once a week, for many years – was the kind of sentimental, romantic language a young man might write to the young woman he loves. There are many mothers who are possessive of their sons and flattered by such demonstrations of affection, but Jennie was not. She wanted his love, of course, but she also wanted him to be his own man.

Just before his death, Winston still had on his desk a copper mould of a hand. It was a cast of his mother's hand, and his own hand was almost its replica.[35]

Nobody knew better than Jennie that what Winston needed most was the support of a strong man. With the Oscar Wilde scandal still stark in her mind, Jennie must have considered this deeply as she journeyed back to Paris in April 1895.

5

'Poor dear Mama. It is so sad. You and Winnie will have to protect and take care of her now and make her happy. . . .'[1] The condolence note to Jack, after his father's death, was from his and Winston's childhood nurse, Mrs Everest.

But far more than care and protection, Jennie needed the enduring love of a man. She seemed to find it in Paris with Bourke Cockran. If happiness in life consists of having something to do, someone to love, and something to hope for, then Jennie and Bourke must have been happy in Paris. It was a whirling world: there was always another restaurant, another party, another theatre, another club. 'It was a very lively life,' remembered Jennie's nephew, who regarded his aunt as 'picturesque, rather mysterious . . . something far more beautiful than any of the actresses we were called upon to admire. . . .'[2]

Bourke Cockran agreed. Jennie was filled with the joy of living, an enormous sense of gaiety and excitement, and Paris was the place for her. The night of the Grand Prix, the great race of the year, was the fête night of Paris. Richard Harding Davis wrote of it:

You will see on that night, and only on that night, the most celebrated women of Paris racing with linked arms about the asphalt pavement which circles around the bandstand. It is for them their one night of freedom in public, when they are permitted to conduct themselves as do their less prosperous sisters, when, instead of reclining in a victoria in the Bois, with eyes demurely fixed in front of them, they can throw off restraint and mix with all the men of Paris, and show their diamonds and romp and dance and chaff, and laugh as they did when they were not so famous.

The theme song of the Nineties was 'The Man Who Broke the Bank at Monte Carlo', and the crowd of thousands sing and shout it in French and English, with a strut and swagger backgrounded by the clashing of cymbals and the big drums and the blaring of brass.

And when they reached the high note in the chorus, the musicians, carried away by the fever of the crowd, jumped upon the chairs, and held their instruments as high above their heads as they could without losing control of that note, all holding onto the highest note as long as their breath lasted. It was a triumphant, reckless yell of defiance and delight; it was the war cry of that class of Parisians about which one always reads and which one sees so seldom, which comes to the surface only at unusual intervals, and which, when it does appear, lives up to its reputation and does not disappoint you.[3]

At the Grand Prix of 1895, people still talked about the previous Grand Prix when the favourite was an English horse named Matchbox. So protective were the horse's owners that they had the horse escorted onto the track by eight gendarmes, seven detectives in plain clothes, two trainers, and the jockey. As one cynic put it, 'Probably if they had been allowed to follow him round the course on bicycles he might have won, and no combination of French jockeys could have ridden him into the rail. . . .' Sophisticated Parisians claimed the sure way to win money at the Prix was to bet *against* any English horse.[4]

Jennie's house in Paris was a natural social centre with a constant flow of people. The American news was that the heat along the Atlantic Coast was an unprecedented 96 degrees in the shade; that a soldier had bicycled from New York to Chicago in 13 days, 7 hours, and 45 minutes; and most important, that the New York State Senate had approved a resolution in favour of woman's suffrage.

The news from Britain was that Lord Rosebery had won one race but lost another. His horse had won the Derby for the second year in succession, but Rosebery had resigned as Prime Minister.[5]

Friends brought news from other parts of the world. Revolution had spread throughout Cuba, and the insurgents had seized several towns. The Japanese had defeated the Chinese and declared a Kingdom of Korea. Sir Edgar Vincent had arrived from South Africa with news of increased friction there.[6] And Harry Cust, who had written delicate love poetry for Jennie and was now editor of the *Pall Mall Gazette*, arrived from Armenia with stories of turmoil and atrocities.

It was a humming household at 34 Avenue Kléber but it was well organized by Walden, who had been Lord Randolph's butler. He superintended a small staff of French servants, aided by Jennie's maid Gentry.

Bourke fitted easily into this *mélange* of activity, completely accepted by both Jennie's sisters as almost part of the family.

All three sisters had planned to accompany their mother's body back to Brooklyn for burial. A New York newspaper reported their plans, noting, 'In their journey across the ocean, the three sisters will be under the care of Bourke Cockran.'[7] But then Jennie decided not to go. The primary reason was that something had gone wrong in her relationship with Bourke.

What, and why? Religion? Bourke was a devout Catholic, an active worker and lecturer for the Catholic Church in New York. But was this difference insurmountable? Probably it was not. What else then? Kinsky? Was the 'opium' of that romance still too strong, was he still too near, were they seeing each other again in Paris? Possibly. But was there another factor: If they were married, where would they make their home? A British reporter commented about Jennie, 'She is allied to both [England and America] with bonds of steel. It is doubtful if she herself could tell to which she is closest.'[8]

Jennie had lived most of her adult life in England. All of her dearest friends were there. Her sons belonged to it. She had absorbed its culture, its graces, its intellectual ferment, its very air. It was true that she retained her American accent, and proudly waved a small American flag when an American horse won the Derby. She was also the main American social focus in London, even more than the changing American Ambassador. But England now was as much a part of her blood and bone as America was. It would rip the whole fabric of her life to give it up. Bourke's roots were deep in America. It was not a matter for compromise: one of them would have to surrender.

That was probably the basic reason for the end of their affair: each of them was too big for surrender. Each was so remarkable a person, so strong a personality, that perhaps they found themselves competing with one another. A love affair can be intense, tempestuous, full of the fierceness and wonder of living, but marriage requires long-range consideration. Ten years earlier, all their doubts and questions and logic would have been swept away by their emotions. But now they were both mature and toughened by the turmoil of their lives; they had learned how to look round all the corners. Their past and future marriages seem to demonstrate that, for a lifetime of living, each needed someone weaker. Each of them married non-competitive mates whom they felt they could more easily control. Bourke and Jennie together were too much of a match.

Leonie was a confidante of both of them, and they both hinted to her of this sort of problem. Bourke told her that Jennie was so overcharged with energy that she wore him out, and Jennie said that it was exhausting to be alone with Bourke, that he really needed a table of guests to whom he could 'show off'.

The pity of it was that they could not face the challenge of each other. As it was, their parting regret must have been deeply felt, but there was no sharp break. Bourke continued to commute to London until he remarried, and it was not just to visit his sister and his niece. Jennie, in turn, depended on Bourke for a variety of advice and assistance. In fact they never stopped seeing each other or writing to each other, even after each remarried. Their letters became much more circumspect, of course, but whenever Jennie really needed Bourke, he never failed her.

When her sisters and Bourke went to America, Jennie went to Aix-les-Bains, the small, fashionable resort in southern France where the warm sulphur springs were said to give guests a new lease on life. For Jennie, however, it meant a lonely interval of solitary walks in the gardens, the baths, the brooding reflections among the Roman antiquities, with the future seeming more and more remote.

Her sons kept up a regular flow of mail. Winston had been to the races at Newmarket and wrote that 'The Prince asked after you as did many others.' [9] On another occasion Winston lunched at the Duke of Connaught's residence. 'The Prince was there and saw me. I had a long talk with Lord Roberts – who had just been made Field Marshal. Everyone of course asked after you. . . .' [10] Another day, the Duke and Duchess of York (later King George V and Queen Mary) came to see the regiment at a field day and Winston was asked to dine with them. 'The Colonel went there also and although everything was exceedingly formal I was very glad to have been asked. I had quite a long talk with the Duke of Connaught about the Election & of course everyone asked for you. . . .' [11]

Then came a sad letter. Their nanny, their childhood nurse Mrs Everest, had died of peritonitis. 'Everything that could be done was done,' Winston wrote:

I engaged a nurse – but she only arrived for the end. It was very sad &

her death was shocking to see – but I do not think she suffered much pain.

She was delighted to see me on Monday night and I think my coming made her die happy. Her last words were of Jack. . . . Please send a wire to Welldon to ask him to let Jack come up for the funeral – as he is very anxious to do so.

. . . Well my dearest Mummy . . . I feel very low – and find that I never realized how much poor old Woom [Mrs Everest] was to me. I don't know what I should do without you.[12]

Winston's need for his mother was not only emotional ('. . . How I wish I could secrete myself in the corner of the envelope and embrace you as soon as you tear it open'[13]), it was also intellectual. He discussed politics and people with her in great detail. Winston felt the new government of Lord Salisbury was 'too strong – too brilliant altogether. They are just the sort of government to split on the question of Protection. Like a huge ship with powerful engines they will require careful steering – because any collision means destruction.'[14]

Taking office for the third time, Salisbury was then sixty-five years old, a bulky man, his shoulders more stooped than ever, his full, curly beard more grey. He was a melancholy, unpredictable man who had a sharp, penetrating mind. Salisbury had distrusted Lord Randolph, but he had always been very appreciative of Jennie.[15] Winston had met Salisbury at his mother's dinner table.

When Jennie and Winston discussed politics, they usually had the advantage of discussing people they knew rather than remote names and abstract policies. In her letters to him, there was none of the condescension of a politically sophisticated woman to a son not quite old enough to vote. Jennie was careful to keep her correspondence on a level of equality, respecting the surprising maturity of her son's opinions and not hesitating to argue when she felt that he was wrong or uninformed. She always believed that his real future was in politics, and she was delighted when he wrote her of army life, 'I do not think it is my *métier*.' Later he commented, 'It is a fine game to play – the game of politics – and it is well worth a good hand before really plunging.'[16] He was counting on her, he said, to look out for the 'good hand'.

Her two sons were very different in their emotional make-up, their personalities, their abilities, their needs. Jack, not yet sixteen, was the quiet one. He was of medium height but would grow taller than Winston, and he was also the better looking of the two. He idolized his brother, who was everything that he was not – outgoing, adventurous, exuberant – although Jack was very likely the better horseman. He also had more of his mother's elegance and charm, and certainly all of her musical ability. Winston was tone deaf.[17]

Jack's son, John Churchill, later wrote of his father, that 'people sought his company, but frankly, he was not what I would call intelligent. Although he shared my passion for Wagner, he had no real understanding of art, and his love for his first-class library hardly went deeper than admiration for the covers and bindings, especially first editions; he seldom actually read the books.'[18]

Despite John Churchill's assessment that his Uncle Winston had 'pinched all the brains in the family',[19] Jack Churchill did very well indeed at Harrow, even though he was the youngest boy in his class. The Reverend J. E. C. Welldon wrote to Jennie of him: 'His conduct in the House is excellent; there is no better boy, and I think you may look with very great satisfaction upon his character.'[20]

Jack was the kind of boy who kept a precise record of his expenses, studied hard enough to get good marks – particularly in English and History – and never had a school punishment. He was a loving boy, who adored his mother. Jennie, in turn, loved Jack as much as she did Winston, but in a different way because their needs were different. She was clearly more solicitous of Jack, more maternal, more concerned about his health. She called him 'Darling Puss', urged him to go to bed early, chided him for his poor spelling,[21] and often wrote, 'I miss you very much. I love you more!'

What worried Jennie most about Jack was that he lacked drive and direction. Unlike Winston, he did what she wanted him to do and seldom argued with her. But what he lacked in excitement, he made up for in dependability. When Jennie needed something done – especially in later years – she went to Jack, not Winston. Jennie was always doing things for Winston and Jack was always doing things for Jennie.

Jennie always reserved a large part of her life for herself, but whatever she gave to her sons, she gave with intensity and concentration. She let both of them know that she loved them deeply, and she proved it again and again. This, she felt, was giving them the strongest root of all. Everything else they could forgive.

'Jack and Winston have helped their mother in every way, even by not going to the University in order to work, and both absolutely adore her,' Jennie's sisters Leonie had told her son. 'I have done everything and given my boys everything, but they don't seem to care for me at all.'[22]

Both sons had joined Jennie in Paris for the short Easter holiday, and Jack joined her again in August 1895 for a trip through Switzerland. Winston was unable to go, as he was laid up with a 'sprung vein' caused by too much riding.

After returning from Switzerland, Jennie went on to the Isle of Wight for Cowes Week. It was an event she never missed, as it was very social but in a relaxed kind of way. Yachting had been a love of her father's, and he had passed it on to his daughters.

The main rivalry this year was between the Prince of Wales and his nephew, Kaiser Wilhelm II of Germany. The Prince thoroughly disliked his nephew, and Princess Alexandra detested him. But even this did not spoil the light-hearted spirit of the event.

At Cowes Jennie was soon surrounded by her fashionable friends. Women's fashions had evolved toward the Gibson Girl figure – full-bosomed, full-bottomed, a tinier waist than ever before, and a flowing skirt. It suited Jennie well. The leg-o'-mutton sleeve, which had periodically shrunk and swelled, was at its zenith. Tall, tight collars covered most throats, and skirts again swept the floor.[23]

Hair was kept close to the head in a bun, although many women soon began to wear it fluffed out. During the 'bun' period, a dignified nobleman complimented Jennie on her 'bum'. Suddenly realizing what he had said, he felt very embarrassed, but Jennie made light of it.[24] Also fashionable then were the wide-brimmed picture hats that seemed to float on top of the head and were called hatpin hats. Women skaters, however, had to be warned how to fall properly – 'Falling on your back can drive your hatpin into your head.'[25]

During that week in August 1895, everybody seemed to be wearing white: the men, white trousers and white shoes. Jennie and her sisters wore white serge sailor suits, with sailor hats that had been made fashionable by Princess Alexandra.

One of the more sprightly but snobbish guests was Jennie's American cousin, Kitty Mott, a niece of her mother's. Kitty and her millionaire husband arrived on a luxurious three-masted schooner, the *Utoawana*. Jennie noted that the one thing that seemed to depress Kitty was the fact that her husband's iron works specialized in lavatories and his name was emblazoned on all of them.

Jennie and Leonie took some of their time to befriend a shy, teenage girl. 'They saw me standing about, looking lost and bewildered, for I knew no one, so they came up and spoke to me in a gay, friendly way, transforming the day I had rather dreaded into a glorious episode of my hitherto quiet life. . . .' [26] The shy girl, who became the Duchess of Sermoneta, later considered the two sisters among her most intimate friends.

Jennie, however, did not spend all her time wih Leonie and their friends. The Prince of Wales, who had left Cowes early, wrote to Jennie of a report he had heard that she was frequently seen in the company of Hugh Warrender. Mixing some jest with obvious jealousy, the Prince wondered 'where your next loved victim is . . .?'

Hugh Warrender seemed a likely candidate. A handsome, twenty-seven-year-old officer in the Grenadier Guards, he would periodically reappear in Jennie's life. Even her sons were conscious of the feeling between them and made references to Hugh in their letters. 'Turn on the devoted Warrender,' Winston wrote to his mother when he wanted more correspondents.[27]

Jennie's nephew mentions that his aunt seemed to have a particular attraction for young men. He remembered one who proposed marriage to her thirteen times but was always gently refused. He might have been Warrender.

Cowes Week over, Jennie went to London for some intensive house-hunting. During the summer, Winston had written, 'I am longing for the day when you will be able to have a little house of your own and when I can really feel that there is such a thing as home. . . .' And while she and Jack were in Switzerland, he wrote, 'I do look forward to having a house once more. It will be too delightful to ring the bell of one's own front door again. . . .' [28]

Jennie had been thinking the same thing. The gay, aimless, wandering life in which she had been free and easy for the first time was a tonic she had needed. But now she needed a home, not only for her sons, but for herself. She soon found what she wanted. It was not in fashionable Mayfair, but on the wrong side of Oxford Street: a quiet, respectable address, 35A Great Cumberland Place, within sight of Marble Arch and only a short distance from Hyde Park. It was a handsome, seven-storey Georgian house with a large library. Clara later sold her own large house opposite the Russian Embassy in Chesham Place and took a smaller one directly opposite Jennie's, at Number 37.

Leonie, too, soon moved nearby, to Number 10. It was rumoured that Number 4 was inhabited by the phantom of a butler who had committed suicide. The ghost, it was said, still answered the doorbell in a most disconcerting manner – at least disconcerting enough for that house to have changed tenants ten times while Jennie lived in Great Cumberland Place. Much more alive was another neighbour, the celebrated Australian soprano Nellie Melba (originally Helen Porter Mitchell). Nellie and Jennie became friends, and they played piano duets and even sang together. But it was Jennie and her sisters who gave Great Cumberland Place its own social reputation, so much so that it came to be known as 'Lower Jerome Terrace'.[29]

Most of the socially important American residents of London lived within a mile of Hyde Park Corner. The more favoured ones faced the park itself, as Jennie had when she lived at Connaught Place. Americans were moving into most of the gracious mansions. Lansdowne House, which had been a British institution of social grandeur, would soon be rented by William Waldorf Astor. And the magnificent Dorchester House, with its spectacular grand stairway, glass cases enclosing Shakespearian folios, and a splendid carriage drive laid down in ground red brick, would become the American Embassy.

On October 3 Jennie wrote to Clara:

I shall go to Mintos for a few days & then to London to look after '35A *Greater* Cumberland Place' as the boys call it – I hope to get into it the end of November; but you know how long it takes to do anything & I am going to have it all painted from top to toe, electric light, hot water etc. . . . How nice it will be when we are all together again on our 'owns'! The boys are so delighted at the thought of 'ringing their own front door' they can think of nothing else. . . .

But Winston was thinking of others things too:

My dearest Mamma,

I daresay you will find the content of this letter somewhat startling. The fact is that I have decided to go with a great friend of mine, one of the subalterns in the regiment, to America and the W. Indies. . . . We shall go to New York & after a stay there move in a steamer to the W. Indies – to Havana where all the Government troops are collecting to go up country and suppress the revolt that is still simmering on; after that back by Jamaica and Hayti to New York & so home. . . .

Now I hope you won't mind my going my dear Mamma – as it will do me good to travel a bit with a delightful companion who is one of the senior subalterns. . . .[30]

Jennie was worried and tried to dampen the idea.

You know I am always delighted if you can do anything which interests and amuses you – even if it be a sacrifice to me. I was rather looking forward to our being together & seeing something of you. Remember, I only have you and Jack to love me. You certainly have not the art of writing & putting everything in their best lights but I understand all right – & of course darling it is natural that you shd want to travel & I won't throw cold water on yr little plans – *but* I'm very much afraid it will cost a good deal more than you think. N.Y. is fearfully expensive. . . .[31]

She made a strong point in her letter of saying, 'I *must* know more about yr friend. What is his name? Not that I don't believe you are a good judge but still I shd like to be sure of him.' Winston's friend was Reggie Barnes, the same young man who was involved in the Bruce case and the racing scandal.

Jennie also added a maternal criticism: 'Considering that I provide the funds I think instead of saying "I *have* decided to go", it may have been nicer and perhaps wiser – to have begun by consulting me. But I suppose experience of life will in time teach you that tact is a very essential ingredient in all things.'

At the end of her letter, however, she suddenly gave up the whole idea of being a careful and restraining mother and wrote, 'P.S. I have had a talk with the Tweedmouths over yr plans & they can help you much in the way of letters to the Gov of Jamaica & in suggesting a tour. . . . Would you like me as a birthday pres to pay yr ticket?'[32]

The first of his mother's friends whom Winston contacted was Sir Henry Drummond Wolff, Her Majesty's Ambassador in Madrid and one of Jennie's oldest admirers. She had met him at Cowes before her marriage and described him afterwards as 'the best of the company . . . with a pink-and-white complexion that a girl might have envied, and a merry twinkle which hid behind a pair of spectacles . . . a godsend if anything went wrong, and a joke from him saved many a situation.' It was Wolff who had suggested starting the Primrose League, a politico-social organization through which Conservatives could meet and work together, regardless of their social class. Jennie was part of the original group of twelve who helped organize it, until it became a working coalition of almost two million people. Wolff was cynical, flippant and unflappable, but a man of great warmth who was very fond of Jennie. Winston wrote to him, and Wolff promptly replied. 'After receiving yesterday your letter, I saw the Minister for Foreign Affairs [The Duke of Tetuan] & spoke to him about your wish to go to Cuba. . . . He said he would get you a letter from the Minister of War & give you one himself to Marshal Martinez Campos who is personally his great friend.' [33]

Campos, who had been Minister of War and Prime Minister, was now the Captain-General of the Spanish Army. Wolff also asked about Jennie and sent his love. He followed up with a very official letter from the Minister of War to Marshal Campos 'which I hope will obtain for you the facilities you desire.' [34]

Winston also got Colonel Brabazon's approval, and Brabazon sent him to see Viscount Wolseley, who was then Commander-in-Chief of the Army and another friend of Jennie's. 'He said he quite approved,' Winston reported to his mother, 'but rather hinted that it would have been better to go without asking leave at all.' Wolseley, however, sent Winston to Military Intelligence for maps and background. 'We are also requested to collect information and statistics on various points & particularly as to the effects of the new bullet — its penetration and striking power. This invests our mission with an almost official character & cannot fail to help one in the future.' [35]

Now that the expedition to Cuba was settled, Winston was suddenly remorseful. 'When are you coming to London?' he asked Jennie. 'Do send me a wire to let me know. I must see a little of you before we go.' He also remarked that he planned to bring back a great many Havana cigars 'some of which can be "laid down" in the cellars of 35 Great Cumberland Place.' At the end of the letter he added, 'Longing to see you.' [36]

Only to her did he fully reveal himself. Only to her did he reveal his driving ambition. Only with Jennie was he always open and unabashed. She chided him for his conceit, but she believed in him. And for the rest of her life she would tap the men and open the doors to prepare the complicated pattern of stepping stones to his future.

6

It is a rather extraordinary woman who can turn to a recently rejected lover and ask him to be host to her son. But Jennie scarcely hesitated. There was no need to. The love they had shared had enriched them both, and this favour would bring further mutual enrichment.

Bourke would never have a son of his own. His only child had been stillborn. This was a great lack in a man like Bourke Cockran, who had so much that he wanted to pass on. Now Jennie was giving Bourke a son for a time, just as she was giving Winston a father.

For Bourke, Winston must have seemed a double image. On the one hand, he had the courage, the intelligence, the ambition that Bourke himself had as a young man. And on the other, these qualities, in addition to the boy's remarkable self-confidence, no doubt reminded Bourke of Jennie.

For Winston, Bourke loomed not only as a father figure, but also as a man of enormous wisdom and experience, a great orator, a man of taste and style, much the model of the man he himself wanted to be. More than that, Bourke was much the model of the man Jennie wanted Winston to be.

Bourke was at the dock to meet Winston on his arrival in New York, and took him to his home. He had a spacious apartment at 763 Fifth Avenue, 'beautifully furnished and fitted with every convenience'.[1] The chairs were soft and deep, the library was large, and Bourke served the best brandy, the finest food, the longest cigars. It was one thing for Winston to spend weekends at the country homes of his mother's British friends; it was quite another to live in the apartment of a brilliant aggressive American, a man's man. 'Mr Cockran is one of the most charming hosts and interesting men I have met,' Winston immediately informed his mother.[2]

'I have never seen his like, or in some respects, his equal,' he later added. 'His conversation, in point, in pith, in rotundity, in antithesis and in comprehension exceeded anything I had ever heard.'[3]

This was an extraordinary statement from a young man who had been in contact with the finest minds of England: Gladstone, Salisbury, Rosebery, Chamberlain, Balfour, and his own father. Bourke Cockran was not just a man with a fine mind and an eloquent tongue; he was also a superb listener. And with Winston, Bourke Cockran showed that he truly cared what the young man said, that he respected him.

They talked until very late almost every night. Bourke not only revealed the breadth of his experience and the depth of his mind, but he taught Winston how to use language. 'What people really want to hear is the truth – it is the exciting thing – speak the simple truth.'[4]

Avoid cant, he said, avoid mannerisms, invective, egotism. The two men analysed their mutual admiration for the great English orator of a previous century, Edmund Burke. 'Burke mastered the English language as a man masters the horse,' Cockran said. 'He was simple, direct, eloquent, yet there is a splendour in his phrases that even in cold type reveals how forcibly he must have enthralled his visitors. . . . How I should have loved to have heard him.'[5]

Winston wanted to hear Cockran speak, and he persuaded him to read some of his speeches. What was so memorable to Winston was Cockran's titanic vigour, his poetic vision, the fire without frenzy. There were phrases of Cockran's that Winston never forgot. Many years later, he told an American audience:

I remember when I first came over here, in 1895, I was a guest of your great lawyer and orator, Mr Bourke Cockran. I was only a young cavalry subaltern, but he poured out all his wealth of mind and eloquence to me. Some of his sentences are deeply rooted in my mind. 'The earth,' he said, 'is a generous mother. She will provide in plentiful abundance food for all her children, if they will but cultivate her soil in justice and peace.' I used to repeat that so frequently on British platforms that my wife very strongly advised me to give it a holiday, which I have done for a good many years. But now, today, it seems to come back with new pregnancy and force, for never was the choice between blessing and cursing more vehemently presented to the human race.

There was another thing Bourke Cockran used to say to me. I cannot remember his actual words, but they amounted to this: 'In a society where there is democratic tolerance and freedom under the law, many kinds of evils will crop up, but give them a little time and they usually breed their own cure.' Now, I do not see any reason to doubt the truth of that. There is no country in the world where the process of self-criticism and self-correction is more active than in the United States.

You must not – you must not indeed – think I am talking politics. I make it a rule never to meddle in internal or party politics of any friendly country. It's hard enough to understand the party politics of your own! Still, I remain, as I have said, a strong supporter of the principles which Mr Bourke Cockran inculcated into me on my youthful visit before most of you were born.[6]

Winston Churchill even repeated Cockran's words in his historic Iron Curtain Speech at Fulton, Missouri:

I have often used words which I learned fifty years ago from a great Irish-American orator, a friend of mine, Mr Bourke Cockran. 'There is enough for all. The earth is a generous mother; she will provide in plentiful abundance food for all her children if they will but cultivate her soil in justice and in peace.'[7]

How remarkable to have retained whole sentences for half a century. But both men had amazingly retentive minds. Bourke explained to Winston how he prepared for his speeches: studying the subject in detail, storing in his memory material from a wide range of reading, trying to simplify the most abstruse questions with familiar, easily understandable illustrations, and then trusting to the inspiration of the moment for the phrasing of sentences.[8] Until then, everything Winston knew about oratory derived from his own analysis of what he himself had heard. Now for the first time he was learning basic techniques from an expert.

But it was more than technique, more than fine phrases that Winston absorbed. It was the spirit of oratory, something he already had within him but that was now suddenly made more exciting.

Jennie was delighted to get Winston's enthusiastic reports from New York. 'I have great discussions with Mr Cockran on every conceivable subject from Economics to yacht racing.'[9] And in a later letter, he added, 'We have made great friends.'[10] No other man in Jennie's life could have given her son all that Bourke Cockran now gave him.

This was Winston's first trip to his mother's homeland, and there was much to do and see. Bourke planned a full itinerary. 'We have engagements for every meal for the next few days about three deep. . . .', Winston wrote. 'Last night we had a big dinner here to ten or 12 persons all of whom were on the Judiciary. Very interesting men – one particularly – a Supreme Court Judge – is trying a *cause célèbre* case here now. . . .' [11]

Winston sent further details about this to his brother:

There is a great criminal trial going on now – of a man who shot a fellow who had seduced his sister. I met the judge at dinner the other night and he suggested my coming to hear the case. I went and sat on the bench by his side. Quite a strange experience and one which would be impossible in England. The Judge discussing the evidence as it was given with me and generally making himself socially agreeable – & all the while a pale miserable man was fighting for his life. This is a very great country my dear Jack. Not pretty or romantic but great and utilitarian. Everything is eminently practical and things are judged from a matter of fact standpoint. Take for instance the Courthouse. No robes or wigs or uniformed ushers. Nothing but a lot of men in black coats & tweed suits. . . . But they manage to hang a man all the same, and that after all is a great thing. . . . [12]

How Jennie must have laughed with pleasure at Winston's almost boyish excitement with everything he was seeing and doing in the United States. She had opposed his trip to Cuba because she had a mother's concern for her son's unnecessary exposure to combat. She had even expressed doubts about his enjoying New York. If he had been put into the hands of Jennie's elderly and very proper female cousin in America, Winston's enjoyment would indeed have been limited. Her decision to involve Bourke Cockran, however, had changed the whole tone of the trip.

'Mr Cockran, who has great influence over here, procured us orders to visit the Forts of the Harbour and West Point – which is the American Sandhurst,' Winston wrote to Jack.[13] And to his mother, Winston commented, 'I was treated like a general.' [14]

There was also the Horse Show, a trip on a tugboat, and the Fire Department:

The other night, Mr Cockran got the Fire Commissioner to come with us and we alarmed four or five fire stations. This would have interested you very much. On the alarm bell sounding the horses at once rushed into the shafts – the harness fell onto them – the men slid half-dressed down a pole from their sleeping room and in 5½ seconds the engine was galloping down the street to the scene of the fire. An interesting feat which seems incredible unless you have seen it. . . .

What an extraordinary people the Americans are! Their hospitality is a revelation to me and they make you feel at home and at ease in a way that I have never before experienced.[15]

This was his mother's country, his mother's people, his mother's heritage, and therefore a part of his too. 'I am a child of both worlds,' he later said. But even as he wrote about his new world with wonder, he could still be critical. The comfort and convenience of elevated railways was 'extraordinary' he noted, but the use of paper-dollar currency was 'abominable'; and the essence of American journalism was 'vulgarity divested of truth'. American vulgarity, however, was not totally a bad thing, as he explained to Jack:

I think mind you that vulgarity is a sign of strength. A great crude, strong young people are the Americans – like a boisterous healthy boy among enervated but well-bred ladies and gentlemen. . . .

Picture to yourself the American people as a great lusty youth – who treads on all your sensibilities, perpetrates every possible horror of ill manners – whom neither age nor just tradition inspire with reverence – but who moves about his affairs with a good-natured freshness which may well be the envy of older nations of the earth. Of course there are charming people who are just as refined and cultured as the best in any country in the world. . . .[16]

Some of the vulgarity that winter of 1895 was evident in the garish interiors of many of the mansions neighbouring Cockran's apartment. One of them had a reception hall 'conspicuously larger than the Supreme Court of the United States.' Then there was Lillian Russell appearing in a white serge cycling costume with stylish leg-o'-mutton sleeves, riding a gold-plated bicycle with mother-of-pearl handlebars which bore her monogram in diamonds and emeralds, the hubs and spokes of its wheels also set in jewels.

However, there was also a growing informality to parallel the vulgarity. Young men were discarding frock coats, replacing 'boiled shirts' with soft shirts with detachable starched cuffs and collars. Women were seen wearing the new 'rainy-daisy' skirt that cleared the ground by a 'scandalous' six inches.

Winston scarcely had time to examine much of this in detail. He and Reggie Barnes were soon en route to Cuba via Florida in a private compartment thoughtfully arranged for by Bourke Cockran. 'I hope in England to renew our discussions and I can never repay you for your kindness,' Winston wrote to him.[17]

While Winston was in the New World, Jennie, who was a part of both the New World and the Old, suddenly found that her identification with the United States took on a new dimension. In December 1895 President Grover Cleveland sent a message to Congress which was almost an ultimatum to Great Britain. It concerned the boundary between Venezuela and British Guiana. The United States had economic interests in Venezuela, and the Venezuelan government was laying claim to a large part of British Guiana. Negotiations had dragged on unsuccessfully, and now Cleveland informed Congress that he would appoint an American Commission to define the boundary and impose its decision on Great Britain – by war, if necessary – in the name of the Monroe Doctrine.

'Twisting the lion's tail' was then a popular political ploy, especially with a presidential election due the following year. Stocks were down but jingoism was up. An Anglo-American war not only seemed likely, but was quite an acceptable idea.

It is not difficult to imagine Jennie's reaction and that of her American friends in England. A few left for the countryside or the Continent or tried to become socially invisible. But Jennie, in her typical way, galvanized her closest friends in a quiet campaign behind the scenes. Their objective was to persuade government leaders and prominent editors that the war talk was manufactured by political propagandists and that it would soon disappear. This campaign consisted of small dinners, private parties, and seemingly casual encounters, but its calming effect was considerable.

Jennie and the other American women had a powerful base of influence. The British liaison in this crisis was Joseph Chamberlain, the new Secretary of State for the Colonies. Chamberlain's American wife was part of Jennie's circle, and the Secretary listened thoughtfully to Jennie, whom he had long admired. George Curzon, the Secretary of State for Foreign Affairs, who had known Jennie since he was a young man, had also married an American. He similarly needed little prodding to make his voice heard on this issue. There were no doors, official or unofficial, which were closed to these insistent women. And as always, Jennie had the ear of the Prince of Wales.

An American general in England returned to the United States and told the press that Lady Randolph Churchill was the active leader of ten American women,

> true daughters of the United States, who are working quietly and mightily to prevent war between the two countries that are looking at each other in a sinister way. For these women, the war means a thousand times as much as it does to other American women; and they have untold power of international arbitration. . . . These particular ten are so situated that they are in the midst of the greatest powers that rule England today. Their influence, thrown upon the scales, would turn it whichever way they bent themselves.[18]

Jennie's activity did not escape British notice either. 'If there should come hard war talk,' wrote one British correspondent, 'Lady Randolph Churchill would set out lecturing, as she did when she elected her husband a few years ago. And her talks would put things straight in a short time. She has a clear and concise way of delivering them that robs them of the term "lectures". . . . And she would be convincing.' [19]

'LADY CHURCHILL WAS U.S. "BEST" AMBASSADOR', headlined a Boston newspaper.[20]

Jennie's influence in cooling the critical situation can, of course, be overestimated. Nevertheless, the intensity of her activity on this issue was important. She, too, was 'a child of both worlds'.

Just when one war threat was eased, another began to loom. The scene this time was the Transvaal, South Africa. Cecil Rhodes, whom Jennie knew well, was Prime Minister of the adjoining British Cape Colony. Rhodes had authorized Dr Leander Jameson to organize an armed force to invade the Transvaal in support of a planned uprising of the British against the Boers, settlers of Dutch ancestry, in Johannesburg. However, the Johannesburg rising did not take place and Dr Jameson, not informed of this, plunged in with his tiny force. The raid was a fiasco. Jameson's raiders were quickly captured by the Boers, and the incident made England an international laughing stock. But it was all a prelude to a bitter war that was slowly brewing, a war in which Jennie and her sons were fated to play important roles.

Jennie's immediate concern, however, was the war in Cuba and Winston's activity there. She had written to Jack before Winston left saying she thought the Cuban trip was 'a foolish business'. She turned out to be right, but for other reasons. From the standpoint of experience and excitement, Winston was delighted. It was almost as if every action in his life – even the mistakes – seemed to have some predestined purpose in his development. Some aspects of the Cuban War, however, did disappoint him:

One conspicuous feature of this war is the fact that so few men are killed. There can be no question as to the immense amount of ammunition expended on both sides, but the surprising truth remains that ridiculously little execution is done. It has always been said, you know, that it takes 200 bullets to kill a soldier, but as applied to the Cuban War 200,000 shots would be closer to the mark.[21]

At the same time, Winston did find some action and he wrote to his mother: 'We advanced right across open ground under heavy fire.' He recorded on the day of his twenty-first birthday that 'for the first time I heard shots fired in anger and heard bullets strike flesh or whistle through the air.'[22] He kept one bullet that struck and killed a Spanish soldier who was standing close to him.

Jennie was relieved when Winston had finally returned to New York by mid-December 1895. He again stayed at Bourke's apartment, although this time Cockran was in London with Jennie. Cockran had a long history of fighting for causes, and this romantic one was his own. Jennie had made up her mind, but what woman would not have been flattered by such persistent admiration? A firm friendship established with Winston, Bourke may have felt that he held stronger cards with Jennie. Indeed, he probably did. Winston wrote in his memoirs that after he was twenty-one his mother 'never sought to exercise parental control'.[23] The evidence shows otherwise, but the Cuban escapade at least illustrates how increasingly difficult it would be for Jennie to exercise such control. Winston did need Bourke. So did Jennie. But how could she go back to America now? She could fight for America, and she had. But go back? The breach was too wide.

Winston's return to England stirred up considerable resentment in the press against this young lieutenant who fought for Spain against the Cuban nationalists. Winston protested that he did not fight at all, that he simply observed. But the negative impressions remained. Jennie's intuition about the 'foolish business' had proved correct.

Jennie also heard from Sir Henry Drummond Wolff, the Ambassador to Spain, who sent her copies of letters from Winston to the Duke of Tetuan and Marshal Martinez Campos, wryly noting that they all called each other by their Christian names.[24] Winston, at twenty-one, might have felt an equality with these mature leaders; he had written to his mother, 'I am getting absurdly old.' In a sense, he always had been.

Bourke Cockran had waited in England for Winston's arrival, and the two men now had more time together to deepen their relationship. Seeing this relationship grow before her eyes, Jennie had cause for further reflection. Who had the greater need, her son or herself? Every need had a price, but was the price right? She wanted and needed Bourke, but on her terms. So did Winston. They wanted and needed him in England.

Winston wrote and illustrated an article about his Cuban experience for *The Saturday Review*,[25] and Jennie sent copies to her most influential friends. A response came immediately from Joseph Chamberlain, who had played such a vital role in resolving the Venezuelan crisis. 'It is the best short account I have seen of the problems with which the Spaniards have to deal, & agrees with my own conclusions.'[26]

Winston, however, was more interested in the reaction of Bourke Cockran, who had returned to New York by the end of February. 'I am much interested in the action of the United States as respecting Cuban belligerency. . . . I should very much like to know what your opinion is upon the whole question . . .', he wrote to Cockran. 'Of course I won't think of giving you away. . . . I hope the United States will not force Spain to give up Cuba. . . . Do write and tell me what you do think.'[27]

Cockran completely disagreed with Winston about Cuba, as did most of the British and American people. Indeed, Cockran had addressed a mass meeting in New York protesting Spanish rule in Cuba. Perhaps his arguments influenced Winston, who later changed his views on the issue.

Their correspondence was not confined to the Cuban question; it ranged the world. Winston recommended books – '. . . rather a good book . . . "The Red Badge of Courage". . . . Believe me it is worth reading . . ." [28] – and Bourke sent him copies of his speeches, one of them on Irish Home Rule.

'It is one of the finest I have ever read,' Winston replied. 'You are indeed an orator. And of all the gifts there is none so rare and precious as that. Of course – my dear Cockran – you will understand that we approach the subject from different points of view and that your views on Ireland could never coincide with mine. . . .' [29]

About Irish Home Rule, which Cockran urged so strongly, Winston was certain that:

the civilized world [will not] compel us as you suggest to a prompt settlement. How could they with justice? Does Russia give up Poland? Does Germany surrender Alsace and Lorraine? Does Austria give up Hungary? Does Turkey release Armenia – or Spain grant autonomy to Cuba? One more instance shd the United States accede to the demand for Confederate Independence? And one more argument. You may approve of Home Rule in principle. But I defy you to produce a workable measure of it. He will be a bold man to rush in where Mr Gladstone failed.

Finally, let me say that when I read your speech I thought that Ireland had not suffered in vain – since her woes have provided a subject for your eloquence. Do write to me again. . . . [30]

Cockran's answer was immediate:

. . . With your remarkable talent for lucid and attractive expression you would be able to make great use of the information to be acquired by study of these two branches [sociology and political economy]. Indeed I firmly believe you would take a commanding position in public life at the first opportunity which arose, and I have always felt that true capacity either makes or finds its opportunity. I was so profoundly impressed with the vigor of your language and the breadth of your views as I read your criticisms of my speech that I conceived a very high opinion of your future career. . . . [31]

This was heady praise indeed for twenty-one-year-old Winston. Winston also mentioned to Bourke, 'My mother has been rather ill and is gone to Monte Carlo.' [32] Cockran answered that he was immediately returning to Europe and would stop briefly in London on his way to

France. There he planned to see Jack, who was in Paris on holiday, and then, surely, to go on to Monte Carlo. It was his third trip to Europe that year.

Jennie had decided to go to Monte Carlo for a brief change of scene, as well as for reasons of health – psychological as well as physical. Before she left, she asked her friends to look after Winston, who was at Aldershot, taking a signalling course. As a result, he was invited to a variety of dinners, and he wrote to his mother about one at Mrs Adair's:

Such an interesting party. Mr Chamberlain – Lord [sic] Wolseley, Mr Chaplin – Lord James, Sir Francis Jeune, and in fact all the powers that be. Chamberlain was very nice to me and I had quite a long talk with him on South Africa. . . . Tonight I am dining with Lord James, who has the Duke of Devonshire and a lot of 'notables' so I hope to be quite '*au fait*'.[33]

It is difficult to exaggerate the value of such meetings for Winston's future. The political *élite* of London was a closed circle of small circumference. You were in or you were out. If you were in, the potential for leverage was great. Being 'in' not only opened the necessary doors and warmed the welcomes, but it lit the cigar, poured the brandy, gave the knowing smile. It often meant the difference between getting something done and not getting something done.

Jennie made certain that Winston attended all the important parties while he was in London. And when she returned home that summer of 1896, she again made Great Cumberland Place a social centre: 'During this vivid summer my mother gathered constantly around her table politicians of both parties and leading figures in literature and art, together with the most lovely beings on whom the eye could beam,' Winston wrote.

On one occasion, however, she carried her catholicity too far. Sir John Willoughby, one of the Jameson raiders then on bail awaiting trial in London, was one of our oldest friends. In fact it was he who had first shown me how to arrange my toy cavalry soldiers in the proper formation of an advanced guard. Returning from Hounslow, I found him already arrived for luncheon. My mother was late. Suddenly the door opened and Mr John Morley was announced.[34] I scented trouble; but boldly presented them to each other. Indeed, no other course was possible. John Morley drew himself up, and without extending his hand made a stiff little bow. Willoughby stared unconcernedly without acknowledging it. I squirmed inwardly and endeavoured to make a pretence of conversation by asking commonplace questions of each alternately. Presently to my great relief, my mother arrived. She was not unequal to the occasion, which was a serious one. Before the meal was far advanced no uninformed person would have noticed that two out of the four gathered round the table never addressed one another directly. Towards the end it seemed to me they would not have minded doing so at all. But having taken their positions they had to stick to them. I suspected my mother of a design to mitigate the unusual asperities which gathered round this aspect of our affairs. She wanted to reduce the Raid to the level of ordinary politics. But blood had been shed; and that makes a different tale.[35]

Both of her sons were home often now, and both were delighted to be part of the social whirl. Winston knew the value of it and Jack enjoyed its pleasures. The activity at Great Cumberland Place now had a frenetic quality: parties, dinners, recitals, discussion groups. Shane Leslie remembered the homes of his mother and his two aunts as places that were

full of servants all of whom looked as if they needed a holiday by the seaside. Footmen seemed constantly harassed, cooks in a suicidal state tho cheering up when royalty consented to praise the soufflé, which had collapsed into a pancake on the stairs. The successive ladies' maids were as ambitious as their mistresses, but usually reached tearful state before the 'Miss Jeromes' came out to an important dinner. One footman was so impressed by the frivolity that surrounded him that he fled the scene and, to his immense credit, took holy orders in the Church of England.[36]

It all cost money, however, a great deal of money, and Jennie's finances were always pinched. Her impulses and her far-ranging eye always exceeded her budget. She could no more change her style of living, though, than she could change her love of books or music or life.

Jennie was not the only one of the Jerome sisters with this problem. Leonie had the substantial financial resources of her husband's family to rely on, but Clara was often in critical need. 'It was a common sight to see her running across the street to borrow a fiver from one of her sisters to pacify the butcher or candlestick maker.'[37]

'Our finance is indeed involved!' Winston wrote to his mother. 'If I had not been so foolish as to pay a lot of bills I should have the money now.' Rarely was a son so like his mother.[38]

Indeed it is difficult to understand how Jennie managed to keep afloat. All she really had was the annual income from the rental of her father's house in New York. Since her mother had left her nothing and most of her husband's money was in trust funds for their sons, the upkeep of her new home was certainly beyond what she could afford. She must have been a marvellously adroit juggler of bank and insurance loans, but there must also have been a certain number of personal loans from friends, which were ultimately written off as gifts.

This need for money made Jennie especially vulnerable to a variety of 'get-rich-quick' schemes. She again invested some money with her brother-in-law Moreton who 'has just left on a journey, for the 500th time, to make a fortune.' But it is one thing to lose money within the family; it is quite another to be duped. The man responsible for the latter was James Henry Cruikshank, who was introduced to the three sisters through the highest auspices – none other than the son of the highly respectable Lord Cadogan. Cruikshank collected £4,000 from Jennie and her sisters and friends, promising that the money would be multiplied through some clever process. Instead, he simply spent it.[39] The loss was disastrous for Jennie.

There were few small secrets in London Society, and Jennie's financial condition was not among them. Perhaps this was partly responsible for the many rumours of her imminent marriage.

To the Countess of Warwick Jennie wrote: 'I am *not* going to marry anyone. If a perfect darling with at least £40,000 a year wants me *very much* I might consider it. . . .'[40]

There was one particular man who seemed to want her very much. He was not, perhaps, a *perfect darling*, but he did have much more than £40,000 a year. Furthermore, he and Jennie had known each other for many years. As an American magazine had noted, 'Older New Yorkers recall the fact that Mr Astor admired Lady Randolph before her marriage.'[41] *The New York Times* had reported on its front page:

The most interesting bit of society news which has been sent by cable from London of late is the engagement of Lady Randolph Churchill to William Waldorf Astor. This report will not occasion much surprise, for Mr Astor's attentions to Lady Randolph Churchill have been so marked as to create no small amount of gossip. Letters received in New York by prominent people from friends in London from time to time, have contained hints of the probabilities of such an alliance. This announcement of the engagement will undoubtedly be received with enthusiasm by New York society. Although Lady Churchill who is a daughter of the late Leonard Jerome, and Mr Astor, who is the son of the second John Jacob Astor, have lived a long time in England, they are thorough Americans. Had it not been for an unfortunate family jar,[42] several years ago, Mr Astor might never have decided to make England his home. Lady Churchill, who is a cousin of Mrs Clarence Gray Dinsmore, Mrs David Thompson, and Mrs Jordan L. Mott, is a most charming woman, and has been in the past somewhat of a power in English politics, her late husband owing much of his promotion to her influence, notwithstanding she is an American.[43]

'Wealthy Willie', as he was often called, reputedly had the largest fortune in America – a total of $200 million (£77 million) with an annual income of $6 million (£230,000). A Frenchman visiting America wrote of him: 'This man, this individual, who has only two arms and two legs, yes, and even a limit to his capacity for enjoyment, could stroll down Broadway or Fifth Avenue and stretch his arms hither and yon, saying, "Mine! Mine! All mine!" '[44]

For all his money and property, Astor was a lonely and hated man, particularly in America.[45] When he moved to England, he referred to it as 'a country where a gentleman might live'.[46] Of America, Astor said, 'Why travelled people of independent means should remain there more than a week, is not readily to be comprehended.'[47]

In England, he had bought Cliveden, the great and lovely country estate noted for its spectacular views of the Thames. He furnished this Italian-style palace with exquisite panelling, magnificent tapestries, and the finest continental cooks. 'The place is splendid,' Jennie wrote to her son Jack from Cliveden. 'Mr Astor has a great deal of taste.'[48]

Jennie found much in Astor to appreciate besides his money and his good taste. A blue-eyed, ruggedly handsome man of firm character and great courage, he had a first-rate mind and a broad interest in history and languages. Besides having been Ambassador to Italy, he had also written two novels.

There was little question that Astor wanted to marry Jennie. He had the reputation of being reserved, so perhaps he needed her warmth. It hurt him to hear himself called a traitor in America, and Jennie's popularity could have enhanced his image. Moreover, Jennie's entrée would have been invaluable to him in his desire to be completely accepted in British society.

Astor's father had chosen his first wife for him, not even asking whether or not she was to his taste; [49] now he wanted to pick his own wife – the loveliest, brightest woman he could find. Jennie was a woman who could crumble any reserve, lift any gloom, fill any emptiness.

What a fantastic temptation it must have been for Jennie! She had only to say 'yes' and she would have been the richest woman in the world. All those niggling debts and piled-up bills would be gone forever. She could have done anything within the realm of her creative imagination – writing, painting, operating a publishing company, supporting a whole movement of young authors, artists, musicians, creating her own theatre, as her father once had – all this would have been possible for her. She could have been the hostess of the greatest literary and political salon of her time. She could have made herself and her husband a significant political force in England. She could have torn down the glass-topped wall around Cliveden's three hundred acres and made it the social centre of all Europe.

The challenge and the inclination probably would have been overpowering – for almost any other woman. Perhaps Jennie had the inclination, and assuredly she recognized the challenge, but she simply did not love Astor. She denied to the press the report of her engagement.

At the height of the rumours, the Prince of Wales was planning a house party in Scotland. He noticed William Waldorf Astor's name on the suggested guest list and crossed it off. 'Not Mr Astor,' said the jealous Prince. 'He bores me.'

The Prince still saw a lot of Jennie. They were together at the Derby when the Prince's bay horse Persimmon won the race. 'It was a very popular win and the crowd cheered tremendously,' Jennie wrote to Jack.[50] Her brother-in-law Moreton added in another letter, 'As H.R.H. came down to lead Persimmon in, the Books shook hands with him and slapped him on the back, and one big Ringman roared out, "Three cheers for the bloody crown!"'[51]

The Prince's victory lent an added gaiety to Cowes Week that year. For Jennie there was a pride of admiring men trying to be more persuasive than ever. 'What fun you must be having!' Winston wrote to her. He said that his friend, 'Bino' Stracey (Sir Edward Stracey) 'had seen you there in great form – all over the place in a launch.'[52]

After Cowes, the Prince of Wales was guest of honour at a weekend party at Deepdene to which Jennie secured an invitation for Winston. It was a great honour for a second lieutenant. Among the guests was his commanding officer Colonel Brabazon.

'I realized that I must be upon my best behaviour: punctual, subdued, reserved, in short display all the qualities with which I am least endowed,' Winston remarked. Unfortunately, he caught a delayed train that arrived much later than scheduled. He expected to slip in unnoticed at the dinner table and to apologize afterwards.

When I arrived at Deepdene, I found the entire company assembled in the drawing room. The party it seemed without me would be thirteen. The prejudice of the Royal Family of those days against sitting down thirteen is well known. The Prince had refused point-blank to go in, and would not allow any rearrangement of tables to be made. He had, as was his custom, been punctual to the minute at half past eight. It was now twelve to nine. There, in this large room, stood the select and distinguished company in the worst of tempers, and there, on the other hand was I, a young boy asked as a special favour and a compliment. . . .

'Don't they teach you to be punctual in your regiment, Winston?' said the Prince in his most severe tone, and then looked acidly at Colonel Brabazon, who glowered. It was an awful moment! [53]

His mother did not try to save him from that one. However, she did start to intervene for Winston in something more important. The 9th Lancers were leaving shortly for South Africa and needed extra subaltern officers. Winston wanted to go.

. . . my dearest Mamma you cannot think how I would like to sail in a few days to scenes of adventure and excitement – to places where I could gain experience and derive advantage – rather than to the tedious land of India where I shall be equally out of the pleasures of peace and the chances of war. . . . I cannot believe that with all the

influential friends you possess that I could not be allowed to go . . .
You really ought to leave no stone unturned to help me at such a
period. . . .[54]

Winston was probably referring to the fact that Jennie had already
tried to turn a few stones for him, with little success. Now he wanted
her to try turning some more. Earlier that summer her requests for
help from Viscount Wolseley, Commander-in-Chief of the Army, and
the Marquess of Lansdowne, Secretary of State for War, had been fruit-
less. At that time the British Army was rigidly departmentalized into
areas of influence. Lansdowne had made this clear when he answered
Jennie, 'The management of the operations in S. Africa is under Sir F.
Carrington, & we are not in any way directing them, or interfering with
the composition of his staff – I fear therefore that we can do nothing to
find employment for Winston and I hope *you* may not be too much disappointed.'[55]

Lansdowne had then offered some personal advice:

May I, as a friend, add this? I am not quite sure that in view of the
enquiry which has been promised into the charges made recently
against some of the officers of the 4th Hussars, it would be wise on
Winston's part to leave England at this moment. There are plenty of
ill-natured people about, and it is just conceivable that an attempt
might be made to misrepresent his action.[56]

Truth magazine had taken up the still-simmering racing scandal
and the Bruce case in May; in June the charges made against some of
the 4th Hussars were to be debated in the House of Commons.

Jennie accepted Lansdowne's advice and halted all her efforts to get
Winston transferred to South Africa. For his part, Winston reconciled
himself to the inevitable and wrote to Bourke Cockran, 'I sail for India
the 11th of September. I hope we shall meet again soon – if possible
within a year. I may return to England via Japan after a little of India
so perhaps I shall once more eat oysters and hominy with you in New
York. Please send me press cuttings of your speeches.'[57]

At about the time Winston would have arrived in India, Jennie
wrote to him, '. . . My darling, . . . take care of yrself & peer into that
Bible sometimes, & love me very much. . . .'[58]

7

The next two years were restless years for Jennie – restless and rootless. She had her own home, exquisitely refurnished, and she had made it a lively social centre for her friends who reached into most strata of society, and she was spending more time visiting them all over England. She also spent an increasing amount of time at the Prince of Wales's country home at Sandringham. There were trips to France or Monte Carlo when she could afford it – and even when she couldn't. It was all very social, very time-filling, and yet very empty. Even though Winston was in India, her relationship with him seemed gradually to fill a large part of that emptiness. The regular correspondence between mother and son demonstrates how much they were in each other's thoughts at this time. The mail boat sailed once a week, and their letters seldom missed it. They were usually long, loving, revealing letters.

'The house is full of you – in every conceivable costume and style,' Winston wrote to her, soon after his arrival in India.

My writing table is covered with photographs . . . my cigarette box that you brought me from Japan . . . my books. . . .[1]

I have thought of you so much, my darling boy. . . . Darling boy how I wish you were with me & that we cld have a good talk about every-thing. . . .[2]

. . . Your letters . . . my dearest Mamma . . . I get none except yours. . . .[3]

Winston really had no one else. His brother Jack was barely seven-teen and still at Harrow. As much as Jack admired and idolized his older brother, the distance between them – not simply the years, but their tastes and temperaments as well – was always too great to cross easily. Bourke Cockran's importance in Winston's life was growing, but he was of another world. Winston's world was essentially England, and there he had no close, personal friends. It would take unusual people to penetrate his ego and his overwhelming self-confidence, to reach inside and find the troubled human being.

Jennie therefore had to be everybody for Winston – mother, friend, sister, sweetheart. Her letters were packed with all the English news: politics, books, social gossip. Above all, they were personal letters, unsparing of what was on her mind or in her heart. And his were the same. 'I devote a great deal of time and thought to my letters to you and endeavour to make them not only worthy of the writer but even of the recipient. (Rather good that!)' he wrote.[4]

Winston had quickly acclimatized himself to all the comforts he could find in India. Together with Reggie Barnes and another officer, he had rented a palatial bungalow which he described as 'all pink and white, with heavy tiled roof and deep verandahs, sustained by white plaster columns, wreathed in purple bougainvillea.'[5] Land elsewhere was 'bare as a plate, hot as an oven',[6] but Winston's two acres had 250 rose trees. 'We built a large tiled barn with mud walls containing stabling for thirty horses and ponies. Our three butlers formed a triumvirate in which no internal dissensions ever appeared. . . . Thus freed from mundane cares, we devoted ourselves to the serious purpose of life. . . .'[7]

This serious purpose was polo three times a week, butterfly collecting ('My garden is full of Purple Emperors, White Admirals and Swallowtails'),[8] and cutting three great basins of flowers every morning.

Jennie admonished him. 'I hope you will find time for reading,' she wrote. 'Think how you will regret the waste of time when you are in politics & will feel yr want of knowledge.'[9]

Winston had already become sensitive to this lack in himself. He told Jack, 'I shall envy you the enjoyment of a liberal education, and of the power to appreciate the classical works,'[10] and in his memoirs he noted, 'The desire for learning came over me. I began to feel myself wanting in even the vaguest knowledge about many large spheres of thought.'[11]

Jennie enthusiastically began to make her contribution. She sent him the eight volumes of Gibbon's *Decline and Fall of the Roman Empire*, which had so influenced the thinking and style of her husband. It had a similar impact on Winston. 'I was immediately dominated both by the story and the style. All through the long glistening hours of the

Indian day, from when we quitted stables till the evening shadows proclaimed the hour of Polo, I devoured Gibbon. I rode triumphantly through it from end to end and enjoyed it all.'[12]

Jennie also sent him twelve volumes of Macaulay – eight volumes of history and four of essays. He described his reading of it as embarking on a 'splendid romance, and I voyaged with full sail in a strong wind.' Winston described Gibbon as 'stately and impressive' and Macaulay as 'crisp and forcible. Both are fascinating. . . .'[13] The combination of Gibbon and Macaulay made a lasting impression on both his writing and speaking styles. It gave him, he said, 'the feel for words fitting and falling into their places like pennies in the slot.'[14]

Jennie continued to send him a selected library of books, mostly history and philosophy – Plato's *Republic*, Aristotle's *Politics*,[15] Darwin's *On the Origin of Species*, Malthus's *On Population*, Pascal's *Provincial Letters*, Adam Smith's *Wealth of Nations*, and the entire twenty-seven-volume set of the *Annual Register*.

'The method I pursue with the *Annual Register* is [not] to read the debate until I have recorded my own opinion on paper of the subject – having regard only to general principles,' Winston informed her.

After reading, I reconsider and finally write. I hope by a persevering continuance of this practice to build up a scaffolding of logical and consistent views which will perhaps tend to the creation of a logical and consistent mind.

Of course the *Annual Register* is only valuable for its facts. A good knowledge of these would arm me with a sharp sword. Macaulay, Gibbon, Plato etc must train the muscles to wield that sword to the greatest effect.[16]

Jennie was absolutely delighted to play such a vital role in the development of her son. At his request she sent him 'the detailed Parliamentary history (Debates, Divisions, Parties, cliques) . . . of the last 100 years. . . .'[17] Every book, every letter became a forum for discussion and cross-comment between mother and son. Of course in the process Jennie was stretching her own mind as well as Winston's. A later critic commented that she must have had an 'inordinate belief in his capacity to digest' because she had sent him Lecky's work on the *Rise and Influence of Rationalism*, which was 'stiff reading even for a well-educated man'.[18] But Jennie knew the reach of her son's mind. Winston himself later characterized it as 'an empty, hungry mind, and with fairly strong jaws; and what I got, I bit.' [19]

Winston had earlier sent his mother a book, also, one entitled *Making Sketches*, 'which interests me very much and which I am sure will please you still more — as you will have seen many of the scenes herein described.' [20]

Jennie, meanwhile, maintained her customary maternal protectiveness, reminding him to be careful 'of what you drink'.[21] But she was particularly concerned about his horse-racing in India. His American aunt, Duchess Lily, the widow of Randolph's brother the Duke of Marlborough, had given him a typewriter, a charger, and was now sending him a racing pony. 'I want to talk to you very seriously about the racing pony,' his mother wrote.

It may be dead for all I know, but if it is not I want you to promise me to sell it. I had a long talk with the Prince . . . & he begged me to tell you that you ought not to race, only because it is not a good business in India — they are not square & the best of reputations get spoiled over it. *You* don't know but everyone else does that it is next to impossible to race in India & keep clean hands. It appears that Colonel Brab[azon] told the Prince that he wished you hadn't this pony. I am sure you will regret it if you don't [sell it].[22]

But Winston did not agree.

. . . When I see *all* those with whom I have to live and many whom I respect owning ponies — I must confess I do not see why you should expect me to deprive myself of a pleasure which they honourably and legitimately enjoy — or why you should distrust my ability to resist the temptation to resort to malpractice. . . .[23]

As an obedient son, however, he added, '. . . If you still wish me to get rid of the pony — after you have considered what I have written here — I will do so . . . but . . . I beg you not to ask me. . . .'

She answered, '. . . Do tell me in yr next that you have taken steps to sell the pony. You have no idea how it worries me. . . .' [24]

Winston then took another tack: '. . . Tell His Royal Highness — if he says anything further about racing in India — that I intend to be just as much an example to the Indian turf as he is to the English – as far as fair play goes.' [25]

Jennie probably did not expect to win this contest of wills, and she later wrote to Jack, 'Of course I have given in about Winston's pony – and I hope he will sell it after it has won a race – if it ever does!' [26] The purpose of her exchange on this subject was to remind Winston of the scandal with which he had been associated only recently. Thanks to her well-placed friends in the Army and Government, the brush had tarred him only lightly. But it must not happen again. If ever he wanted to do anything in public life, he must be more than careful, he must be utterly irreproachable. Without saying any of this directly, Jennie had made her point.

Winston has described his daily life in India in a series of vivid pictures:

Just before dawn, every morning one was awakened by a dusky figure with a clammy hand adroitly lifting one's chin and applying a gleaming razor to a lathered and defenceless throat. By six o'clock the regiment was on parade, and we rode to a wide plain and there drilled and manœuvred for an hour and a half. We then returned to baths at the bungalow and breakfast in the Mess. Then at nine, stables and orderly room till about half-past ten; then home to the bungalow before the sun attained its fiercest ray. . . . Long before eleven o'clock all white men were in shelter. We nipped across to luncheon at half-past one in the blistering heat and then returned to sleep till five o'clock. Now the station begins to live again. It is the hour of Polo. It is the hour for which we have been living all day long. I was accustomed in those days to play every chukka I could get into. . . . I very seldom played less than eight and more often ten or twelve.

As the shadows lengthened over the polo ground, we ambled back perspiring and exhausted to hot baths, rest, and an 8.30 dinner, to the strains of the regimental band and the clinking of ice in well-filled glasses. Thereafter those who were not so unlucky as to be caught by the Senior Officers to play a tiresome game then in vogue called 'Whist' sat smoking in the moonlight till half-past ten or eleven at the latest signalled the 'And so to bed'. Such was the long, long Indian day. . . .[27]

'Life out here is stupid, dull and uninteresting,' he wrote to his mother. '. . . This is an abominable country to live long in. Comfort you get – company you miss. I meet few people worth talking to. . . .' [28]

He had already had occasion to write, 'I do wish, my dear Mama, you could come out . . .',[29] and he had invited Bourke Cockran, too. 'You can't think how interesting this country is. . . . You must come out here – if only for a flying visit. . . .' [30]

His correspondence with Cockran dealt with a broad range of subjects. Winston, for example, expressed his disapproval of William Jennings Bryan's demand for sweeping changes in currency. 'Even if you prove to me that our present system is radically bad – my opinion is unaltered. . . . A man suffering from dyspepsia might pray for fresh intestines but he would fare badly while the alteration was being effected. . . . What Bryan has done is like an inebriate regulating a chronometer with a crowbar. . . .' He also congratulated Cockran on William McKinley's election to the Presidency and discussed the expense of presidential elections in America compared to the lesser cost in England. He then added, 'Yours may be the government for gods . . . ours at least is suitable for men.' [31] His words, indeed, were falling into their proper places 'like pennies into a slot'.

In his letters to his mother, Winston was equally critical of British politicians:

Among the leaders of the Tory Party are two whom I despise and detest as politicians above all others – Mr Balfour & George Curzon. The one – a languid, lazy, lack-a-daisical cynic – the unmonumental figurehead of the Conservative Party; the other the spoiled darling of politics – blown with conceit – insolent from undeserved success – the typification of the superior Oxford prig.[32]

This letter must have jolted Jennie, for Balfour and Curzon were not only old and valued friends of hers, but they would prove to be of enormous help in advancing the career of her cynical son. Jennie, however, had always taught her sons to express their opinions about anybody or anything, and she would not counsel them differently now.

Jennie only wished that Jack had more of his brother's directness. 'He is not given to strong opinions,' Winston said of Jack, 'and it is very difficult to get at what he really thinks.' [33] Jennie earlier had suggested to Jack the possibility of a career in an infantry regiment, where her contacts were so firm that she felt he would be accepted despite his bad eye. When Jack demurred, she answered, 'I do not wish to stand in your way if your heart is not on going into the Army.'[34] Jack seemed to change his mind a year later, and Jennie answered,

Darling I don't want to make any tiresome remarks, but you must remember that your want of decision as regards your likes and dislikes and choice of a career has been a drawback to you – I have never heard you before really express a real desire to go into the Army. It is not too late. . . . Bless you, my child. Don't fret. All will come right for you, I am sure.[35]

Jack again changed his mind and now preferred the Bar, but despite his uncertainty about his career, the one thing of which he was certain was that he wanted no more of Harrow. Jennie was sceptical. 'Your last report, just in, is very good and they seem to think you are doing well. Perhaps it would be a mistake to start a fresh place in the winter. Well! You must say what you want. If you are *very* keen to come away, I won't keep you there.'[36]

Jennie went to Harrow to visit the Headmaster James Welldon, and she reported to Winston that Jack

is too mature for school life – even Welldon thought so. . . .

I have been very busy arranging things for Jack. I went to see Welldon and had a long talk with him as to his future. I am much against his going in the Army. I can't afford to put him in a smart cavalry regiment & in anything else he wld be lost & unhappy. Besides at the best it is a poor career. I think he might do [better] at the Bar. He has plenty of ability and common sense, a good presence, & with perseverance & influence he ought to get on. The City he hates. He is going to leave Harrow this term, spend a year or more in France & Germany, then study Greek for six months with a tutor & go to Oxford. He seems to like the idea. Meanwhile he is coming with me to Blenheim for Xmas.[37]

Taking up the issue with his brother, Winston told Jack:

If you feel no desire to go into the Army, I should be the last person to press you to do so. . . . If you are not keen when you start you will never do any good in the Army. . . . But does this not apply with greater force to the Bar? . . . If you go to the Bar equipped only (as you put it) with 'moderate work, little brains & lots of people to help you' you will inevitably end as a 'briefless barrister'. . . . You see, when people go to a lawyer – or when they go to a doctor – they don't ask for good manners & lots of influence – what they want is a man who will win their cases or cure their diseases. . . . Don't think of drifting languidly and placidly – as your letter apparently suggests to the Bar. . . .

I think you have great talents, Jack . . . but I *am* perfectly certain that unless you start full of enthusiasm and keenness, you will never develop your abilities. . . .[38]

To his mother, Winston wistfully observed, 'What a strange inversion of fortune – that I should be a soldier and Jack at college.'[39]

As Jennie had told Winston, Jack would spend Christmas with her at Blenheim. Christmas at Blenheim Palace, the Marlborough ancestral home, was a family tradition that could not be ignored, even though Jennie and her mother-in-law were at best only on polite terms with each other: '. . . Between you and I,' Jennie told Winston, she [Frances, the Dowager Duchess of Marlborough] is not making herself pleasant to me & we have not exchanged a word – but I do not mind & perhaps it is as well. To the world we can appear friends, anything of the kind in private is impossible.'[40]

The Dowager Duchess had never stopped grieving for her son Randolph, and she was bitter that Jennie was not similarly grieving. Her ill-will extended beyond Jennie to her grandsons, particularly to Winston. Thus when nineteen-year-old Consuelo Vanderbilt had become the ninth Duchess of Marlborough the previous year, the Dowager Duchess had told her that 'Your first duty is to have a child, and it must be a son, because it would be intolerable to have that little upstart Winston become Duke. Are you in the family way?'[41]

Consuelo and Jennie had quickly become very fond of each other, and despite the Dowager Duchess, Jennie's relations with the rest of the family were always mutually affectionate. Even Randolph's sisters were her friends. Of her sister-in-law Fanny, Lady Tweedmouth, Jennie said, 'Without exception the noblest character I have ever met . . . her sympathy and advice were a tower of strength to all who came in contact with her.'[42]

Even if there had been no such relationship with Randolph's sisters,

Jennie would have maintained her link with the Marlborough family. Her own position in British society was solid enough so that she did not need the association for herself, but she did want to keep it intact for her sons. There is no question that Blenheim Palace and the historic Marlborough name were prestigious and influential factors in Great Britain.

Duchess Lily, the mother of the ninth Duke of Marlborough, was also close to Jennie, not only because the Duchess was an American and had been widowed but because Jennie had been her social buffer in the early days. The Duchess was now married to Lord William Beresford, and it was to their home at Deepdene that Jennie went when, as in that winter of 1896, she wanted the quiet of the countryside. Her iron nerves had been upset by the persistent publicity of the scandal about Winston, the rumours of her engagement to Astor, and Cruikshank's fraud.

Winston was luckier that winter: he found the one thing Jennie lacked for him – romance. The young lady's name was Pamela Plowden. 'The most beautiful girl I have ever seen – bar none,' Winston wrote to his mother.[43]

It might have made Jennie a little jealous to find her son so taken with the beauty of another woman, when he had so often written that there was no one more beautiful than his mother. On his twenty-second birthday, Jennie wrote, 'I wish I cld give you a good kiss. . . .' [44] Instead she sent him a cheque for £50, and made no reference to Pamela.

Jennie had met Pamela and knew her father, Sir Trevor John Chichele Chichele-Plowden, then British Resident at Hyderabad. Pamela was pretty enough to have been the object of many men's affections, and there was no indication how serious she felt about Winston. Jennie knew that Pamela could cope with Winston but she did not know if Winston could cope with Pamela.

Winston's feeling for Pamela, however, was obviously not overpowering enough to divert him from his main goal. He was determined to join Kitchener's army in Egypt in the advance up the Nile to reconquer the Sudan. 'I should never forgive myself if an expedition started next year and I felt that it was my own fault I was not there . . . *Please do your best*,' he wrote to his mother.[45]

Jennie wrote directly to Kitchener, whom she knew rather well, but earlier she had explained to Winston:

I am going to wire you today to write at once & apply to the War Office to be allowed to go to Egypt. . . . The chances of being taken are extremely remote as the competition is tremendous – but there is an outside chance of Sir H. Kitchener's personal influence being brought to bear & I am going to try it for you. Should it succeed you must know & remember that it means signing a paper to the effect that you will serve in the Egyptian Army for two years – & there will be no getting out of it if you don't like it – On the other hand should this fail you must not let it unsettle you & make you take a dislike to your work in India. Life is not always what one wants it to be, but to make the best of it as it is, is the only way of being happy – Of course the War Office will take no notice of yr application but as soon as you have applied I will write to Kitchener & if he asks for you you will probably be allowed to go. In my heart of hearts I have doubts as to whether it wd be the best thing for you – but Fate will decide.[46]

This was the kind of letter Jennie wrote to both her sons at every turning point in their lives. It was a way of training their point of view, giving direction to their attitudes, offering a method of analysis. They received this from no one else. Winston particularly needed someone to temper his youthful enthusiasm, sober his daydreams, clarify the alternatives.

For many Englishmen, Horatio Herbert Kitchener was becoming the personification of the whole concept of British imperial expansion. The new Sirdar (Commander-in-Chief of the Egyptian Army) was a complex man. An intensely self-disciplined man who would not tolerate inefficiency or excuse failure, he was equally impatient of criticism or opposition. Margot Asquith had once written of him: '. . . He is either very stupid or very clever, and never gives himself away.' [47]

Kitchener set the fashion of the strong, silent man, never in a hurry. Winston Churchill later said that Kitchener 'will never be fettered by fear, and not very often by sympathy.' And G. W. Steevens wrote of him, 'Erect, six foot and more of flesh and bone, but mainly wire, tanned and moustached, yet with "no body to carry his mind, no face to keep his brain behind".' [48]

I don't know how soon I may hear from the Sirdar [Jennie wrote to Winston] but I will wire & if he takes you, you will have to square yr Colonel – but I don't suppose you wld join them until the end of

March. In any case, when you receive this make enquiries & find out how much money you will want & answer by return – should you be taken – as I shld have to find it for you & it cannot be done in a moment.[49]

But a week later, Jennie said that she was beginning to think the situation 'is more than doubtful, as I am told Kitchener won't take anyone under 27. . . .'[50]

'Well, my dearest Mummy,' Winston replied on January 7, 'I hope we may meet in Cairo but I begin to fear from your silence that the answer is adverse. Perhaps however as the Sirdar has been up at Dongola your letter will have been delayed.'[51]

Winston was right. Kitchener was at Dongola, the first stage of his advance up the Nile, and Jennie finally received the note he had written to her on December 30 from his Frontier Force headquarters:

My dear Lady Randolph,
    I will note your son's name for special service and if he wishes to serve in the Egyptian Army he should send in his application through his Colonel to the A.G. [Adjutant General] Egyptian Army Cairo. I have however at present no vacancies in the cavalry but I will have his name put down on the list.[52]

Winston felt that meant there was still hope. 'Keep pegging away about Egypt. I do not mind waiting and you will never make me believe there is anything which you could not in time achieve.'[53] And again: 'You will see that if I go to Egypt & if things turn out well, it might almost be worth my while to stick to soldiering. . . . I beg you to leave no stone unturned in your endeavour to obtain a vacancy for me.'[54]

Jennie could not have been pleased to hear from Winston that he might 'stick to soldiering', as she had already cautioned him, 'How little one hears of any of the Generals in time of peace. There is really very little honour & glory to be got out of the Army. A moderate MP gets better known in the country & has more chance of success than a really clever man in the Army.'[55]

Earlier she had put it more plainly: 'I am looking forward to the time when we shall live together again & all my political ambitions shall be centred in you.'[56]

Consciously or subconsciously, she had more and more intertwined the ambitions of her son with her own ambitions. There was no limit to their combined drive, their combined determination. She had not been able to make her husband Prime Minister, but now she had a fresh chance with her son. It had been no idle whim when she refused to surrender her husband's robes of office after his resignation as Chancellor of the Exchequer. 'I am saving them for my son,' she had said.

Now it all became clear. How could she marry Bourke Cockran and go to the United States? Her son needed her in England. She could not desert his ambition because his ambition was now her own.

8

Early in 1897 Jennie had returned to Paris, primarily to install Jack with a family in Versailles, where he could live for the year and study French. The persistently attentive Bourke Cockran synchronized his plans so as to be in Paris at the same time. Jennie also dined with the Breteuils, and she and Breteuil's wife, both Americans, must have scrutinized each other carefully. There was still another of Jennie's admirers in Paris, the legendary Cecil Rhodes, after whom the then British territory of Rhodesia had been named.

The monumental blunder of the Jameson Raid in the Transvaal had forced Rhodes's resignation as Premier of the Cape Colony, but he was still a British colossus in South Africa and one of the richest and most powerful men in the world. He was also the kind of man who would and did go unarmed to meet the leaders of a native rebellion and persuade them to thrown down their spears.

Rhodes's brother expressed the wish that Rhodes might marry Jennie. 'Colonel Rhodes told me that he would sooner his brother marry you – if you would have him – than any other woman in the world!' [1]

Rhodes had a passion for diamonds, power, and flattery. He had no use for sports or society or the ordinary amusements of rich men. He also was contemptuous of most women – Jennie being one of the few exceptions. Jennie, however, was not stirred by Rhodes: 'He does not give the idea of a clever man – a strong one, if you like, determined and dogged, but intellectually weak.' [2]

Jennie decided not to linger in rainy, muggy Paris, but to continue to Monte Carlo. The Marquis de Breteuil had told her he would be delighted to invite Jack to his home whenever Jack was free, and Bourke had promised to spend some time with him before leaving Paris. 'I hated leaving you, dear boy,' Jennie wrote to her son. 'I am writing you a line before I go to bed so that you may get it tomorrow & know that your Mama is thinking of you. . . . Good night my darling Jack – work hard and don't get "mopy". Fill your life . . . & the time will fly. . . .' [3]

'Jack darling,' she wrote afterwards,

the temptations of a big town are strong, I know; and you are very young, but you are sensible beyond your years and a great dear – and I am sure my confidence in you would not be displaced. Keep the good society and the friends I have introduced you to, and you would come to no harm. . . . Darling child, remember this year is the only one of your life you can give up entirely to French. Make the most of it – Do, like Winston, talk incessantly! [4]

Jennie, though, had sharper words for Winston, who had overdrawn his account, even after a warning from the bank:

I *must* say I think it is *too* bad of you – indeed it is hardly honourable knowing as you do that you are dependent on me & that I give you the biggest allowance I *possibly can*, more than I can afford. I am very hard up & this has come at a very inopportune moment & puts me to much inconvenience. . . . I have paid it. But I have told them at Cox's not to apply to me in the future as you must manage yr own affairs. As for yr wild talk & scheme of coming home for a month, it is absolutely out of the question, not only on account of money, but for the sake of yr reputation. They will say & with some reason that you can't stick to anything. You have only been out 6 months & it is on the cards that you may be called to Egypt. There is plenty for you to do in India. I confess I am quite disheartened about you. You seem to have no real purpose in life & won't realize at the age of 22 that for a man life means work, & hard work if you mean to succeed. . . . It is useless my saying more – we have been over this ground before – it is not a pleasant one. I will only repeat that I cannot help you any more & if you have any grit in you & are worth yr salt you will try & live within yr income & cut down yr expenses in order to do it. You cannot but feel ashamed of yrself under the present circumstances – I haven't the heart to write more.[5]

That was, of course, the kind of stern lecture that a father ordinarily would have given. It was comparatively easy for Jennie to be a surrogate father for an obedient son like Jack, but Winston had the same kind of stubborn, imperious nature she had. He, in turn, framed his answer coolly, discussing many other things first, and then bringing up the overdrawn account but blaming the bank. Jennie simply could not maintain her sternness. 'What an extraordinary boy you are as regards yr business affairs,' she wrote.

You never say a word about them, & then spring things upon one. If you only told me when you were hard up – & why – perhaps I shd not be so angry. But I don't believe you ever know how you stand with yr account at the Bank. . . . Dearest, this is the only subject on which we ever fall out. I do wish you wld try & reform – if you only realized how little I have, & how impossible it is for me to get any more. I have raised all I can, & I assure you unless something extraordinary turns up I see ruin staring me in the face.[6]

She then detailed her income and expenses:

Out of 2700 pounds a year 800 of it goes to you 2 boys, 410 for house rent and stables, which leaves me 1500 for everything – taxes, servants, stables, food, dress, travelling – & now I have to pay money in interest borrowed. I *really* fear for the future. I am telling you all this darling in order that you may see how impossible it is for me to help you – and how you *must* in future depend on yrself.[7]

Two weeks later she stressed the matter again:

. . . Darling I lay awake last night thinking about you & how much I wanted to help you – if only I had some money I wld do so. I am so proud of you & all yr great and enduring qualities. I feel sure that if you live you will make a name for yrself. But I know to do it you have to be made of stern stuff & not mind sacrifice & self denial. I feel I am reading you a lecture & you will vote my letters a bore – but you know that I do not mean it in that way. . . .[8]

How could Jennie lecture Winston on money, when she herself was so much like him? Her own fantasy was that she would one day make a fortune at Monte Carlo. Newspapers played up the stories of those who did, particularly one American who purportedly broke the bank several times, winning almost £60,000.

Jennie had no such luck at Monte Carlo this time, but she did have a visitor. 'The Prince came over from Nice and dined with me,' she wrote to Winston. 'I told him of your wish to come home & he begged me to tell you that he was very much against it & thought you ought to take the opportunity to go to the frontier & see something of the country.'[9] To Jack, Jennie added, 'The Prince told me he had spoken to the Queen about him [Winston].'[10]

There also had been other news of her sons. Bourke had written in detail about his discussions and activities with Jack in Paris. And Brabazon had informed her that he had made a special trip to a meeting of the Turf Club to sponsor Winston successfully for membership.[11] And 'Bimbash' Stewart, a friend of Kitchener's and Jennie's, had told her that Kitchener wanted Winston to have the first vacancy. 'But you must take Bimbash's statement with a grain of salt,' Jennie had warned Winston.[12]

Winston, however, had more immediate and exciting plans. On April 21 he wrote to his mother: 'I am afraid you will regard this letter somewhat in the aspect of a bombshell.' With the declaration of war by Turkey on Greece, Winston wanted to serve again as a war correspondent. But he was unsure which side to go on.

> This, my dearest Mamma, must depend on you. . . . If you can get me good letters to the Turks, to the Turks I will go. If to the Greeks – to the Greeks. . . . In thinking all this out it has occurred to me that Sir Edgar Vincent could probably do everything for me in Constantinople & could get me attached to some general's staff etc. as in Cuba. On the other hand, you know the King of Greece and could of course arrange matters in that quarter. . . . Of course nearly every paper has one [correspondent] there already, but I have no doubt you will find one to avail themselves of my services. . . . These arrangements I leave to you and I hope when I arrive at Brindisi I shall find the whole thing cut and dried. . . .
>
> . . . Of course my dear Mamma – if you don't want me to go I won't.[13]

But as usual, Winston threw in his standard final plea, which nearly always worked: 'I know you will not stand in my way in this matter.'[14] Jennie considered it 'a wild scheme', but consulted her friends at the Foreign Office and confided to Jack, 'Luckily the war will be over by the time he gets home.'[15] As she informed Winston, it was 'like a damp firework'.[16]

Bourke Cockran had returned to London and kept up his correspondence with Winston. Before his homecoming, Winston had written, 'I am looking forward to seeing you and hearing some account of your rhetorical successes, so much so that it makes me feel quite tired to wait.'[17]

Jennie kept Jack informed about Winston. 'You may imagine what talks Winston and I have been having,' she wrote to him shortly after Winston's return. 'He looks very well, I think, and is more quiet.'[18] She also advised Jack that she was sending him copies of the *Daily Graphic*, some money for horse-back riding and dancing lessons, and would contact him about a music teacher as soon as Breteuil has found one. 'Politics are so interesting just now, and you must be *au fait*,' she added.[19] She was also expecting him to join them soon in London.

In 1897 horses were still very much a part of the London scene. Young boys continued to chase in and out of traffic collecting horse dung to sell as fertilizer. For most people, the bells on the hansom cabs still sounded more romantic than the blare of the rare automobile horn. However, the science section of the *Annual Register* reported: 'Prominent among the matters of general scientific interest has been a development of mechanical propulsion for road-carriages. In this country, the use of such carriages or 'motor-cars' is restricted by the act preventing any such vehicle exceeding a speed of more than four miles an hour. . . .' The Mayor of Tunbridge Wells had put a number of horseless carriages on exhibition and one critic noted, 'The new invention was generally derided. Besides, the law required that a man with a red flag should always precede a mechanically-driven vehicle on the road.'

These new mechanical monsters did not acquire the seal of social approval until 1898 when the Prince of Wales took his first motor-car drive. There is a photograph of the occasion showing Prince Edward with three other passengers, one of whom is Jennie. 'The motor-car will become a necessity for every English gentleman,' the Prince announced.[20]

This might have been so, but the bicycle was still enormously popular. 'I went across Albert Bridge from Cheyne Court at 9.15,' wrote one diarist.

The Park Road was already full of bicyclists and many were already having coffee and rolls. I rode for a while with General Sir Evelyn Wood and Sir Francis Jeune, the divorce judge. Colonel Brabazon, Mr Claude Lowther, Mr Sidney Greville, Lady Sykes, who rides a horse better than she does a bicycle, Mrs Brown Potter the actress, Lady Essex, Princess Dolgorouki, Mr Lewis Waller, the actor, and so on. Mr Henry Chaplin stood on the sidewalk looking on. He told me he prefers to ride an 18-hand-high horse that hasn't got wobbly wheels. . . .[21]

Jennie was a bicycle devotee and bought one to send to Jack: 'I have got you a very good bicycle for 8 pounds. . . .'[22] She also reported, 'I have been initiated into the mysteries of golf, and I like it . . . but I am quite sworn off poker which is a good thing – sixpenny bezique is now my form!'[23]

The year 1897 was the Diamond Jubilee, marking the sixtieth year of Queen Victoria's reign. The Queen had occasionally gone to Regent Street in an unpretentious open carriage, without even special traffic arrangements, but one day she was recognized near Hyde Park Corner. Someone called out, 'It's the Queen! God bless her!' Suddenly all the traffic around her came to a halt as everyone stared at this little white-haired woman dressed completely in black.

And then an electric thrill seemed to go round. The passengers inside and outside the vehicles sprang up; the prim coachmen and footmen in their private carriages, usually as stolid as wax dolls, rose to their feet and shouted like schoolboys; the foot passengers swelled the cheering; such a cheer! It was a sight I would not have missed for worlds, that forest of waving hats and handkerchiefs, the faces of the people, startled for once out of their British reserve. Everyone in the crowd fixed eyes on the Queen as on a dearly-loved friend; everyone shouted that came near, 'God bless you, Ma'am!' 'How well she looks!! A long life to her! Hurrah!' As for the Queen, she burst into tears, and bowed right and left, making spasmodic attempts to dry her eyes with her black-bordered handkerchief, between the bows.[24]

For the formal Diamond Jubilee Procession from Buckingham Palace to St Paul's Cathedral the Queen was in command of her dignity and carried a little sunshade. The weather had been misty and cold, the sky threatening, but just as Her Majesty left the palace, the sun broke through, bright and warm, to produce the proverbial 'Queen's weather'. She seemed aged and fragile, still dressed in black, but now with cream-coloured feathers in her bonnet. She rode in an open landau, drawn by eight cream-coloured horses, and along the way the lamp-posts were decked with flowers.

'No one ever, I believe, has met with such an ovation as was given me,' the Queen wrote in her diary. 'Every face seemed to be filled with real joy.'

Jennie's nephew Shane Leslie described the occasion. 'The slower the procession went, the more gorgeous it seemed. The Queen herself might have been playing her own part in a film of the future.' [25] Leslie remembered overhearing someone say, 'Imagine having seen a little lady whose Grandpa actually owned all America!' [26] The dome of St Paul's Cathedral was floodlit by powerful spot-lights and the streets were lined with coloured lamps. There was the fine selection of British troops from all over the Empire, Field Marshal Roberts on his white charger, prime ministers from a dozen colonies, the German Emperor, and various potentates.

'There was a large tent in the garden at Buckingham Palace for the guests,' one witness recalled.

But, apparently, the question of ventilation for the guests had been overlooked. The result was that, when the tent was full, the heat was so great that many nearly fainted. Reggi Brett (afterwards Lord Esher) was at that time Secretary at the Office of Works, and there-fore, everybody appealed to him. He said that obviously a current of air was necessary, and that if windows were cut in the canvas at each end of the tent, that would solve the difficulty. As there appeared to be no one capable of cutting holes in the canvas, he determined to do this himself. He was in Court dress and had a rapier at his side. This he drew, and at once thrust it through the canvas side of the tent. To his horror, there was a piercing yell, and it turned out that a house-maid was on the other side, looking through a crack. Mercifully, she was not hurt.[27]

Several weeks later the season's ball was held at Devonshire House in Piccadilly. More than a ball, it was a spectacle. The guests were the most prominent people in England, including the Prince and Princess of Wales and other royalty. 'Everyone of note and interest was there representing the intellect, beauty and fashion of the day,' Jennie wrote.[28] They had all been asked to come dressed as a famous person in history, and *Town Topics* reported that '. . . those who were present say that it was a sight . . . never to be equalled within living memory. . . .' [29]

Jennie described the frenzied thought and preparation that had gone into the costumes:

> . . . Great were the confabulations and mysteries. With bated breath and solemn mien a fair dame would whisper to some few dozen or more that she was going to represent the Queen of Cyprus or Aspasia, Fredegonde or Petrarch's Laura, but the secret *must* be kept. Historical books were ransacked for inspirations, old pictures and engravings were studied, and people became learned in respect to past celebrities of whom they had never before heard.
>
> The men, oddly enough, were even more excited about their costumes than the women, and paid extravagant sums for them. There is no doubt that when a man begins to think about his appearance, he competes with women to some purpose, money, time and thought being of no account to him. On the night of the ball, the excitement rose to fever heat. Every coiffeur in London and Paris was requisitioned, and so busy were they that some of the poor victims actually had their locks tortured early in the morning, sitting all day in a rigid attitude or . . . 'walking delicately'. [30]

The Prince of Wales came as the Grand Prior of the Order of St John of Jerusalem, adorned with a dazzling diamond cross, and a carefully managed ruff to suit his short neck, looking 'as if he had stepped off the stage of "Les Huguenots".' Princess Alexandra was Marguerite de Valois, attended by female nobility. [31] The Duke of Devonshire was the Emperor Charles V, and the Duchess was Zenobia, Queen of Palmyra, 'a dazzling vision of golden suns, jewels, peacock feathers, gems of all kinds, and a high crown with two startling horns, and a lovely pear-shaped pearl hung low on her lovely smooth brow.' [32]

The Duke and Duchess 'received on a raised dais at the end of the ball-room the endless procession who passed by, bowing, curtsying, or salaaming, according to the characters they represented'. [33]

Daisy, Princess of Pless was the Queen of Sheba. Dressed in a blue silk gown covered with diamonds and turquoises, she 'looked like a lily in a vase of purple and gold,' and was 'surrounded by a retinue in Oriental garb, some of whom so far sacrificed their appearance as to darken their faces.' [34] One of the sacrificers was the Princess's younger brother, George Cornwallis-West, who would soon begin spending a significant part of his life with Jennie. That evening, though, he left early, cursing the designer who had created his costume of 'a multi-coloured bed-quilt'.

The woman who had loved Jennie's father, Mrs Fanny Ronalds, represented Music as she had once before at a ball in New York, but this time her head-dress was lit by electricity instead of gas. Lady Maud Warrender was most impressed by the two sisters who came as the 'Furies' and 'wore hairnets to keep their heads tidy!' [35]

Jennie also noted, perhaps a little cattily, that a certain Lady who had covered herself with priceless jewels was actually on the verge of bankruptcy. But she appreciated Lady Tweedmouth dressed as Queen Elizabeth 'with eight gigantic guardsmen surrounding her, all dressed as yeomen of the guard.' And she remarked upon the well-known baronet who 'had been perfecting himself for weeks in the role of Napoleon, his face and figure lending themselves to the impersonation. But what was his dismay at finding in the vestibule a second victor of Austerlitz ever more lifelike and correct than himself. It was indeed a Waterloo for both of them.' [36]

Jennie was dressed as the Byzantine Empress Theodora, a most interesting choice. For precedent there was, of course, 'the divine Theodora', the leading character in Disraeli's novel *Lothair*, who wore a diamond star on her forehead, as Jennie did at one time. The similarity was not coincidental, as Disraeli had been a friend and admirer of Jennie's. The Empress Theodora was almost as multifaceted as a diamond star. The daughter of an animal trainer, she had become an actress, a dancing girl, a courtesan, and finally the mistress and wife of the sixth-century Emperor Justinian I. Justinian was a man of considerable energy, but he was neither strong-willed nor profoundly intelligent. Theodora possessed many of the qualities he lacked. In addition to an imperious will and a piercing glance, she had intellectual brilliance and an extraordinary beauty. As Gibbon wrote in his *Decline and Fall of the Roman Empire*, 'Either love or adulation might proclaim that painting and poetry were incapable of delineating the matchless excellence of her form.' Moreover, Gibbon added, 'The prudence of Theodora is celebrated by Justinian himself; and his laws are attributed to the sage counsels of his most reverend wife, whom he had received as the gift of the Deity. Her courage was displayed amidst the tumult of the people and the terrors of the Court.'

Justinian named Theodora as Empress of the Byzantine Empire, with ruling authority equal to his own. The governors of all the provinces had to swear an oath of allegiance to her, too. She was evidently an extraordinary person, 'born to shine in any situation of life'.

Jennie's costume was as flamboyant as the woman she portrayed. It was a heavily embroidered Byzantine robe, apparently copied from the mosaic portrait in the apse of the church in Ravenna. Ornate circular designs, worked in jewels and rich braids, were repeated throughout the gown. Encircling her forehead was a crown with pendants of pear-shaped pearls in the centre and at the temples. Hanging from the crown was a filmy veil, and on her arms were veils of tulle and sparkling brilliants. Her neck was covered with pearl chokers, and her long black hair flowed forward over her shoulders almost to her waist. In one hand she held a giant lily and in the other the golden orb of power.

Her costume caused considerable comment in the press, and Winston later requested of her 'some photos of you in Theodora costume – for my table.' [37]

'She didn't need a costume to make her look like Theodora,' her nephew accurately commented, 'she *was* Theodora.' [38]

All was not serene, however. Jennie wrote,

> Towards the close of the ball two young men disputed over a certain fair lady. Both losing their tempers, they decided to settle the matter in the garden, and pulling out their weapons, they began making passes. But the combatants were unequally armed, one being a crusader, with a double-handed sword, and the other a Louis XV courtier, armed with his rapier only. He, as might be expected, got the worst of it, receiving a nasty cut on his silk stocking.[39]

Jennie did not mention that the courtier who got the cut was her son Jack. Winston had served as his brother's second in the duel.

It was strange that the calm, equable Jack was the one to fight the duel while his exuberant brother served as his second. Jack was only seventeen and it must have been a matter of high moment for him to find himself in the more dramatic position while his dashing brother watched from the sidelines. There were not many such moments in Jack's life.

Perhaps tempers were so short because it was too hot to dance, and besides, the weighty costumes made most kinds of dancing impossible.

The Prince of Saxe-Coburg wore a heavy suit of armour with the visor down, but the heat soon forced him to open the visor so that he could breathe more freely. Jennie's sister Leonie also arrived helmeted, with sword and shield as well, representing her favourite Wagnerian character, Brünnhilde.

Fortunately, the supper tent was built around the pond where it was cooler, and the area was lit by coloured electric lamps hanging from the branches 'like living jewels'. Soon this would all be part of a vanished world, long before Devonshire House and its marvellous marble staircase would be demolished and an automobile showroom built on the site.

Within a week after the ball, Winston made his first public address, speaking at a meeting of the Primrose League of Conservative Party supporters. His mother, who had been one of the founders of the League, was still an active member. In deciding where to make his maiden effort, Winston surveyed the prospects 'with the eye of an urchin looking through a pastry-cook's window. Finally, we selected Bath.' [40]

He spoke about the Workmen's Compensation Bill, which was then being debated before Parliament, having first discussed the speech in detail with his mother. Comments in the press about the speech were very favourable, one magazine dubbing it 'an auspicious début'.

Jennie arranged a large party at her home afterwards. Some of the guests were people whom Winston either did not know well enough or did not like well enough, such as Arthur James Balfour. The party was important for Winston, though, because he would soon need Balfour's help. Balfour was still in his late forties, the tall, handsome nephew of Lord Salisbury, whom Jennie correctly believed he was destined to succeed. He had a nonchalant manner, but he was said to have 'the finest brain that has been applied to politics in our time'.[41] In 1895 he had published his second major work, *The Foundations of Belief*, which William James had read with 'immense gusto'. But to some, Balfour's soft, bland face made him seem mysterious. 'No one could tell what banked fires burned behind it, or whether they burned, or even if they existed.' [42]

Balfour was a wealthy bachelor, his blood as blue as his eyes, and he deeply admired Jennie's beauty. Their friendship dated from the early days when they worked in politics together, but there had never been any hint of romance between them.

It is not known what Winston and Balfour talked about at that party, but the importance of such parties is hard to over-estimate. Upper-class British reserve often disappeared on these occasions, and people were more easy and open with each other. Matters that might have lingered unresolved through a long correspondence were often settled with a few words. It was at such a dinner party a year before that Winston had received a promise from General Sir Bindon Blood that he could accompany him if he headed another expedition in India.

Reports of a revolt of the Pathan tribesmen on the Indian frontier arrived when Winston and his mother were at Goodwood watching the races. The newspapers further announced that General Blood would head an expedition of three brigades to quell the revolt. Winston promptly sent a telegram to the General, reminding him of his promise, then kissed his mother good-bye and raced to catch the next boat to India.

It was at another party that Jennie had spent a long evening discussing the British political situation with 'Old Lawson' — Edward Lawson, owner of the *Daily Telegraph*. Therefore, when Winston wrote to his mother that General Sir Bindon Blood had suggested Winston join him 'as a press correspondent',[43] Jennie immediately contacted Lawson. Just as promptly, Lawson agreed, saying, 'Tell him to post picturesque, forcible letters.'[44]

'I have faith in my star,' Winston wrote to his mother.[45]

'I believe in your lucky star as I do in mine,' Jennie answered.[46]

And then she wrote to Jack, who by now had returned to France, 'I shall feel very lonely without either of you.'[47]

9

'Look after Mamma,' Winston wrote to his brother, 'and write often to her. I am afraid she will be worried about me. She certainly would if she were here.'[1]

Yet Winston's own letters to Jennie spared her none of the grisly details of the war. This again revealed the multiple role she played in his life. She was not just his mother whom he wanted to shield from worry. She was his closest friend, the one he told about all his experiences. And she wanted to know. She shared with him a love of action, and she lived it with him through his letters. She shared his love of language and served as his best audience, so he left little to her imagination.

'It is a war without quarter. They kill and mutilate everyone they catch, and we do not hesitate to finish their wounded off.'[2] Earlier he had told her about

an awful rout in which the wounded were left to be cut up horridly by these wild beasts. I was close to both officers when they were hit almost simultaneously and fired my revolver at a man at 30 yards who tried to cut up poor Hughes' body. He dropped, but came on again. A subaltern – Bethune by name – and I carried a wounded Sepoy for some distance. . . . My pants are still stained with the man's blood. . . . It was a horrible business. . . . Later on I used a rifle which a wounded man dropped and fired 40 rounds with some effect at close quarters. I cannot be certain, but I think I hit 4 men. At any rate they fell.[3]

His attitude about performing such acts seemed to be summed up in a later letter: 'Bullets – to a philosopher, dear Mamma, are not worth considering. Besides, I am so conceited. I do not believe the gods would create so potent a being as myself for so prosaic an ending.'[4]

Jennie forwarded all of Winston's letters to Jack, but she reminded him with each letter, 'Mind you send it back at once.' In one of her letters to Jack, she remarked, 'You may imagine how thankful I am to have received a cable from him every day since the fighting, so that I know he is all right.'[5]

Winston had sent each of his columns for the *Daily Telegraph* to his mother with such comments as, 'Use your own discretion in editing it – as I am too tired to write more now and then post it off.'[6] '. . . Forgive this scribble – and believe I love you. . . .'[7]

> Darling Winston
>
> . . . You may imagine how much I think of you, & how in my heart I shall be glad that the war will be over soon, & that I shall know you safely back at Bangalore – & yet I am more than glad for yr sake that you managed to get up there. . . . But I think of all the hardships you are going through & I feel for you darling. . . .
>
> . . . I read yr letters for the D.T. to Ld Minto who thought them excellent – but begged me not to sign yr name. He said it was very unusual & might get you into trouble. The 1st one appeared yesterday headed 'Indian Frontier – by a young officer.' The Editor wired to say they wld give 5 [pounds] a column. . . . I wrote to the Prince & told him to look out for yr letters. Also to lots of people. You will get plenty of kudos (can't spell it). I will see that you do darling boy. . . .[8]

Winston was displeased with the amount of payment, even more displeased that the columns did not have his name on them. '. . . . Poor Winnie,' Jennie wrote to Jack. 'He thinks his letters are not a success – *but they are!*'[9]

Despite his disappointment, Winston responded to his mother's suggestion about putting his columns together in a pamphlet. 'Perhaps you will have them put in a book,' he wrote. 'It would of course sell well and might do me good.'[10]

Winston never stopped reaching for recognition:

> I rode on my grey pony all along the skirmish line where everyone else was lying down in cover. Foolish perhaps, but I play for high stakes and given an audience there is no act too daring or too noble. Without the gallery things are different . . . quality not quantity is after all what we should strive for. Still I should like to come back and wear my medals at some big dinner or some other function. . . .[11]

Behind this public façade, with only his mother as audience, he could reveal, 'I am a little lonely here at times as I have never a friend to talk to. . . .'[12]

On another occasion he cautioned her, 'If I am to do anything in the world, you will have to make up your mind for publicity, and also to my doing "unusual" things.'[13]

Evidently Jennie was concerned about his penchant for self-promotion, because during this period she wrote to him:

You have done more than well my darling boy & I am as always proud of you. Forgive a piece of advice – which may not be needed – but be modest. All yr feats of valour are sure to come out & people will know. Let it be from others & not from yrself. One must be tempted to talk of oneself in such a case – *but resist*. Let them *drag* things out.[14]

Neither was it really necessary for him to remind her, 'You must get people to do things for me',[15] for she never stopped doing that. Colonel Brabazon wrote to her that Sir Bindon Blood was speaking '*very* highly of our "young officer",'[16] and at the same time, Blood wrote to Jennie, 'You may depend on my looking after him if there is another opportunity for him.'[17]

Jennie remembered to send Winston the photos he requested of her 'as the wicked "Theodora",'[18] and she also asked him to give one to Kincaid-Smith, a handsome Captain in Winston's outfit with whom she had been corresponding. Winston knew about this correspondence and perhaps was demonstrating a pang of jealousy when he deprecated Kincaid-Smith's polo playing, which, he said, 'has not got the dash of younger men'.[19]

That November Winston was twenty-three, and his mother cabled her congratulations to him. 'I knew you would remember,' he answered.[20] Jennie had also written, '. . . if you don't go to Egypt . . . I will come and stay with you next year. . . . We will have great fun. . . .'[21]

Winston later let his mother know just how much her letters meant to him: '. . . . your letter is the central point of my week. If I thought mine could give you half as much pleasure, I should write all day';[22] '. . . when the mail comes in with no letter from you, I get in such a state of despondency & anger that I am not approachable by anyone and fly to my inkpot to let off steam.'[23]

With the initial frontier action over, Winston informed his mother that he had been under fire 'for ten complete times', and observed that it was 'quite a foundation for a political life'. He added:

> . . . You must keep your eye on the political situation. Although I know & hear nothing out here, it is evident to me that a very marked reaction against the decision of the last general election has taken place. These numerous bye elections might, had I been in England, have given me my chance of getting in. However my experience out here has been of greater value and interest than anything else would be, or perhaps can ever be. Of course should a vacancy occur in Paddington – you must weigh in for me & I will come by the next ship. They would probably elect me even if I could not get back in time. I suppose Ld Salisbury's retirement is now only a matter of months. There might be sweeping changes after that.' [24]

Winston still pressed his mother to renew her efforts to get him transferred to Egypt. 'Indeed, my life here is not big enough to hold me. I want to be up and doing and cannot bear inaction or routine. . . .' He wanted her to 'stimulate the Prince into writing to Kitchener.' [25] He would later suggest she renew her own personal application on his behalf directly with the Sirdar: 'Strike while the iron is hot & the ink wet.' [26]

Jennie had other work to do for Winston. First she had to find a publisher for his book, *The Malakand Field Force.*

> Arthur Balfour . . . has been too nice about you. I told him all about yr book (the Campaign), & he is going to put me in the way of a good publisher and everything. You need only send me the MS & I will have it all done for you. A.B. said he had not read yr letters – but he had heard more than flattering things about them. The letters have been read & appreciated by the people who later on can be useful to you. [27]

It is easy to visualize Jennie doing all these things for her son – writing letters, persuading the Prince, cornering Balfour, arranging a *tête-à-tête* with a prominent person. Of course, it wasn't only for her son. Her priorities would soon change somewhat, but at this time Jennie's life and future were integrated with Winston's. Moreover, she enjoyed working at it. How she revelled in persuading people to do something in which she deeply believed! There was an excitement, a challenge in it, a feeling of action and reaction, and, most of all, the satisfaction of tangible results. At a time in her life when the sequence of the social seasons seemed ever more repetitive and boring, she could gear her activity toward a specific goal. And there was no goal closer to her heart than Winston's future.

Perhaps, too, this was a way of compensating for guilt feelings about Winston's early years, when to some extent she had neglected him in favour, first, of her husband's ambitions, and then of his illness. In those days she could give Winston and Jack only whatever time she had left – which was not enough. Yet, somehow, they were never embittered by this period of neglect; on the contrary it seemed only to amplify their love for her. Winston wrote later that as a child he had loved her as 'a fairy princess; a radiant being possessed of limitless riches and power. . . . She shone for me like the Evening Star. I loved her dearly – but at a distance.' [28] Now that they were grown, the distance had been closed. But now Jennie had to determine how to divide her time between Winston and Jack according to their needs.

Winston was not shy about making his needs known. She had recognized his potential early and helped shape his direction. He knew where he was going and the roads to take, and he knew the vital part his mother had to play to help him get there. He demanded everything from his mother and got it.

Jack's need was different and in some ways stronger. He adored his mother, idolized his brother, and realized his own shortcomings in comparison with them. He did not have their dazzling kind of intellect, their drive, their ambition; and Jennie's attitude towards him was far more maternal and protective. During Jack's stay in Paris, Jennie's letters to him conveyed her worry about his ear infection, his spelling, his reading habits, his clothes – 'I would send you the patterns & you cld choose & send me your measures.' If he had an unplumbed potential, he did not know what it was at this time. He was eighteen and unsure of what he wanted or where he was going. (Jennie had thought of getting Jack into the Foreign Office '. . . if he did pass the Exams – but I fear he is not clever enough.') [29]

To Jennie Jack was a good boy, a loving boy, who represented her own softer and more quiet side. She knew his want of her, but there was Winston as demanding as her husband had been. Jack did not really demand anything. How should she divide herself?

Jack had completed his year in Paris, and the question now was what he would do next. He had written Jennie a long letter:

I can remember at Harrow one or two boys who had suddenly to change all their plans for their futures, but I don't think you could easily find one who changes every year! I have been 'going to be' everything under the sun and as you know I have always had a great abhorrence of being a 'something in the City', with the chance of becoming nothing. I have been 'going into' the Army, the City, the Bar, the Foreign Office, or Diplomacy and now I am to change again to the City. Each time I have been told that I have lots of time, but I have no more, I am nearly 18 and must be settled.

It is not wholly my fault that I have changed so; I am built heart & soul for the Army; but you asked me to give it up because it was expensive and not lucrative because it might leave you alone and because it was 'no career'. I am afraid that many are called & few chosen in anything.

I began to like the idea of going to Oxford, of going where Winston had not been and even of plodding away at the Bar. But now you want me to go under the old gas lamp in the City. The life of a Cavalry Officer appeals to me more but I will do it if it is necessary & if you want me to.

Your letter did not tell me much about your 'serious financial crisis'. Have things gone wrong in America? Or did they get muddled in England? Lord Vernon prophesied to me a year ago that you would either marry! or have a crisis in the next two years! ...

... The only part of your letter with which I agreed, was the wish that we should be more together. ... If you could imagine how much I long to come home to you & Cumberland Place, you would realize that my only wish is to please you & to do whatever you wish.[30]

It was a rather extraordinary letter for Jack to write. He had matured in the preceding year, but his frustration of indecision must have been welling up within him for a long time before he could write about it. How revealing that one of the attractions of Oxford was that it was 'where Winston had not been.' Above all, he did not want to compete with Winston or with the image of Winston.

The further significance of this letter was its tone of freedom and intimacy. In most upper-class British families there was a chasm of reticence between generations which was surrounded by a framework of propriety. There were many unspoken rules about things one did not do and things one never said. It was remarkable that a son would write to his mother of Lord Vernon's prophecy that 'you would either marry! or have a crisis in the next two years!' That he was able to do so was the result of Jennie's consistent encouragement of her sons to say exactly what they thought and felt.

Jack could say almost anything to his mother – as could Winston – because all of them knew that the bond of love between them was indivisible. 'How I long to come home to you', Jack wrote; 'my only wish is to please you and to do whatever you wish.'

On receiving this declaration from her son, Jennie answered somewhat defensively:

Your last letter saddened me, but my darling boy, you can be certain of one thing, and that is that your happiness is the one thing I want above all others, and that I will make any sacrifice necessary to insure it. . . . Darling I don't want to make any tiresome remarks, but you must remember that your want of decision as regards your likes and dislikes and your choice of a career has been a drawback to you – I have never heard you before really express a real desire to go into the Army. . . . It is not too late – if you are content to have a small allowance and live on your pay – and be a Major at 45 on 600 a year! Bless you, my child. Don't fret. All will come right for you, I am sure.[31]

In December 1897, as was customary, Jennie and Jack were invited to Blenheim for Christmas. The Churchill family had decided to put on an amateur play on behalf of charity, and the show would be open to the general public. 'The whole of Oxford may turn up,' Jennie wrote to Winston '. . . 10 [shillings] to see the Churchills playing the fool! . . .'[32] To Jack she added, 'I am dying to see you, you darling. We go to Blenheim on Monday to begin rehearsing this terrible burlesque; but it cannot be helped. I am sending you the second act. You are a Chinaman.'[33]

The playlet was called 'An Idle Hour', and Jack was called Li-Down-Do, while Jennie was Mrs Jubilee Junius, a newspaper reporter, and the

Duke of Marlborough was another main character. Whoever wrote the piece managed to make some digs at Jennie.

She was introduced in the play by the lines:

> J is for Jennie and Jubilee June,
> She's bright and she's clever, but sings out of tune. . . .

Jennie herself sang:

> I'm called Mrs Jubilee 'June'
> (Mrs Perkins is that the right tune?)
> A Lady Reporter
> Belle's Letters own daughter,
> The wife of the Man in the Moon.
>
> My life is a terrible hash
> From county to county I dash:
> To interview Mayors
> And Bishops and Players,
> I stir up the lot with my lash.[34]

The family entertainment seems to have received broad coverage, for Winston wrote to his mother: 'I laughed a great deal reading the account of the Blenheim Theatricals, all of which the Indian Papers solemnly printed. Capital! I am so glad it went off well.' [35]

Jack fully described to Winston his discussions with their mother about his future, and Winston wrote to Jennie about Jack's renewed interest in the Army. Then he added, quite perceptively:

I do not gather that the idea of sending him into the City precludes his going to Oxford. I should be very sorry if it did & I hope you will try to send him there. His letters to me for some time have expressed much eagerness for a University education. Indeed I have rarely known him express such a decided opinion. Also I think his mind is *reflective* rather than *inventive*. If so he needs fuel & knowledge to work upon. This a University education would provide. I hope you will be able to secure one for him. If money prevents I could borrow a further £500 wh he might repay me when he came of age. I think he had set his heart on it. Perhaps the book may be a financial suc-

1 Jennie about 1895, the year of
Lord Randolph Churchill's death

2 Bourke Cockran

4 The Prince of Wales takes
his first automobile ride, June 1898;
Jennie at front left

3 Jennie as th
Empres
Theodor

5 William Waldorf Astor   6 Paul Bourget

7 Jennie and George (far right) at Ruthin Castle
with (left to right) Colonel Cornwallis-West,
the Prince of Wales, Mrs Mary Cornwallis-West,
Lord Marcus Beresford, Muriel Wilson,
Miss Cornwallis-West

8 Winston during the Boer War

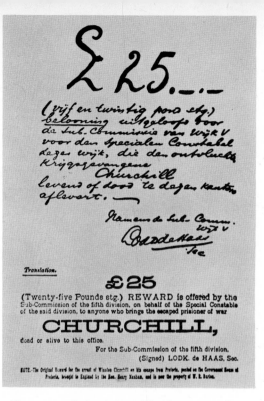

Translation.

£25

(Twenty-five Pounds stg.) REWARD is offered by the
Sub-Commission of the fifth division, on behalf of the Special Constable
of the said division, to anyone who brings the escaped prisoner of war

CHURCHILL,

dead or alive to this office.

For the Sub-Commission of the fifth division.
(Signed) LODK. de HAAS, Sec.

NOTE.- The Original Reward for the arrest of Winston Churchill on his escape from Pretoria, posted on the Government House of
Pretoria, brought to England by the Hon. Henry Massham, and is now the property of W. B. Burton.

9   The poster offering a reward for the capture of
Winston Churchill on his escape from Pretoria

o   The gun at Chieveley Camp named after
Lady Randolph Churchill

11 Jennie and her son Jack aboard the *Maine*

12 The hospital ship *Maine* at Durban, South Africa

13 The Prince of Wales at fifty-seven

14 Mrs Alice Keppel, the Prince of Wales' mistress

15 Sir Ernest Cassel

16 The Marquis de Soveral

17 Herbert and Margot Asquith

18 Jennie's nephew Sunny, the Duke of Marlborough

19 Consuelo, Duchess of Marlborough

cess. Mind you write and say nice things to me about it. Tell me what parts you like. I love praise.[36]

Winston also had mentioned the idea of Jack's joining the Army and Jennie answered:

You talk glibly of Jack going into the Army – but you know he wld never pass the medical examination with his eyes – & besides how could I give him an adequate allowance? Everyone thinks my plan for him is the best. He will go to Germany for a year, learn bookkeeping(?) & German, & one of these days make a fortune. He is quite reconciled to it now. He has joined the Oxford Yeomanry & will have a month's drill at Aldershot & his 10 days before he goes to Berlin. It will set him up & give him a nice uniform for all requirements. How I am to pay for it I do not know! [37]

To Jack, Winston now wrote: 'The whole thing is your own fault for not expressing decided opinions. If you had made up your mind what you wanted – insisted upon it – no one would have stopped you. As it is you will probably be making £5,000 a year and playing polo at Hurlingham when I am struggling on a pittance – as a newspaper hack. I shall come down on you like a cartload of bricks.' [38]

The money problem had become increasingly serious. Earlier Winston had written to Jennie, 'Do not worry about money my dearest Mamma. If the worst comes to the worst you can let the house – and however annoying that might be you will always find lots of places glad to receive you while you remain the dearest & most beautiful woman in the world.' [39]

But Jennie did worry about money, for early in 1898 she had to find £17,000, which she needed to 'buy up all the loans I have made in different Insurance offices' [40] and also to clear up some pressing debts. Her security for the loan was to be the life-insurance policies on her life and on Winston's. Winston was now required to guarantee at least the premiums on these life-insurance policies, amounting to £700 per year, which would also cover the interest on the loans. Winston wrote to his mother:

. . . Speaking quite frankly on the subject – there is no doubt that we are both, you & I equally thoughtless – spendthrift and extravagant.

We both know what is good – and we both like to have it. Arrangements for paying are left to the future. My extravagances are on a smaller scale than yours. I take no credit to myself in this matter as you have kept up the house & have had to maintain a position in London. At the same time we shall vy soon come to the end of our tether – unless a considerable change comes over our fortunes and dispositions. As long as I am dead sure & certain of an ultimate £1,000 a year – I do not much care – as I could always make money on the press – and might marry. But at the same time there would be a limit.

... I sympathize with all your extravagances – even more than you do with mine – it seems just as suicidal to me when you spend £200 on a ball dress as it does to you when I purchase a new polo pony for £100. And yet I feel that you ought to have the dress & I the polo pony. The pinch of the whole matter is that we are damned poor. . . .[41]

Writing to Jack about the loan, Winston noted: 'I recognize that it is a necessity for her to have the money. Indeed unless she has it – she could not continue my allowance – or pay for your education.'[42]

Arthur Balfour meanwhile had kept his word to Jennie, and sent her the name of his literary agent, A. P. Watt. 'I think you will find him invaluable for the work you want. If he thinks such a course practicable I strongly recommend for Winston's sake a *royalty* on the sale, rather than any such arrangement as either half profits, or a lump sum down. Watt will however be a good adviser.'[43]

Within a short time, Watt had arranged for a contract with the highly respected firm of Longmans. 'I received yr book & rushed off to Watt's with it,' Jennie wrote to Winston, and also informed him that another author was preparing a book on the same subject. 'I don't think you need mind – as I hope yours will be out first.'[44] The next morning, she wrote still another letter:

I've received this morning Mr Watt's letter which I copy for you – I am awfully sleepy still as we danced till 3. Everything very well done. I have to finish before breakfast in order to get it off by today's mail.

... I am going to show this to Mr Cassel & to Mr Lawson who is here before wiring – but I have no doubt it is the best that can be done. For Mr Balfour told me Watt was very good at making a bargain

& it is a great thing that yr first book shld be published by such a good firm as Longman, also that it shld be done at their cost.[45]

Winston had told his mother: 'All financial arrangements in connection with it – I shall leave entirely in your hands. But please have no false scruples or modesty about bargaining – as "the labourer is worthy of his hire", and as I have quoted from Dr Johnson to you before, "No one but a blockhead ever wrote – except for money." '[46]

In the same letter, he added, 'I hope the book will please you. After all it is your applause that I covet more than any other. Indeed I think that would include all others.'

Of course, royal praise was also gratifying. 'The Prince showed me yr letter,' Jennie told Winston. 'He was very pleased with it.'[47]

The Prince of Wales also wrote to Winston:

Accept my very best thanks for your letter of 4th which I have read with the greatest possible interest – as I did also your letters which appeared in the *Daily Telegraph*. You were very fortunate to have taken part in the campaign in the North West Frontier – & I only regret that you were not able to remain with Sir Bindon Blood. It does seem hard that when he applied for you to join him again that you were not allowed to do so. . . . Your mother & Jack are staying with us this week & she tells me that you are bringing out a book with an account of your recent campaign which I shall look forward to read – as you have great facility in writing. . . .[48]

Winston was still hoping to receive a transfer to Egypt in time for the approaching campaign. 'You must work Egypt for me,' he had pleaded to Jennie in January. 'You have so many lines of attack. . . . Now I beg you – have no scruples but worry right and left and take no refusal.'[49] Then, a few days later he added, 'Oh how I wish I could work you up over Egypt! I know you could do it with all your influence – and all the people you know. It is a pushing age and we must shove with the best.'[50]

'I wrote to Sirdar 10 days ago,' Jennie answered.

Lady Jeune has written to Sir Evelyn [Wood], & Brab has been to the War Office & they promise to 'note' your name. There is to be no advance until July or August so there is plenty of time. . . . bless you

123

my darling don't fuss – we'll get you up there if it is possible. I may go to Cairo myself for a little, if I do I can perhaps work the Sirdar at nearer quarters with more chance of success.[51]

She also sent an extract of one of Winston's letters to Lord Roberts. Roberts replied, 'What a capital letter Winston writes. When he comes home I must have a talk with him about the Frontier question. . . .'[52] However, Lord Roberts had previously advised Jennie, 'I would, with the greatest pleasure, help your son, but it would be no use my communicating with General Lockhart as Sir George White is all powerful, and, as he refused to allow Winston to join General Blood's Staff, after his having previously served with that officer in the Malakand Field Force, I feel sure he would not consent to his being sent with the Tirah Field Force.'[53]

Earlier Jennie had written to Winston:

I had a letter from my Highlander friend Caryl Ramsden from Cairo. He said on his way out he heard Gen Gatacre & a lot of military men talking of you – as the most 'promising youngster out' but that you wrote too well to remain in the Army – where yr talents wld be wasted – & where yr writings wld sooner or later get you into trouble. Up to now however you have managed to be discreet.[54]

Major Ramsden, the 'Highlander friend' Jennie mentioned, had made a deep impression on her, and the two had been keeping up an intimate correspondence. Fourteen years younger than Jennie, Caryl John Ramsden was such a handsome ladies' man that he had earned the nickname of 'Beauty' Ramsden. Having spent a boring year with his battery in Malta and Crete, he had just been ordered to rejoin his regiment for Kitchener's campaign up the Nile, and Jennie decided to meet him in Cairo.

Jennie appeared to be specifically encouraging younger men. She was still a striking beauty and the young men responded to her charms.

Young Lord Rossmore wrote:

The first time I saw her was at Ascot when I was on a coach belonging to the 1st Life Guards. Suddenly my attention was arrested by the appearance of a lady who was walking in my direction, and who was accompanied by a half dozen men. I thought her the most beautiful creature imaginable and, dressed in white and wearing a big white hat, she was perfectly delightful to look at, and I cried out impulsively, greatly to the amusement of my brother officers, 'Good heavens! Who's that?' ... [She was] the loveliest woman I have ever set my eyes on (my wife, of course, excepted).[55]

As soon as she had decided to go to Egypt, Jennie wired Winston. He, of course, assumed that she was going only for his sake, to further his cause with Kitchener. 'Your telegram reached me on Saturday – and I can assure you I feel vy grateful indeed to you for going to Egypt – It is an action which – if ever I have a biographer – will certainly be admired by others. I hope you may be successful. I feel almost certain you will. Your wit & tact & beauty – should overcome all obstacles.'[56]

Staying with Ramsden at the Continental Hotel in Cairo, Jennie kept up a steady stream of messages to Kitchener. 'I have noted your son's name,' Kitchener finally answered, 'and I hope I may be able to employ him later in the Sudan.' Satisfied with this news she and Ramsden then took a trip on a *dahabeyah*, a riverboat, travelling up the Nile. Major Ramsden soon received orders to rejoin his unit at Wadi Halfa, and Jennie returned to Port Said to embark for London. There she was informed that her ship would be delayed for several days, so she hurried back to Cairo just in case Ramsden had not yet left.

He had not, but neither was he alone. Jennie entered his room without knocking, and there she found him embracing Lady Maxwell, wife of the Army Commander. Jennie's anger was unleashed loudly enough to be heard throughout the hotel.[57]

The echoes of that incident reached the Prince of Wales. 'You had better have stuck to your old friends than gone on your Expedition of the Nile! Old friends are the Best!' he teasingly wrote.[58]

Jennie drafted a reply to him in London and read it aloud to her sister Leonie: '*So* grateful for your sympathy – as your Royal Highness knows exactly *how* it feels after being jilted by Lady Dudley!'[59] Leonie begged her sister not to send the letter, as she was fearful the Prince would never speak to her again. But Jennie replied that she didn't care. In that case, Leonie said, she would post the letter as she had to go to the post office. Leonie went to the post office, but she never sent the letter, and Jennie never knew.

The Prince, however, heard about Jennie's displeasure with his note and he answered: '*Ma chère Amie*: I must ask your pardon if my letter pained. I had no idea "*que c'était une affaire si sérieuse!*"'[60]

Apparently the Prince was anxious to be forgiven, as the next week he asked her to arrange a dinner at her home and then promptly expressed his gratitude: 'I must write to thank you for your charming dinner of last night. . . . I thought your party was exceptionally successful.' And perhaps to appease her further, he added, 'I am delighted with Winston's book – admirably written and most interesting.' [61]

The Prince followed this with a letter to Winston:

I cannot resist writing a few lines to congratulate you on the success of your book! I have read it with the greatest possible interest, and I think the descriptions and the language generally excellent. Everybody is reading it, and I only hear it spoken of with praise.

. . . You have plenty of time before you, and should certainly stick to the Army before adding MP to your name.[62]

The Prince's praise was undoubtedly sincere, for he also sent a copy of the book to his mother, Queen Victoria, saying that for having been 'written by so young a man, [it] shows remarkable ability'.

Winston quite openly appealed to his mother for her own reaction: 'Write to me at great length about the book and be nice about it. Don't say what you think, but what I should like you to think. . . .' [63]

After reading the proofs, Jennie tried to raise Winston's spirits: 'I think [the book] is capital – most interesting & well written. It does you great credit & ought to be a gt success – but of course one cannot tell. I will "boom it" judiciously.' [64]

Her judicious booming included letters to G. C. Buckle, editor of *The Times*, Frank Harris, editor of *The Saturday Review* and a close friend of her late husband's, and Henry Norman, assistant editor of the *Daily Chronicle*, 'asking them to review yr book favourably when it appears, which will be in a fortnight or so, *so* expeditious have Longman been.' [65]

'I owe you a great deal for all the trouble you have taken,' Winston answered, 'and I feel *most* grateful for the spur which your interest and your applause give to my ambitions. . . .' [66]

As soon as the book was published, Jennie had copies sent to all her important friends who might be able to push it, particularly men in the military. Most of the critics were enthusiastic, as the sample from *The Athenaeum* indicates: '*The Story of the Malakand Field Force* (Longmans) needs only a little correction of each page to make its second edition a military classic.' [67]

126

Corrections were probably necessary because Winston had asked Jennie to persuade his Uncle Moreton to correct the text of the book. This turned out to be a mistake. Frewen's copy editing left the book full of errors, and perfectionist Winston writhed when he read it. He realized that he would have done far better to have asked his mother to work on it, and he soon informed her: 'If there is a second edition, I have told them to send them [the proofs] to you for revision.' [68]

He also told her that he was sending her a short story, 'wh I want you to sell, signed, to one of the magazines. I think the *Pall Mall* wd like it & would pay my price. You should not get less than £20 for it, as it is a very good story – in my opinion. So don't sell it without a good offer.' [69]

Some months later he told her about a novel he was writing, a 'political romance', that must 'be entirely rewritten and polished, but I hope to send you the MS in about four weeks. . . .' He felt, though, that the manuscript had a major fault. '. . . you must help me with the woman in the novel. . . . She is my chief difficulty.' [70]

Winston had three months' summer leave due to him in the spring of 1898, and he told Jennie that he planned to stop off at Cairo, then continue to England. Sir Evelyn Wood said that if he did get this leave, he himself 'would see that I got to the front'.[71] Winston also wrote to Sir Ian Hamilton, then General, who was returning home with the manuscript of Winston's first novel, to be delivered to Jennie: 'Please say nice things about me to everyone at home. If you would call on my mother – 35A Gt Cumberland Place – she would be very grateful for news of me & to meet one who has shown me much kindness.' [72] The next day, Winston wrote to his mother saying that he had asked General Hamilton to call on her. 'He has been vy kind to me & I shall be very grateful if you will be amiable to him – should he call. He is a brilliant soldier and will one day be in high command.' [73]

In his next letter, Winston was more specific: 'Please be effusive. You will recognize him in a minute as his left hand was smashed to pieces by a bullet at Majuba Hill. . . . Were they to send another Brigade to Egypt he would vy likely get it. . . .' [74]

Of Jennie's own writing:

When are you going to publish your Impressions of travel etc. We must talk about that when I come home. The Russian article might well be worked in. These things sell. And besides – if for no other reason – they amuse and interest others. So many people travel but so few observe – and of these a minority can express their thoughts & impressions.[75]

A week or so earlier he had told her:

The desire to see England before again going to the wars was very strong upon me. . . . Your letter of last week's mail decided me. . . . I shall be home on about July 2nd. . . . I hope I shall be able to see a good deal of you and that you will try and accept few invitations during my flying visit. . . .

He also listed several things he wanted her to do for him:

(1) Sir B. Blood is . . . coming home by this ship and I want you to ask him to dinner and Lady B. (who is charming) and have some distinguished people – possibly the Prince – to meet him. . . .
(2) I want to have at least two good public meetings during my flying visit. Can you not arrange one at Bradford. . . . I have the material for several speeches of some value ready and can easily bring it up to date & locality. . . .[76]

You might arrange one or two dinners – and get me a few invitations. I want to see people and to get about. Try and get me a pleasant Sunday somewhere. I will go down to Deepdene for one day.
Au revoir, my dearest Mamma. I am looking forward above all things to seeing you. If possible, let us dine alone together on the night I arrive – with Jack, of course.[77]

Jennie's income in 1898 had dropped to only £900 – inclusive of her allowance to Winston and Jack. When she informed Winston how matters stood, he answered, 'The situation as described by your letter is appalling. As you say it is of course impossible for you to live in London on such a pittance. I hate the idea of your marrying – but that of course would be a solution.'[78]
Clearly, his feelings were ambivalent: he was jealous of any possibility of his mother's remarriage. As he had put it to her in a previous letter: 'I have also to reckon on the possibility of your marrying again – perhaps some man I did not like – or did not get on with – and of

troubles springing up – which might lessen your affections for me.'[79] But now he had to recognize their need for money.

Jennie, meanwhile, was busy securing Jack's future. She consulted her long-standing friend and financial confidant, Ernest Cassel, who promised to get Jack a position in the City. Cassel was a remarkable man. *The Times* described him as a person of 'great wealth, a great heart, great influence . . . whose claim to rank among the outstanding figures of the last 20 years is indisputable.'

Of German-Jewish descent, Ernest Cassel was several years older than Jennie, a widower who had never remarried. He had been instrumental in financing the first Aswan Dam in Egypt, the Central Tube Railway in London, the Atchison, Topeka and Santa Fe Railway in the United States, as well as the economic structure of Argentina. He was also well known for his unstinting support of numerous charities, his love of horses and mountaineering, and his close friendship with the Prince of Wales.

Sir Sidney Lee tells the story of the Prince of Wales asking a friend whether he had seen the play, *The Importance of Being Earnest*. The friend replied, 'No, sir, but I have seen the importance of being Ernest Cassel.'[80] Jack's career could not have been in better hands.

At the same time, Winston's career was coming under the influence of the Prince of Wales. The character of the Prince was changing perceptibly. The world thought of him as a pleasure-loving nonentity, and so perhaps he was. One of his friends, Margie Chandos Pole, had once taken him to a clairvoyant in Homburg, an old woman who seemed to know things about him that no one else knew. She predicted that he would not succeed to the throne, that Queen Victoria would outlive him. Some of his friends asserted that the Prince began to believe this prophecy, and that this might have contributed to his decision to lead a pleasure-seeking life.[81]

But now he was becoming increasingly serious about Great Britain's place in the world and he gathered about him men of vast experience in foreign affairs. He had the instinct for selecting the right people for the right information, but he was careful about whom he trusted and worked to develop a keener sense of discretion. Despite these personal reforms, he still adored beautiful women and, as Oscar Wilde had said of himself, he could 'resist anything except temptation'.

The Prince had kept a kind and sharp eye for the development of young Winston, and even made a friendly comment in one of his speeches about Winston's 'Malakand' book. He also let it be known to Sir Evelyn Wood, then Adjutant General of the Army, that he personally favoured Winston's placement on Kitchener's staff. Despite his efforts, however, Wood had to inform Jennie:

Dear Jennie,
    The Sirdar declines to take Mr Churchill, and I wrote to show you the correspondence in order we may concert as to future measures – I will call tomorrow, either at 9 on my way home cycling – or about 10 on my way to the office.

Yours affect[ionately,]
Evelyn Wood.[82]

General Wood also enclosed a copy of a telegram he had sent to Kitchener: 'Personage asked me personally desires you take Churchill. . . . I strongly recommended Churchill as good value for you and Army.'[83]

The day before, Kitchener had telegraphed to Wood: '. . . do not want Churchill as no room.'[84] Even Lord Salisbury, who was then Prime Minister, felt that he could not intervene. 'The matter is absolutely in Kitchener's hands,' he advised Winston, 'and he may think that it is too late now to make any change on previous decisions. I shall greatly regret it, but like Sir Evelyn Wood, "I can do no more".'[85]

Winston meanwhile had written an article for a magazine and had asked Jennie to try to have it 'printed in a July number so that I can see it when I arrive. Also the article which will reach you next week "Ethics of Frontier Policy". This goes to *U.S. Magazine* [*United Service's Magazine*, London] who know all about it. But I want the proofs of both revised & punctuated by some good scholar.'[86]

As the time for the public meeting at Bradford approached, Winston became much more specific in his instructions to Jennie. 'I want a real big meeting, at least 2,000 men,' he wrote. 'Compel them to come in. I am sure I can hold them.'[87] Jennie knew Bradford well, as she had attended a great many political meetings there with her husband. Winston was quite satisfied with the arrangements and the reception he received. On July 15, he wrote to his mother from Bradford,

The meeting was a complete success. The hall was not a vy large one – but it was closely packed. I was listened to with the greatest attention for 55 minutes at the end of which time there were loud & general cries of 'Go on' . . . many people mounted their chairs and there was really a very great deal of enthusiasm.

. . . The conclusions I form are these – with practice I shall obtain great power on a public platform. My impediment is no hindrance. My voice sufficiently powerful – and – this is vital – my ideas & modes of thought are pleasing to men.

It may be perhaps the hand of Fate – which by a strange coincidence closed one line of advance and aspiration in the morning – and in the evening pointed out another with an encouraging gesture. At any rate – my decision to resign my commission is definite.

P.S. They cheered you several times last night with great cordiality.

You might drop a line to Oliver Borthwick and thank him for the vy excellent report in the M.P. [*Morning Post*]. He is also reporting my speech tonight at Heckmondwicke.[88]

Jennie received a message from R. V. Haldane, who had read the speech in the *Morning Post*. 'I thought it very good – broad in tone – fresh & vigorous,' Haldane wrote. 'I hope he will soon be in the House, for there is in his voice something of the strong quality of one that is – alas – still – to the loss of all of us, & of you most of all.'[89]

In the meanwhile, Jennie's persistent activity to get Winston assigned to Egypt caused considerable resentment on high official levels. Winston himself described this resentment:

Who the devil is this fellow? How has he managed to get to these different campaigns? Why should he write for the papers and serve as an officer, at the same time? Why should a subaltern praise or criticize his senior officers? Why should Generals show him favour? How does he get so much leave from his Regiment? Look at all the hard-working men who have never stirred an inch from the daily round and common task. We've had quite enough of this – too much indeed. He is very young, and later on he may be all right; but now a long period of discipline and routine is what 2nd Lt Churchill requires.[90]

Others proceeded to be actually abusive, and the expressions, 'Medal-Hunter', and 'Self-Advertiser', were used from time to time in some high and some low military circles.

None of this deterred Jennie. She and Lady Jeune gingerly suggested to Sir Evelyn Wood that perhaps there was an alternative way to circumvent Kitchener. Wood himself had said in Lady Jeune's presence at a dinner-table conversation that Kitchener was going too far in picking and choosing among particular officers recommended by the War Office. Kitchener did have absolute power for his Egyptian Army but there were several regiments of an Expeditionary Force over which the War Office had complete control. Moreover, Winston had received the endorsements of the Prime Minister and the Prince of Wales.

Two days after this dinner-table conversation, Winston S. Churchill was attached as 'Supernumerary Lieutenant to the 21st Lancers for the Sudan Campaign'; 'You are to report at once to the Abassiyeh Headquarters, Cairo. It is understood that you will proceed, at your own expense, and that, in the event of your being killed or wounded in the impending operations, or for any other reason, no charge of any kind will fall on the British Army funds.' [91]

Jennie's two-year campaign had finally succeeded. As Winston later wrote, '. . . She left no wire unpulled, no stone unturned, no cutlet uncooked. . . .' [92] And now she again kissed her son good-bye as he went off to another war.

With Winston gone and Jack settled, Jennie began seeing her friends more often. They swamped her with attention, affection, and invitations to spend weekends at their country homes.

The great country houses of England at the turn of the century served as a kind of pressure valve for the aristocracy. They provided a haven of tranquillity and remoteness from the world. A few social commentators thought the British country home a kind of lounge and pleasure garden so comfortable and secure that it sapped the energy of the upper classes. Some even believed that this comfort made the British leaders incapable of matching the great achievements of the past.

Whether this was true or not, upper-class society felt the need for a refuge from the strictures of custom and convention. In London one travelled with footmen and left calling cards. There were so many functions at which attendance was obligatory. And one usually had the feeling of being on a stage, subject to the critical examination of curious outsiders.

There was no such atmosphere during the four-night weekend spent at a country house. These estates were far away from city life and they were enormous. Chatsworth, belonging to the Duke and Duchess of Devonshire, accommodated almost five hundred guests.[1] Furthermore, the guests were all carefully selected, most of them so well known to each other that they needed no social pretences, no strained courtliness, no polite hypocrisy.

Jennie was genuinely relaxed on these weekends because they always provided an option: lose yourself in the laughter of a crowd, a game of bridge, the prattling talk, a walk in the woods, an amateur theatrical, a piano concerto. Or find a confidante, charm a man.

There were numberless assignations among the guests. For some, they brought an ease from loneliness; for others, love. At this level of society, a great many marriages were arranged by parents and lawyers, and since they were marriages of convenience, divorce was usually out of the question. The number of 'secret' affairs, therefore, was not so surprising. Every conscientious hostess knew exactly who was paired with whom: '. . . The name of each guest would be neatly written on a card slipped into a tiny brass frame on the bedroom door. The question of disposition of bedrooms always gave the Duchess and her fellow hostesses cause for anxious thought. It was so necessary to be tactful, and at the same time, discreet.' [2]

'It doesn't matter what you do in the bedroom,' the great actress Mrs Patrick Campbell wryly commented, 'as long as you don't do it in the street and frighten the horses.' [3]

There was always the tantalizing possibility of a new affair: eyes meeting across a dining-room table, a quick but meaningful pressure of a hand, an unexpected turn in the garden.

An example of the sort of thing that went on at these country weekends involved one of Lady Warwick's closest friends, the novelist Elinor Glyn. It was in the garden of Warwick Castle that Elinor found herself the unexpected object of amorous attention. The ardent pursuer was none other than her hostess's husband, whose former title was Lord Brooke. Elinor managed to struggle free. Later, while dressing for dinner, she told her own husband of the incident. Her husband gaped at her and said, 'Did he, by Jove!' Then, smiling, he remarked, 'Good old Brookie', and finished tying his tie. [4]

Lady Warwick was similarly unperturbed when she received an amusing note from Jennie with the postscript, 'Tell Brookie I have designs on him. . . .' [5] Indeed, Lady Warwick, whom Jennie called 'Daisy', had her own designs on some of the men in Jennie's life: Count Kinsky, William Waldorf Astor, and the Prince of Wales. [6] But the two friends did not usually compete for the same man at the same time.

Daisy claimed that she was descended on one side from Nell Gwyn, the mistress of Charles II, and on the other from Oliver Cromwell. Her genealogy actually showed, however, that the Cromwell was not the famous historical figure and that the Gwyn was one 'Old Mother Gwyn' who had died drunk in a ditch near the site of Buckingham Palace. Daisy's husband, Lord Francis Brooke, had become the fifth Earl of Warwick in 1893. [7]

Warwick Castle, with its battlemented walls and towers, stood on a rock rising sheer out of the River Avon and had been a Warwick family possession since the Middle Ages. Its interior was largely completed in 1604, when it was described as 'the most princely seat within these midland parts of the realm'. It had an approach which was cut through solid rock and wound from the porter's lodge to an outer court. Inside, there was a great hall overlooking the Avon, the galleries lined with portraits of Warwicks and royalty, by Rubens, Van Dyck, Holbein, and Lely. Daisy added two portraits of herself, one of which was by John Singer Sargent.[8]

Daisy had a party at Warwick Castle for the Prince of Wales in early July 1898.[9] As usual, Daisy invited Jennie, whom she described as 'scintillating . . . a marvellous diamond – a host of facets seemed to sparkle at once. . . . She was as delightful to women as to men. . . . One never thought of giving a party without her. . . .'[10]

Any party for the Prince required enormous preparation. A full orchestra had to be hired and given specific instructions: the Prince did not like classical music and often left when it was played. The Prince also made things difficult by bringing his own retinue of servants: two orderlies and two grooms, two valets, a gentleman-in-waiting, a couple of equerries, two loaders for the shooting, and his own footmen in royal livery to stand behind the table and serve his meals.

What is more, the Prince was most particular about his food. He was a gourmand as well as a gourmet – he liked the best, and lots of it – and best of all, he liked ptarmigan pie. In fact, J. B. Priestley, writing about the period when the Prince had become King Edward VII, observed that

No Edwardian meal was complete without ptarmigan. Hot or cold.

The Edwardian breakfast alone would make one of our Christmas dinners look meagre. First-comers arrived about eight o'clock, late-comers finished eating about ten-thirty. There was porridge and cream. There were pots of coffee and of China and India tea, and various cold drinks. One large sideboard would offer a row of silver dishes, kept hot by spirit lamps, and here there would be poached or scrambled eggs, bacon, ham, sausages, devilled kidneys, haddock and other fish. On an even larger sideboard there would be a choice of cold meats – pressed beef, ham, tongue, galantines – and cold roast pheasant, grouse, partridge, and of course, ptarmigan. A side table would be heaped with fruit – melons, peaches and nectarines, rasp-berries. And if anyone was hungry, there were always scones and toast and marmalade and honey and specially-imported jams.

This kept the guests going until luncheon, usually taken at 1:30, and it might consist of from 8 to 12 courses, some of them very rich, indeed. Then, after a walk in the park, it was time for tea, just to keep body and soul together until dinner. And there was no cup-and-a-biscuit nonsense about this tea: toast and brioches and hot scones and all the jams again; a fine choice of sandwiches; several kinds of rich, sticky cake. And if King Edward happened to be there at teatime, he would probably insist upon having his usual lobster salad. Dinner at 8:30; a dozen courses perhaps, with appropriate wines, and even richer food, probably including, if the chef were up to it, one of those quasi-Roman idiocies, in which birds of varying sizes were cooked one inside the other like nests of oriental boxes. And surely that is enough? But no, a fellow can feel peckish after a few rubbers of bridge; so 'round about midnight, in a neighbouring room, he would help himself to sandwiches, devilled chicken or bones, the brandy and whisky and soda; and then he could get through the night and be ready to welcome his early-morning tea and biscuits.[11]

One of the many other guests Lady Warwick invited to her July weekend party was a young lieutenant named George Cornwallis-West. A tall, handsome man just two weeks older than Winston, he was the son of William Cornwallis-West of Ruthin Castle in North Wales, and although theirs was a family of important connections, they had little money.[12] George's mother was Jennie's age, and she, too, had shared the affections of the Prince of Wales. Both Jennie and Mary Cornwallis-West had been known as 'PB's, professional beauties, whose photographs had sold in stores throughout the country.[13]

Mary Cornwallis-West had a more practical mind than Jennie, particularly in money matters. She later helped one of her daughters marry the very wealthy Duke of Westminster. Her other daughter, whom George greatly resembled, had married His Serene Highness, Prince Hans Heinrich of Pless. The Princess explained why:

I was never told I must marry rank or money but I think it must have been an understood thing, because, for our position and the scale on which we lived, we were poor.

In Germany, every bride, whatever her rank, provides furniture, linen, trousseau, everything. . . . I could provide nothing; and my family could not even give me my trousseau on a fitting scale. Henry, knowing all this, dazzled me with descriptions of life in Silesia. I was to have hunters, jewels, castles, two ladies-in-waiting, visit England every year, and goodness knows what. It all sounded splendid and romantic. I did not realize it clearly at the time, but I was just being bought. . . .[14]

The Cornwallis-West family considered George a very eligible heir, and his parents fully expected him to select a bride from among the wealthiest, most noble young ladies in Britain.

A fellow officer in the 1st Battalion of the Scots Guards, John van der Weyer, described George as a 'good-looking fellow; but short on brains'.[15] He had other qualities though: he played a good game of tennis, enjoyed yachting, was a superb shot and an excellent horseman. He was also a godson of the Prince of Wales.

It was this last that may have qualified him to be a guest at Daisy Warwick's weekend party for the Prince. George later said he was flabbergasted to receive the invitation. He was in the middle of a musketry course, and getting excused from it 'was an almost unheard-of-thing'.

On the other hand, an invitation to meet His Royal Highness almost amounted to a command. I went up to see the Commandant, Colonel Hamilton, and he gave me leave. That visit to Warwick was a very eventful one for me, as it was there that I first met . . . Lady Randolph Churchill. Jennie, as she was always called by her friends — was then a woman of 43, still beautiful, she did not look a day more than 30, and her charm and vivacity were on a par with her youthful appearance. I confess that I was flattered that so attractive a person should have paid any attention to me, but she did, and we became friends almost immediately.[16]

George was obviously overwhelmed. His experience had been mainly with younger, more fragile, wide-eyed women. He was not easily flustered, but his memoirs indicate that with Jennie he felt as if he were accompanying a famous stage star, a living legend. She knew everyone, had been everywhere, seen everything, while he was just a poor, young lieutenant.

His first letter to Jennie — one of several hundred — was dated July 29, 1898, and decorated with hearts. In it he wrote, 'I thought about you all yesterday & built castles in the air about you & I living together. . . .'[17] And Jennie was equally smitten. It was marvellous to be loved so completely.

It was a simple matter for Jennie to confide to her closest friends how pleased she would be if they invited George for country weekends when they invited her. They were delighted to oblige. Making their affair even more convenient was the transfer of George's Battalion of Scots Guards to London. Could Jennie have had a hand in that? It is entirely possible.

Jennie cancelled most of her social appointments so that she could give George as much of her time and attention as possible, and she entertained him at her home in a way that he had never been entertained before. His letters rhapsodized about the soft, exquisite kimonos she wore, instead of the conventional whaleboned gowns.

'Of course, the glamour won't last forever,' Jennie told a friend, 'but why not take what you can, and not make yourself or anyone else unhappy when the next stage arrives?' [18]

She wrote to her sons about George in the casual way she told them about everything. In return, Winston sent news of the front to George via Jennie. Winston and George probably had met, for they were of the same age, they had mutual friends, and their mothers had known each other well.

It is unlikely that Jennie was thinking seriously about George now – after all, he had been born the same year that she had married Lord Randolph Churchill. Her exact thoughts and feelings cannot be known, but she did something very revealing at this point. One of her closest friends and oldest admirers, George Nathaniel Curzon, had just been appointed Viceroy of India and was then assembling his staff. Jennie wrote to him recommending George.

Going to India at this stage of their romance could scarcely have been George's idea. It must have been Jennie's. Was this her way of ending their affair before the inevitable family bitterness began? Or was she thinking of her brief fling with 'Beauty' Ramsden – how it had ended on such a humiliating note? Perhaps this time she wanted to be in control of the romance; this time she wanted to decide how and when it should end.

Curzon's answer, however, was cool and unresponsive: '. . . You recommended young Cornwallis-West. He seemed a nice boy at Warwick but I don't suppose there is a chance of my having room for him, as I fancy I can only take one English officer here & I have 50 applications. . . .' [19] In addition to the practical difficulties of granting Jennie's request, Curzon may in fact have been jealous of this handsome young man who had achieved what he himself never could.

It was almost as if Curzon's refusal had lifted a veil of guilt from Jennie's conscience. She had tried to end the affair and had failed. Why shouldn't she now enjoy this intense, fervid romance as long as it lasted? Except for her relationship with Count Kinsky, she had seldom been as happy. As for George, it would be torture for him to be turned away now. Why shouldn't they enjoy their love for each other 'until the next stage arrives', as Jennie put it?

That September Jennie and George were guests of Olive Guthrie, sister of Jennie's brother-in-law John Leslie, at Duart Castle on the Isle of Mull. 'This is the most delightful place I've ever been in – too lovely,' Jennie wrote to Winston.[20]

Jennie's twelve-year-old nephew Shane Leslie was also there, and George took him fishing, 'with myself to carry his net and fly. When I netted a record trout for him, he gave me a gold piece.' [21] Indeed, George's passion for Jennie was almost equalled by his obsession with fishing and hunting. Every letter to her, no matter how romantic, also contained detailed accounts of the pheasants he had shot or the fish he had caught or the quality and range of his newest gun or fishing rod.

One day at Duart, George went out stalking deer on a nearby hill with two men. After they had been away eight hours, Jennie put on her walking shoes and set off toward the moors to meet them. '. . . I was elected to accompany Jennie in his pursuit,' Shane Leslie wrote. 'We missed our way and Jennie broke an ankle. We had to crawl back and I half-carried her home.' [22]

The ankle was not actually broken, but it was badly sprained. 'Fancy what a bore for me,' Jennie wrote to Jack, '– I have sprained my ankle and can hardly put my foot to the ground. I was four miles from home when I did it, and managed to hobble back – but today it is so swelled I have to send for a doctor.' [23]

The Prince of Wales consoled her: 'I hope your ankle is better, but you should be very careful. *Tout à vous.* A.E.' [24] But from two Leslie great-aunts Jennie received little sympathy. Jennie's great-niece gave the general verdict as: 'Chasing George – determined to get him – ruining the man's sport . . . serves her right.' [25]

II

Winston was now with Kitchener's 20,000-man force in the Sudan. Near Omdurman they awaited the charge of 60,000 fanatical Muslim Dervishes. With a religious fervour and fury that one would have imagined had disappeared after the Crusades, the Dervishes came like a tide, armed with spears and rifles and roaring their cheers for God, his Prophet, and his Holy Khalifa. Against them, Kitchener threw the Camel Corps and his full force of modern artillery. Then he ordered the 21st Lancers to charge. It was history's last great cavalry charge, and Winston was in it.

Immediately after the Battle of Omdurman, he sent a telegram to his mother, with the message: 'ALL RIGHT WINSTON',[1] and Caryl Ramsden sent another: 'BIG FIGHT. FINE SIGHT. WINSTON WELL.'[2]

Soon afterwards Winston described the battle to his mother:

> I fired 10 shots with my pistol – all necessary – and just got to the end of it as we cleared the crush. I never felt the slightest nervousness and felt as cool as I do now. I pulled up and reloaded within 30 yards of their mass, and then trotted after my troop who were then about 100 yards away. I am sorry to say I shot 5 men for certain and two doubtful. The pistol was the best thing in the world. . . . The Dervishes showed no fear of cavalry, and would not move unless you knocked them over with the horse. They tried to hamstring the horses, to cut the bridles – reins – slashed and stabbed in all directions and fired rifles at a few feet range. Nothing touched me. I destroyed those who molested me and so passed out [of the battle] without any disturbance of body or mind.[3]

He told of friends who had been killed or slashed, and continued: 'I speculated on the shoddiness of war. You cannot gild it. The raw comes through. . . . There are 7,000 bodies lying there. . . .'[4]

'. . . I thought about you a great deal my dearest Mamma – before the action,' he wrote later. '. . . I fear it must have been with a beating heart that you read the telegrams and looked down the casualty list.'

George Warrington Steevens, the brilliant special correspondent of the *Daily Mail*, who had observed the Battle of Omdurman and the twenty-four-year-old Winston Churchill, wrote an article entitled, 'The Youngest Man in Europe':

In years, he is a boy; in temperament, he is also a boy; but in intention, in deliberate plan, purpose, adaptation of means to ends, he is already a man. . . .

He is what he is by breeding. From his father, he derives the hereditary aptitude for affairs, the grand style of entering upon them. From his American strain, he adds to this a keenness, a shrewdness, a half-cynical, personal ambition, a natural aptitude for advertisement and, happily, a sense of humour . . . qualities which might make him, almost at will, a great popular leader, a great journalist, or the founder of a great advertising business. . . .

. . . He is ambitious and he is calculating; yet he is not cold. He has a queer, shrewd sense of introspection . . . he has not studied to make himself a demagogue. He was born a demagogue and happens to know it.

. . . He has the 20th century in his marrow. . . .

What will he become, who shall say? At the rate he goes, there will hardly be room for him in Parliament at 30, or in England at 40.[5]

At the moment, however, Jennie was not pleased by Winston's continued friction with Kitchener. The Sirdar was furious with Sir Evelyn Wood for sending Winston to the Sudan and had told people that Winston was 'only making a convenience' of the Army. Winston's opinion of Kitchener was no higher. 'He may be a general – but never a gentleman,' he commented to his mother.

Writing to Jack, Jennie remarked: 'Of course, he talks like that about the Sirdar, but only to me, I think – he wouldn't be so silly as to air his views in public. From the Sirdar's point of view, I daresay he is right – I had hoped W wd have made friends with him & that is the best way of clipping your enemy's claws. . . .'[6]

Winston would soon be returning to London, and the Prince of Wales invited him to come & see me and tell me all about the recent campaign & about your future plans.

I can well understand that it must be very difficult for you to make up your mind what to do, but I cannot help feeling that Parliamentary & literary life is what would suit you best as the monotony of military life in an Indian station can have no attraction for you – though fortunately some officers do put up with it or else we should have no army at all! [7]

Meanwhile, Jennie had arranged two political meetings at which Winston was to speak, one at Bradford and the other Birmingham. By the simple expedient of inviting the editor of the *Morning Post* to lunch with her, she also managed to have two letters published which Winston had written to him, airing some of his views about Egypt.

Jennie not only laboured on behalf of Winston's career but also kept busy entertaining the stream of friends he sent to visit her while they were in London. Jennie made them all welcome, and no doubt enchanted them. But there were times during that winter of 1898 when she questioned the value of her ability to enchant.

Her romance with George was an affair of grand passion, but she seemed uncertain, dispirited, fearful. How long does beauty last? How long would this love last? What could she finally expect from life?

As always, Jennie sought advice from her friends. One was George Curzon, who had recently married Mary Leiter, one of the wealthiest women in America. People who did not know Curzon well compared him to German baroque architecture, 'perhaps most admirable when viewed from a distance'.[8] But Jennie knew that one reason for his cold, stiff appearance was a brace he wore on his back, and she remembered him with fondness as the witty young man who had once borrowed a nightgown from her during an unexpected overnight stay at Blenheim Palace.

Curzon was about to leave for India and his post as Viceroy. At a farewell dinner given for him by the Duke and Duchess of Portland, Jennie was seated next to him and later described the conversation:

... We got on the subject, which, without my knowing it at the time, was fraught with great importance for me. In a despondent mood, I bemoaned the empty life I was leading at the moment. Lord Curzon tried to console me by saying that a woman alone was a godsend in society, and that I might look forward to a long vista of country-house parties, dinners and balls. Thinking over our conversation later, I found myself wondering if this indeed was all that the remainder of my life held for me. I determined to do something, and cogitating for some time over what it should be, decided finally to start a review.[9]

It was a spectacular idea, bold and to the point. Jennie needed to work at something to give her life direction. The fact that she then knew nothing about organizing and running a literary magazine did not deter her. She had an abiding interest in literature and a deep respect for writers. She knew many of the literary lions of the time and counted some of them among her intimates. Although she did not understand finance, she knew men who did; she had no knowledge of printing and other production matters, but she would find those who were experts. And while publishing was almost exclusively a man's world, Jennie moved easily among men.

But first she needed a clear concept.

'My ideas were of the vaguest, but they soon shaped themselves,' she wrote. 'I consulted my friend, Mrs Craigie . . . whose acquaintance I had made . . . at the Curzons.'[10]

In fact, Jennie had known Pearl Craigie for several years, but their relationship had remained somewhat formal. Until February 1899, Mrs Craigie's letters to Jennie always began with the salutation, 'My dear Lady Randolph Churchill'. Then this was changed to, 'My dear Jennie (since you insist!),' and several months later, it was 'Dearest Jennie'. Before the year was over Pearl Craigie became Jennie's closest friend.

At first glance, it seemed an odd association. Jennie was basically an extrovert; Pearl Craigie was usually reserved, distant, mysterious, full of 'still deeps and silent pools'.[11] She said of herself, 'I not only think twice before I speak or move – but twenty times. If I could only be natural once, I should feel rested, but this eternal restraint, this unending, "Shall I say this?" "Is it wise to say that?" "Is this wrong?" "Will this be misunderstood?" "Will this give a wrong impression?" tires me to death. . . . People scare me out of my wits. . . .'[12]

Yet, although Pearl Craigie was more than a dozen years younger than Jennie, the two women had a good deal in common. They were both Americans who had been brought to Europe as children, both loved music and were expert pianists, and both had had unhappy mar-

143

riages. Like Jennie, Pearl Craigie had married at nineteen; she was separated several years later and divorced in 1895. She had one child, John Churchill Craigie. (Could her admiration of Jennie have been responsible for her selecting that name?)

Beyond these similarities was Pearl Craigie's apparent adoration of Jennie. It was as if Jennie were the image of everything she herself wanted to be. She had written such things as,

There is no woman who does not love to be loved.
There is only one obligation in life, and that is courage. . . .
Life is not what we find it, but what we make it. . . .
People say, 'Gather the roses while you may.' I'd gather them fast enough if I could see them. But where are they? When you find them, they have to be bought and paid for.[13]

Pearl Craigie must have seen in Jennie a woman who had the courage to love, to gather her roses, and what was most essential to the task of making of her life what she wanted it to be — an unshakeable belief in herself. She also saw in Jennie the kind of striking beauty that made it easier to have those qualities. Pearl did not have that beauty. Gertrude Atherton described her as 'a short, dark woman who would have been plain but for a pair of remarkably fine eyes.'[14] But her large, attractive eyes often seemed sad, and her pale refined face with its tight narrow lips was softened only by a dimple in each cheek.

Her father, John Morgan Richards, a distant cousin of the Jerome family, had made a fortune in the patent medicine business[15] and moved his family from Boston to London when Pearl was a child. A man of magnetic personality, he loved books and wrote one himself about England. Pearl's neurotic, eccentric mother was a witty woman and an ardent advocate of peace. When war between the United States and Spain was imminent, she sent a telegram: 'ITALY, POPE, VATICAN, ROME. STOP WAR. RICHARDS.'[16]

With her first book, Pearl decided on the *nom de plume* 'John Oliver Hobbes'. She chose John because it was the name of her father and her son, Oliver because of the warring Cromwell, and Hobbes because she liked the work by the philosopher of that name. Her first novel, *Some Emotions and a Moral*, was published when she was twenty-four and became an enormous success. It was essentially a satire on 'Smart Society', rich in epigram and with implications that required careful reading to be perceived.[17] 'You might as well flirt with the Ten Commandments as fall in love with your wife,' she wrote.

Pearl Craigie wore 'flowing Watteau gowns, lived in over-furnished rooms with stained glass lampshades' and spent much of her time in bed suffering from fatigue or vague illness. She was neither modest about her ability nor shy about her ambition, and perhaps, like Jennie, she envied the degree of freedom that men enjoyed. She most admired, she wrote, the fact that 'if a man really wants a thing, he will ask for it.' On the other hand, she felt that the clever woman had to go in for 'blimming'. 'Blimming,' she explained, 'is just talking and talking pleasant things, and saying nothing. This was a way to keep the world off. No one ever finds out that a blimming woman is cleverer than her husband. It's one of the great conservers of marital bliss.'[18]

Pearl herself was expert at 'blimming'. As Jennie said, 'a brilliant and clever conversationalist, she could hold her own with all manner of men, and yet in the more frivolous company, which she often frequented and thoroughly enjoyed, she never talked over people's heads. She had the art of drawing everyone out and making them appear at their best. So different to some clever woman writers I have met.'[19]

Pearl Craigie's admiration for Jennie appeared boundless and Jennie surely found it flattering. Pearl was a celebrity, having written books, magazine articles, and a highly successful play. Important people paid court to her, yet with her characteristic self-effacement, her early notes to Jennie were written as if she felt she were intruding on Jennie's time: 'Are you quite sure that there will be room for me this evening? . . . I should go in any case, solely for the pleasure of seeing you, and I would see you better when there were not a number of guests to claim your attention. . . .'[20] And another time: 'I hope you will find a little moment to spare for me. . . .'[21]

But Jennie also admired and appreciated Pearl. 'On looking back at the early period of the *Review*,' she wrote, 'I often wonder how I should have succeeded without Pearl Craigie's intelligent help and advice. A woman of great sympathies, her unselfishness has been realized by all who ever came in contact with her, and her valuable time was always at the disposal of anyone she could help.'[22]

In addition to the personal qualities which made it almost inevitable that these two talented women should gravitate towards each other, there was the basic fact that they were two of the very few women on the London literary scene. Indeed, they were among the few women who dared to make a life for themselves outside the home. Despite the growing freedom of the Naughty Nineties, it was still a man's world. The Woman Suffrage Bill, introduced by Faithful Begg in 1897 and supported by 257,796 signatures, received only two readings in the House of Commons before its defeat by seventy-one votes. An unmarried mother was permitted to earn a living only if she gave up her child. And the child's father could escape legal responsibility for it with a payment of twenty pounds, which brought immunity from inspection for the boarding house that received his child. Moreover, in 1899 the law (*Regina v. Clarence*) held that 'a husband could not be held guilty of committing rape on a wife who tried to refuse intercourse, even if he was suffering from a disease of which he was aware, though she was not.' [23]

As Francis Power Cobbe wrote, men treated women 'uniformly as minors'. A significant breakthrough had occurred in 1892 when seven government departments hired some 'type-writer girls'. But a woman who tried to qualify in a profession was often told, 'You surely don't imagine that men would ever put real confidence in one of your sex?' [24]

It was perfectly permissible for the Victorian woman to play the piano, sing, act on the stage, and write private poetry, but relatively few women had been able to make their mark on England's literary world – Jane Austen, early in the century, the Brontë sisters, Elizabeth Barrett Browning, George Eliot (Mary Ann Evans) and Pearl Craigie – and they were considered phenomena. A woman organizing a literary magazine, making critical judgments and business decisions, must have caused a thousand British clubmen to cringe and curse. The kind of quarterly Jennie was considering was in itself unique, but her temerity in wanting to create it, to be editor and publisher, was outrageous.

But Jennie had never been daunted by 'No' or hindered by 'Never'. Challenge was the zest of her life. Not that she was unaware of the countless problems involved in the project, nor of her ignorance and in-experience; she knew she would need all the help she could get.

Among the most important men Jennie met at one of Pearl Craigie's many dinners was John Lane. A former railway clerk, Lane had become one of the most successful publishers in Great Britain. His 'Bodley Head' published a surprising amount of successful poetry and 'daring novels', as well as high-level literary criticism by some of the youngest and most talented authors in England, which created new literary fashions and taste.

Lane's next move was to establish a literary quarterly. Probably more than in any other country, quarterlies have ebbed and flowed through the literary history of England. But in 1898 there was not yet a magazine that had successfully struck the modern note of the nineties.

Yellow seemed to be the colour of the nineties. One of the most popular novels was *The Yellow Aster* and one of the most popular books of poetry was called *Le Cahier Jaune* (The Yellow Notebook). Cashing in on this trend, John Lane gave his literary quarterly the title, *The Yellow Book*. 'Its flaming cover of yellow, out of which the Aubrey Beardsley woman smirked at the public for the first time' made a powerful impact. Nothing like it had ever been seen before. 'It was novelty naked and unashamed. People were puzzled and shocked and delighted.' [25]

Aubrey Beardsley was a delicate, effeminate young man of great talent and enormous nervous energy. Oscar Wilde described him as having 'a face like a silver hatchet, with grass-green hair'. Lane had a nerve-wracking time with Beardsley's persistent attempts to slip some indecency into his cover drawing, and he had to spend considerable effort examining the covers, even submitting them to his friends for further checking before publication. Even so, one issue went to press before a particularly 'audacious impropriety' was discovered, and Lane had to cancel the issue. Beardsley, like Wilde, was a doomed figure. He would die of tuberculosis at the age of twenty-five, a devout Catholic, begging his friends to destroy his 'obscene drawings'.

Lane was in New York at the time of the Wilde scandal. A headline in one of the Sunday papers read: 'ARREST OF OSCAR WILDE, YELLOW BOOK UNDER HIS ARM.' 'It killed The Yellow Book, and nearly killed me,' Lane said.[26] Crowds threw stones at his windows, and six of Bodley Head's authors threatened not to let Lane publish any more of their books unless he suppressed Beardsley's work and eliminated Wilde from the catalogue. Lane surrendered: Beardsley left.[27]

Courage was not one of John Lane's prominent characteristics. A trend-setting magazine such as *The Yellow Book* needed audacity, but Lane brought to it an air of compromise. 'Publisher John Lane had no objection against thin ice, provided he felt reasonably sure it would not let him through,' wrote a critic of his *Yellow Book*.[28] He began to substitute more and more of the 'safer', more established writers for the newer, bolder ones, and within two years *The Yellow Book* was dead.

The short, dandified Lane married a large, rich Bostonian, described as 'an ice-covered Brunnhilde'.[29] As an American, she soon found herself in Jennie's social circle and was an early supporter of Jennie's project. But it was not Jennie who had the the first formal business meeting with Lane about the review; it was her son.

This was an eventful occasion in the changing relationship between Jennie and Winston. Until then, Jennie had always been doing things for him, and as long as she lived, she would be his advance guard. But now, gradually, Jennie and Winston acted more and more like a sister and brother. He was, of course, not only helping her but also asserting his own manhood.

Jennie was away for a weekend at Welbeck, the Duke and Duchess of Portland's estate, when Winston wrote to her: 'Lane lunches with me tomorrow. I will write you the results of our interview which should cover the whole ground. I have written to Mr Cassel about the investment of the surplus loan I have raised.'[30]

Two days later Winston wrote again:

Mr John Lane called on me yesterday, and after lunch we had a long talk. We agreed on nothing, but I cannot help thinking you will find him vy satisfactory. This, or something like this, should be the scheme. You would have to guarantee, say, £1,000, the chance of loss on four numbers. £350 of this would be paid towards the first number. This will be your whole liability in the matter, and should the magazine show a balance profit, this would of course not be wanted, and you would not lose anything. Given the guaranteee – Lane will produce the magazine on an agreed scale – paying the writers, printing, publishing, advertising, etcetera – on a scale previously fixed.

In order to assist the production of the magazine he would do everything at cost price, and would take no profit until the enterprise was successful. Should it become successful you and he would divide profits. Lane thought these might amount to about £800 each. Harmsworth however said it would not be worth your while unless you had at least £2,000 out of it. I dissent. I think that even £800 for a beginning would enable you to live in the house – apart from the pleasure of influencing thought and opinion and becoming generally known as literary and artistic. I confess I do not think the ½ profit good enough. You had better get Moreton [Frewen] to go into the matter – or better still Harmsworth. I should much prefer a 25% on the total sales v.i.z. [sic], threepence in every shilling sold.

However, these are, after all, details. The three features of the schemes are:

1. A guaranteed amount.
2. A Fixed scale of Production.
3. A division of Profits.

In what proportion these are to be fixed is a matter for bargain and contract – in which you must be represented by a clever man.

I think Lane has a considerable clientele of his own. He certainly has lots of ideas, and is full of enthusiasm. One of his ideas struck me as good. He is the great authority on bindings. He suggested that the magazine should come out each quarter – bound like some famous old book. This alone would command a public interested in bindings. All this you must talk to him about. I will leave his address, and you should write to him at once – and arrange an early interview. He is a gentleman-like fellow, and would probably be willing to do a good deal.[31]

Jennie arranged her first business meeting with Lane on December 3, 1898. The formal note, still among Lane's papers, reads, 'Lady Randolph Churchill presents her compliments to Mr Lane, and in the absence of her son, who left for India last night – would like to know if it would be agreeable to him if she called between 11 and 12 0-c this morning.'

Lane probably thought that he would be able to control Jennie and also handle the administration and finances of the project. Jennie, in turn, probably thought Lane would do all the production, reporting to her on the details. Neither was correct.

By this time Jennie had decided exactly what kind of review she wanted. It was to be unique, an international literary magazine that really would be international and really would be literary. She would get the best talent on both sides of the Atlantic. Everything about the magazine would be of high quality – the content, the art, the binding and the paper. It would look like a book and be almost as expensive. No one had ever produced anything like it before. That was the kind of challenge Jennie relished.

12

The last year of the century brought a fresh beginning for Jennie. Of all the envious women who watched her from the sidelines, a great number gladly would have taken that one year of Jennie's to fill the whole of their own lives.

Winston especially shared her excitement about the review:

. . . you will have an occupation and an interest in life which will make up for all the silly social amusements you will cease to shine in as time goes on and which will give you in the latter part of your life as fine a position in the world of taste & thought as formerly & now in that of elegance & beauty. It is wide & philosophic. It may also be profitable. If you could make £1,000 a year out of it, I think that would be a little lift in the dark clouds.[1]

One of Jennie's acquaintances suggested that the review was merely a means of further enveloping her 'literary young man friend'.[2] But George Cornwallis-West was already thoroughly enveloped. Besides, at that time George was more interested in sports than in sonnets. It was gratifying for Jennie to have such an ardent lover always available, but the new and growing excitement of a review gave her a particular buoyancy.

The man she wanted to share this with was Bourke Cockran. Cockran was in London at the time, so the two met often. Bourke's maturity and wisdom were in strong contrast to George's callowness. Jennie could talk to him about financial matters, such as the idea of forming a syndicate of six major contributors to supply the funds for the first year of publication. She could talk to him about the magazine's content – her desire for 'lots of American talent to write for me. . . .' She could talk to Bourke about all her hopes and dreams of finding fulfilment, of doing something important with her life.

George was more romantic and impressionable, a young reed whom

Jennie could bend and turn at will; Bourke was a solid oak, a strong, mature man who had cultivated his individuality. 'You were a tower of strength to me,' Jennie wrote to him after he had left London, and then asked him to 'find me a really clever man for my "American Notes" – and oh! do find me a name for my magazine.'[3]

When George came into her life, Jennie had relegated Bourke to a different level but had things changed again? Jennie was a woman of so many facets that it seemed she needed a variety of men to suit them. George's passion suited one need; Bourke's mature understanding and sensitivity suited another.

However insoluble the differences between her and Bourke must have seemed – her subconscious need to drive and dominate, the irreconcilable question of leaving England and her sons – deep within her Jennie still must have felt that Bourke was more the man for her, 'Don't forget about me when you get home . . .' she had written to him.[4]

The magazine, which Jennie and her friends called 'Maggie', was now taking on its own life and making its own demands on Jennie's time. Finding a proper name for 'Maggie' was one of the niggling problems. Jennie had asked Bourke to think of a title and she was now asking everyone. One friend had seriously suggested *The Mentor of Mayfair*. Other titles proposed were even worse. 'It seemed as difficult to find an unappropriated title as though I were naming a racehorse, instead of a book,' Jennie wrote.[5]

'I beg you not to be in a hurry,' Winston had wisely written, 'a bad name will damn any magazine.' She should search for a title, he said, that would be 'exquisite, rich, stately . . . something classical and opulent. . . .'[6]

For an exquisite, opulent title, Jennie asked an exquisite, opulent man, one of her former lovers, Sir Edgar Vincent. He suggested *Anglo-Saxon*, and Jennie was enchanted. 'How simple! It sounded strong, sensible and solid.' She soon learned, however, that someone else had already registered the same title, and Pearl Craigie, who had obtained this information at a party, warned Jennie that the owner 'will wait, probably, till your circulars, advertisements [are out] . . . & then apply for an injunction, claiming damages and compensation. . . .'[7] Jennie had a simple solution: she merely added the word 'Review' and she had her title – *Anglo-Saxon Review*.

But that was an easy problem compared to the search for a basic concept and style. Jennie sought out all those whose talents she most admired and asked them what *they* thought, what *they* wanted. She kept her questions sharp, her mind receptive, and tried to let her own imagination and ideas act as a filter for everything she heard. 'Sometimes I became a little bewildered at the conflicting advice and suggestions I received.'

'Why don't you have three articles and three languages?' said one. 'That would damn it at once,' said another. 'Mind you, have something startling in the first number – "new ideas on free love" or "sidelights on Royal courts".' 'Be lofty in your ambitions; set up a poetical standard to the literary world.' 'Why not get a poem from the Poet Laureate?' 'Or an essay on Bi-Metallism from Mr Henry Chaplin?' 'Aim at a glorified *Yellow Book* – that's the thing!' How amusing it all was![8]

One of the less elegant suggestions was to emphasize the bond between England and the United States with a motto for the magazine: 'Blood is thicker than water.' Jennie told this to Winston and he exploded, saying that it should be 'relegated to the pothouse Music Hall', that it 'only needs the Union Jack & The Star-Spangled Banner to be suited to one of Harmsworth's cheap Imperialist productions. . . . People don't pay a guinea for such stuff . . . I confess I shivered when I read your letter.'[9] Jennie eliminated the motto. She wanted, after all, an elegant magazine that might be read with interest and pleasure by educated people anywhere, a luxurious-looking magazine with writings of significance and artistry.

At a guinea a copy, furthermore, it was enormously expensive. It greatly restricted her and made financial matters very delicate. Winston pleaded with her, therefore, to delay a final commitment until his return home as he felt he could more easily deal with John Lane than she could. He suggested that all agreements with Lane should be made on an annual basis only. He also wanted to make his own investment in the magazine, but he said, 'I do not like Lane's 12½ per cent of the gross profits. It is enormous!'[10]

Jennie agreed and wrote to Lane, 'I should like to know, and to have explained to me, how you are entitled to so large a percentage – Of course, I only want what is fair between us. . . .'[11]

She soon made it plain to Lane that she was in charge, that he worked for her. Lane had printed a subscription form on which payment was to be made to his own bank. Jennie rejected that idea immediately. 'I shall expect the order to be payable to my bank,' she said curtly.[12]

Jennie had adopted Lane's idea of a quarterly, each issue bound, as Winston put it, 'like some famous old book', and she prevailed upon Cyril Davenport of the British Museum to help her choose the most beautiful bindings from earlier periods. Then she wrote to Lane saying that she hoped he was '*quite* satisfied' with the bindings, but she had already selected and decided on them.

To supervise other historical matters she went to Arthur Strong, librarian of the House of Lords, 'and he will do all I want'.[13] She also used Strong's support to get Lionel Cust of the National Portrait Gallery to be responsible for the illustrations.

But Jennie was beginning to have doubts about herself. What were her literary qualifications? She was well-educated for a woman of her time and her experience was broad and varied, but she was neither as educated nor as experienced as the men she was dealing with. She was essentially a dilettante. Her taste was excellent, but her judgments were instinctive. She knew nothing of being a professional editor. Cecil Rhodes tried to encourage her: 'After all, women, remember, have great imagination and much more delicate instinct than my sex, who are rough and brutal. I think you should have a fair chance.' [14]

In her pessimism, however, Jennie must have written an unhappy letter to Pearl Craigie, who replied: 'What do you mean by calling yourself uncultured, un-literary & old? You must be "going crazy" – to use our country's cheerful idiom. You are perfectly charming & your judgment in artistic matters is distinguished. These things you know in your heart, already, so I cannot be accused of flattering you.' [15]

Winston agreed that she needed expert editorial assistance and volunteered his services. 'I know I can help you in ways scarcely anyone else *can* and nobody else will.' [16] He also saw in that prospect an opportunity of earning £200 a year – 'a very sensible addition to the advantages we derive from the venture.' [17] However, Winston had to admit that he was probably no better qualified and no more experienced than Jennie, and that, in the initial stages, it was better to have an experienced man.

'I am quite prepared to do it alone,' Jennie had told Lane, but she didn't really believe it.[18] Her great need, she thought, was for someone on whom she could rely to read manuscripts and to advise her on the selection of ideas for articles.

She found the ideal candidate one evening at a dinner party at Pearl Craigie's. He was Sidney Low, a slightly balding man with a very thick moustache and penetrating eyes.

The brilliant Sidney James Mark Low, three years younger than Jennie, had been the editor of the *St. James's Gazette* (1888–97) and then the Literary Editor of the *Morning Standard*. The author of the *Dictionary of English History*, he was later co-author of *The Political History of England*. Even more significant for Jennie, Low had the reputation of having a keen eye for vital young talent. He was credited with having discovered a number of young writers, including Rudyard Kipling and James Barrie.[19]

John Lane and Sidney Low were vastly different men. Lane was a sharp businessman, whereas Low said his principal concern was with 'spinning words'.[20] Lane was a collector of things – books, pictures, furniture, old glass; Low was attracted to talented people – especially women – and the more celebrated they were, the more they fascinated him. For a literary man and serious scholar, Low had an unusual fondness for the social swirl. Few men more greatly appreciated the society of a beautiful, witty, and accomplished woman of the world. Jennie asked him to escort her to a succession of parties, which Low described in his diary. Of one, he wrote:

Dined with Lady Randolph Churchill. Present: the Prince of Wales, Duke and Duchess of Devonshire, Cecil Rhodes, Countess of Warwick, Lady Gerard, Miss Plowden, Lord Hardwick, Sir Henry Burdett, Winston Churchill and his brother, and Mr Ernest Cassel. Sat between Winston C. and the Duchess of Devonshire. Talked with Rhodes on South Africa. The Prince of Wales talked to me after dinner. Deplored imperfect knowledge of foreign languages by Englishmen. Spoke of the Dreyfus case and its scandals, and the state of France. Said he did not think there was any chance of an Orleanist restoration, and the Bonapartists were too lazy and unenterprising to do anything. Told me he had once met [the French General, Georges] Boulanger and thought him a poor creature. He also spoke of our hostess' venture, the *Anglo-Saxon Review*.[21]

As Low's biographer remarked, Jennie was 'irresistible': she had 'not only traditions of culture, but very great energy, and these allied to beauty, brilliance and wit. . . .' Jennie had completely captivated Low. 'She solicited his help, advice and contributions in support of her new *Review*, and freely he gave all these.'[22]

Low personified a great deal of the literary substance of the *Review*, but Jennie was its soaring spirit. John Lane's file soon bulged with memoranda from her:

After I have seen Mr Wightman's article, I shall better be able to judge, whether we can have it signed or not. I am glad you find him all I had heard of him. . . . I shall write to W. D. Howells, – a story from him for September wd do well. We have enough fiction for the first no. I shall read with interest E[dith] Wharton's book. I hope you will like Robins' article on Lady M.M. I am glad that it is long, as we have so many pages to fill up. I have just returned from Paris, where I did considerable work, and have got a good many subscribers and some good contributors. I have come to the conclusion with Mr Low, Mrs Craigie and a few others that there is no harm in having one French contributor in each no.: even the first, [Paul] Bourget will write for the first, and he is as well-known here as in America and France. I must consider my foreign subscribers – besides, 250 pages takes a great deal of filling, and it will not be easy to find good contributors. . . . I will let you know about Prof. Waldstein – as it is for Sept., it can wait. Meanwhile, I have not heard one word from Prof. Thornton – and am trying to get an article on 'Wireless Telegraphy' from Prof. Lodge, which will do well. . . . I am glad to hear of the interest the *Review* is awakening in the States – I have orders and cheques sent to me from there. . . .[23]

I write a line to catch the post, to tell you that the first no. is now nearly completed, and I think it is very good – the J.F. cover is the greatest success. I saw Mr Leighton this morning, and he, too, is very pleased with it. I shall see Mr Davenport tomorrow. . . . The contributors are slow in sending in their stories, and it takes some reminding to get them![24]

Jennie was meticulous about detail, and a contemporary recalled the vision of her 'on some of the numerous occasions when she called, maybe a bunch of proofs in her hand, to discuss . . . the format of the

Anglo-Saxon Review. . . .'[25] She was also highly critical of imperfection, and Lane bore the brunt of her anger.

I am horrified in my old complete copy – the same mistake as to the word 'received'. . . . I thought you had settled it. . . .[26]

I return to you the list and proposed proofs. You will see the centre is missing from 16 to 40. . . .[27]

I am not going to be made ridiculous by publishing stuff which makes no sense. . . .[28]

As work on the *Review* progressed, Jennie became increasingly critical of Lane. She was unhappy that he had made both their names in the masthead 'a trifle large'. Further, she had not received the prospectuses or the dummies she had asked for. And again: 'I do not think you ought to get commissions on the subscriptions I get. . . .'[29] Worst of all, she was annoyed about his projected trip to America in May – with the first issue scheduled for publication on June 15. 'It is unfortunate that he absents himself at such a moment. . . .'[30]

Her memoranda to Lane came in a steady stream:

. . . I hope to send you next week articles by Mr Whitelaw Reid [publisher of the New York *Tribune*], Lord Rosebery [former Prime Minister], two from Mr Strong, Mr Henry James, Prof. Thompson and Prof. Lodge. I have heard from Mr Low this morning. He seems to think that unless you have all the copy by the first of May, the *Review* cannot appear this season. This need not be so, particularly as it need not be published until the end of June.[31]

I am expecting other MS in a few days. The photogravures are in hand. Mr Strong has been ill, and is at Versailles, but returns the 17th. . . . I have seen Mr Cust about various matters, and Mr Davenport. The latter has chosen two other bindings; therefore, with the 17th-Century French one we have, and the James I one we are having made, our year will be covered.[32]

. . . I will do what I can with regard to Mr Bryce and the stories you mention, but they are not wanted for the first no. . . . I am going to ask Lord Hugh Cecil to write something on the church; he is very clever and bold. Mrs Craigie has sent me a drama in two acts, 'Osbern and Ursyne', which I think is beautiful. It has not been published – and will not be for months, and will not be acted until July. . . .[33]

. . . I have written to Mr Leighton to add the word 'Review' to the designs for the back, and hope that he will be able to send me a rough sketch tomorrow. Then we can go ahead.[34]

. . . It will be necessary to have seven illustrations in the first no. . . . I shall consider the frontispiece, 'The Queen', as an extra for the first no. I have written to Miss Wharton, and shall hope to see her. . . .[35]

Jennie kept her own list of the pieces for the first issue, with the author's name, the length, and the price paid for each. The price paid ranged from £10 to Charles Davenport for three bindings, to £50 for the Political Summary. Mrs Craigie received £40 for her play, which ran to thirty-three pages; Prof. Oliver Lodge £25 for his article on Wireless Telegraphy; Algernon Swinburne was paid £15 for a poem; Henry James £40 for his twenty-five-page story. There was no price listed for Lord Rosebery's article of twenty-three pages on Sir Robert Peel, which may have been given to Jennie as a gesture of friendship. There were also five letters from the Duke of Devonshire, for which he was paid £25. Cecil Rhodes was to have been paid £5 for an article which was apparently not received. And C. Robbins was paid £31 and 10 shillings for a twenty-eight-page article called 'A Modern Woman'.

Heightening the frenzy of the beginnings of 'Maggie' was the fact that Lane was away for more than a month; Low was sick, and so was Strong for part of the time. The full responsibility was on Jennie, but she had a decisive, organized mind and tremendous energy.

Through it all, she managed to maintain both a busy social schedule and a heady romance; she even found time to perform at concerts. 'I must tell you that you were an angel,' Pearl Craigie told her, 'you played beautifully and I was immensely proud of you.'[36] Jennie also persuaded Pearl to play with her[37] and Mademoiselle Maria Janotha at another concert at Queen's Hall. They played Bach's *Concerto in D Minor for three Pianos*, with an orchestra from the Royal College of Music conducted by Sir Walter Parrott. Janotha, who had been Court pianist to the German Emperor, was a great favourite of Queen Victoria. Before any performance at Court, she knelt at the Queen's feet and presented her with some white heather. She also kept a mascot on the piano while she played, to repel the evil eye.[38] On this occasion it apparently worked, for their concert was a tremendous success and they received a rousing ovation. 'This was the only time I ever remember enjoying playing in public,' Jennie wrote.[39]

Pearl Craigie began to make herself more and more indispensable to Jennie, both personally and professionally. She not only suggested stories and contributors ('How about Anatole France?'), found her a secretary ('She is clever, industrious . . . can mind her business and be depended on . . . not at all on the Woman Journalist lines . . .'), but she was also watchful of Jennie's health and morale ('Do be careful & remember that you are precious. . . . You are looking lovely . . .').[40]

It was extraordinary how rapidly their relationship had taken on new dimensions. At first Pearl had leaned heavily on Jennie; now the need was more mutual. They were regularly seeing one another, writing notes, exchanging ideas.

Despite her involvement with the *Review*, Jennie gave a lot of time and thought to Pearl's play, which was then being prepared for production.[41] During a country weekend she wrote her a long letter explaining why she thought a certain actor would be ideal for the lead. Jennie's love of the theatre was another bond between her and Pearl.

A major element in their friendship was the fact that, unlike almost everyone else, Pearl Craigie asked little of Jennie. She seemed to get great satisfaction from just being her friend, a part of her work and her life. As for Jennie, she could ask almost anything of Pearl, and Pearl was quick to oblige. When Jennie asked her to play with her in the concert, she hesitated only because she had not performed for a long time. But she put herself to the task, taking a dozen lessons from one of the best teachers in London, Signor Bisaccia, who commented that 'She plays with her brain.'

Pearl Craigie seemed to depend upon her brain in all aspects of her life, usually keeping her emotions strictly contained. After her divorce she revealed herself to few people other than Jennie. Jennie understood Pearl's problems, her longings, her unhappiness, and her great gifts. She accepted her effusive attachment and returned to her some peace and love.

But as the pressures increased, Jennie had less time for her personal life. 'Maggie' was not yet in print, but it had already become an irresistible target for cartoonists, satirists, columnists, rumour-mongers and society wags. Some of their comments were genuinely funny, and Jennie laughed along with them, as was the case with this poem, which Jennie enjoyed reciting for her friends:

Have you heard of the wonderful Magazine
Lady Randolph's to edit, with help from the Queen?
It's a guinea a number, too little by half,
For the Crowned Heads of Europe are all on the staff;
And everyone writing verse, fiction, or views –
The best blue-blood ink must exclusively use;
While (paper so little distinction achieves)
'Twill wholly be printed on strawberry leaves;
And lest the effusions, so dazzlingly bright
And brilliantly witty, should injure the sight,
A pair of smoked glasses (of ducal design)
Will go with each copy to shelter the eyne.
The articles promised already, or written,
Suggest what a treat is preparing for Britain.
The Princess of ———— will describe a new bonnet;
The Spanish Queen Mother has offered a sonnet,
Provided that all whom its scansion may beat
Will refrain from indelicate mention of feet;
And the Duchess of ———— has accepted the section
Devoted to 'Babies, their Tricks and Correction.'
The Czar will contribute a fable for geese,
'On Breaking up China and Keeping the Peace';
The Porte sends a batch of seraglio tales,
And our Prince will review 'Mr Bullen on Whales'.
Mr Primrose, who also has thoughts of the sea,
Addresses the captains of every degree.
A treatise profound, yet delectable, too,
On 'How to be a Father-in-Law to a Crew(e)';
While William of Potsdam, the ablest of men,
Will fill every gap with one stroke of his pen,
And, lest art be slighted 'midst hurry and rush,
Will illustrate all with one flirt of his brush.

Such, such is the hint of the new Magazine
Lady Randolph will edit, with help from the Queen.[42]

The London correspondent of a New York magazine offered some kindly opinions: 'Lady Randy is sure to have a clever magazine, for she is so clever, brilliant, keen of wit. She is highly educated, observing, and has as varied a knowledge of the world and society as it is possible for a woman to have. . . . Lady Randy's acquaintance is limited only by the confines of the earth. . . .' The same correspondent later reported seeing 'Black Jennie' almost every evening in the House of Commons, lobbying for articles and subscriptions. 'Poor Arthur Balfour, who is intensely lazy, has promised to write an article for the first number, but according to my latest intelligence, he has not come up in time. Viscount Peel [son of Sir Robert], the ex-Speaker, has promised to write an article on the licensing question, and Emperor William was to write on yachting. . . . H.R.H. [the Prince of Wales] has even been induced to put his pen to paper for the fascinating Jennie. . . .' And he pointed out that Whitelaw Reid, publisher of the New York *Tribune* and a former Ambassador to France, had written a revealing article not for his *Tribune* but for the *Anglo-Saxon Review*.[43]

'I think Lady Randolph made a great mistake in not calling her publication, *The Transatlantic*,' the American correspondent continued. That title, he said, had been awarded the prize at a dinner at Arthur Balfour's house where the question was supposed to have been decided. '*Anglo-Saxon*, as I have said before, will not succeed in this country.'[44]

This was an ominous note from a friendly commentator, and some of the other comments were more discouraging – sufficiently so that Pearl Craigie felt it necessary to try to boost Jennie's morale:

As for criticism, if one gives work to the general public, one has to accept the fate of an Aunt Sally, so far as the journalists are in question. They detest every educated influence. . . . They fear the brightening of the average intelligence – for in the imbecility of the mob (well-dressed and otherwise) is the hack journalist's strength. But the times are changing rapidly. The mob – as a mob – is becoming well-read, even philosophical, the Press in England has less power, and the country more power every day.[45]

Meanwhile, Winston had returned home, having resigned his commission in the Army. 'I can live cheaper and earn more than a writer,' he explained.[46] Jennie put him to work on the *Review*, and the two of them worked on the Preface for the initial issue – their first literary collaboration.[47] (The quotation from Samuel Johnson in the second paragraph was a favourite of Winston's; he had used it twice in letters to his mother.)

The explanation of the production of another Review will be found in the number of those already in flourishing existence: the excuse must be looked for in these pages. Yet a few words of introduction are needed by this newcomer, who comes into the crowded world thus late in the day, lest, in spite of his fine coat, he be thought an unmannerly intruder. I desire to say something of his purpose, of his aspirations, of his nature, in the hope that, if these seem admirable, good friends, instead of jostling, will help him through the press, and aid him somewhat in his journey towards the golden temple of literary excellence.

The first object of every publication is commercial. 'No one but a blockhead,' says Dr Johnson, 'ever wrote except for money'; and the *Anglo-Saxon* is not disposed to think lightly of his wares, or set low value on his effort, for otherwise his green-and-gold brocade would soon be threadbare. But after the vulgar necessities of life are thus provided for, reviews, and sometimes reviewers, look to other and perhaps higher ideals. It is of those that I would write, for are they not the credentials which must carry the ambitious stranger on his way?

Formerly, little was written, but much of that little was preserved. The pamphlets, the satires, the lampoons, the disquisitions – above all, the private letters – of the 18th Century, have been carefully stored for the delight of succeeding generations. Now, the daily production of printed words is incalculably vast. Miles of newspapers, tons of magazine articles, mountains of periodicals, are distributed daily between sunrise and sunset. They are printed; they are read; they are forgotten. Little remains. And yet there is no reason why the best products of an age of universal education should not be as worthy of preservation as those of a less-cultivated era. The literary excellence of the modern review is high. How many articles, full of solid thought and acute criticism, of wit and learning, are born for a purely ephemeral existence, to be read one day and cast into the wastepaper basket the next? The most miserable lampoons of the reign of Queen Anne are still extant. Some of the finest and cleverest productions of the reign of Queen Victoria are almost as difficult to find as ancient manuscripts. The newspapers of today light the fires of tomorrow. The magazine may have a little longer life. It rests on the writing-table for perhaps a month, and thereafter shares the fate of much that is good in an age that, at least in art and literature, takes little thought for the future. The sure knowledge that their work will perish must exert a demoralising effect on the writers of the present day. Newspapers and periodicals become cheaper and cheaper. To satisfy the loud demand of the enormous and growing reading public, with a minimum of effort, is the modern temptation.

I do not imagine that the *Anglo-Saxon Review* will arrest these tendencies. But its influence may have some useful effect. This book is published at a price which will ensure its respectful treatment at the hands of those who buy it. It will not be cast aside after a hurried perusal. It appears, too, in a guise which fits it for a better fate. After a brief, though not perchance unhonoured, stay on the writing-table, it may be taken up into that Valhalla of printed things – the library. More than this, that it may have company, another of similar character but different design, will follow at an interval of three months, until a long row of volumes – similar but not alike – may not only adorn the bookshelves, and recall the elegant bindings of former times, but may also preserve in a permanent form something of the transient brilliancy of the age.

It is with such hopes that I send the first volume out into the world – an adventurous pioneer. Yet he bears a name which may sustain him even in the hardest of struggles, and of which he will at all times endeavour to be worthy – a name under which just laws, high purpose, civilizing influence, and a fine language have been spread to the remotest regions.

Lastly, I would in this brief note express my sincere thanks to all those who have helped to fit the *Anglo-Saxon* for the battle of life – not only to those who have, as subscribers, furnished him with his costly habit, but also to those who, like the fairy godmother in the child's story, have given him something of their energy, their wisdom, and their brains.[48]

Jennie gave a luncheon to introduce the *Review*. Its fate was then up to the critics and the public. Lady Warwick called it 'a thing of splendour . . . its contents almost equalled its binding'.[49] *The Saturday Review*, however, said that it was a swindle to charge a guinea for a copy which was not in real leather and not tooled by hand. But to do that, Jennie said, it would have cost at least a hundred pounds to produce a copy. Another critic thought it 'The Yellow Book in court dress and bedroom slippers . . .' and the New York World commented: 'You can pay five dollars for this magazine. It may be good, but you can buy the World for a cent.' The Pall Mall Gazette provided the most careful and perceptive review:

Why should not an effort be made to preserve some, at least, of the best work of the day? Lady Randolph Churchill has set herself to answer that question, and she has done so in an eminently practical way. She has realized – and this is the distinctive feature of her venture – that there is no better method of insuring respectful treatment for any article offered for sale than to make the purchaser pay handsomely for it. Provided that good value be given for good money, there is, we most firmly believe, no surer way to commercial success. And certainly the Anglo-Saxon Review bids fair to perform that condition alike in the material form and the literary substance of its production. Let us proceed 'from without inwards', as the anatomists say, and begin with what is the special feature of the Review – the binding, paper, and print.

To say that the cover alone is worth the money – considering that the money is a whole golden guinea – would, no doubt, be an exaggeration. But it is clear that no one who loves books well enough to pay that price will likely throw away a volume bound in green calf, richly-tooled in gold, according to a design which is a facsimile of a binding executed for King James I. That sapient monarch, 'the most learned fool in Christendom', as Sully called him, was a considerable connoisseur in book-binding, as Mr Cyril Davenport shows in a scholarly note on the binding of this volume. . . . And this beautiful binding encloses paper and print which are a joy to the senses of touch and sight. Selecting her contributors, Lady Randolph Churchill, as might be expected from the title of the Review, has gone to American as well as to English sources. The United States is represented by Mr Whitelaw Reid, Mr Henry James, and Miss Elizabeth Robins. The most interesting contributions, however, and those which may give that abiding interest to the number which the editor desiderates, are those of Lord Rosebery and Mr Algernon Swinburne. Lord Rosebery's appreciation of the life and character of Sir Robert Peel not only helps to throw new light on the personality of that statesman, but also affords the ex-Premier the opportunity of expressing his own views on the functions and the position of an English Prime Minister. They are well worth consideration. Mr Swinburne's lines on the Centenary of the Battle of the Nile have an intense earnestness of patriotism, albeit something lacking in the lyric 'surge and thunder' one is accustomed to expect from the poet. Dr Sir Rudolph Slatin writes of the Soudan with his unique experience, and the Duchess of Devonshire contributes some amusing unpublished letters of the beautiful Duchess Georgiana. A word of praise is due, likewise, to the seven charming photogravures with which the Review is illustrated. In short, there is nothing but good to be said of this unprecedented venture in periodical literature.[50]

'Maggie' was launched. 'I am perfectly delighted and congratulate you with all my heart,' wrote Pearl Craigie.[51] To Lane, Jennie wrote: 'The book had a great success, and so it ought!'[52]

The dilettante had become a professional. She had created something unique. Although she had received a great deal of advice and technical help, it would not have been born without her. The *Anglo-Saxon Review* was a publication of quality and substance. It had imagination and style. What its fate would be was another question, but the overwhelming fact of its birth could be credited only to Jennie.

There was little time for Jennie to revel in success. The second volume was waiting.

13

Both Jennie's sons were in London in the summer of 1899. Jack was with a firm of brokers in the City and doing well; and Winston, pursuing 'the larger ends of life', had finished his new book, *The River War*, and was looking out for a political opportunity.

The opportunity came unexpectedly. He had been invited to speak at a public meeting of the Oldham Conservatives, and two days before the meeting, Oldham's senior Member of Parliament died. Winston was asked to stand as Conservative Party candidate.

'Everything is going capitally –' he told his mother.

> Owing to the appearance of a Tory Labour Candidate it is quite possible we shall win. There is no meeting Monday but on Tuesday night I make my big opening address. I would like you to come down for that. There is no hotel but this house is very comfortable, and Wittaker [Chairman of the local Conservative Association and former Mayor of Oldham] is a very nice fellow. He will be delighted to put you up. Come if you can, by the 12 o'clock train (look it up). You can return early the next morning. There is practically no local society – only multitudes of workers.
>
> My speech last night at the club produced great enthusiasm and there is no doubt that if anyone can win this seat I can. . . . Find out if Pamela would like to come down – and wire me. Send me a box of good cigarettes – Jack knows the sort – and let me have all my letters to this address. Write every day. . . . Good luck to the Magazine.[1]

The next day Winston wrote again telling his mother that the women of the local Primrose League wanted her to attend a reception they were to hold at the Conservative Club. Then, after discussing the time of her arrival, he went on to say: 'If you bring *Pamela* with you there will not be room for your maid nor for hers so that if you cannot conveniently do without your maid for one night it would be necessary to tell *Pamela* that there is no accommodation *and put her off.*' [2]

Apparently his romance was not going smoothly. Winston had had little experience with young women. He could make interesting conversation and write endearing letters, but Pamela had often protested that he was not demonstrative enough. She was more experienced than he and knew how much attention she was entitled to expect from a young man who presumably loved and wanted to marry her. However, the pattern of love and marriage pre-eminent in Winston's mind was undoubtedly that of his parents. By the time he understood anything of their relationship, the romance was dead and his father was distant and harsh with him. Winston therefore came into his first courtship awkward and unsure. Although he had invited Pamela to attend this meeting, which he fully expected would be significant to his career, he was obviously relieved when she declined. 'I quite understand your not coming,' he wrote, 'it would perhaps have been a mistake. . . .' [3]

Jennie knew Oldham well. She had campaigned there for her husband and still had friends in the borough. And now she moved with more than her usual zest. She had long been urging Winston to leave the Army and enter politics, and since he had at last done it, it was up to her to help in any way she could, despite any other work she had to do. But it was fun for her, too, and after the frenzy of starting 'Maggie' this was a refreshing change of pace. It brought back pleasant memories of the days when she had conducted Randolph's campaigns.

Winston, of course, realized the political importance of his mother's presence in Oldham. The Oldham *Daily Standard* on Tuesday, June 27, 1899, announced:

TONIGHT'S MEETING
LADY RANDOLPH CHURCHILL
EXPECTED

Oldham Conservatives will learn with the greatest satisfaction that Lady Randolph Churchill will attend tonight's meeting at the Theatre Royal, at which her son, Mr Winston Churchill, and Mr James Mawdsley will deliver their first public speeches in support of their joint candidature. Lady Churchill, talented mother of a talented son, is naturally deeply interested in this election, and she may be certain that not only for her late husband's and her son's sake, but for her own, she will receive a most cordial welcome to Oldham. There are thousands of true hearts in this constituency, which have a warm corner for Lady Randolph Churchill.

The next day, the same newspaper reported on the meeting and noted:

Lady Randolph Churchill had a most enthusiastic reception, as she accompanied Alderman Wittaker on the platform. Her charming and graceful presence gave an added interest to the proceedings. She listened intently to the speeches, and seemed especially pleased and amused with Mr Bottomley's vigorous and humorous address.

Jennie went with Winston everywhere: the mass meetings at the big halls, the open-air meetings, the small gatherings at individual homes. She bowed, she smiled, she made brief speeches. She was proud and she showed it. One newspaper reported that 'Lady Randolph Churchill had a most enthusiastic reception at the Co-operative Hall meeting, and repeatedly during the evening had she to gracefully bow her acknowledgments to the hearty cheering.'

On the same day the *Standard* reported:

A gathering of the lady members of the Oldham Habitation of the Primrose League took place on Tuesday evening at the Central Conservative Club, Union Street, when about 200 Dames attended. Alderman Woddington introduced Lady Churchill to the meeting, and she was most cordially greeted by the assembly. Her Ladyship addressed a few words to the gathering, and stated she had no idea there would be so large and representative an audience in attendance. She was delighted in the interest that was shown in the cause which they had all so much at heart, and she hoped they would do everything in their power to further it by returning the two Conservative candidates at the head of the poll. (Applause.) Lady Churchill then retired, and subsequently accompanied her son to an open-air meeting at Glodwick.

Before his mother's arrival in Oldham, however, Winston, who had always consulted her about his political strategy, went out on a limb of his own choosing. He announced that he would not support the Government position on the Clerical Tithes Bill, a controversial measure intended to benefit the clergy of the Church of England and the Church schools. This put him in opposition to his own Party on an important issue. Then, as now, a Member of Parliament – and especially a candidate – was expected to show firm party loyalty. As Sir Ivor Jennings has written,[4] members of a British political party 'realize that their chance of office depends upon maintaining the unity of the party. . . . The unity of the party implies . . . the loyalty of party members to their leaders. . . . "Our men" must rally round their leaders because party divisions tend to "let the other fellows in".'

Labour candidates, therefore, proceeded to taunt the Conservative government that their own candidate had repudiated them. The *Manchester Evening News* was moved to say of Winston that 'as a politician, he hardly is out of his swaddling clothes.'

This was something Jennie could not undo, but she put up a brave front on polling day in Oldham: '. . . dressed entirely in blue . . . [she] arrived in a landau and pair with gaily-ribboned and rosetted postillions. . . .' She was with Winston when he received the news of his defeat. 'Lady Randolph Churchill, who had listened to the results with a tinge of regret, bore herself proudly as she retired from the room with her talented son', the Oldham *Daily Standard* reported.

Jennie wasted no time in writing to all her friends in politics, emphasizing that Winston had lost by fewer than 1,500 votes against a very popular opponent and that his defeat was only a slight blemish, not a stain. She appealed for their declarations of support in the future.

Their replies were prompt:

Arthur Balfour: 'Never mind – it will all come right; and this small reverse will have no permanent ill effect on your political fortunes. . . .'[5]

H. H. Asquith: '. . . Winston's good fight at Oldham gives him his spurs, & perhaps (as you hint) there are more desirable constituencies to be found. . . .'[6]

The Prime Minister, Lord Salisbury: 'Winston made a splendid fight. . . .'[7]

Winston answered Salisbury: '. . . I take the opportunity of making my excuses for my ill success at Oldham and of thanking you for the

168

lenient allusion you made to the contest in a letter which you recently wrote to my mother. . . .'[8]

Winston was so exhilarated by the encouraging responses to his mother's letters that he asked her to plan '. . . my little political dinner on Thursday, only 6 or 7. They will all be in town on account of Parliament.'[9] He also sought further advice from another of his mother's close friends, Joseph Chamberlain, then Colonial Secretary.

He was most forthcoming, and at the same time, startlingly candid and direct. His conversation was a practical political education in itself. He knew every detail, every turn and twist of the game, and understood deeply the moving forces at work in both the great parties, of whose most aggressive aspirations he had in turn been the champion. . . . South Africa had begun again to be a growing topic. The negotiations with President Kruger about the delicate, deadly question of suzerainty were gradually engaging national, and indeed, world attention. The reader may be sure that I was keen that strong lines should be taken, and I remember Mr Chamberlain saying, 'It is no use blowing the trumpet for the charge, & then looking around to find nobody following.' Later, we passed an old man, seated upright in his chair on the lawn on the brink of the river. Lady Jeune said, 'Look, there is Labouchere'. 'A bundle of old rags!' was Mr Chamberlain's comment, as he turned his head away from his venomous political opponent. I was struck by the expression of disdain and dislike which passed swiftly but with intensity across his face. . . .[10]

Henry du Pre Labouchere, the Radical M.P., was not only a bitter opponent of Chamberlain's in Parliament, but as editor of *Truth* magazine he had persistently attacked Winston on the scandalous allegations of homosexuality and race-fixing. The damage such a man could do to a political career was already evident to Winston.

Whereas earlier Jennie had cautioned her son to avoid notoriety, it was now his turn to be concerned about her activities. Jennie had gone to Goodwood for the annual races and Winston wrote:

. . . I also beg you not to bet or play cards. You have so much to make life interesting that there is no excuse or sense or reason for taking refuge in the desperate forms of excitement which the brainless butterflies of the world long for. I feel a little worried about this because I know you played and gambled last year vy high at Goodwood: and it can if repeated only end in bringing the most terrible misery upon us all. Already we feel the sting sharply. Forgive my lecture. It is an appeal.[11]

Gambling was one of Jennie's vices. Her father had been one of the great gamblers of his day – the New York stock market, horse races, cards – and her husband had had a similar appetite. The Prince of Wales loved to gamble; indeed, most of the men she knew well were gamblers. She probably acquired the taste for it from them, but gambling was also compatible with her own personality. It offered excitement and challenge. And with her finances frequently ebbing towards disaster, gambling provided hope of a sudden recoupment. E. F. Benson remembered playing cards with Jennie. 'And after a hectic hour's hard work,' he wrote, 'she won exactly a shilling. She greedily seized it. "Is this all mine?" she asked. "Someone will now want to marry me for my money."'[12]

George was with Jennie that weekend at Goodwood, as he was with her almost every weekend. During the week he was stationed at a nearby camp, but wrote to her almost daily. They were most unusual love letters. He coupled his intense ardour for her with detailed discourses on the quality of his guns, the number of birds or animals he had shot, why there was too much wind for fishing on a particular day, and so forth. Had Jennie been less in love, all this would probably have been unbearably tedious.

Apparently George still tried to shroud their relationship with some degree of subterfuge. When at the end of one weekend Jennie went with him to the station, and someone saw them together, George later told his fellow officers that Jennie was his sister. 'They believed me,' he told her. 'Some day soon, I hope to be able to say wife instead of sister.'[13]

Their affair had already lasted a year and there seemed to be no abatement. George's parents, who had tried to ignore the situation, now decided to try another tactic. They were entertaining the Prince of Wales at Ruthin Castle one weekend, and they invited Jennie.

The weekend must have been a severe test for Jennie. The Cornwallis-Wests would have certainly been polite, but hardly warm. Other members of George's family must have stared and gossiped. The Prince of Wales would not have treated her cordially. Jennie's courage had survived colder receptions than this, but there could be little question that the situation was trying and unpleasant. There was general agreement, however, that Jennie and George looked 'smashing' together.

Jennie then returned the favour. She took George and Winston for a weekend at Blenheim Palace. This was still another turning point of social acceptance. Sunny, the young Duke of Marlborough, had always deeply admired his aunt Jennie, and Consuelo, his Duchess, considered Jennie one of her closest confidantes. Nevertheless, this visit would not have been possible except for the fact that Jennie's mother-in-law, the Dowager Duchess of Marlborough, had died the preceding month.

This rotund, dowdily-gowned Duchess who always travelled with cages of birds and Blenheim spaniels, this disagreeable, embittered woman had so idolized her son Randolph that no daughter-in-law could ever have been good enough. But Jennie had also had the disadvantages of being an American, of being stronger than the Duchess's son, and of being more beautiful and talented than her daughters. Yet despite the enmity between them, these two unusual women had had a grudging respect for each other.

Blenheim Palace with its giant trees and beautiful grounds was full of memories for Jennie. She had first come here as a nineteen-year-old bride, and the townspeople had unhitched the horses of the Churchill carriage so that they themselves might pull the young couple to the palace. How overwhelmed she had been: the ornamental lake, the miles and miles of magnificent park, the hundreds of rooms, the gold dinner plate, the unrelenting formality. And her handsome, brilliant husband Lord Randolph – what would he have thought of George?

Jennie saw Winston and George together at Blenheim: two young men of the same age, one her son, the other her lover. There was no question that Winston was the more brilliant, the more ambitious, the more energetic, but George was more attractive.

It does not seem unfair to suggest that Winston was jealous of George's relationship with his mother and that George was jealous of Winston's accomplishments. Their relationship was most proper, but there were subtle references in letters, occasional demeaning criticisms: 'I saw Winston today in St James Str,' George wrote to Jennie. 'Don't tell him I said so, but he looked just like a young dissenting parson, hat brushed the wrong way, and at the back of his head, awful old black coat and tie, he is a good fellow, but very untidy. . . .' [14] Winston, in turn, did not keep from his mother his strong reservations about the possibility of her marrying George.

Such a possibility however, was still distant in Jennie's mind. More immediate was the *Review*. Part of Jennie's job was extracting from authors the articles they had promised to write. Cecil Rhodes was difficult: 'I will come and see you, if you will let me, on my return in about three weeks. . . . I will try to write something for you on board ship, but do not announce it.' [15]

George Bernard Shaw was more punctual in producing an article called, 'A Word More about Verdi'. But when Jennie invited him to a luncheon, he responded by telegram: 'Certainly not! What have I done to provoke such an attack on my well-known habits?' [16]

Jennie replied in another telegram: 'Know nothing of your habits; hope they are not as bad as your manners.' [17]

Then she received the following letter from Shaw:

. . . Be reasonable. What can I do? If I refuse an invitation in conventional terms, I am understood as repudiating the acquaintance of my hostess. If I make the usual excuses, and convince her that I am desolated by some other engagement, she will ask me again. And when I have excused myself six times running, she will conclude that I personally dislike her. Of course, there is the alternative of accepting; but then I shall endure acute discomfort and starvation. I shall not have the pleasure of really meeting her and talking to her any more than if we happened to lunch at the Savoy on the same day by chance. I shall get no lunch, because I do not eat the unfortunate dead animals and things which she has to provide for other people. Of these other people, half will abuse the occasion to ask me to luncheons and dinners, and the other half, having already spread that net for me in vain, will be offended because I have done for you what I would not do for them. I shall have to dress myself very carefully and behave properly, both of which are contrary to my nature.

Therefore I am compelled to do the simple thing, and, when you say, 'Come to lunch with a lot of people,' reply flatly, 'Won't.' If you propose anything pleasant to me, I shall reply with equal flatness, 'I will.' But lunching with a lot of people – carnivorous people – is not pleasant. Besides, it cuts down my morning's work. I won't lunch with you; I won't dine with you; I won't call on you; I won't take the smallest part of your social routine. And I won't ever know you, except on the most special and privileged terms, to the utter exclusion of that 'lot of other people' whose appetites you offered me as an entertainment. Only if I can be of any real service at anytime, that is what I exist for; so you may command me.[18]

Jennie found it more and more enjoyable to be associated professionally with so many literary celebrities. She had met most of them before at parties, dinners, teas, and some of them she knew very well. There was, however, a monumental difference between knowing them as an admiring woman and as a demanding editor. The distinguishing factor was power. She had exerted social power before and political power, but this was her first experience with literary power, and she liked it very much indeed. Her feeling of power filled her memoranda to John Lane:

... I suppose you are *'en retraite'* enjoying your holiday. You have not let me know ... your opinion as to Mr Leighton's letter in reference to the bindings – I have decided not to have the better leather until the magazine is more established. But I have written to Mr Leighton that I will have the end papers and tooled gold lines inside the boards, which will add sixpence to the cost of every vol.: I think this is necessary as the book looks unfinished as it now stands. . . . No. 2 fills up slowly. I am to have an article on the 20th by Mr Gorst, the financial adviser to the Khedive – he writes well, and is much thought of – Sir Henry Wolff is trying to get me an article from some prominent Spaniard on the situation in Spain, and I have one or two other 'irons in the fire'. You will be glad to hear that Mr [George] Meredith has promised me his next work. I wish I could have got that poem 'Cruisers' from Mr Kipling – but I dare say the *Morning Post* paid him 200 pounds for it. I can't say I admired it much – so rough and informal. . . . I hope early next week to hand to the printers the order in which they can make the ten pages up to date. . . . No. 2 . . . will be a very readable number, perhaps more so than Volume I. But nothing brilliant or startling. . . . It has been very difficult to get any prominent politicians. They all want to enjoy their holidays. I admire Mr Phillips' poem very much, and have written to tell him so. It is exceedingly fine. . . . Am waiting to hear from America. . . .[19]

At the end of each week, Jennie was transformed from a tough editor to a tender woman. However, her absences during the week served to strengthen George's resolve to marry her. But she was reluctant. 'Jennie and I had discussed it many a time,' George later wrote, 'and she had always said that the difference in our ages made marriage out of the question.' [20]

It is one thing, however, to understand a fact with your mind, and it is quite another to accept it with your heart. Jennie was forty-five years old, but she looked and felt much younger. She wanted to keep feeling young, and George could help her to do that. To her, her spirit still seemed as young as his.

Meanwhile, as George noted, 'people began to talk.' The popular magazine *Gentlewoman* remarked that 'a handsome American woman is to marry a handsome young man about the age of her son. . . .' Often the talk was snide and cruel. Winston told his mother about one clipping he had seen which compared the expected marriage to that of 'Lobengula [a Zulu king] with a white woman'. 'I tore it up,' he said, 'and I don't know why I waste my time in repeating such trash. . . .' [21]

Nevertheless, Jennie and George had already decided to announce their engagement. The announcement would be made during Cowes Week, the first week in August, on the Isle of Wight. The choice of time and place could not have been mere coincidence. It was from the Isle of Wight that the first Jerome had sailed to America in 1710. But more significant, it was on the Isle of Wight that Jennie had first met and fallen in love with Lord Randolph Churchill, and it was there, during Cowes Week, that he had proposed marriage and she had accepted. Why did she now choose that place and that time to become formally engaged again? Was it an attempt to cut across time? Was it her singular way of defying society? Or was it the longing of a romanticist to return to one of the most unequivocal feelings she had known?

The headline in *The New York Times* read:

LADY CHURCHILL TO WED
Lord Randolph's Widow Engaged
to Lieut. Cornwallis-West
BRITISH SOCIETY ASTONISHED [22]

British society was more than astonished; it was incensed. For a woman of Jennie's position to dally with a young man might raise a few eyebrows, but for her actually to marry him was downright scandalous. She was the leader of Anglo-American society in Great Britain, a member of the royal circle, an intimate of some of the very important people of the world. She could have chosen a husband from among many of the mighty men of her time. And whom did she pick – a callow young man who was also plainly improvident.

Pressures against the marriage mounted immediately and one of the most forceful was wielded by the Prince of Wales. George later wrote:

> . . . I had been invited on board the Britannia at Cowes, and the Prince of Wales took the opportunity of taking me aside and pointing out to me the inadvisability of my marrying a woman so much my senior. He admitted that this was the only argument against our engagement, told me that no one could possibly say what might happen within the next three months, and begged me to do nothing in a hurry. 'If there *is* war,' he added, 'you are sure to go out. There'll be time enough to consider it when you come back.' [23]

Perhaps the Prince was thinking more of himself than of George. Jennie was one of the favourite women in his life, and he counted on her in many particular ways, as he did on very few others. He liked her to be available to arrange parties, dinners, entertainments; he relied on her for sympathy, understanding, confidence. Were it to be a marriage of convenience – he would probably have thought it an advantage. Such a marriage simplified matters because it kept the woman in his orbit, giving her some protective social status. But a marriage of love meant that the woman was no longer available. To that the Prince objected – and he objected vehemently.

Of course George also heard from his father as well as the rest of his family and friends. In view of their disapproval of the relationship, it is not unlikely that the Colonel told his son to expect no future income from him, and he may even have threatened disinheritance. George's commanding officer, Colonel Arthur Paget, also became involved; he requested 'a verbal understanding that I would not marry or become engaged before leaving' for South Africa.[24] The Colonel was a good friend of Jennie's, but he was a better friend of the Prince of Wales.

How reminiscent the whole scene must have seemed to Jennie. The Duke and Duchess of Marlborough had made similar attempts to stop her marriage to their son. George, however, was not a Lord Randolph. He was an anxious young man very much in love but overwhelmed by the concerted pressures against him. He buckled.

On the front page of *The New York Times* the day after the engagement announcement appeared the following report:

Lady Randolph Churchill's Son Denies
That His Mother Will Marry Young Cornwallis-West.

COWES, Isle of Wight, August 4 – Lieut. Winston Leonard Spencer-Churchill, the son of Lady Randolph Churchill, asked the Associated Press to deny the reported engagement of his mother to Lieut. G. F. M. Cornwallis-West, brother of Princess Henry of Pless.

The matter continued to be the subject of much conversation among their friends. Neither Lady Randolph Churchill nor Lieut. Cornwallis-West has been seen about since the engagement was reported.[25]

How it must have delighted Winston to be the one to deny that his mother would marry George.

Jennie left immediately afterwards for her favourite spa, Aix-les-Bains. Jennie had a great deal to think about as she soaked in the baths. Several months before, Caryl Ramsden had come to say good-bye before returning to Cairo. Jennie, who concealed little from her sons, then wrote to Winston, 'I told him I did not think England . . . would feel any colder for his absence. He has too many irons in the fire to be able to concentrate. . . .'[26] To Jack she remarked: 'Who knows what a butterfly like him thinks of, and shall I add, Who cares!'[27]

But this sad merry-go-round with George was a more serious matter, and she did care.

A letter from Winston followed immediately. 'I do hope the cure will do you good and that you will not find the time hanging heavy on your hands. I am afraid so. I wish I could have come with you – no humbug. The book alone prevented me. . . .'[28]

Knowing that the marriage plans were forestalled but not abandoned, Colonel Cornwallis-West now wrote to Winston and forcefully declared the inadvisability of any future relationship between his son and Winston's mother. He asked for Winston's support in thwarting the relationship.

However much Winston agreed with the Colonel, his loyalty to his mother was unswerving. He forwarded the Colonel's letter to Jennie and asserted: 'I don't want to be dragged into their [Cornwallis-West] family cabal. Whatever you may do or wish to do, I shall support you in every way. But reflect most seriously on all the aspects of the question. . . . Fine sentiments & empty stomachs do not accord.' [29]

On September 3, Winston wrote to his mother from Blenheim:

I have had a second letter from Colonel West, which since he has not marked it *Private* — I send you, but you must destroy it and not tell anyone that I showed it to you, as I rather think he meant it to be looked on as private. There is not much in it and I did not think it necessary to answer. It is for George to settle with his family: for you to consult your own happiness. . . .

Please send me a telegram when you get this letter to say that you love me and will write the same sentiment at a greater length.

And in a postscript, he remarked, 'After all I don't believe you will marry. My idea is that the family pressure will crush George.' [30]

Winston was nearly proved right. The family pressure could have crushed George, as his and Jennie's economic circumstances were even more critical than the difference in their ages. They had little money and, what's more, no friendly support. They had their love, and it was strong enough for Jennie, but was it strong enough for George? He did not have Jennie's fibre. It seemed, then, as if the romance had run dry, the last chapter finished. But unexpectedly, there would come news that would change everything. Within two months Great Britain would be at war with the Boers in South Africa.

14

By the turn of the century, Britain's foreign policy had changed from 'splendid isolation' to 'swaggering imperialism', from an era of conspicuous peace to a time of turmoil. The poet and critic Wilfred Blunt wrote:

> Of the new century, I prophesy nothing except that it will see the decline of the British Empire. Other worse empires will rise perhaps in its place, but I shall not live to see the day. . . . For a hundred years we have done good in the world, for a hundred, we shall have done evil, and then the world will hear of us no more.[1]

Rudyard Kipling had written his famous poem, 'The Recessional' for the Diamond Jubilee two years earlier, ending on the note:

> Lord God of Hosts, be with us yet,
> Lest we forget — lest we forget.

But pessimism and humility were not the mood of the British people in the autumn of 1899. Sensationalism was the mood. Jingoism was the mood. War was the mood.

The excitement of the Jameson Raid into the Transvaal and the gory drama of the Battle of Omdurman seemed to have whetted a national appetite. The young Lord Harmsworth, publisher of the *Daily Mail*, commented that what his readers wanted most and what his newspaper supplied best was 'a good hate'.[2]

Since the abortive Jameson Raid three years earlier, the Transvaal had been rearming heavily. It was one of three Republics bordering the British Cape Colony, which constituted the southern part of South Africa. The British had once annexed the Transvaal, but the Boers of the Transvaal had beaten them at Majuba Hill and asserted their independence in 1881. South Africans of Dutch descent, the Boers (meaning 'farmers') were rugged and fiercely individualistic.

With the discovery of gold in 1866, the Transvaal rapidly became the most industrialized and wealthiest land on the African continent. Gold also brought an influx of 'outlanders', mostly British, and this became the point of international tension. President Kruger of the Transvaal refused to grant outlanders the right to vote. Jennie's good friend, Sir Alfred Milner, the new High Commissioner of the Cape Colony, became the most ardent advocate of the outlanders. He wrote to the Colonial Secretary, Joseph Chamberlain, saying:

> The spectacle of thousands of British subjects permanently in a position of helots, constantly chafing under undoubted grievances and calling vainly to Her Majesty's Government for redress does steadily undermine the influence and reputation of Great Britain and the respect for the British Government within the Queen's dominions.

After unsuccessful negotiations with President Kruger, Milner reported back to the Colonial Secretary, 'There is no way out of the political troubles of South Africa except reform in the Transvaal or war.'[3]

Shortly afterwards, Chamberlain and Jennie were weekend guests at Chatsworth. 'One night at dinner,' Jennie said, 'we discussed the situation, and he frankly told me he considered [war] inevitable.'

Joseph Chamberlain was the dominant figure in Lord Salisbury's Conservative Government. Once opposed to Imperialism, Chamberlain had not only learned to 'think imperially', but had placed himself at the crest of the rising imperialist wave. This elegant man with his monocle on a black ribbon was now known to the public as 'Pushful Joe', and when war came many called it 'Joe's War'.[4]

Jennie's own views were mixed. She had friends in both camps. She feared, as her husband had almost twenty years before, that 'the final triumph of the British arms, mainly by brute force, would have permanently and hopelessly alienated it [the Transvaal] from Great Britain.'[5]

Winston, however, was completely at one with the new mood. 'Imperial aid must redress the wrongs of the Outlanders' he had written in 1897. 'Imperial troops must curb the insolence of the Boers. There must be no half measures. The forces employed must be strong enough to beat down all opposition from the Transvaal and the Free State; and at the same time win over all sympathizers in Cape Colony. . . . For the sake of our Empire, for the sake of our honour, for the sake of the race, we must fight the Boers.'[6]

Much of the press was fanning this jingo imperialism into a patriotic fury. The historian R. C. K. Ensor later noted: '. . . It is often said that distemper caused the war; and it may be true, though not in the most obvious sense. . . . If the Boers became united by the mistaken conviction that a British Government wanted their blood, it was largely because they heard a British public calling for it.'[7]

In early October 1899, President Kruger of the Transvaal sent an ultimatum to Great Britain: withdraw British troops massing along his frontiers and stop any further reinforcements. There was a three-day deadline for a reply, after which war was inevitable.

The Boers had 50,000 troops,[8] twice as many as the available British force. They were ready for guerrilla war and the British were not.[9] The British Commander-in-Chief, Sir Redvers Buller, was soon *en route* with reinforcements, and aboard his ship was the war correspondent for the *Morning Post*, Winston Churchill.[10] Jennie had made some of the preliminary contacts and Winston had made the final arrangements.

The Prince of Wales, meanwhile, had not forgotten his conversation with George West about Jennie. 'I was told by my C.O.,' George wrote, 'that Lord Methuen had applied for a junior officer from his old regiment to go as his Aide-de-Camp, that it must be someone who could ride, and that my name had been sent in. It came as a surprise to me, as I had done nothing to bring it about. The explanation was soon forthcoming, however, as I found a note from the Prince of Wales awaiting me when I went home':

My dear George West,

    I had the opportunity of speaking to Lord Methuen at the station yesterday when I took leave of Sir Redvers Buller, and strongly urged him to take you on his staff, so I hope it may be all satisfactorily settled. I envy you going out on active service with so fine a battalion, and wish you good luck and a safe return home.

                                                Yrs. very sincerely,
                                                Albert Edward.[11]

The arm of the Prince of Wales was long and his friends had expedited his wishes. He may have thought, as George's parents did, that an enforced separation would cool the couple's ardour. Nearly twenty-five years before, the Duke and Duchess of Marlborough had mistakenly thought the same thing about Lord Randolph and Jennie.

For the short time remaining, Jennie cancelled all her appointments so that she could be with George as much as possible. She even excused herself from one of the season's prized social events, the annual country house party given by Lord and Lady Wolverton for the Prince of Wales.

Formerly, George and Jennie had been reasonably judicious about being seen together in London, but now they appeared to flaunt their relationship. Jennie also accompanied George on his extensive shopping tours, and it was rather mockingly reported that they were seen together at a play called *Elixir of Youth*.

The Boer War was one of the last of the so-called 'gentlemanly wars'. Officers going to the front were permitted to bring with them some of their favourite foods, spirits, guns, horses, clothing. Fortnum and Mason instituted a special 'South African War Service', and other well-known stores followed suit. 'They brought their own dressing cases, with silver or gold fittings; they brought their splendid shotguns by Purdy or Westley-Richards; their magnificent hunters saddled by such masters as Gordon of Curzon Street. They brought their valets, coachmen, grooms and hunt-servants.' [12] The Prince of Wales made his final inspection of George's regiment before its departure. 'I shall never forget our march from Chelsea Barracks to Waterloo Station at about five o'clock on a dark autumn morning,' George later wrote.

> There was a slight fog and, comparatively speaking, the streets were badly lighted in those days. A good many wives and sweethearts accompanied the men from the Barracks and linked arms, and naturally nothing was done to prevent them. . . . Over Westminster Bridge, our ranks almost degenerated into a rabble, so great was the crush of civilians. . . . Some of the scenes were particularly heartrending. . . . [13]

The regiment embarked from Southampton on a small ship called *The Nubia*. The British correspondent for a New York magazine reported:

> When Mr West started for South Africa, the tears were rolling down his face, while Lady Randolph, who was more or less in hiding at the hotel, as so many of his own relatives had come to see him off – was

quite prostrated with grief. . . . Lady Randolph herself told a friend that she had promised George not to touch either port or champagne until they met again. . . .[14]

Twenty-four hours after *The Nubia* had sailed, a London newspaper reported with blaring placards that the ship had sunk with all hands on board. When the fog lifted, however, *The Nubia* was found steaming dead slow not more than half a mile from shore. The false news about the ship only intensified Jennie's anxiety. How she must have regretted her obstinacy in refusing to marry George so many months before. It would have been different if they themselves had decided to end their relationship, but George's going to war gave the situation an aura of drama and foreboding.

Winston tried to ease her mind. He assured her that he would look up George in South Africa, and he said he expected that George would probably be back in England in time for that year's Derby.

Jennie tried to divert her mind to the *Anglo-Saxon Review*, but her early enthusiasm took an emotional downward turn. She had assigned and collected copy for the third volume, and when the second issue appeared it, too, received critical praise. Its green cover was tooled in gold, and its contents included articles on subjects ranging from the Dreyfus Case to the Marlborough Gems.

Just at this time, Jennie received a visit from Mrs A. A. Blow, the American wife of the manager of one of South Africa's richest mining syndicates. Mrs Blow was very excited about an idea she had, but it was one that would never be realized, she said, unless Jennie took it in hand. The idea was to provide an American hospital ship to care for the wounded in South Africa.

At first Jennie was hesitant. No American group in England had ever done anything like this before. The practical part of her mind foresaw giant tangles of international red tape. Furthermore, a major part of the American public was pro-Boer, seeing in the Transvaal a small country fighting for its independence against the mighty British Empire. Indeed, a large segment within England itself, led by Jennie's friend John Morley, was similarly against this war. But Jennie discussed the idea with another friend, Sir William Garstin, who strongly urged her to take up the project. 'Believe me,' he said, 'you will be making history, apart from the excellence of the work.'[15]

'Then and there,' Jennie said, 'I made up my mind to do it.'[16]

Florence Nightingale, who had organized a unit of nurses for the Crimean War in 1854, had written an article entitled 'Cassandra' in which she posed the question, 'Why have women passion, intellect, moral activity — these three — and a place in society where no one of these can be exercised?'

Some women have an intention like a battering ram, which, slowly brought to bear, can work upon a subject for any length of time. They can work for ten hours just as well as two, upon the same thing. . . . What do you suffer — even physically — for the want of such work, no one can tell. The accumulation of nervous energy, which has nothing to do during the day, makes them feel every night when they go to bed as if they were going mad; and they are obliged to lie long in bed in the morning, to let it evaporate and keep it down.[17]

Jennie's thinking on these matters followed the same lines, and she had arrived at similar conclusions as to the role and abilities of women. On October 25, 1899, the first committee meeting for the organization of a hospital ship was held at Jennie's home. Mrs A. A. Blow was elected Honorary Secretary; Fanny Ronalds, Treasurer; Mrs Cornelia Adair, Vice-Chairman; and Jennie, Chairman.[18]

'A large and influential general committee was formed' Jennie wrote.

All worked with zeal and enthusiasm, and soon the whole thing was well in train. There was a general impression that the war would be short and sharp. Hospitals of all kinds were greatly needed, and we hurried with feverish activity. Funds and the ship — those were the two great and immediate preoccupations. No stone was left un- turned to procure money — much money — and it had to be all American money. It is useless to deny here that the war was viewed with disfavour by my countrymen. They had a fellow-feeling for the Boer, fighting, as they thought, for his independence. But the plea of humanity overran their political opinions, and the fund once started, money poured in. A resolution carried at the meeting of the Executive Committee was embodied in our appeal to the public:

'That whereas Great Britain is now involved in a war affecting the rights and liberties of the Anglo-Saxon people in South Africa, and has under arms 70,000 troops to maintain its rights and liberties;

'And whereas the people of Great Britain have, by their sympathy and moral support, materially aided the people of the United States of America in the war in Cuba and the Philippine Islands, *it is therefore resolved*:

'That the American women in Great Britain, whilst deploring the necessity for war, shall endeavour to raise, among their compatriots in America, a fund for the relief of the sick and wounded soldiers and refugees in South Africa. It is proposed to dispatch immediately a suitable Hospital Ship, fully equipped with medical stores and provisions, to accommodate 200 people, with a staff of four doctors, five nurses, and 40 commissioned officers and orderlies.

'To carry the above resolution into effect, the sum of 150,000 dollars (£30,000) will be required.' [19]

There were fund-raising concerts, matinées, and entertainments of all sorts. Large firms contributed so many medical supplies that the committee found some difficulty in storing them. Cheques and donations, from a few shillings to a thousand pounds, poured in. On the other hand, there were also some rebuffs. Jennie sent a telegram to a New York millionaire asking for a contribution. He replied that he had 'no knowledge of the scheme', to which Jennie retorted, 'Read the papers.' [20]

A British paper remarked upon the intensified feeling of kinship between the two nations in times of trouble and crisis. It went on to praise 'our American cousins' for their independence, their capacity, their methods, 'and, we may add, their strong sense of humour.' Discussing the generosity of the American women in Britain and their offer of a hospital ship, it commented: 'It is noticeable that they have formed a strong committee, with Lady Randolph Churchill as its head. It is to be supposed, therefore, that the result will be a great success. . . .' [21]

Winston later wrote that his mother 'raised a fund, captivated an American millionaire, obtained a ship. . . .' [22]

This was true. She had wanted an American ship and contacted her distant cousin, Theodore Roosevelt, then Governor of New York, to ask if he could help. Unfortunately he had no suggestions to make. It was then that she found the American millionaire: forty-five-year-old Bernard Nadel Baker. Founder of the Atlantic Transport Company in Baltimore, Baker had spent all his adult life in the shipping business. At a special meeting of his Board of Directors, on December 12, 1899, Baker reported that without an opportunity to consult the Board as a whole, he had taken the responsibility of tendering to the British Government the use of one of the company's transport ships for the duration of the war in the Transvaal.

It was an unusual gift, particularly since Baker had offered that the hospital ship as well as the crew would be maintained at his company's expense. This represented a gift of some £3,000 to £4,000 a month.

The ship was called the *Maine* after the vessel that had been sunk in Havana Harbour before the start of the Spanish-American war. Unfortunately, she was an old cattle boat.[23] How does one convert such a ship into a floating hospital? Jennie asked experts in the Army and the Red Cross, but they were of little help. There was no precedent for this kind of conversion and no existing plans or procedure, so Jennie and her group had to find people to draw up plans and procedures.

What about doctors, surgeons, and nurses? Jennie wanted most of them to be American. She remembered that Mrs Whitelaw Reid had provided nurses for the Spanish-American War from the Mills School of Nursing, which her father had founded. Jennie knew the Reids well, and Whitelaw Reid had written an article for the first issue of the *Review*. Mrs Reid was pleased to accept the responsibility of providing an American medical staff.

The next task Jennie set for herself was to get the *Maine* officially designated a military hospital ship. She went directly to the Marquess of Lansdowne, the Secretary of State for War, and Lord Goschen, the First Lord of the Admiralty, as she had known both men on a first-name basis for a long time. The *Maine* gots its military designation as well as Lieutenant-Colonel Hensman, a surgeon from the 2nd Life Guards, and some men from the St John Ambulance Brigade.

During October and November, the committee met almost daily. A series of defeats in South Africa had caused gloom and depression in Britain, but for Jennie it was one of the most absorbing times of her life. She urged and badgered the War Office and the Admiralty. 'Would they supply us with this? Would they guarantee us that? We would not take No for an answer,' Jennie recalled.

At the first meeting of the General Committee, Jennie reminded them:

A little more than a fortnight ago, the scheme was not in existence. Today we have a ship, we have a magnificent staff, and, what is even more important, we have £15,000, hundreds of donations and our fellow countrymen are working for us in all parts of the world. We may differ as to the policy which necessitates the sending of so many gallant soldiers to the front. It is always easy to criticize, but as a gifted compatriot wrote to me, 'The wounded are the wounded, irrespective of creed and nationality.' And, indeed, we can have but one mind in this matter: If we can alleviate sufferings and at the same time comfort the many aching and anxious hearts at home, shall we not be fulfilling our greatest mission in life? These are 'Women's Rights' in the best sense of the word. We need no others. We have heard of the friendship between England and America. These are better than words, and we greatly hope that the hospital-ship *Maine* may do more to cement that friendship than years of flag-waving and pleasant amenities.[24]

The New York Times revealed further news about the project:

The possibility of Lady Randolph Churchill accompanying the American hospital-ship *Maine* to the Cape of Good Hope has aroused much interest here. Her ladyship said today:

'The question of my going is dependent upon several contingencies. It is quite possible that I may go, but the matter has not yet been fully determined.'

Lady Randolph Churchill has taken the most active part in the scheme to fit out the *Maine*, obtaining privileges from the War Office, which otherwise would have been impossible, in favor of the American nurses, and her friends are now anxious that she should see the matter through personally.[25]

It was finally decided that she would go, and several days later, Jennie was quoted as saying:

The *Maine* is to be essentially an American women's ship. We are not only to aid the wounded, but are to show the world that American women can do the good work better than anyone else can do it. I am going to the Cape in the *Maine*, not because my son is there, for he will be a thousand miles away, but because I want the generous efforts of American contributors to be carried out under the personal supervision of a member of the Executive Committee.

I am going because I think I may prevent any kind of friction between the American nurses whom Mrs Whitelaw Reid is sending out
on Saturday, and the British officials, in case such friction should
arise. I contribute that much time and service gladly.[26]

The value of what she was doing, however, could not still the voices
of the gossip-mongers. One magazine remarked: 'Everyone in London
is wondering what Lady Randolph will do when she arrives in South
Africa. It is well known that her one object in going out with the *Maine*
was to follow Mr George West. . . .' [27]

Similarly, Consuelo Vanderbilt, Duchess of Marlborough, who was
working with Jennie in outfitting the hospital ship, wrote in her memoirs
'that everybody knew that Lady Randolph was going out on the ship,
to join her son Winston. We knew that she was equally anxious to see
young George Cornwallis-West.' [28]

The Sunday Sketch even quoted punsters saying that Jennie was
going to South Africa to remove George West 'from the field of danger
by *Maine* force. . . .' [29]

Jennie took no public notice of such comments, and in a newspaper
interview, she clarified her role:

. . . I am not going to do any amateur nursing, because I don't believe
in it; it really is not at all fair to the patients. . . . I shall superintend
the correspondence, which is certain to be heavy, and I am taking a
secretary to assist me. For the rest, I have no doubt that I shall find
plenty of work to do – in fact, I mean to help in any way I can. . . .
Where we shall go first, I have no idea. We are entirely in the hands
of the Government, and they will naturally send us where we shall be
of most use. When shall I be back? How can I tell you how long the
war will last, and I certainly mean to see it through.[30]

Queen Victoria met the American staff on the ship and told them how
much she appreciated their kindness 'in coming over to take care of my
men'. Two days later, Jennie was invited to 'dine and sleep' at Windsor,
and had a long conversation with the Queen about the war and the
Maine. The Queen remarked, 'I think the surgeons look very young.'
Whereupon Jennie answered: 'All the more energetic therefore.' [31]

The royal blessing later helped resolve a storm in a teacup at a
Maine fund-raising function in New York. The celebrated actress, Lillie

Langtry [32] – who had once captured the varied hearts of the Prince of Wales,[33] and both Jennie's father and brother-in-law Moreton Frewen, among others – was appearing on the New York stage and Jennie obtained her help. Lillie announced a concert and tea featuring a variety of entertainment, as well as an 'American Bar'. She told the press that the programme would be sponsored by New York's leading society women, and that she herself would invade Wall Street to sell tickets.[34]

Word soon circulated that prominent actresses and society women would serve as barmaids in short skirts. The Women's Christian Temperance Union organized full opposition, saying that the 'spectacle would be degrading . . . a blot on the reputation of the women of this city . . . and a violation of State laws. . . .' The *New York Journal* printed an editorial about the tea, under the headline, 'Should Good, Pure Women Associate with Mrs Langtry, Even for the Sake of Charity?'[35]

Reinforcement was forthcoming from the Society for Political Study, which claimed that 'the women belonging to The 400 who are taking part in this tea are no more representative American women than the submerged tenth. . . . They represent money and society, but not the brains. We clubwomen represent the brains.'[36]

New York society leader Mrs William Backhouse Astor announced that she would not attend the tea, and advised her friends to do likewise. Lillie cabled Jennie: 'Cold shoulder. What's to be done?'

Jennie knew exactly what to do. The best weapon against snobbery is snobbery, so she appealed to the Prince of Wales. Through the appropriate channels, the Prince immediately let it be known that unless Mrs Astor changed her mind and attended the tea, he would see that her daughter in England would not be in royal favour.

What would *the* Mrs Astor do? Would she continue to assert her prerogatives and her principles? Could she possibly demean herself to associate with that notorious actress for such a questionable project? Indeed she could, and did. And trooping along with her went the rest of New York society's leaders.

The tea was a phenomenal success; it raised more than $5,000 (£2,000) for the *Maine*. As part of the entertainment, a strongman demonstrated muscle-developers and sold them on behalf of the fund. Lillie Langtry, wearing a gown of lace and ermine, recited Rudyard Kipling's 'The Absent-Minded Beggar'.[37] A detective wearing a light-check sack coat, red shirt, and lavender trousers was 'secretly' present to make sure there were no short-skirted barmaids. The Earl of Yar-

188

mouth was the amateur bartender, wearing a white apron over his velvet-collared coat and unblushingly accepting tips 'that would even make a Waldorf-Astoria waiter lose his presence of mind'. *The Times* quoted the Earl as having said that his role in the affair 'may make a bit of a stench here, but it will do me a lot of good with the Prince.'

Jennie had no such problems with her final fund-raising party at Claridge's in London. Sir Arthur Sullivan had arranged for the use of the ground floor of the hotel, and Jennie and her friends had it converted into a garden of chrysanthemums, roses, and multi-coloured lights. A large contingent of British royalty arrived, accompanied by an escort of the Life Guards in their brilliant white-and-scarlet uniforms, drummers and drum-majors, and Scots Guards in tartans. The casts and orchestras of two musical shows, *The Belle of New York* and *El Capitan*, were also there, and the featured singer was Mrs Brown Potter, one of the Prince's favourites.

Describing the event in great detail, the London correspondent of *The New York Times* noted:

> Lady Randolph Churchill looked in for a few minutes, but was deeply distressed, owing to her anxiety as to the fate of her son, Winston Churchill, believed to be a prisoner in the hands of the Boers, and left before the guests arrived. The absence of the leading spirit in the movement, due to the uncertainty as to the death or capture of her son, gave a tragic tone to the gathering.[38]

The Boers had ambushed an armoured train in which Winston was a passenger. Walden, who had been Lord Randolph's valet and now served his son, wrote to Jennie:

> ... The driver [of the train] was one of the first wounded, and he said to Mr Winston: 'I am finished.' So Mr Winston said to him, 'Buck up a bit, I will stick to you', and he threw off his revolver and field-glasses and helped the driver pick 20 wounded up and put them on the tender of the engine. . . . He [the driver] says there is not a braver gentleman in the Army. . . .[39]

Telegrams of concern arrived from the Prince of Wales ('pray he may be safe and sound . . .'), Empress Eugénie, who had lost her only son in the Zulu War; and George West ('How anxious you will be, my poor darling. How I wish I could help you . . .').[40] But the message that warmed her most was a telegram from her son Jack: 'Don't be frightened. I will be here when you come home.'[41]

Jennie had been away for the weekend when she first heard the news, and she rushed back to London where Jack was indeed waiting. Her relationship with Winston had reached a turning point some months before and now so did her relationship with Jack. At this time, she needed him as a man whose strength she could lean upon.

Good news soon arrived – a letter from Winston. He was uninjured but was being held in a Boer prison camp in Pretoria. 'You need not be anxious in any way but I trust you will do all in your power to procure my release.'[42] To Bourke Cockran, Winston wrote: 'I am 25 today – it is terrible to think how little time remains!'[43]

Jennie called upon all her influential friends, and asked them to exert their leverage to get her son released from prison. He was, after all, officially a newspaper correspondent and not a soldier.

George, too, had been in the thick of the war. He had sent word to her after a battle saying that he was safe and asking her to forward the news to his mother. 'It's been a very stiff fight,' he wrote, 'and thank God so far I am unhurt.' In his next letter, he said that he had been involved in the

hardest fight that has taken place in any part of the colony . . . 13 hours' hard fighting was the time the Battle of Modder River lasted. I can tell you it was a near shave. . . .

The men started without breakfast and went the whole day without food and water, having finished their water long before noon. It was a terribly hard day, and the heat was terrific. I was knocked over by sunstroke at 3 p.m. and don't remember anything till the evening, when I found myself in the hospital . . . four days' tomorrow. . . . I am sick of this war, three big battles in six days is enough for any man, and I think most of us think the same. . . . How busy you must be with your ship, which appears to be a great success, and *Maggie*. I do hope this number will be a success. . . .[44]

Jennie, however, spent little time with the daily workings of the *Review*, and Sidney Low capably carried on for her during the time of her intense activity for the *Maine*. Now there was added impetus to hurry the conversion of the cattle-boat. *The Nursing Record and Hos-*

pital World inspected the result and called the *Maine* 'the most complete and comfortable hospital ship that has ever been constructed.' [45]

Then one day in mid-December, Jennie received a call from the *Morning Post*: 'All I could hear,' she recalled, 'was, "Hurrah! Hurrah!" repeated by different voices, as one after the other seized the instrument in their kind wish to congratulate me.' [46]

CHURCHILL ESCAPED

was the headline carried by the *Post*.

Winston later described the feat:

> Now or never! I stood on the ledge, seized the top of the wall with my hands, and drew myself up. Twice I let myself down again in sickly hesitation, and then with a third resolve scrambled up and over. My waistcoat got entangled with the ornamental metal-work on the top. I had to pause for an appreciable moment to extricate myself. In this posture I had one parting glimpse of the sentries still talking with their backs turned fifteen yards away. One of them was lighting his cigarette, and I remember the glow on the inside of his hands as a distinct impression which my mind recorded. Then I lowered myself lightly down into the adjoining garden and crouched among the shrubs. I was free! [47]

The Boers offered £25 for Winston's recapture and described him in a circular as 'about five foot eight or nine inches, blond with light, thin, small moustache, walks with slight stoop, cannot speak any Dutch, during long conversations he occasionally makes a rattling noise in his throat. . . . Speaks through his nose, cannot pronounce the letter "s". . . .' [48]

Winston had escaped, but he was still three hundred miles from the frontier. He walked, ran, hid in ravines, jumped onto a train, and finally, by the sheerest of luck, stumbled into friendly hands. 'Thank God you have come here,' the man said. 'It is the only house for twenty miles where you would not have been handed over. But we are all British here, and we will see you through.' [49]

Jennie was relieved, proud, exultant. Now she made final plans for the launching of the *Maine*. She wanted the ship to fly the flags of the United States and Great Britain. Queen Victoria was pleased to agree and promised to send a British flag to the ceremony with her son, the Duke of Connaught. President William McKinley, however, did not agree with Jennie's contention that 'it would carry no political significance'. Americans were predominantly pro-Boer, and there would be a presidential election in less than a year. McKinley's refusal to personally send an American flag placed Jennie in an awkward position at the ceremony. 'Under the circumstances,' she wrote, 'I thought the best policy was to preserve a judicious silence.'

The Duke of Connaught presented the flag on behalf of the Queen and, after thanking the 'large number of American ladies', said:

> Never has a ship sailed under the combined flags of the Union Jack and the Stars and Stripes; and it marks, I hope, an occasion which brings out that feeling of generosity and affection that the two countries have for each other. . . . Therefore, I ask Lady Randolph Churchill to accept, in the name of all those who have worked with her, the thanks, both of the Sovereign of our country and of all Englishmen and women in this splendid present which has been made in aid of our wounded soldiers in South Africa.

Jennie herself made a short speech, in which she said, '. . . All who have been interested in this work have made it a labour of love. We hope that the *Maine* will be more than useful on her errand of mercy, and that our charity will be as widespread as possible, irrespective of nationality.'

The Duke hoisted the British flag to the mainmast as the Scots Guards band played 'Rule Britannia'. The music changed to 'The Star-Spangled Banner' as the Stars and Stripes were run up the mizzen, and the Red Cross flag to the foremast. 'Add to these the Admiralty's transport flag at the helm, and it is not surprising that we felt much beflagged and bedecked,' Jennie said. 'It was a great moment for us all, and I confess I felt a lump in my throat.' [50]

The ship was in a state of chaos. Ten thousand people had visited her the previous Sunday, leaving the decks covered with mud and the paint no longer clean. What is more, the reconstruction itself had not yet been completed; painters, carpenters, plumbers and engineers were still to be seen in every corner; the wards were littered with wood shavings, paint-pots, ropes, scaffoldings and debris.

On that final hectic day of departure, a small crisis developed when three male nurses left the ship because Colonel Hensman had told them to serve his five-man staff. They said they would serve themselves and the wounded, but not Hensman's men. Hensman was nominally the officer in charge, and Major Julian M. Cabell of the U.S. Army Medical Department, who had been granted special leave of absence by the Secretary of War, was the senior American surgeon on board. Cabell let it be known before sailing that he was 'virtually head and is to do all the work'. This conflict in command made Jennie's presence during the voyage essential for easing tension between the British and Americans.

Jennie's sister Clara had been ill with a cold, but despite this came to the sailing with her two sons, Hugh and Oswald. Neither was Jennie without an admiring man to help her – he was Allison Vincent Armour, a member of the Chicago meat-packing family, whom Jennie kept busy getting last-minute supplies at the Army & Navy Stores.[51]

Jack was also there and planned to stay aboard after everyone else left. But the rolling of the ship made him ill, and he left with Clara.

Even though everyone else at the dock was jubilant, cheering and waving, Jennie, as Clara wrote afterwards to Leonie, 'seemed depressed. . . .' She had just received a telegram:

INVALIDED. PROBABLY RETURNING HOME ALMOST
IMMEDIATELY. REPEAT TO MOTHER. GEORGE.[52]

In a letter that reached her too late, he asked her to postpone her departure until he arrived, or they would miss each other, 'which would be too awful'.

As the *Maine* moved out from the dock, 'the fog was so thick one could not see an inch'. Jennie stood on deck listening to cheers.[53] She had probably anticipated this moment as one of elation but her mood now matched the sad bleating song of the foghorn.

15

On Christmas Day 1899 the *Maine* sailed into a full gale in the Bay of Biscay.[1] Jennie had been on many ships in many gales during her travels around the world, but this was the worst.[2] It lasted six days — into the new year and the new century.

> ... no fiddles can restrain your soup from being shot into your lap, or the contents of your glass into your face [Jennie wrote] . . . I never realized before how one can suffer by colour. The green of my attractive little cabin, which I had thought so reposeful, became a source of acute suffering. . . . The sound of the waves breaking on the deck with the report of cannon-balls . . . and I remember thinking, as I rolled in sleepless wretchedness, that if we went to the bottom, at least we should be counted as victims of the war.[3]

She told Leonie that the gale had often made sleep impossible and so she 'sat up in a secure chair & read'. And in a postscript she added, 'Look after Jack and George. Write to me all he says. . . .'[4] George West had left Africa for England at just about the time that Jennie had left England, their ships probably crossing somewhere in the ocean. There was no knowing when she would see him again. She was committed to the purpose of this trip and she could not desert that purpose. As Winston told her in a letter, 'Your name will be long remembered with affection by many poor broken creatures. Besides, it is the right thing to do, which is the great point.'[5]

Late in the evening on January 2, the *Maine* anchored off Las Palmas, in the Canary Islands. The air was soft and balmy, and the low verandahs of the houses were covered with bougainvillea of varying shades. Jennie was reminded of Monterey, California: 'the same square pink houses, with green shutters and centre court or patio, tropical vegetation, and the sea at the door.' For Jennie, Las Palmas was merely pretty, 'whereas Monterey, with its 17-mile drive, unparalleled gardens, and unique, storm-swept cypress-groves overlooking the ocean, is probably one of the most beautiful spots in the world.'

> We returned to the ship laden with spoils — birds, parrots, fruit, plants, coffee-pots, and Heaven knows what else. I had an opportunity of judging the appearance of the *Maine* as we came alongside. Alas! The brilliant green stripe, denoting our status as a military hospital ship, was a thing of shreds and patches, many of our stanchions were bent and twisted, and our would-be immaculate white paint a foggy grey.[6]

In the letter in which Winston had praised Jennie for doing her duty, he had gone on to inform her:

> I have another piece of [news] that will surprise you. . . . Jack sailed from England on the 5th, and I have obtained him a lieutenancy in the S.A. Light Horse [Brigade], too. I feel the responsibility heavily, but I knew he would be longing to come and I think everyone should do something for the country in these times of trouble & crisis. I particularly stipulated that Cassel should agree, and I hope you will not mind.[7]

Jennie minded very much indeed. Jack was nineteen, barely old enough to grow a moustache, and his vision in one eye was so poor it could be a hazard in battle. Then, too, such was Jack's adoration of his brother that a need to prove his courage might make him foolhardy. 'This adds to my worries,' Jennie wrote to Clara.[8]

Adding even more to her worries was the news from Winston that General Buller had given him a lieutenancy with the South African Light Horse, while still permitting him to retain his correspondent's status. 'There is a great battle — the greatest yet fought — impending here . . .' Winston said. 'If I come through alive, I shall try to run down to Cape Town — or perhaps you will come to fetch the wounded from Durban.'[9]

The phrase 'if I come through alive' must have acted upon Jennie's ready imagination. Now the lives of both her sons were in danger.

Soon the *Maine* was at sea again and her decks were busy. There was much to do on the seventeen-day voyage to Cape Town. There had been no time to batten down the mass of articles brought on board at the last minute, and the gangways and hold were in complete disarray. 'The filth and dirt . . . something awful . . .' Jennie wrote.

In addition, there was a continuing clash of ideas, methods, and personalities between the British and the Americans on board. Some of the personnel assigned to specific wards, for example, would order others not to walk through their wards, or someone would say, 'Be good enough to keep your wet feet off my clean [mat]. . . .'[10] Jennie also felt that some of the men were acting like priggish young medical students, not mature doctors. 'I may change my mind,' she said. 'I hope I will. . . .'[11] As head of the Hospital Committee and its representative, she had final authority, but she reserved its use. Instead, she called upon all her charm, tact, and firmness to engender a sense of camaraderie.

One of the personal problems was particularly acute:

. . . I am sorry to tell you that Sister Barbara is a great thorn in our side. . . . I have tried to befriend her but honestly, everyone in the ship thinks she is rather mad – She has fought with everyone from the Captain to the Stewards – The Ship's Officers went in a body and said they would dine in their rooms, she insulted them so – She and Mrs Hancock [wife of the Medical Officer] fight all day. Hibbard [Superintendent of Nurses] isn't on speaking terms with her. . . . I have begged her to be less antagonistic to everyone. I told her how suicidal such a course was to her – She alternately tries to flirt with the men on board – or insults them. . . . I will try to get one of the transports to take her back – Poor wretch, she hasn't a penny, I suppose I shall have to give her some.[12]

With the British Colonel and the American Major both jealous of their prerogatives, Jennie's presence was often required to smooth differences and calm tempers. She had two strong allies on the ship: one a personal confidante, the other a professional medical worker.

The professional was Superintendent of Nurses Mary Eugenie Hibbard. She had been in charge of the Grace Hospital and Nursing School in Detroit, and was later to become Chief Nurse of the U.S. General Hospital at Savannah, Georgia. Mary Hibbard was tall and dignified, with attractive grey hair rolled back from her brow. She had a soft, well-modulated voice and a keen mind. It was perhaps inevitable that she and Jennie would clash over the prerogatives that went with her nursing activities, but at the outset their working relationship was correct and efficient.[13]

Jennie's other ally was Eleanor Warrender, her companion, secretary and librarian, who did 'a thousand things'. She was a pale, quiet girl, the elder sister of Jennie's persevering admirer, Hugh Warrender. Hugh and his family had decided that Eleanor needed a change of scene and had persuaded Jennie to take her along. Jennie called her 'a capital girl . . . she and I understand each other perfectly. She is intelligent, and a lady – and the whole ship swears by her. . . . I think she is quite happy.'[14]

But Jennie was not happy, even though the *Maine* celebrated her birthday on January 9 by 'dressing' the ship, all flags flying. She was forty-six years old, not an age she especially wanted to accept. The man she loved seemed more remote than ever. And the great achievement and adventure of the hospital ship had been diminished by petty squabbles. Later she would remember star-gazing at the Southern Cross one evening and gloomily observing, 'I thought its beauty a delusion.'[15] The single happy note was that Jack would join her at Cape Town.

Two weeks later, the *Maine* slowly sailed into Cape Town's bay, the sun rising through the breaking clouds above nearby Table Mountain. For the first time Jennie felt the immediacy of war. Filling the bay was a forest of ships' masts – the transports were disembarking troops and supplies at a furious pace.

The Governor of the Cape Colony, Sir Alfred Milner, who had known Jennie for many years, organized a reception for her at the Mount Nelson Hotel.[16] They ate strawberries in a pretty garden, but Jennie kept thinking of the streets filled with soldiers. Jack had not yet arrived and the war news from Winston was bad. Redvers Buller was in retreat, and critics were already calling him 'Reverse' Buller.

For Great Britain, there had already been Black Week: three serious defeats with the loss of several thousand men.[17] One of them was the only son of Lord Roberts, who was now appointed to supersede Buller as commander, with Lord Kitchener as his Chief of Staff.[18]

'Swaggering down the highway of the world', Great Britain had been beaten by an untrained army. Queen Victoria, however, set the tone of British resoluteness when she told Arthur Balfour, 'Please understand that there is no one depressed in *this* house; we are not interested in the possibilities of defeat; they do not exist.'[19] Reinforcements comprising the entire British Army outside India were already on the way to South Africa, as were volunteer forces from England and the colonies.

On the day the *Maine* arrived in Cape Town, Jennie received a change in orders from Cape Town's Chief Medical Officer. He felt that the current war situation called for an alteration in priorities, and he gave the *Maine* a new mission: proceed directly to Durban, take on the wounded, and return immediately to England.

Another woman might have been overjoyed. Here was the chance to return to an anxious lover waiting in England. Moreover, the decision was not hers – she was being *ordered* back, so no one could fault her.

But Jennie was infuriated. The *Maine* was not a transport for patients; it was designed as a floating hospital with a staff of superior surgeons and nurses and the latest operating room facilities including an 'X-ray installation'. Its purpose was to stay close to the war and the wounded, a symbol of international concern and goodwill. That mission was more important than the wishes of any individual. Jennie made it clear that she would appeal against the Medical Officer's decision at Durban. Jack arrived just before the *Maine* sailed. 'No time to write, off to Durban,' Jennie wrote to Clara. 'Best love. Jack with me.' [20]

Jack wore a dashing sombrero hat – one side up, the other down. But for Jennie he must have been an unsettling sight, this handsome young man with a thin moustache, armed and in uniform, yet looking so young and vulnerable. The idea of Winston as a soldier was already familiar, but to Jennie seeing Jack must have given her a feeling of dread. Jack had tried to explain that he wanted to go to war because '. . . I should be a fool not to accept a chance of going & doing what I have longed to do so often. . . . I am afraid I am in for a rough time but I am sure I shall like it. . . .' [21]

Before setting off, they sent a telegram to Winston telling him to try to meet them at Durban for a family reunion – 'After all,' Winston had written to Jennie earlier, '. . . there are only us three in the whole world. . . .' [22]

Jennie has provided us with a description of the voyage.

And we emerged to bask in the sun like lizards. I gazed for hours through my glasses at the shore, which was only three or four miles distant. The soft green hills and bright sandy beaches, with kraals dotted here and there, gave it such a cultivated appearance that one could hardly realize that this was 'Savage South Africa'. As we approached Durban, the wind began to blow, and an ominous bank of grey cloud came up, with lightning flashing on the horizon. I shall never forget the astonishing storm which suddenly burst upon us. The electric barometer in my cabin dropped perpendicularly. Torrents of hailstones beat down on us as large as small plums; the wind increased to a hurricane, and was so violent that the ship stood still, although we had been going at 10 knots. The awning aft was violently blown into the sea, carrying with it all its rafters and stanchions, smashing one of the big ventilators, and only just missing some of the sisters, who were crouching on the deck. The sea, meanwhile, presented a most curious appearance, being covered with millions of little jets about a foot high, due to the force with which the hailstones fell, and as they floated for a while, it was quite white in a few minutes.

Inside my deck-cabin, the din was terrific, the noise of the hailstones striking the skylight and windows, sounding like bullets. It was impossible to speak. One window was smashed, and the water and ice poured in everywhere. The hailstones were solid lumps of ice, each with a pattern like an agate. With the decks covered with ice, the thermometer at 82 degrees seemed an anomaly, and reminded one of the Scotsman who, during a rainstorm, threw out his rising barometer, shouting after it: 'Go and see for yourself!' Luckily, the storm did not last long, and we were soon able to emerge and look at the damage.[23]

Waiting for them at Durban was the port's British Medical Officer, who was equally determined that the *Maine* immediately fill up with wounded and set forth for England. Within the next few days, Jennie used her powers of persuasion with 'the government of Natal, Sir Redvers Buller, and other influential friends' in Durban and successfully frustrated three attempts to make the *Maine* a transport.

Winston was waiting for her in Durban. The reunion was a moving one. 'And so we three met all together again, about 7,000 miles from where we expected each other to be,' Jack wrote.[24] Jennie and her sons had two days for themselves, and the Governor of Natal, Sir Walter Hely-Hutchinson, invited them to go to Pietermaritzburg. It was a picturesque trip on a twisting railway through hills of ever-changing colours. For two days, in this peaceful place, they all tried to push from their minds the impending bloody battles for the relief of Ladysmith. But all too soon the boys left to join their brigades. 'It was hard to say goodbye to my sons. . . .' [25]

Frederic Villiers, the noted war correspondent, and Captain Percy Scott of H.M.S. *Terrible* met Winston and Jack while all of them were going to the front. 'Winston introduced his brother to me,' said Villiers, 'who at once told me that he had heard me lecture before the boys when he was at Harrow, and said he especially remembered that I threw a portrait of his mother on the screen in the act of firing a revolver.'

Villiers had taken the photograph in 1894 aboard the *Empress of China*, on which Jennie and Lord Randolph were travelling to Manchuria. To help pass the time, Villiers and some Japanese officers were practising with their revolvers, shooting at empty beer bottles slung over the stern of the ship. Jennie, who was a good shot, joined them.

Villiers told Jack and Winston that he had flashed that same photograph of their mother onto a screen during a lecture at the University Club in Madison Square, New York. 'To my surprise,' he said, 'the whole room stood up and cheered with great enthusiasm, and it was some time before I could proceed with my lecture.' Later he learned that the mansion that housed the University Club had been built by Jennie's father for his young family, that he had given it to Jennie as her dowry, and that the present lecture hall had once been Leonard Jerome's private theatre. 'Why, Lady Randolph used to act on that very platform!' one of the members said.[26]

The conversation later shifted to the war. They were arguing a point about Kitchener's campaign in the Sudan when Winston said, 'I know I'm right, for I put it in my book.'

He reached for his grip-sack on the rack, and produced his book on Khartoum, from which he immediately quoted, and, I must admit, his view was a very sound one. He went on reading till we were all nearly asleep. Presently I roused to a decided opinion on another point. I was about to clinch it at once by waking Winston, who was by now fast asleep, when his brother said –

'For heavens sake, don't wake him, or we shan't have any rest at all tonight! He's got another volume of that book up in the rack!' [27]

The wounded from Spion Kop were already making their way to the *Maine*, moving along by day in their jolting wagons and lying all night on the hillside. When the first ambulance train arrived near the dock, Jennie and the staff of the *Maine* were ready. The *Central News of Durban* reported: 'Lady Randolph superintended their reception, personally directed berthing, and flitted among the injured as an "angel of mercy".' [28]

Of the typical soldier Jennie said, 'Out of his uniform he is a big child, and wants to be kept in order, and too much spoilt. I am afraid we were inclined to do this!' [29] 'I had long and frequent talks with many of them.'

Jennie also wrote letters for them, and if they paused, finding it difficult to think of anything else to dictate, she would suggest things. ' "Won't you send your love to anyone?" I asked. "Not out of the family," was the answer, with a reproving look. One very gallant Tommy, who lay with a patch over his eye, and inflamed cheek and the broken arm, asked me to add to his letter: "The sister which is a-writing of this is very nice." ' [30]

All the nurses wore simple uniforms consisting of a long white skirt and a short white jacket, a brassard with *Maine* and a Red Cross embossed on it, and a white cap that peaked in the middle. Jennie wore the uniform too, and many of the men called her 'Sister Jennie'.

One of the first wounded officers to arrive carried a note that was to be delivered to Jennie. It was from Chieveley Camp, in Natal, and it began, 'My dearest Mamma'. It was, of course, from Winston. 'It is a coincidence,' he said wryly,

that one of the first patients on board the Maine should be your own son. Jack, who brings you this letter, will tell you all about the skirmish and the other action he took part in. He behaved very well and pluckily and the Adjutant, the Colonel and his squadron leader speak highly of his conduct. There was for ten minutes quite a hot fire. And we had about ten men hit. Jack's wound is slight though not officially classed as such. The doctors tell me that he will take a month to recover and I advise you not to allow him to go back before he is quite well. He is unhappy at being taken off the boards so early in the game and of course it is a great nuisance, but you may be glad with me that he is out of harm's way for a month. There will be a great battle in a few days, and his presence – though I would not lift a finger to prevent him – adds much to my anxiety when there is fighting.[31]

Later Winston would write:

It was a great joy to me to have my brother Jack with me, and I looked forward to showing him round and doing for him the honours of war. This pleasure was, however, soon cut short. On February 12, we made a reconnaissance six or seven miles to the east of the railway line, and occupied for some hours a large, wooded eminence known to the Army as Hussar Hill.

After quitting Hussar Hill and putting at a gallop a mile between us and the enemy, our squadrons reined in into a walk and rode slowly homewards up a long, smooth grass slope. On this occasion, as I looked back over my shoulder . . . I remarked to my companion, 'We are still much too near those fellows.' The words were hardly out of my mouth when a shot rang out, followed by the rattle of magazine fire from two or three hundred Mauser rifles. We leapt off our horses, threw ourselves on the grass, and returned the fire with an answering roar and rattle. Jack was lying by my side. All of a sudden he jumped and wriggled back a yard or two from the line. He had been shot in the calf, in this, his very first skirmish, by a bullet which must have passed uncommonly near his head.[32]

Jack described the conclusion of the incident in a letter to his Aunt Clara:

Thank goodness it had turned out to be nothing, but it hurt a good deal at the time. I mounted again as the squadron continued to retire, but after going about a mile, Winston made me get into an ambulance; and so my military career ended rather abruptly. It was very bad luck being hit the first time I was under fire. But I saw a very good day, and while it lasted, I heard as many bullets whiz past as I ever want to.

I went straight on to the *Maine*, and there I remained until she sailed for the Cape. . . .[33]

Listening to Jack's dramatic account of the fighting only increased Jennie's desire to visit the war zone. She wrote to Winston to this effect, and he answered: '. . . I can easily arrange for you to come to Chieveley – if the fighting stops. . . . '[34]

Winston soon managed a few days' leave and again visited his mother and brother aboard the *Maine*, which was still lying at anchor. Helping Jennie entertain her sons was her new friend and protector, Captain Percy Scott, the Commander of H.M.S. *Terrible*. Captain Scott, whom Winston called 'the greatest swell in Durban', was an inventor as well as a sailor.[35] He had invented, among other things, a gun carriage which enabled the 4.7 naval gun to be taken up country to the front. Captain Scott lavished every courtesy on Winston and Jack. He showed them all the wonders of his armoured cruiser, one of the two largest warships afloat, and displayed the 4.7 gun which he had named *Lady Randolph Churchill* – Jennie fired the test round before the weapon was shipped to the front.

The *Maine* was now almost filled with wounded soldiers. 'We were busy from morn to night. Indeed, one never seemed to have a moment to write or read: the one difficulty on board ship at any time, and more particularly on a hospital ship, is to be alone, and when alone, to be able to concentrate.' [36]

Jennie was particularly bothered by the fact that a number of sick and wounded men sent to the *Maine* from other hospitals arrived still wearing the tattered garments in which they had been taken from the battlefield. She wrote of some wounded being taken aboard the *Maine* from a tug, 'one man wearing only shreds of some khaki trousers, another still with only a pocket handkerchief tied round his wounded leg.' There were many like that, some of whom had already been transferred to several hospitals, always sent out again in the same rags they had worn on arrival.[37]

The medical situation during the Boer War was described in a book by W. L. Burdett-Coutts as 'hopelessly insufficient'. He told of patients 'dying like flies for want of attention. . . . Three doctors for 300 patients, and no nurses, few trained orderlies. . . . Not enough beds, stretchers on the ground. . . . Delirious patients wandering in the wards at night. . . . The hospital death rate almost 8% . . . and at one hospital, a 21% death rate. . . . Robberies by orderlies. . . .' [38]

Jennie wanted to visit the front and see conditions in the hospitals at first hand. With the backing of Captain Scott, she got permission to go to Chieveley Camp, along with Eleanor Warrender and Colonel Hensman. Scott had planned to escort them, but emergency duty delayed him at the last moment and he sent his coxswain instead.

Jennie described the trip: 'The train was full of officers and men returning to the front. Although we were travelling at night, I was kept awake by the thought that I was going to pass those well-known, and, to me, peculiarly interesting places. . . .'

In the middle of the night, the train was searched for spies.

Every pass was then minutely examined, every face scanned, and I saw with keen interest two individuals dragged out of the next compartment. . . . Both were marched off – to what fate, one wonders!

I was asleep when we reached Frere at five a.m. A vigorous tap on the window awoke me. 'Lady Randolph Churchill, are you there?' 'Yes, very much so,' I answered, as I dropped the shutter and put my head out, finding an officer of the Seaforth Highlanders on the platform. 'I knew you were coming up, and thought you would like a cup of coffee,' he said – 'If you will accept the hospitality of my tin hut, 50 yards from here; you won't get anything more for a long time.' In my eagerness, I was proceeding to jump down, when he remarked that I had no shoes on, and, with a glance at my dishevelled locks, suggested a hat. As I walked to the hut, dawn was just breaking. A long orange-red streak outlined the distant brown hills; through the haze of dust showing on the skyline, trains of mule-carts were crawling along, and in the plain, little groups of soldiers and horsemen were moving about, emerging from every tent. My host seated me on a stool in the tiny verandah, and gave me an excellent cup of coffee. He was so delighted to have someone to speak to that the words and questions came tumbling out, waiting for no answers. In one breath, he told me how he had been there for months, broiling with heaps of uncongenial work to do, all responsibilities and anxiety, and no excitement or danger. He lived in daily hopes of getting some fighting. Meanwhile, 'Someone has to do the dirty work, and there it is.' [39]

When the train was underway again, a guard rushed to tell Jennie that they were passing the place of the armoured-train disaster where Winston had been taken prisoner. The train was still lying on its side, a mangled and battered wreck. A few yards away was a grave with a cross.

Finally, they reached the camp at Chieveley and Jennie observed the weather-beaten and in many cases haggard men, with soiled, worn uniforms hanging on their spare figures; the horses, picketed in lines or singly covered with canvas torn in strips to keep off the buzzing, plaguing flies; the khaki-painted guns; the ambulance-wagons with their trains of mules; and above all, the dull booming of 'Long Tom'. . . . She also saw the gun that Captain Scott had named after her, and the gun crew gave her an empty cartridge case as a souvenir.

Having briefly borrowed the General's tent, Jennie was scribbling a note to her sons when a rider galloped up, calling out in a cheery voice: 'General! Are you there?' 'His look of blank astonishment when he caught sight of me was most amusing. A woman in the camp, and in the General's tent! I explained, and after a few laughing remarks, he rode off.' [40]

Jennie spent some of her time in visiting an area where two thousand horses were resting before being sent to the front. Hundreds of them had just arrived from South America. Jennie, who loved horses, could not help visualizing the trip they had endured: penned up for days on a rolling ship, then crammed into an open truck under a blazing sun, to be taken out, stiff, sore, and dazed. With two days' rest, they were to be sent up to the front, only to be fodder for Boer bullets.

When Jennie returned to the hospital ship, the soldiers wanted to know what she had learned of the war. 'Any news?' 'Ladysmith? – Nothing?' 'What, back again at Chieveley Camp? That Buller, he's unlucky.' In one of the wards, she hung a large framed map with flag pins that represented the military situation. But every day a few more Boer flags were found stuck in the frame, their places taken by Union Jacks. Whenever there was a victory, 'a grand cheer went up from the men; lights were flashed, messages heliographed from Captain Percy Scott's electric shutter on board the *Terrible* to all ships in the harbour, the band played itself out, the men sang themselves hoarse, and at last, after a bouquet of fireworks, we went to bed.'

Jennie was dining with Captain Scott aboard the *Terrible* on March 29 when news came of the relief of Ladysmith.[41] The city of Durban 'went mad'. Jennie described the demonstration at which the cheering was so continuous that none of the speakers could be heard. In London, crowds massed in the streets and sang 'Soldiers of the Queen', strangers embraced each other, poured water on each other, drank toasts together, and fireworks went off everywhere.[42] Robert Browning's lines were fitting:

> How bad and sad and mad it was,
> But, Lord! how it was sweet!

The time had come for the *Maine* to take its patients to England.

While the ship was being prepared for the voyage, Jennie, Winston and a Captain Thorp, who was one of her discharged patients, went to Ladysmith on a special pass from General Buller. They saw the carcasses of horses, the masses of spent shells, the newly made graves. At one point, they crossed a small sandbagged bridge over which British soldiers had run single-file under a barrage of fire from three hills. The dust of the battle area was up to their ankles, the sun was scorching, misery and desolation were everywhere. On their way into the town, they got a ride atop a pile of haversacks on a Scottish mule cart. Jennie thought they made a strange sight 'but no one noticed us'. The faces of the townspeople were 'empty and resigned'.[43]

Jennie borrowed a wild horse which had never before been in harness and she rode with Winston and Thorp to the camp of the South African Light Horse Brigade 'where we had some tea out of bottles and tin mugs. By this time, I was too tired to take in any more, and the hazardous drive back in the semi-darkness quite finished me.'[44] The next day she returned to the *Maine* on a Red Cross train filled with wounded men.

She had come a long way from savouring the strawberries in the garden of the Mount Nelson Hotel. She had seen war as it was: the mangled bodies, the eyes of despair, the unmitigated desolation.

George now seemed remote from her, their love affair was part of another world. She had written to him, but she had little time to yearn for him. But on her return to the ship, she found a letter from George awaiting her. He had written from his father's home:

I have just received your wire, re-directed – saying you are going to remain at Durban a month – I thought and hoped that, once you had arrived at Durban and got things started on board the *Maine*, you would think of returning. . . . I am alone with my father, who never misses an opportunity of dropping hints about financial difficulties, and how easily they could be overcome if I married an heiress. . . .[45]

Such a letter might have worried her more at another time, but now the *Maine* was ready to set sail from Durban and Jennie would soon be back in England. The other crews in the harbour cheered them as they moved out to sea. In a column as dispassionate as could be expected, war correspondent Winston Churchill reported:

The Maine left yesterday for Cape Town with 12 officers and 175 soldiers, mostly serious cases.

During the two months the ship has been at Durban, more than 300 cases have been treated, and many difficult operations have been performed successfully.

Lady Randolph Churchill has been untiring in her attention to the management, and I impartially think that her influence has been of real value to all on board. . . .' [46]

From the ship, Jennie wrote to her 'Darling boys', telling them she was anxious to get the war news so that she could figure out, even indirectly 'where you two boys are'. 'One more week, and then home,' she added. 'I shall find all my work cut out for me there.' [47]

When the *Maine* arrived at Cape Town, Jennie learned to her dismay that there were orders for the ship to unload the wounded and wait for other patients.[48] Aboard ship the wounded men, filling every berth and still dreaming of home, were thrown into despair by the news. Jennie hurried ashore, found the Medical Officer, and declared that it was her intention that the *Maine* would leave at daybreak the next morning, as previously arranged, 'and that I was cabling to the Minister of War to back me up. . . .' [49]

That evening, the Marquess of Lansdowne did back her up, and at daybreak the *Maine* sailed for home.

The weather was perfect, and the men who were well enough sat on deck. They talked about their hopes and their plans, they sang, and sometimes Jennie sang with them. These men had become a part of her life. She had written to the Prince of Wales: 'I am satisfied with the Mission the *Maine* has fulfilled – & if I may say so my connection with it. It has been hard work & sometimes the temptation has been great to fly off in a mail steamer for home – but I am glad I resisted. . . .' [50]

It had been four months and a day since the *Maine* left England. Jennie had been depressed then. Now as the ship docked at Southampton, she stood on deck radiant in a white straw hat with a blue ribbon on which were embossed the British and American flags. On her blue serge dress, she wore the *Maine* badge over the left breast, and on her red cravat was a Red Cross pin.[51]

As her friends crowded aboard ship, they told her how wonderfully healthy she looked, at least fifteen years younger. Someone gave her a large bouquet of roses.

And then she saw George.

16

Colonel Cornwallis-West had discovered a telegram Leonie had sent to George informing him of the time of Jennie's arrival in Southampton. The Colonel bitterly accused Leonie of assisting Jennie 'in her insane infatuation for my son.'[1]

The Colonel was wrong if he thought Jennie was simply infatuated with George; she loved him. Yet she had been changed by the war and was no longer certain what she wanted. She was, after all, what some thought of as 'an older woman'. The Empress Eugénie, whom Jennie loved, had said that a woman over forty 'begins to dissolve, loses colour, grows dark like a cloud.' And Emilie du Châtelet, mistress of Voltaire, had written in her 'Treatise on Happiness' that the older woman has only three pleasures left: gambling, study, and gourmandizing at the dinner table.[2]

Jennie's life, however, contradicted both of them. At forty-six she was in her prime. She had kept pace with the world in a rather remarkable way. Those who were envious often accused her of having 'a man's mind'. How else, they said, could she have so successfully invaded the private preserves of Power? First, politics; then, publishing; and now, war.

Her political power had been exercised indirectly, manœuvring and campaigning for her husband and then her son. Her publishing power was a real literary force. But her successful organization of the *Maine* represented a maximum of administrative efficiency and dedicated purpose. Never had she felt more effective, more vital.

'I hate leaving the ship,' she wrote to Winston. 'People are gradually understanding the work I have done, and in any case, I have my own consciousness of something accomplished. . . . The H.R.H. and everyone seems to take it for granted that I am not going again and that I shall have done enough.'[3] But she herself felt that she had not done enough, and she talked of going back to the *Maine*. As late as May 26, she told Winston, 'I shall probably go out on the third voyage.'

This resolve naturally made a difference in her personal relations, and her new attitude about marriage to George was reflected in a letter to Winston: '. . . There are so many things against my doing it — that I doubt it's ever coming off. . . .'[4]

George was even more changed than Jennie. He had returned from the war to recuperate at his father's home. His family combined pampering their only son with steady and less than subtle pressure. They maligned the marriage he hoped to make as 'ill-assorted' and 'doomed'. The Colonel had let it be known that 'if this marriage takes place it will estrange the whole of my family from my son and so I have told him.'[5] George particularly resented the continuous inference that if only he would choose a young heiress, he could replenish the family fortune. His father pointedly stressed their need for money to restore Ruthin Castle and to keep alive the heritage of the Cornwallis-Wests.

None of this impressed George. He was no longer the callow, impressionable young man, 'the spoiled darling'. The father he had admired now disappointed him, and he had never liked his mother, who had given her love to many men, but seldom to her son. (In fact, so strong was his hostility towards his mother that he insisted that he did not want to be buried near her.) He was close to his two sisters, but at this time he was confiding in almost no one.

George's growing maturity was largely the product of his brief but vivid contact with war. He had come home depressed about the carnage on the battlefield, which had only been emphasized for him by the ghastly work of burying the dead after they had lain for some time under a blazing sun. 'A magnificent specimen of an old Dutchman, lying dead, with a look of marvellous calm upon his face, very like Rembrandt's picture of Joseph Trip in the National Gallery. For the first time, it struck me that we were fighting against men of a splendid type, whose sole idea was to protect their own country from invasion.'[6]

The change in Jennie did not mean that she no longer cared for George, although her ardour had been tempered by the companionship of the brave, dashing, brilliant Captain Percy Scott of H.M.S. *Terrible*. Captain Scott had offered the wisdom of a more mature man, and Jennie had that contrast to consider, too. But her love for George had lasted for more than a year, and it was not a relationship she could easily dismiss. Cooled passions can start smouldering again, and romance was an art George knew.

George had recovered sufficiently to be sent to Pirbright as a musketry instructor for recruits and reservists. While there he stayed with Consuelo, Duchess of Manchester, who had taken a house near Windsor that year. Consuelo was one of those friends on whom Jennie could always depend for love and laughter. The other Consuelo, the young Duchess of Marlborough, had written that Jennie had a fund of *risqué* stories which she told with a twinkle in her eye. Most of these had first been told to Jennie by the older Consuelo.

The Duchess of Manchester had been born Consuelo Iznaga. Her father was Cuban and her mother American. Before moving to England, they had lived on a Louisiana cotton plantation and in New York. Consuelo's husband, the Duke of Manchester, had died in 1892. Besides her husband's estate, she had inherited her brother's property valued at over two million dollars, which she generously shared with her sisters.[7]

Consuelo had a graceful figure, golden hair, large dark eyes, and an angelic expression. Yet she was the kind of woman who, while riding in a carriage to a Court Ball, decided that her stays were too tight and that she was going to remove her corset. And so she did, twisting and wrenching it out over her breast, much to the astonishment of her escort.

She was probably also the 'American Duchess' who upon returning from Ireland was asked whether she had seen the Blarney Stone. 'Yes, certainly I have,' the Duchess replied.

'Well,' the man said with a smile, 'they do say that the virtues of the Blarney Stone can be conveyed to another by a kiss.'

'I guess that may be,' she answered, 'but I don't know anything about it, because I sat on it.'

Jennie, of course, was also at Consuelo's house near Windsor for weekends when George was there. George used to 'hack a pony over every morning so as to arrive at Pirbright in time for parade' and then return in the afternoon.[8]

Many years later, Jennie wrote:

If people sufficiently prominent for one reason or another succeed in surrounding themselves with an atmosphere of mystery, the interest of the public is aroused. . . . There are men and women we well know who can, through their personality, live down scandals, whereas the less-favoured go under, emphasizing the old saying that, 'One may steal a horse while another may not look over the wall.'[9]

Jennie was certainly one of those people who aroused 'the interest of the public'. Reporting on the on-again, off-again marriage rumours, *The New York Times* stated, 'Mr Cornwallis-West's family . . . have cut Lady Randolph Churchill dead. . . .'

Other press reports indicated the wide variety of rumour:

The engagement of Lady Randolph Churchill and young Cornwallis-West is absolutely broken. They have both promised to give up the idea of ever becoming man and wife. . . .

The engagement . . . has been reported so many times and contradicted so often, that people are inclined to believe that the interesting rumour – probably on account of its vitality – has a good deal of truth in it. . . .[10]

Dr Samuel Johnson had said: 'I believe marriages would in general be as happy, and probably more so, if they were all made by the Lord Chancellor, upon a due consideration of characters and circumstances, without the parties having any choice in the matter.'[11] It is not difficult to predict what the Lord Chancellor would have said about Jennie and George.

Jennie truly did not know what she wanted. Her letters were full of indecision, questions, and longings. Complicating matters for her were additional problems: her two sons were still in combat in South Africa and she knew more intimately now what a bullet or shell could do to a human body; her sister Leonie was expecting another baby soon, 'and as she had not had one for 11 years, it is always rather bad. . . . She is counting on me . . .';[12] and the *Anglo-Saxon Review* needed Jennie's complete attention to save it from a premature death. She had obtained financial support for only the first year, and now she had to find more funds.

Jennie sent George a note apologizing for being 'snappy and tired', but she had good reason to be. Her irritating relationship with John Lane was becoming more turbulent. Earlier, she had complained to Lane about a new prospectus which he had issued

without telling me anything about it – and that my name figures in it in such microscopic type, I wonder you put it on at all! Considering that I am the proprietor and the editor, and you merely the publisher, it is rather audacious – I must say I am exceedingly surprised at the line you are taking, and considering the circumstances of the case, my patience is very nearly exhausted. . . . Also, Mr Thompson is to see that all sums to the credit of the *Anglo-Saxon Review* . . . at the office are to be paid over to the Second National Bank as agreed upon between you and Mr Thompson. I really cannot see how we are to get on if you are to go back on your word like this and not to be counted on. . . .[13]

Lane had answered: '. . . I really don't know what "line" it is that surprised you, or what I am doing to exhaust your patience. . . .'[14] He then went into great detail about the new prospectuses and the quality of his sales force in both America and England.

Jennie was angered because she felt he was printing too many copies of the *Review*, not notifying subscribers about renewals, and not informing booksellers that back issues were available. She was also curt in her comment on some articles he suggested: 'I do not like them.'

Sales of the early issues had been below expectations, particularly in America. The interest there seemed to have been more snobbish than literary. Perhaps if there had been no Boer War and no relationship with George, Jennie would have gone to the United States on a promotion tour for 'Maggie'. A survey of publications of the time, however, indicates that this kind of magazine was generally short-lived and seldom a viable proposition. Such people as Ernest Cassel and Bourke Cockran had invested in the *Review* with no great expectations of profit. They had put in their money more as a personal matter than a financial one, and even Jennie knew the limit of their responses.

Jennie's sub-editors had ably carried on in her absence, particularly Sidney Low. Low had sent an issue of the *Review* to the editor of the popular magazine *Sphere*: 'I hope you may find time to cast a glance at it. I am interested in the magazine. I look after it during Lady Randolph's absence. . . .'[15] But neither Low nor any of the other editors had Jennie's persuasive powers for getting contributions from well-known authors and celebrities. When Jennie set herself on an assignment, few could refuse her. One potential contributor who had failed to come through was her son Winston, but he was most apologetic: 'I have never had a moment either to write your *Anglo-Saxon* article, nor to write the three American articles for which I was offered £300.'[16]

Winston had no qualms, however, about making more demands on his mother.

I have very nearly made up my mind to stand again for Oldham. They have implored me not to desert them.

Mind you send me all the reviews on my new book on this war, and I do hope you will realize the importance of making the very best terms you can for me, both as a writer and lecturer.[17]

I do hope you will have been able to arrange good terms for me to lecture in the United States, probably during December, January and February, and we can consider the desirability of my undertaking to lecture in England during the autumn when I come home. . . .[18]

'I am doing all the things you want', she had written. She had seen his publisher, Longman, to complete financial arrangements for his new book; she had checked into the American lecture bureau of Major Pond and found it highly reputable. ('I believe he *is* the man.') She was also sending him a fat collection of reviews of his book. ('I trust they will satisfy your greed.') [19]

She continued to tell him that '. . . Pamela spoke to me about your idea of a play, but I discourage it. Honestly, it would not do. People would not stand any war play. . . . It would be thought bad taste. Even a year after the Civil War, nothing could be given at that time, of that kind. . . . You will find plenty to write about without it. . . .' [20] Jennie convinced him.

Then, in a reminiscent mood, Winston wrote to Leonie:

I have had many adventures, and I shall be glad of a little peace and security. I have been under fire now in 40 separate affairs in this country alone, and one cannot help wondering how long good luck will hold. But I stand the wear and tear pretty well. Indeed, my health, nerve and spirits were never better than now, at the end of seven months of war. I saw Jack for a day in Cape Town, on his way to Beira. He will have a very interesting position on Carrington's staff, and should not, under ordinary circumstances, run into much danger. Don't worry. . . .[21]

Jennie, meanwhile, was worrying about Jack.

Of course, I have been following Buller's advance, and have had some bad moments, thinking of you, but have trusted you for the best, and think you capable of looking after your skin as well as most. I am glad to think that the end is approaching, and that the war must soon be over now. I am also glad that you are moving, anything is better than stagnation in an unhealthy camp. How fit you must be, as riding suits you, I know. I am much more frightened of fever than of bullets, so don't be rash as regards water, etc. I have a long letter from Winston today, from Bloemfontein, dated March 1st. He seems to have had a narrow escape at Dewetsdorp, from falling into Boers' hands, as an advance party met the enemy. Winston's saddle turned and I understand his horse galloped away, but luckily, his own people turned back for him. He did not give me this account himself. I suppose I shall see it in the papers. Meanwhile, Pamela had heard it from someone and told me. I am sure that you, like him, are heartily sick of the whole thing. Everyone is; and all longing for peace and home.[22]

Jennie was careful not to mention George in her letter to Jack. She knew that both of her sons were unhappy about the possibility of her marrying, but that Jack was particularly sensitive to it. Winston had a carefully patterned future and a romantic interest in Pamela, and though he still needed his mother for important things, Jack needed her for nearly everything. He had had no career until his mother mapped one out for him. Jack's initiation into war was the only thing he could call his own, and even that was, at least in part, a way of competing with his brother. He was a young man in search of an anchor and a frame of life.

The war in South Africa was still raging, but in May Mafeking was relieved. For 216 days the small British garrison there had held out. Lord Roberts had promised to end the Boers' siege by May 18, and on that date the Lord Mayor of London proclaimed that the siege had been lifted.

Mafeking had become the British symbol of stubborn courage. When the Boers first surrounded the garrison and asked the Commanding Officer to surrender to avoid bloodshed, his answer was: 'When does the bloodshed begin?' Now London went wild. Men draped themselves with the large posters announcing the news. Performers stopped their shows to sing the national anthem. People spontaneously formed pro-

214

cessions and marched through the city in every direction. Strangers hugged and kissed each other. The fears and tensions of war were momentarily overcome by joy.[23]

But Jennie's personal life was still in turmoil. Her inner debate about marrying George was revealed in a letter to Winston:

... added to the reasons in favour of it, is his extraordinary devotion to me through all these trying times, and my absence – Also, the fact that it is possible for him to help me in a money way in the future, if not at present. There is no doubt that you will never settle down until you have a home of your own, and in the four years that I have had this house, you have spent about 3 months in all in it – I mention this to show you why I do not feel that I would be breaking up our home if I should marry.

... You know what you are to me, and how you can *now* and *always* count on me – I am intensely proud of you, and apart from this, my heart goes out to you and understands you as no other woman ever will – Pamela is devoted to you, and if your love has grown as hers – I have no doubt that it's only a question of time for you to marry – What a comfort it will be to you, to settle down in comparative comfort – I am sure you are sick of the war and its horrors – You will be able to make a decent living out of your writing, and your political career will lead you to big things – Probably, if you married an heiress, you would not work half so well – but you may have a chance in America – tho I do not urge you to try – You know I am not mercenary, either for myself or you boys – More's the pity![24]

Finally the question was resolved. The persistent and loving George at last persuaded Jennie to let him announce their engagement.

The Prince of Wales had talked to Jennie at length about the subject and she was quoted as saying that 'she knew her own mind a great deal better than the Prince'. He also expressed his views in a letter which she angrily tore up and answered in blistering terms. The Prince responded, almost sadly:

It has been my privilege to enjoy your friendship for upwards of a quarter of a century – therefore, why do you think it necessary to write me a rude letter – simply because I have expressed my regret at the marriage you are about to make? I have said nothing behind your back that I have not said to your face – You know the world so well that I presume you are the best judge of your own happiness – but at the same time, you should think twice before you abuse your friends and well-wishers for not congratulating you on the serious step you are going to make! I can only hope that we shall all be mistaken.[25]

George, too, was still under pressure:

On the Thursday morning of that week my engagement was announced in the *Daily Telegraph*, and I received a peremptory order from the officer commanding my battalion, Colonel Dalrymple Hamilton, to go up and see him. He told me at the interview that if I married Lady Randolph, I should have to leave the regiment. Considering that she had a host of friends, including himself, and was liked by everybody, and that there was no rule in the regiment against subalterns marrying, I considered such an ultimatum outrageous and saw red. If I had had any doubts as to the wisdom of what I was about to do, they were blown to the four winds by what I considered nothing less than a piece of unwarrantable interference, and it made me obstinate. I dashed off in a hansom to the War Office and sent in my name to the Adjutant-General, who was then Sir Evelyn Wood, whom I just knew. A few minutes later, I caught him going out of his office, and he said: 'I've no time at the moment unless you can go with me in a cab to where I am lunching, and tell me what I can do for you.'

On our way down Piccadilly, I told him what had happened, and asked whether it was in accordance with Queen's Regulations that an officer should be told to leave his regiment because he wished to marry a woman admittedly older than himself, but of whom nothing else could be said except in her favour. Sir Evelyn reassured me, and promised to do what he could to help me.[26]

Shortly afterwards George was ordered to report to the regimental orderly room, to see Colonel Fludyer, who commanded the regiment.

[Fludyer] poured out the vials of his wrath upon me for having dared to go to a man whom he described as 'the enemy of the Brigade of Guards'. Why, heaven knows! He made it quite clear to me that my presence in the regiment would no longer be desired or expected. I felt more angry than ever, and after consultation with Jennie, wrote to the Prince of Wales, asking if I might have an interview. When I saw him and told him all about it, he came to the point at once: 'Is it your intention to make soldiering your profession for the rest of your life?' he said. 'If it is, then I advise you to sit tight. If, however, it is not, why make enemies of men who have been your friends and who probably will continue to be your friends after all this has blown over? My advice to you is to go on half-pay for six months or a year, look around and see if you can find something else to do, and then make up your mind at the expiration of the time.' [27]

Jennie would not simply wait quietly. She had made her choice. This was the man she wanted. For her, that meant that she would fight for him in every way she could. She went directly to the Secretary of State for War, the Marquess of Lansdowne, and later that day Lansdowne advised her:

I have spoken to the Commander in Chief, who was very sympathetic.

It is clear that Mr West could not be required to leave the regiment except by the military authorities, with the concurrence of the Commander in Chief. Until, therefore, an attempt has actually been made to bring about his removal, you can afford to disregard vague threats such as those which you mentioned to me this morning.

I would venture to urge you strongly to adopt this line, and not to gratify the busybodies by taking serious notice of the incident which you described to me.

May I as an old friend tell you how sincerely I wish you all possible happiness. . . . [28]

George followed the Prince's advice and applied for half-pay duty, determined to seek another way to make a living.

Now Jennie's main concern was to reconcile her sons to the marriage. 'It is rather hard on me not to have a word from either of you boys,' she wrote to Jack.[29] Winston accepted the situation, but apparently without enthusiasm. He had long ago said he would quit the war only after Pretoria had been retaken. That having been accomplished, he now agreed to come home for his mother's wedding. She accordingly arranged for the wedding to coincide with his return at the end of July.

Next she had to persuade Jack to come home, too: 'I hope this will find you with your face more or less turned towards home. I dined with Cassel last night, and he said that he thought that now that the war was almost over, you had done your duty by your country, and that you ought to come home and attend to your business.' [30]

Jennie asked Winston to try to influence Jack, and Winston urged him: 'Please telegraph Mamma what you propose to do. It is all very well being consistently loyal to the South African Light Horse, but at the same time, when the war becomes merely an affair of guerillas, I think you would do much better to come home to the quills of the city and the arms of the ladies'.[31] Jack answered: 'I envy you going home, and was much tempted when I received your wire to "chuck" the regiment and catch you at Cape Town. However, although I am very sick of all this here, I should feel unhappy if I were home before it is over. The quills of the city can I think wait a little while and so can the arms of the ladies. . . .'[32]

It was natural for Jennie to want Jack to attend her wedding, but she also wanted him home so that she could try to reconcile him to the marriage. But Jack was resistant, and his worst fears may have been realized when he received her letter of June 23:

Now listen, darling boy, I have thought over everything and have come to the conclusion that, for many reasons, it would be unwise for either you or Winston to live with us, once we are married. Knowing how fond I am of you both, you will believe that I have not come to this conclusion hastily. It seems hard, and it gives me a pang every time I think of it, but I know it is the nicest plan. I should like you and Winston to have rooms together, which I would furnish for you, and arrange, and your life, as far as your material comfort goes, to the best of my ability. I need hardly say you will always be more than welcome here. You can both look upon it as your home for everything but sleeping. George is helping me in every way possible, to make my income larger by putting my affairs straight. As I wrote to Winston, I hope to make you both independent of me by giving you a certain amount of capital. Of course, this would have to be worked out when you come of age, next year. Meanwhile, if all goes well, George and I propose geting married very quietly (but not at the Registry Office) on the 28th of July. Have many things to settle and arrange – I shall go to Paris and then to Aix, and after that, here. God bless you,

my darling boy. . . . You must stand by me. I have, & will, always
stand by you. . . .

Your loving mother.[33]

Jennie must have recognized that her words had been neither very
motherly nor very tactful, as she wrote again in a different tone a week
later:

My darling Jack:

Surely, darling boy, you would not stay out much longer? You
will find Cassel ready to receive you – and your 'Mommer' with open
arms. Winston will be here in time for my wedding, if all goes well –
It will be very quiet – No breakfast – except for the family. But I
won't do it in a 'hole-and-corner' fashion, as if I was ashamed of it.
I pray from the bottom of my heart that it would not make you unhappy. You know how dearly I love you both, and the thought that it
may hurt you is the one cloud on my happiness. But you won't grudge
me the latter? Nothing could exceed George's goodness and devotion,
and I think we shall be very happy. Everything I can do for you, I
will. Meanwhile, my real friends are most kind, and have given me
charming presents; and they all like him so much that they are
reconciled. . . .[34]

Then, on the very day of her marriage, she again wrote to Jack:

I am more than distressed to think that my letters, with the exception
of one, have not reached you. You must know that your 'Mommer'
would not forget you. I wired you and Winston that I was going to
marry George, and here am I, actually at the day. I would give much
if you were here and could give me a big fat kiss. I could assure you
with my own lips what you already know, and that is that I love you
and Winston dearly, and that *no one* can ever come in between us. I
shall always remain yours, your best friend, and do everything in
the world for you. You both can count on me. I am glad to think you
know & like George. He has behaved like a brick. By the next
mail, I shall write and tell you all about the wedding. Sunny [her
nephew, the Duke of Marlborough] is giving me away; and I am well
supported by the Churchill family. People here have been most
kind. . . . I want you to come home as soon as you decently can. Both

Winston and I hate to have you away. I have all sorts of plans for you, and I want to make your life as pleasant as possible. God bless you, *my darling boy.* . . .[35]

The New York Times carried a detailed account of the wedding:

LADY RANDOLPH
WEDS LIEUT. WEST
Many Notables Attend the Nuptials
in London
QUIET WEDDING BREAKFAST
Marlborough Gives the Bride Away —
Many Rich and Handsome Gifts
Received.

LONDON, July 28. — Lady Randolph Churchill (neé Jerome) was today married to Lieut. George Cornwallis-West at St Paul's Church, Knightsbridge. The church was thronged with handsomely dressed women. There was no restriction upon the number admitted to the church to witness the ceremony, but only relatives and intimate friends were bidden to the subsequent wedding breakfast, and no reception was held.

The usually quiet neighborhood of Wilton Place, where St Paul's Church is located, was this morning early astir with excitement. Before 9 o'clock crowds had collected outside the church gates. The scenes which ensued gave some idea of the interest or curiosity the public took in the wedding. By 10.15 o'clock the crowds had swelled to large proportions. The late opening of the church doors caused great inconvenience to early guests. When the gates were opened, a rush was made to enter the church. It was only with the aid of policemen that they were in any way controlled.

The Duke of Marlborough, who gave the bride away, arrived in Summerlike attire — a gray suit and blue shirt — and wore a crimson flower in his buttonhole. Directly after he had performed his official duties, he took a seat near his young American wife, who was one of the first to arrive. She was dressed in pale gray, with a fashionable bolero, a waist belt of two shades of rose color, and a small black toque. The next most interesting guests were Lady Georgiana Curzon, Lady Sarah Wilson, and Winston Churchill, a son of the bride.

Lady Randolph's attire was quite up to date, and she looked as if just arrived from Paris, instead of the South African veldt. Lady Tweedmouth, another sister-in-law of Lady Randolph's was present. Lady Blandford, mother of the Duke of Marlborough, brought Lady Norah Churchill. Mrs Jack Leslie, sister of the bride, whose child was christened yesterday, arrived with Lady Randolph. Mrs Moreton Frewen, another of the bride's sisters, was attired in a soft black and white gown, with hat to match. She brought her little girl, while Moreton Frewen acted as usher.

A great many Americans were present, among others, Ambassador Choate and several attachés of the Embassy. Mme von André, in white muslin and a black and white hat, sat near the front of the church. Mrs Dudley Leigh wore a pink and white Liberty satin gown and a white hat, wreathed with roses. Mrs Arthur Paget came dressed in a pretty black and white muslin gown, carrying pink roses. Mrs Ronalds wore a mauve and white muslin dress and a toque of rose leaves. She was accompanied by Mrs Blow, who had on a gown of pale pink and white. Mrs Adair wore dark gray, a white tulle boa, and a pale-blue toque, with pink malmaisons.

Among other important people present were M. de Soveral, Lord and Lady Londonderry, Lady de Grey, Lady Granby, Lady de Trafford, Count Albert Menadorff, Baron and Baroness Eckhardstein, Lady Limerick, and Mrs Willie Grenfell.

The arrival of Lady Randolph Churchill with the Duke of Marlborough was the signal for a general rush of enthusiasts outside the church, all eager to catch a glimpse of the bride as she walked slowly up the path. There was some little delay at the church door, and the Duke, who was carrying a large umbrella, handed it, with great ceremony, to a friend, before proceeding to give his arm to Lady Randolph. His Grace was very serious, almost severe, as was Lady Randolph, as they walked up the aisle. The bride was wonderfully handsome and young-looking in a gown of pale blue chiffon, with real lace and ostrich feathers in her toque.

The register was signed by Mrs Moreton Frewen, the Duke of Marlborough, Winston Churchill, and the best man, Lieut. H. C. Elwes, a brother officer of Lieut. West in the Scots Guards. Directly they entered the vestry Winston Churchill gave his mother a tremendous hug and then spoke to Lieut. West. Afterward, as they came down the aisle, Lady Randolph looked radiant, as did the young bridegroom, who was smiling and nodding to friends.

After the ceremony, the wedding party repaired to the residence of the bride's sister, Mrs Moreton Frewen, where the wedding breakfast was served to fifteen people, at six small tables decorated with roses. Mr Frewen proposed the bride's health, and the bridegroom in responding, said:

'Jennie's friends are my friends. I thank you all from the bottom of my heart and the bottom of Jennie's heart for all of your good wishes.'

After the breakfast the bride and bridegroom started for Broughton Castle, which Lady A. G. Lennox had placed at their disposal for the honeymoon.

Lady Randolph's going-away dress was a pale blue batiste. Lieut. West was attired in a flannel suit. Showers of rice were thrown after the couple as they departed. The Prince of Wales called on Lady Randolph Churchill yesterday and bade her good-bye. He also sent a present.

Among the presents received by Lady Randolph was an exquisite pearl and diamond tiara, the joint gift of A. J. Balfour, the Duke and Duchess of Devonshire, Lord and Lady Londonderry, the Marquis and Marchioness of Lansdowne, Lily, Dowager Duchess of Malborough, Lady Georgiana Curzon, Henry White, Mrs Arthur Paget, Mrs George Cavendish-Bentinck, the Countess of Crewe and Essex, and many others. Another gift was a splendid jug of beaten silver and two massive tankards from the officers of the Scots Guards, comrades of the bridegroom. Lieut. West's gift was a beautiful pearl and diamond necklace. Sir Ernest Cassel gave a pearl and diamond aigrette. There was a great deal of plate and some handsome gold boxes.[36]

It was a lovely wedding, and even the weather had turned fine. The day before, it had been stormy, but on Saturday the sun came out.[37]

Lady Dorothy Nevill, who had recently contributed an article for Jennie's *Review*, also contributed an acrid comment on the marriage. Strolling among the children in Hyde Park, the distinguished seventy-year-old matriarch of London Society was asked what she was doing there. 'Well,' she answered, 'if you want to know, my dear, I am searching in the perambulators for *my* future husband.'[38]

A newspaper account of the wedding described George as 'a fair young man, rather like his sister, Princess Pless. He is very good at lawn tennis.'

Daisy, the Princess of Pless, was not exactly forthright in her comment on the occasion: 'In spite of the disparity in their ages,' she said, 'we were all pleased with the marriage, and hoped it would bring about lasting happiness to them both.' [39] Not a single member of the Cornwallis-West family was present at the wedding. Colonel and Mrs Cornwallis-West left for Ireland the day before.

Winston described the wedding to his brother:

Mama was married to George West on Saturday, and everything went off very well. The whole of the Churchill family, from Sunny downwards, was drawn in a solid phalanx, and their approval ratified the business. The wedding was very pretty, and George looked supremely happy at having at length obtained his heart's desire. As we already know each other's views on the subject, I need not pursue it. [40]

Despite the disapprovals and the open criticism, Jennie's mail was full of messages from well-wishers in all parts of the world. There was one card, however, that must have made her tremble as she opened it. It was from the Chancellor of the Austro-Hungarian Embassy in St Petersburg. The card had a black border, and on it was the simple inscription in French: 'Toujours en deuil' (Always in mourning).

It was from Count Charles Kinsky. Theirs had been the kind of love that not even the happiest marriage would obliterate. It had been a chapter in Jennie's life that she had closed but could never end.

17

Broughton Castle,
Banbury

My dear Winston,

   . . . This is an ideal place for any couple to come to, honey-moon or otherwise, we are most comfortable, the best of food, drink and everything, besides a most delightful old, rambling, weatherbeaten, stone-roofed house of the 14th century.

My dear Winston, I cannot impress upon you how much I appreciate the line you have taken as regards my marriage to your mother. I have always liked and admired you, but I do so ten times more now. I only wish, as I wrote and told my father, that my family could have taken a leaf out of your book. Nothing could have exceeded the sympathy and kindness which you, and all the Churchills have shown me. I hope always, as now, to be a real true friend to you, and never to come in between yourself and your mother. If I ever do, which God forbid, you can always refer me to this letter, which is a record of the feelings I have in the bottom of my heart towards you and yours. We arrive tomorrow at 2.15. Will you order lunch for three unless you have another coming. *A demain*, my dear friend.

Always *your sincere friend*,
George C-W.[1]

As much as anything else, Jennie and George wanted acceptance of their marriage. Although they did not expect it from the Cornwallis-West family for some time, they did hope to get at least grudging approval from Winston and Jack. George's letter to Winston was a preliminary.

As time passed, George would realize more and more the varied facets of his wife's personality. Even on their honeymoon Jennie's zealous mind never stopped working. George later smilingly told Shane Leslie that Jennie had brought along hampers of correspondence and articles for the *Anglo-Saxon Review*. She even brought a pile of unpaid bills, explaining to George the need to be 'business-like'.

'Of course, I was eager to put her affairs in order,' George said, 'but I found it a bit thick when I was expected to pay for Lord Randolph Churchill's barouche, purchased in the 8o's.' [2]

All her life Jennie complained of 'trying to cope with bills and bores'. This was not an uncommon condition for women in her situation. Society widows, pinched for funds, paid only their most pressing debts and learned how to juggle the others. It was customary for the new husband to settle whatever claims he could. Fortunately for George, his father did not disinherit him; he continued to get a small allowance from his family, and he had some money of his own. Jennie also continued to receive the annual rental from her New York home. She and George, therefore, had enough money to take a prolonged honeymoon trip to Belgium and France, with the last few weeks spent in Scotland.

Winston intruded on his mother's honeymoon to tell her, '. . . Indeed I require a brand-new outfit of socks & pocket handkerchief, etc. I send you a specimen sock for a pattern and I know you will know best what to order.' Winston had made it clear in an earlier letter that he intended his letters to her to be private: 'I hope you will always understand that these letters are written for your eye alone, and I could not write with any freedom if I felt they were ever to be read by anyone else. Not that there is anything very intimate in this.' He signed the letter, 'Goodbye my dearest.' [3] In his first letter after her marriage, he had not even mentioned George. A week later, however, he did close a letter with 'Best love to George.'

Winston had moved to an apartment in London made available to him by his cousin Sunny. There was to be another election at Oldham, and Winston was ready to try again, this time with greater hope of success.

He wrote to his mother in Scotland and asked her to contact a number of her friends, such as Lord Rosebery and Viscount Wolseley, and request that they serve as chairmen at several of his lectures. Rosebery was the first to agree,[4] and writing to thank him Winston commented, '. . . I would have written to you myself, but I felt such a request would come better from my mother. . . .' [5]

This election was so important to Winston that he felt it necessary to ask his mother to cut short her honeymoon. 'I hope that you and George will be able to come down here [from Scotland] and stay at the

Queen's Hotel, Manchester, for the last four or five days of the Election. It is thought that your presence here would do good, and if George takes any interest in electioneering, he will have plenty of opportunities of watching or of participating in it as much as he likes during the next fortnight. . . .'[6]

The very next day, he made his invitation more urgent.

I write again to impress upon you how very useful your presence will be down here, providing you really felt equal to coming down and doing some work. Mr Crisp, the other candidate, has brought his wife down and she is indefatigable, going about trying to secure voters and generally keeping the thing going. I know how many calls there are on your time, and from a point of view of pleasure I cannot recommend you to exchange the tranquil air of Scotland for the smoky tumult here, but I think it will be worth your while to see the close of this contest. . . . They have spoken to me several times have the committee as to whether you would be likely to come down. I need not say that it would be very pleasing to me to see a little more of you in that way. . . .

. . . Give my love to George. If he comes to Manchester with you, I suggest your stopping at the Queen's Hotel, that being more comfortable than here. I shall easily find lots of work for him if he will do it, either in speaking or in organization.[7]

Jennie came, but without George. She had also asked Joseph Chamberlain to come to Oldham to speak on behalf of Winston. After the meeting Chamberlain wrote to her: 'I was delighted to speak for your son. . . . He has so much ability that he must succeed – & he is so young that he can afford not to hurry too much.'[8]

This time Winston won a sweeping victory at Oldham. He shared the happy news with Bourke Cockran: 'I have suddenly become one of the two or three most popular speakers in this election, and am now engaged on a fighting tour, of the kind you know – great audiences (five and six thousand people) twice & even three times a day, bands, crowds, and enthusiasm of all kinds. . . .'[9]

Bourke's almost fatherly pride could not compare with Jennie's sweeping enthusiasm. Her son was now truly started on the political career she had long ago predicted and had tried so hard to promote. Of

226

course, she knew that there is no road more uncertain than the political road, so she continued writing to the Prince about Winston, forwarding his replies to her son. She also set up small luncheons and dinners for Winston with political leaders.

Winston arranged his first public lecture in London for October 30, 1900, and Jennie asked for a large number of tickets for influential friends. 'Mamma dear, tickets herewith. Don't give away more than dozen or so; for the space is limited and others may crop up.' [10]

Jennie received an enticing invitation from J. B. Pond, head of the lecture bureau in New York, with whom she had corresponded about Winston's tour: 'Have you any idea how green your memory is here in New York City? I would suggest that you accompany your son on the voyage and witness his reception here. It seems to me it would be a very proud day for you, and your friends here would appreciate it, and I need not add it would doubly enhance the value of the lecture.' [11]

Normally Jennie might have been tempted by such an offer. It would have been a matter of great pride to escort her son to the United States, to share in his success. She was not simply an American – she was an enthusiastic American, and she would have revelled in touring the country with her son.

But she could not leave George. He needed her more than Winston did. He had made a most romantic decision and now had to face up to the hard economic facts of living. He needed to find work, and his qualifications were few. He could hunt, fish, play lawn tennis and bridge, but none of these could earn him an annual income to support an expensive way of life. Even more than money, he needed the dignity of being the man in the house. If he failed at this, his only future would be as a handsome lapdog for an extraordinary wife. Jennie knew this, and she confided her concern to her steadfast friend, Sir Ernest Cassel, who soon took advantage of an opportunity to broach the subject to George.

'Now that I had practically left the Army, and had only a small income, it became necessary for me to seek a new profession,' George wrote later.

The question was: Which? Soon after I returned, I met Sir Ernest Cassel at Lady Lister Kaye's house, and found myself next to him after dinner. It was he who broached the subject and asked me what I thought of doing with myself. I told him that the administrative side of an electrical engineering concern rather appealed to me. 'Not the

City?' he asked. I replied that the prospect of going on a half-commission basis to a firm of stockbrokers and touting for orders from my friends had no allurements for me. He thought a moment and said: 'There are many young men of your class who should never go east of Temple Bar. Perhaps you are one of them.' [12]

Cassel suggested that George might benefit from some technical knowledge. He mentioned the fact that he had some interest in the Central London Railway, which was then nearing completion, and he offered to put George in touch with the Managing Director of the British Thomson-Houston Company, contractors for the line. Soon afterward, George became one of the unpaid members of the company's staff in Glasgow.

I lived at Troon – I couldn't stand Glasgow – and went in every day. Looking back, I am convinced that Cassel's idea of sending me there was to find out whether I really meant to take up a business career seriously or not. Perhaps he thought that if I could stick putting on overalls and acting as a sort of unpaid plumber's mate to the highly paid experts who were building this vast power unit, I might be worthy of help. He had been through the mill himself, and I imagine he felt that nobody could be of use unless he had some sort of similar experience.[13]

After George learned something about the technical side of commercial electricity, he was sent to the company's Managing Director for an interview.

He was prepared to find in me a useless sprig of aristocracy, out of a job, and not particularly wanting one, who at the same time wished his friends to consider that he was 'something in the city'. . . .

'Good morning. Sit down,' he greeted me. 'I know . . . what you have come about. The best thing I can do is to offer you a seat on the board of the Potteries Electric Traction Company, which operates the tramways at Stoke-on-Trent and the Potteries towns. It is one of our biggest concerns, but the fees are only £50 a year. Good bye.'

I was taken aback and replied, 'It isn't a question of money. . . . I want to learn something about the business. Attending a board meeting once a month would teach me nothing. I want an office in this building. Can it be arranged?'

His whole manner changed, and he at once became sympathetic. In three months' time, I was Chairman of the company and of several others, and was also elected a member of the Advisory Committee, and a director of the parent company itself a few years later.[14]

It was an unexpected beginning for their marriage: George working near Glasgow; Jennie in London, busy with the *Anglo-Saxon Review*. They met at weekends, either at her London house or in the country. It was almost as if they were still courting.

But an item in *Truth* magazine pointed out that Jennie's situation had changed: 'Lady Randolph Churchill loses her precedence as widow of the younger son of a Duke, by her second marriage, and also the privilege of the entrée which was granted to her by the Queen as widow of a Cabinet Minister.'

Yet she still had the privilege of retaining the name of Lady Randolph Churchill; indeed, her sister-in-law, the Dowager Duchess of Marlborough, had set a family precedent by keeping her title despite a second marriage. Jennie received a letter on that very question from George Curzon, now Viceroy of India who had 'absolutely no idea what to call you. I suppose you are not Lady Randolph or Lady Jennie. I cannot identify you as Mrs West — "Dear Mrs West" — no, that will never do. On the other hand I dare not essay the bold flight of Jenny, for I think I remember trying it, without success, about 18 years ago. In this, there is something rather touching'.[15]

Jennie did not leave people in doubt for long. She put a notice in *The Times*, and a jingle soon circulated about it:

> The papers give this information
> At Lady Randolph's own request,
> That now her proper designation
> Is Mrs George Cornwallis-West.[16]

Life for Mrs George Cornwallis-West was no less exciting than life for Lady Randolph Churchill had been. Jennie was still Jennie. Discussing her marriage with a friend while they were out motoring, Jennie said, 'I suppose you think I'm very foolish.' Her friend was evasive, and Jennie said, 'But it's worth it. I'm having such fun.' Jennie's kind of fun was quite new for George, and he enjoyed it all thoroughly. Their weekends were filled with a never-ending series of parties. He wrote:

> Another delightful place to which we used to go for weekend parties was Reigate Priory, which was at that time leased to Mr and Mrs Ronnie Greville. Their parties were always amusing, as they contained a leaven of interesting and intellectual people, as well as those who moved in Edwardian society. One of the most entertaining of them, though I doubt very much whether the guests looked upon him as such, was Mrs Greville's father, old Mr McEwan, Scottish millionaire. A frail old gentleman with a beard, he gave one the impression that his one idea was to obliterate himself, although it was indirectly through him that such luxury as one experienced there was possible. I liked the old man immensely, and often used to go for walks with him. One day, I was explaining to him that my sole motive for having gone into business, apart from having something to do, was to endeavour to make sufficient money to pay off the mortgages on my family estates. He stopped in his walk and looked at me with his head on one side, and, with the Scottish accent which was natural to him, he said: 'A most praiseworthy object young man. I hope ye'll succeed, but I doot ye will.'
>
> 'Why?' I asked.
>
> 'Some men are born to make money, it just comes natural to them; others never will. Maybe ye're one of the latter.'
>
> 'I've worked hard all my life,' he went on, 'but it's been an easy thing for me to become rich, I just couldn't help it; and the only pleasure it gives me is the thought that I'm able to give pleasure to others. But money doesn't necessarily come from hard work.'
>
> I thought of Cassel's remark about men who should never go east of Temple Bar, and thought how strange it was that two millionaires should have said practically the same thing. I realized now how true it is that in order for a man to make money, he must have a natural *flair* for it.[17]

For the June 1900 issue of the *Anglo-Saxon Review*, Jennie's friend, the Countess of Warwick, contributed an article which began: 'Love and Misery proverbially go together. There is a popular notion . . . that a lover could not get along without a little misery. . . .' But Jennie's miseries that year concerned 'Maggie', not love. In fact, George, among

230

many others, urged her to sever all connections with John Lane, whose responsibilities to the *Review* did not seem to preclude his being anywhere in the world except England. Lane had been in America for an extended period, most of the time ill with typhoid and nervous prostration. When matters came to a head between him and Jennie it was from Italy that he wrote to her.

Mr Jenkins informs me that you are giving notice of your intention to take away the A.S.R. . . . I am writing to know the grounds of your complaint & to beg of you, under all the circumstances of my absence through illness, to refer the matter to arbitration if there is any serious difference.

I hope you will reconsider your proposal, at any rate, I hope you will not do anything in the matter until I return – certainly within three weeks.[18]

Jennie, however, had made up her mind, and in his next letter Lane took a more practical approach.

After very carefully considering the matter of your dissatisfaction with my publishing the A.S.R., I have decided not to offer any opposition to your withdrawing it from me, but I will offer you my advice, which is simply to stop the Review at once, or most certainly at the end of two years. This is the view I took when I saw Mr Crisp & he certainly was of my opinion & he then encouraged me to tell you exactly what I felt.

I was in America when the first 4 vols were completed & I had much trouble in getting subscribers to renew their subscriptions in most cases. The people only renewed under the impression that it could not last beyond the second year & that sets in consequence would become rare & even valuable. I am convinced that is the only way you will get your money back by stopping with vol. 8 & selling the remainder in sets as a 'limited edition'. But in event of your stopping it with vol. 8, no one here or in America could handle it as well as myself. I know that particular market & let me urge on you the old proverb that it is bad to change horses in crossing the stream. If you will close Vol. VIII, I believe that I could sell a sufficient no. of the Review to clear you *of all loss at least*. . . .

I shall be in town on Wednesday for the day & I would come to see you if you are free & care to discuss the matter with me. I think I could get someone to purchase the title & conduct it on a different line as a 2/6 quarterly, if you decide to stop it. I enclose two poems by Mr Theodore Peters, which seem to me good, though short. I think £21 would satisfy him for either of them.[19]

Jennie answered Lane immediately:

I am in receipt of your letter of the 13th inst., which I have read with much care. I note that you have decided not to offer any opposition to my withdrawing the *Anglo-Saxon* from you. Whilst thanking you for your advice concerning it, I have other views at present. I would only like to remind you that it was a pity that you did not let me know at the end of the first year the conclusions which you had come to, and which you put out at length in your letter. I would be much obliged to you if you would give up the stock you have in hand of the *Anglo-Saxon Review* to the representatives of Mr John Macqueen, who will call for it on my behalf on Wednesday. Mr Yeatman will see you as to the matter of winding up our various accounts, etc. both here and in America.

I am going out of town today, and shall not be back until the end of the holidays, so should not be able to see you at present, but will make an appointment with you later.

Yrs. sincerely,
Jennie Cornwallis-West.[20]

The December 1900 issue of the *Anglo-Saxon Review* listed Mrs George Cornwallis-West as the new publisher, replacing John Lane. She may have felt that it would confuse her readers if she substituted Mrs Cornwallis-West for Lady Randolph Spencer Churchill as Editor, so she used both names, putting the West name in parenthesis under the Churchill name.

She now had several editors helping her. Besides Sidney Low, there were William Earl Hodgson, former editor of the *National Review and Realm*; and Charles Whibley, a distinguished author of political portraits. Lady Cynthia Asquith referred to Whibley in her *Diaries* as her 'literary mentor', but described him as having 'frivolity without humour and cleverness without intelligence'.[21] Whibley's English was characterized as 'so flawless that it makes one ache with the presumptuousness of daring to put pen to paper.' [22]

With the backing of such an editorial team, Jennie could now spend more time searching for money and contributors. Pearl Craigie wrote to her, 'All right. Will prepare essay for March number.' [23] On the lists of authors that Jennie kept, she had placed question marks after the names of those from whom she had expected articles but who had not submitted any. They included her distant cousin Theodore Roosevelt, then Governor of New York, Sir Bindon Blood, H. H. Asquith, Eleonora Duse and Stephen Crane.

Roosevelt had an excuse: he had just been elected Vice President of the United States; and Stephen Crane finally presented her with an article entitled 'War Memories'. The famous young author of *The Red Badge of Courage* finished the piece just before his death at the age of twenty-nine. '. . . War is neither magnificent nor squalid,' he wrote, 'it is simply life, and an expression of life can always evade us.'

Crane and his common-law wife had rented Brede Place in Sussex, the huge, wind-swept house that Clara Frewen had fallen in love with and bought with her husband several years before.[24] Brede Place was a remnant of medieval England, a feudal home built in 1350 that had a chapel, a great hall, straw on the stone floors, a double-sided fireplace that consumed whole tree-trunks, a solarium, timbered inner walls, outhouses, and ghosts. The ghosts were so real that when the Cranes gave a party, the local cook had to 'be bribed to function in the evening, with a bottle of brandy.' [25]

Jennie and her sisters remembered a three-day party that Stephen Crane gave for sixty guests, including Henry James, Joseph Conrad, H. Rider Haggard, and H. G. Wells. Wells invented a game of racing on broomsticks over the polished floors, and the guests revelled until dawn.

H. G. Wells's home in Worcester Park became the site of another literary scene. Jennie's friends had decided that they had discovered the worst novel of the decade, *Irene Iddesleigh*, and they met at Wells's home to read parts of it aloud. One of the choice passages concerned the heroine's first quarrel with her husband: 'Irene, if I may use such familiarity –' begins Sir Hugh, who ends his tirade, 'Speak, Wife. Woman! Do not sit in silence, and allow the blood that now boils in my veins to ooze through the cavities of unrestrained passion, and trickle down to drench me with its crimson hue!' Sir Hugh's suspicions that his wife has a lover are confirmed, and he locks her in her room for a year. But at the end of the year a trusty maid helps her escape, to run off with her lover. Sir Hugh expunges Irene's name from his will. 'With the pen of persuasion dipped into the ink of revenge, he blanked the intolerable words that referred to the woman who, he was now convinced, had braved the bridge of bigamy.' [26]

Jennie loved the spirited fun of the literary world, so different from the formality of the society world. She particularly enjoyed meeting visiting American authors and repeated with glee a story about her friend Mark Twain. At a London gathering he asked Mrs J. Comyns-Carr, 'You *are* an American aren't you?' Mrs Carr explained that she was of English stock and had been brought up in Italy. 'Ah, that's it,' Twain answered. 'It's your complexity of background that makes you seem American. We are rather a mixture, of course. But I can pay you no higher compliment than to mistake you for a countryman of mine.' [27]

Several months later, Mark Twain would introduce Winston to an American audience, saying:

> I think that England sinned when she got herself into a war with South Africa, which she could have avoided, just as we have sinned in getting into a similar war in the Philippines. Mr Churchill by his father is an Englishman; by mother, he is an American, no doubt a blend that makes the perfect man. England and America; we are kin. And now that we are also kin in sin, there is nothing more to be desired. The harmony is perfect – like Mr Churchill himself. . . . [28]

On arriving in America for his lecture tours, Winston had been quoted in the New York *Evening Journal* as having said, 'I am not here to marry anybody. I am not going to get married, and I would like to have that stated positively.' Waiting for him was an invitation to dine with Theodore Roosevelt, and from Boston he wrote to his mother: 'I stayed with Bourke Cockran in New York, who worked indefatigably to make the lecture a success and who gave a large dinner party at the Waldorf before it.

'I should like you to write him a line if you have time because he has treated me in a most friendly way, and that in spite of his strong Boer sympathies.' [29]

Winston had Christmas dinner in Ottawa with another of his mother's admirers, the Earl of Minto, Governor General of Canada. Pamela Plowden was also there. His romance with Pamela had ended months before when he discovered that she was promised to two other young men. After Christmas dinner, Winston wrote of Pamela to his mother: 'We had no painful discussions, but there is no doubt in my mind that she is the only woman I could ever live with.' [30]

The lecture tour had not been as profitable for Winston as he had expected. 'I have decided to come home on the 2nd of Feb.,' he wrote in mid-January. 'As you know, my tour has not been the success I had hoped. I shall, I think, clear £1,600, which though no mean sum, is nothing to what I had anticipated, and I think an inadequate return for all that I have had to go through.' [31] Indeed, his finances were in such poor shape that, even though Ernest Cassel was successfully investing what money Winston had, he had found it necessary to write to Jennie:

I hope my dearest Mamma to be able to provide for myself in the future – at any rate until things are better with you. If you can arrange to relieve me of this loan, with the interest of which I am heavily burdened – £300 per annum – I will not ask for any allowance whatever from you, until old Papa West decides to give you and G. more to live on. Jack in a few years should be self-supporting too. . . . [32]

At least as far as his brother was concerned, Winston's prediction may have been unduly optimistic. Jack had returned from the war still unsure of what he wanted, and Jennie invited him to live with her and George. Jack's commanding officer had written Jennie a note, saying,

I cannot let Jack go without sending you a line to say how well he has done. Of course I always knew he would. . . . Since Ladysmith, the regt has always been at it – with scarcely a week's rest anywhere . . . and had some exceedingly hard work and heavy losses – Jack has always done his share with the greatest keenness – He is most gallant in action, and most trustworthy and hard-working in camp. In fact I am very sorry to lose him. . . . [33]

He was still the same quiet, affectionate young man. There was an initial awkwardness in having him and George in the same household, but George was not often home. He travelled a great deal on business, and it was a comfort to Jennie to have one of her sons with her.

Jennie had received an invitation to accompany her nephew, Sunny, the Duke of Marlborough, on a visit to the Curzons in India. At first she had written to Jack, 'You and George will have to look after each other and keep out of mischief in my absence.'[34] But perhaps she then reflected on something Winston had mentioned about Jack in a letter to George: '. . . He is not yet really grown up; though he seems so old in some things.'[35] At any rate, she decided to stay.

Curzon was disappointed.

Well, I have two things to say. First, we are very much distressed at not seeing you here when we counted upon you to conjure a little vivacity & colour into our humdrum processional lives. I suppose that a too uxorious spouse has kept you at home. Second – I got some time ago from Burma an old silver Burmese bowl, which we meant to offer you as a wedding gift. Our chance having gone, I have had no alternative but to send it to Gt. Cumberland Place, where it should arrive some day.[36]

Jennie's decision to have Jack living in her home seemed to be what he needed. He soon resettled himself in his job in the City, and wrote Winston a bright letter about it. In a letter to his mother, Winston remarked that Jack had sent him '. . . an interesting account of his life on the stock exchange. He writes so well, and if he practised with his pen would I am sure be able to make his name much better known than it is at present, and moreover to add to his interest in life and the balance at the banks.'[37]

Winston also asked Jennie to select some watches for the men and a brooch for the woman who had helped him escape from the Boers: 'I am sure you will choose much better than I shall. . . .'[38]

There was some talk of a dissolution of Parliament, which would have meant another General Election and another campaign battle at Oldham for Winston, 'which I really do not think I should have had the strength to fight. . . .' But Jennie informed Winston that as yet there was no substance to the report.

Jennie was probably right at the time, but within a matter of days the situation was suddenly changed. On January 22, 1901, at 6.30 p.m., Queen Victoria died. Soon after he heard about it Winston wrote to his mother:

So the Queen is dead. The news reached us at Winnipeg, and this city far away among the snows – fourteen hundred miles from any British town of importance – began to hang its head and hoist half-masted flags. A great and solemn event: but I am curious to know about the King [until then, Albert Edward, the Prince of Wales]. Will it entirely revolutionise his way of life? Will he sell his horses. . . . Will he become desperately serious? . . . Will he continue to be friendly to you? . . . Will the Keppel[39] be appointed 1st Lady of the Bedchamber? . . .

I contemplated sending a letter of condolence and congratulations mixed, but I am uncertain how to address it and also whether such procedure would be etiquette. You must tell me. I am most interested and feel rather vulgar about the matter. I should like to know an Emperor and a King. Edward VIIth – gadzooks what a long way that seems to take one back! I am glad he has got his innings at last, and am most interested to watch how he plays it. . . .

P.S. I have been reading, 'An Englishwoman's Love Letters'. Are all Mothers the same? [40]

Queen Victoria had become critically ill in mid-January. 'When the Prince of Wales went in to see the Queen,' wrote Sir Frederick Ponsonby, 'she gained consciousness for a moment and recognized him. She put out her arms and said, "Bertie", whereupon he embraced her and broke down completely.' [41] Another time, during a moment of consciousness, she sent for her dog, a little white one, and called it by its name.

'It was three o'clock before the bells began tolling,' Shane Leslie remembered,

and the one-and-eighty guns thundered salute to the dead. In time, there appeared a very small coffin, surmounted by sceptre and crown, and slowly hauled by bluejackets in their straw hats at the slope. A bunch of Kings and Emperors followed. Grim fates, exiles, dethronements and assassinations were awaiting them. How unimportant they all seemed, the kings of the earth, compared to the little packet of ashes they were honouring with bowed heads and shuffling tread. A cortege of diplomas passed like so many resplendent lackeys. . . .

Lord Roberts passed in tears, looking tiny in his big boots and cocked hat. And the Kaiser was obviously suffering from nerves, for compared to the solemnity of others, he was chafing and twisting round. He had rushed loyally to the funeral, and whispers said he had offered to lift his grandmother into her coffin, but that the Queen's surviving sons had interposed, and lifted her reverently. . . . Incredible how light she was . . . as though some last ray of departing glory had stricken her to a handful of ashes. . . .

On the following Sunday, the Queen still lay in state in St George's Chapel before interment at Frogmore. The body lay in state suffocated by a carnage of flowers. The sweet and sickly air smelt like laughing-gas, and the soldiers toppled over, from time to time, under the fumes.

London was plunged in fog and crepe. Every shop window was streaked by a mourning shutter. The women, old and young, were draped with veils, and most touching was the mourning worn by the prostitutes, in whose existence the old Queen had always refused to believe. Even the crossing sweepers carried crepe on their brooms. Old men were already boasting that they had lived in three reigns. My grandmother prepared to go into perpetual mourning. It seemed as though the keystone had fallen out of the arch of heaven.[42]

Albert Edward, Prince of Wales, had become King Edward VII, and a new era was beginning.

18

'My dearest Mamma, I enclose a cheque for £300. In a certain sense, it belongs to you; for I could never have earned it had you not transmitted to me the wit and energy which are necessary.' [1]

It was a touching tribute from a grateful son.

Four days later, on February 18, 1901, three weeks after Edward's accession, Winston Churchill rose in Parliament to make his maiden speech. Although he defended the war vigorously, he expressed his respect for the Boers: 'If I were a Boer – fighting in the field – and if I were a Boer, I hope I should be fighting in the field. . . .' But he called it a war of duty and hoped the Boers would not 'remain deaf to the voice of reason' and 'refuse all overtures, disdain all terms.' [2]

Listening intently in the gallery, as she had so often listened to Lord Randolph Churchill, was Jennie Cornwallis-West. Before her was her twenty-six-year-old son with the same hand-on-hip stance as his father, the same slight lisp, the same nervousness that Lord Randolph had suffered during his own maiden speech in Parliament. But he spoke with more frankness, more incisiveness, more flashes of humour than his father had done.

Jennie knew what Winston was going to say, as she had been his audience and critic while he rehearsed the speech. As she sat there, proud and anxious, she may have remembered sitting in the same gallery, many years before, with the worried wife of another new Member who literally mouthed every word her husband spoke.

A few of Jennie's friends were worried that the strains of the preceding year had taken their toll on her and that she was not looking as well as she might. Pearl Craigie wrote to her:

Do not forget to keep quiet. You look as fresh & bright as possible, but you must not tax your brain. Read boring books & the daily papers; your mind is too active in the particular circumstances. Later on, you can do as you please. Just now, however & for some months you ought to emulate the milch cow!!

Your new plans are most interesting. Winston, nevertheless, must not tire you. . . .[3]

Pearl Craigie might better have sent that letter to Winston, as he was, in fact, taking a great deal of his mother's time. His requests of her were constant: surely she could find him a new secretary; he wanted a painting for a particular space on his wall; wouldn't she please ask the Duke of Portland to preside over one of the meetings at which he was scheduled to speak? And he needed a hostess to help him greet guests at the White Friar's Club Annual Banquet. 'Please telegraph me if you could care to help me. . . .'[4]

Of course, he was appreciative. And he was thoughtful, too, about helping her when he could. 'I have seen Gen. Ian Hamilton, who will make it his business to see that the *Maine* and its mainstay receive a complimentary allusion in Lord Roberts's concluding dispatch. You may regard this, I think, as settled.'[5]

Later that year, he advised his lawyers, Lumley & Lumley:

While my mother's position remains unchanged, I recognise that it is difficult for her to make me or my brother any allowance, and I feel it my duty, on the other hand, to assist her in any manner possible without seriously prejudicing my reversionary interests. I therefore forego the allowance of £500 a year she and my father had always intended to give me. So I also defray the expenses of the loan of £3,500 I contracted at her suggestion for my brother's allowance and my own from 1897–1900, amounting to £305 per annum.

I view the question of the £1,100 in the same light, and will raise no objection to its dissipation as proposed.

What I desire in my brother's interest, as in my own, is that there should be a clear understanding necessarily not of a legal nature, that in the event of Mr George Cornwallis-West being at some future time in a superior financial position, my mother will make suitable provision for her children out of her own income; in other words, that she will reciprocate the attitude I am now adopting.[6]

Jennie paid close attention to Jack, too, even when she was away on short holidays. '. . . Make Walden [her butler] get you a bottle of hairwash from Floris's – Ask for Col. Clayton's Hairwash, and tell Walden to pay for it. You must use it with a little sponge. Now, do this – Otherwise, you won't have a hair on your head. Poor old boy, I think of you so much. . . .'[7]

On August 10, 1901 the signature of Jennie Cornwallis-West appeared for the first time in the Blenheim Palace Guest Book. Arthur Balfour was also there that evening. Within a year, Balfour, who had long been a political force in England, would succeed his uncle, Lord Salisbury, as Prime Minister.

Balfour was not the Prime Minister that the new monarch would have wished. He was an aloof, unbending man,[8] and Edward VII was a man of warmth and laughter. The Edwardian Age was the era of 'Good old Bertie', 'the first amiable king since Charles II.'[9] Edward was a king who enjoyed being King, and the British people took pleasure in his enjoyment. They loved him, as Lord Granville said, 'because he has all the faults of which the Englishman is accused.'[10]

Edward was fifty-nine years old, portly, bearded, and jovial. He was a polished, sophisticated man who relished pomp and pleasure,[11] 'sweet women and dry champagne'. In contrast with the sombre Queen Victoria, always in mourning and withdrawn, King Edward loved bright uniforms, medals, and decorations, and ceremonial occasions of all kinds; instead of quaint, quiet Court drawing-room receptions, there were now loud, lavish Court balls; instead of peaceful, carefully paced carriage rides in the park, there were horse races, regattas, and automobiles.

> For to him above all was life good,
> Above all he commanded her abundance full-handed,
> The peculiar treasure of kings was his for the taking;
> All that men come to in dreams, he inherited waking.[12]

It was still an age of kings in Europe. Edward's niece was Empress of all the Russias, another niece, Queen of Spain, his daughter was Queen of Norway, the German Emperor was his nephew, and the Kings of Denmark and Greece were his brothers-in-law.

In England the Edwardian Age was a time of opulence, extravagance, and peace. The Boer War may have tarnished the British lion, but the British pound was the most solid and respected currency in the world. However, despite an increasingly large middle class, a third of the British people still knew what hunger meant – they were over-worked and underpaid and lived in wretched slums. The average workman earned only a pound a week. Yet the general public mood of gloom was gone. Education offered hope, universal male suffrage promised change. It was a time of less boredom, less pretence, and increased freedom. As for the rich, 'more money was spent on clothes, more food was consumed, more horses were raced, more infidelity was committed, more birds were shot, more yachts were commissioned, more late hours were kept than ever before.' [13]

King Edward's Danish-born Queen, the lovely and gracious Alexandra, adjusted easily to the new informality of the court. At a ball at Chatsworth, Alexandra and George's sister, Daisy, took off their shoes 'to see what difference it made in our height. The Queen took, or rather, kicked hers off, and then got into everyone else's, even into Willie Grenfell's old pumps. I never saw her so free and cheerful – but always graceful in everything she does.' [14]

The King wanted informal, honest friends around him, rather than flattering courtiers. He had long ago forgiven Jennie what he felt was a mistaken marriage and had taken the initiative in writing to her. In a letter to Jack from Cowes that year, Jennie wrote: 'I had a very nice letter from the King, nicest I've had from him since I married. . . .' [15]

So Jennie was again absorbed into the inner circle, and with her, George.

My wife had a host of friends in London, whom I soon got to know and who were exceedingly kind to me; and thus I became an Edwardian, in the sense that I was a member of that particular set in society with which King Edward associated himself, a set with which a young officer in the Guards or the son of a country gentleman living in the country was not likely in the ordinary course of events, to become particularly intimate.[16]

George called these 'the wonderful days'.

I worked hard all the week, and every Saturday Jennie and I used to go somewhere. . . . Estates which had been for centuries in one family were still intact. . . . Taxation and the cost of living were low; money was freely spent and wealth was everywhere in evidence. . . . I doubt whether in any period of history of the modern world . . . has there been such a display of wealth and luxury as during King Edward's reign. . . . Dinners were Gargantuan affairs . . . champagne, port and old brandy were the order of the day, or rather, night. . . . Women's dresses at dinner parties were very elaborate, and quantities of jewellery were worn. Those were the days of tiaras and stomachers. The blaze of jewels displayed at the opera was really amazing. . . .[17]

It was a time of self-indulgence. Not only did women go to extremes in adorning themselves, but standards of comfort and convenience were exaggerated. Everything was more than lavish. Every estate had multitudes of servants who were themselves stratified within a rigid hierarchy. There were 'upper' servants and 'under' servants. Upper servants included the housekeeper, the cook, the head housemaid, the butler, the lady's maid, the steward. They usually enjoyed many of the upper-class comforts: the choice of the dining-room food, sofas and armchairs in their sitting rooms, coal-fires in their bedrooms. The under servants slept in the basements, in attics, or on folding-beds in the pantries. They worked long hours and slept little. Young scullerymaids were often washing up in the kitchens until one in the morning and then had to be up a few hours later to help prepare the enormous breakfasts. Fires crackled without anyone having seen their being lighted. Curtains were drawn and breakfast brought up without guests being awakened. By eight in the morning lawns were rolled, dead leaves removed, and fresh flowers placed in vases. Servants were silent and invisible. They made possible a rarefied way of life for the British aristocracy, but the Frenchman E. De Gramont remarked that 'this majestic silence got on my nerves. Those great mute corridors, those never-raised voices made me homesick for the Latin hurly-burly; servants shouting, banging pots and pans, slamming doors. . . .'[18]

A few months after Queen Victoria's death, Grand Duke Michael of Russia gave a weekend party at Keele Hall for King Edward. The guests arrived in 'the deepest mourning' and returned to London on a special train. Since it was soon after the King's accession, the train slowed at the major stations *en route* so that the people could see their new sovereign. 'It was a very hot afternoon,' George wrote,

and we were all perspiring freely; and one lady as we neared London produced some *papiers poudres* and began to whiten her nose and generally clean up her face. The King asked what it was she was using, and, on being shown, took two leaves himself and proceeded to powder his nose. The result was comic, but was duly rectified before he stepped out of the train at Euston.[19]

George played a rubber of bridge with Edward and won thirty pounds from His Majesty, 'who produced an enormous roll of notes from his pocket from which to pay me. I had always understood that kings never carried money, which shows how mistaken one can be.' [20]

Where the King went, Jennie and George usually went, too. Races, tennis, bridge, amateur theatricals, long walks, elaborate teas, sumptuous luncheons, enormous dinners. One host had his own private circus, at which he acted as ringmaster. Another provided small carriages drawn by ponies for ladies too tired to walk. And there was always music in the evenings: private orchestras, celebrated singers and musicians in intimate recitals. George remembered a recital by the recently married Fritz Kreisler, who had brought his bride. 'He seemed to play for her alone. To him there might not have been anyone else in the room; and she, on her part, appeared hypnotized by his playing. Her eyes closed and her whole body swayed as if she were about to faint.'[21]

When this social whirl was too much for them, the country home of Lord and Lady Tweedmouth provided Jennie and George with an ideal summer haven. They were there one night when Lord Rosebery, the former Prime Minister, was also a guest, and George wrote of an incident that characterized Rosebery well. Rosebery had just commented on something with a marvellous epigram, when another guest, a youth of seventeen, offered that he had noticed Lord Rosebery studying Marcus Aurelius before dinner. Rosebery stared at the young man 'with those curious cod-fish blue eyes of his' and said, 'All my life I've loved a womanly woman and admired a manly man, but I never could stand a boily boy.' [22]

If Rosebery had been younger, King Edward would have much preferred him as his Prime Minister. Balfour was correct but cold and too intellectual for the King. In contrast, Rosebery and Edward spoke the same language, shared many of the same interests.[23] Rosebery was no less an intellectual than Balfour, but he knew when not to show it.

Jennie and Winston were seeing less and less of each other and were moving in different directions now. But when Jennie complained to him about it, Winston replied:

. . . No, my dear, I do not forget you. But we are both of us busy people, absorbed in our own affairs, and at present independent. Naturally, we see little of each other. Naturally, that makes no difference to our feelings. I remain always,

> Your loving son,
> Winston S. C.[24]

Winston was now twenty-eight, and Jennie wanted to see him married and settled. But he had no grace with young women.[25] He could write romantic letters, but he had little patience for small talk. After his unfulfilled romance with Pamela two other young ladies refused his proposals of marriage: the wealthy Muriel Wilson and the strikingly beautiful young American actress, Ethel Barrymore. The Blenheim guest book of July 13, 1902, shows that Miss Barrymore had been present along with Jennie and her family.

Winston was busy writing, asking Jennie's advice for help with research, borrowing her secretary. His notes to her often ended with a date and the question, 'Dinner?'

King Edward's Coronation had been delayed by the Boer War and by the sudden necessity for the King to have an operation.[26] It was finally arranged for August 9, 1902.

> We'll be merry
> Drinking whisky, wine and sherry,
> Let's all be merry
> On Co-ro-nation Day.[27]

On Coronation Day, in the King's Box in Westminster Abbey, sat a small group of beautiful women whose love and favours had meant much to the King. Among others, they included his current mistress, Mrs George Keppel, and Jennie and her mother-in-law, both wearing diamond tiaras which they had 'begged, borrowed or stolen'.[28] The King's close friend, the Marquis de Soveral, was overheard to remark about them: 'What that lot doesn't know about King Edward. . . .' [29]

Alice Keppel had replaced Lady Warwick in the King's affections. Daisy Pless confided in her diary that she had met Mrs Keppel for the first time at a luncheon. 'Three or four of the women present had several lovers, and did not mind saying so. Alice is fascinating.' [30]

A story was told of a bridge game in which the King and Mrs Keppel were partners. Mrs Keppel bid No Trumps, and was left to play it out. Edward as dummy put down his cards, and there was hardly a trick in them. Mrs Keppel glanced at her hand again, and then at Edward, and said, 'All I can say, Sire, is, "God save the King and preserve Mrs Keppel!" ' King Edward roared with laughter.[31]

Mrs Keppel's husband was Lieutenant-Colonel George Keppel, the younger son of the Earl of Albemarle. The couple had two children, and the younger one, Sonia, remembers Edward well. She called him 'Kingy' and was particularly delighted by his 'kind, deep voice' and his 'plump, be-ringed hands'.[32]

He would lend me his leg, on which I used to start two bits of bread and butter (butter side down), side by side. Then bets of a penny each were made (my bet provided by Mamma), and the winning piece of bread and butter depended, of course, on which was the more buttery. The excitement was intense while the contest was on. Sometimes he won, sometimes I did.[33]

Alice Keppel and Jennie were good friends, and it was Jennie's brother-in-law, John Leslie, who had first introduced Alice Keppel to the King. She was a lovely woman, wih a natural hour-glass figure, large turquoise eyes, and light chestnut hair. Soft-spoken and graceful, she was also unusually quick at repartee. Margot Asquith said of her: 'She is a plucky woman of fashion; human, adventurous and gay, who in spite of doing what she liked all her life has never made an enemy.' [34] One of the reasons she didn't was that she never flaunted her influence.[35]

The Coronation was commemorated in Volume VIII of Jennie's *Anglo-Saxon Review* which paid tribute to the new sovereign with a frontispiece portrait and a lead article by Frederick Greenwood entitled 'Monarchy and the King'. 'The Queen dies,' Greenwood observed, 'and immediately it is as if we marched with our backs to a completed past and our faces to a future of which we see nothing.'

This issue also featured articles by George Bernard Shaw, 'John Oliver Hobbes' (Pearl Craigie), Winston Churchill and Jennie's brother-in-law, Moreton Frewen, who wrote about conservation of fish – half a century ahead of his time. Winston's long-promised article was about the British Cavalry. There was also a piece on 'Decorative Domestic Art' by the editor and publisher, who signed herself 'Lady Randolph Churchill' rather than 'Mrs George Cornwallis-West'. Jennie's article began,

Taste and common sense, with a desire for knowledge, allied to a limited purse, will go farther nowadays to please the eyes and the senses, than the riches of a South African millionaire, spent for him by upholsterers. . . . The rich man often orders hastily and repents at leisure; because he has leisure to repent in. . . .

She was delighted, she said, to see the disappearance of 'the heavy uncomfortable monstrosities of the early Victorian epoch. . . .' And it was important to England, she believed, 'that some of our best artists do not think it beneath their dignity to give designs for the homeliest objects (such as wallpapers and table-linen).' Moreover, she agreed with the current tendency 'to approve everything which pleases the eye, without regard to orthodoxy.' [36]

The article concluded with a warning against snobbishness:

Because a thing is old, its value should not be necessarily enhanced, unless it had beauty or an historical interest attached to it; and most people will prefer a good, solid, well-made copy of a fine model to a rickety, worm-eaten original, with only its antiquity to recommend it.

The *Review*'s next two issues featured articles on everything from the American Revolution to the American athlete, from the 'Great Seals of England' to snuff-boxes, from 'The Absurdity of the Criticism of Music' to 'Celebrated Women of Recent Times'. This was perhaps both the charm and the major fault of the *Review*: it had too much range and no focus.

An article entitled 'The Next Government' was a last-minute substitution made after Jennie had thought the issue was closed, and she had gone off to Scotland for a holiday with George. The article was extremely critical of Lord Rosebery, the former Prime Minister who was one of her friends and a contributor to the first issue of the *Review*. Jennie sent Rosebery an apologetic note, explaining how grieved she was that anything even approaching criticism of him should have appeared in the *Review*. He replied in a characteristic manner, that 'It was very good of you to write. . . . Frankly, I think the introduction of politics into the *Anglo-Saxon* a great mistake. But you are a better judge of this than I am.'

As for the article, he said, 'I think it very unlikely that I shall ever see it, and I am quite sure that, if I do, it will not trouble me. But I tender my humble and hearty thanks to the Editress.' [37]

The *Review* could be hard-hitting. In a regular column called 'Impressions and Opinions' there had been an editorial comment on the Boer War:

The South African War still drags its weary course along. He would be a bold man who should predict that it will be over when this or even the next number of the *Anglo-Saxon Review* is in print. Never was there a campaign which has seemed so often on the very verge of extinction and then has suddenly blazed up again. . . . The fight is not for victory but for conquest. We do not ask for our beaten foes to make terms; we require an unconditional submission and the surrender of their territory. There is no question of treating for peace. . . . We ought not to be surprised if, amid the circumstances, the struggle is slow and desperate.

There was an added note: 'But whatever is done, the British nation is in the last resort responsible. . . . Nothing can be more cowardly than to say to a general: Do what you think proper. Burn farms, starve women, lay waste land, shoot, hang and plunder. But for Heaven's sake don't tell *us* anything about it. . . .' [38]

That had not only been Jennie's feeling about the Boer War, but the growing feeling among the British people. It was not until May 1902 that a peace treaty with the Boers was finally signed.

The future of the *Anglo-Saxon Review* still looked uncertain. Pearl Craigie at first thought that Jennie ought to 'stick to the A.S.R. on its present lines; it is an exotic perhaps – but that is in its favour. – I hope myself that it will prosper, flourish and proceed!' [39]

Pearl's hope notwithstanding, the possibility of proceeding began to look less likely, and the two women talked about a variety of alternatives. They thought of making the *Review* a monthly magazine. 'Do you think that a monthly review would be as successful as a good weekly?' Craigie wrote. 'You might work up one of those already in existence.' Jennie mentioned buying the *St. James's Gazette*, and Craigie replied: 'The *St. James's Gazette* is excellent – at a proper price . . .', and she recommended a staff member of *Punch* magazine as a first-rate editor. But *Punch* publisher Agnew promptly promoted him. 'The Agnews I believe were put on their mettle at once when they heard you had him for the *A.S. Review*. . . .' Craigie also informed Jennie that her father, an astute businessman, 'thinks very well of your new *Review* scheme. . . .'[40]

Pearl's father, John Morgan Richards, was not representative of the many men Jennie approached for money.[41] They all liked and admired her, but this was more a matter of giving good money to go the way of bad, and they discouraged her as kindly as they could.

Reluctantly, Jennie made the tenth issue the last, and quietly folded the *Review*.[42] It must have been very difficult for her to make the formal arrangements and write the necessary letters:

Anglo-Saxon Review

Dear Sir:

Will you please be good enough to instruct your agent in New York to give Messrs Putnams Sons, full particular of stock in your possession, *viz* – of volumes bound, quires, cases, plates, etc., and hand the whole or any part thereof to them on their written order.

Trying to buoy up her spirit, King Edward gave Jennie new royal honours. In 1901 he had made her Lady of Grace of St John of Jerusalem. Now, in recognition of her services on the *Maine*, he invested her with the Order of the Royal Red Cross. He was also increasingly considerate of Winston, who wrote to his mother from Balmoral Castle in September 1902:

I have been vy kindly treated here by the King, who has gone out of his way to be nice to me. It has been most pleasant & easy going & today the stalking was excellent, tho I missed my stags.

You will see the King on Weds when he comes to Invercauld; mind you gush to him about my having written to you saying how much etc etc I had enjoyed myself here.[43]

But the death of the *Anglo-Saxon Review* was a jolt for Jennie. She did not like defeat. It drained her of some of her energetic optimism. She felt tired and would have loved a change of scene and mood. Sir Ernest Cassel offered her just that in the form of a cruise on his yacht up the Nile to the Aswan Dam with a small group of friends, including Winston and Mrs Keppel. But George could not leave his work and Jennie would not leave him.

She had Jack to consider, too. Winston had written to her from Egypt, 'I often think of you and Jack: and feel vy anxious about him. Please concentrate your attention on him. He is rather untamed & forlorn.' [44] Jennie did not need Winston's warning, even though Jack seemed to be flourishing on the stock exchange. A quiet, likeable young man, he had an easier way with women than Winston, but he, too, seemed reluctant about marriage. Jennie and Jack were a frequent twosome that season at concerts, the opera and the theatre.

Jennie had a more difficult case in transforming her niece Clare from a provincial wallflower to a London débutante. She was Clara's daughter, the only female child of all three Jerome daughters. Clare had had a sad childhood, an education at a French convent, and a lonely interval at her father's ancestral home in Ireland. Winston had advised her to 'cultivate a philosophical disposition . . . it is something after all, to be fed and clothed and sheltered. . . .' [45]

But Clare was an awkward, gangly sixteen-year-old who needed love. Under Jennie's tutelage she blossomed.

I grew to love Jennie, as soon as I got over being intimidated by her. One had to admire her; she was resplendent. Jennie's advice was generally worldly, my mother's was sentimental, Leonie's was ethical. . . . My Aunt Jennie became my second mother. . . .

Jennie looked at me in kind of an overhauling way, and said I must pull in my waist and put up my hair. I was still growing, so my dresses had to have big, turned-up hems. It was the fashion for them to touch the ground and for the collars to be kept up by whalebones that dug into one's neck. Veils were worn – it was like being in a cage. I was a wild animal being tamed. The taming process outlasted the London Season. [46]

The three sisters still lived together in their cluster of houses on Great Cumberland Place, and Clare would come across the street to Jennie every morning and read *The Times* leading editorial while she breakfasted. 'After that I had to practise how to do my hair, for I did it, she said, abominably.' Above all, Jennie told her, she had to try to talk and to smile and not look bored whenever anyone else was introduced. 'Remember that you are not invited for your own amusement, but to contribute to the party.' [47]

Jennie practised what she preached. Her own house was perfect for lunches, intimate soirées, and small dinners, but not large enough for the old-fashioned grand salon. Such a salon would have required her to spend more time at home, which would have put her in a restricting social cage. She was too restless for that. She liked to visit. She liked to travel. She presided at flower shows, played at concerts, began writing a book and a play, and became an automobile enthusiast.

Just as Jennie's had been the first home in London to be lit by electric light, she and George were the first in their social set to own a motor-car. 'Although we never went at more than twenty-five miles an hour, I thought it was a thrilling experience,' she wrote.[48]

Driving an automobile at the turn of the century was a rather uncomfortable and hazardous operation. There were no tarred roads and the thick dust whitened women's hair and lashes despite swathes of chiffon. Men wore goggles and more protective hats, but because there were neither windscreens nor side doors, men and women alike took to wearing long canvas coats and other kinds of clothing to help keep them warm. Jennie told Jack about a trip 'in the motor – 156 miles, and did it in under six hours. Too fast, I have a head[ache] in consequence. . . .'[49]

For night driving, courageous motorists took along acetylene torches, which often worked rather badly. Jennie and George were returning from a dinner date one evening when one of their acetylene torches burst into flames – 'fortunately', George wrote, 'without setting fire to the car' – and the other soon followed suit.

We had nothing left but a very small electric torch, with which Jennie, with arm extended in front of her, did her best to throw a feeble light on the road. All went well until we came to a corner which we ought to have turned but didn't, and instead went up a small bank. Fortunately we were going very slowly, but I shall never forget my feelings when I saw my wife fall slowly out, the car remaining perfectly upright – there was, of course, no side door to hold her in. However, she was not hurt; we reversed and arrived home about two in the morning.[50]

Their marriage had started off with surprising success, and even the Cornwallis-West family gradually adjusted to it. George was a very happy man. He had a business position of dignity and growing importance; he mingled among people of wealth and splendour; and his wife was one of the most beautiful, desirable, and important women of their world. His single criticism of her was her attitude towards money.

In money matters she was without any sense of proportion. The value of money meant nothing to her: what counted with her were the things she got for money, not the amount she had to pay for them. If something of beauty attracted her, she just had to have it; it never entered her head to stop and think how she was going to pay for it. During all the years we lived together the only serious misunderstandings which ever took place between us were over money matters. Her extravagance was her only fault, and, with her nature, the most understandable, and therefore, the most forgivable.[51]

But George himself was not without extravagance. Soon after his election to his company's Advisory Committee, he was 'motoring up' from a visit with Cassel to attend his first meeting. Along the way his car broke down; fortunately, he was near a railroad station: 'So I did the only possible thing – chartered a special train.'[52] It cost him about twenty-five per cent of all the fees he would have collected from the company that year.

Certainly Jennie was having fun, and as Pearl Craigie wrote, she was 'looking beautiful and happy'. She was the star attraction of a costume party she attended which had as its theme 'British Society Beauties Dressed as Famous Men in History'. George's mother went dressed as Hamlet, his sister Daisy as Romeo, Lady Sarah Wilson as Bonnie Prince Charlie. But as the *New York Journal* reported:

Historically, the success of the evening was Mrs George Cornwallis-West, formerly Lady Randolph Churchill, who came as a roistering Spanish cavalier. She wore black silk tights, doublet and hose, a dark velvet cloak trimmed with gold; had a sword, a great diamond blazing in her black sombrero, with its drooping feathers; diamond buckles on her pretty shoes, and a black mustache, waxed and ferociously curled, like the Kaiser's.[53]

It was a relatively carefree time for Jennie and George, and Jennie was delighted by George's enthusiasm for people and interesting parties. Even Pearl Craigie, who was the slowest among Jennie's close friends to accept George, now wrote to her, 'I particularly want Mr

Cornwallis-West to come also.'[54] But she would never call him 'George'.

Pearl Craigie was probably jealous of George. Because of him Jennie was giving Pearl proportionately less of her time. Pearl had a possessive nature, and her affection for Jennie was deep. Even when she went to India for a long stay, she wrote: 'My dearest Jennie: I have wished for you every moment since I came out. . . .'[55] And from Paris three months later: 'Dying to see you! . . . I missed you every second. . . .'[56] She even named the leading character in one of her novels 'Jennie'. She loved the name so much, she said, that 'I gave it to someone who was beautiful and charming. . . .'[57]

On her return from Paris, Pearl urged Jennie to join her in organizing a social and professional woman's club. '. . . You are the one woman who can get it going and maintain it. . . .'[58] A new club was not the most exciting of prospects for Jennie, but this was a time in her life when she was not searching for excitement – and so she agreed to help Pearl.

The world surrounding her was searching for peace and quiet, too. France had been hostile towards England for a number of years, but as Jennie's nephew, Shane Leslie, described it, Edward VII's courage and charm dissipated this national bitterness. On a visit to France, King Edward signed his name in French, complimented a French actress on being symbolic of the spirit of France, and did a dozen small things that were favourably publicized in the press. Soon crowds formed wherever he went and turned into rallies. 'The cry of *Vive le Roi* was raised, shouted down, and raised again till it conquered. *La Ville lumière* had become Royalist.'[59] Shortly afterwards an Anglo-French treaty was signed.

King Edward was perhaps less able and industrious than his mother had been, but he had a better understanding of the democratic forces of the new century. He advised the Prime Minister that if a tax on food was pushed through Parliament, he would use the rarely exercised royal veto.

At the time, the major political issue in the country was the old question of Free Trade versus Protectionism. Balfour's Conservative Party favoured Protectionism, the Liberal Party stood for Free Trade. Winston was in a quandary: he was a Conservative who believed in Free Trade. Jennie, who was in a similar dilemma, had her own views on the issue. She sent a sharp letter to the Randolph Churchill Habitation of the Primrose League:

I understand, from the notice sent to me, that at the General Annual Meeting of the Randolph Churchill Habitation of Primrose League, which is to be held on December 1st, Mr J. Ratcliffe Cousins, Secretary of the Tariff Reform League, is to address the meeting in favour of Tariff Reform. Under these circumstances, I am afraid I cannot see my way to preside that evening. In the first place, I am not a Protectionist, and do not desire to associate myself in any way with this retrograde movement, and secondly, I should like to enter my protest against the Randolph Churchill Habitation giving its countenance to views which go far beyond those of the Government and of the Prime Minister. I can quite understand the Habitation desiring to enlighten itself on the great question which is filling all minds at the present moment, but that only one side of the case should be stated is unworthy of the Primrose League, which has always been open-minded on all questions outside the terms of its Constitution. As one of the Vice-Presidents of the Executive Committee, and one among the first twelve members of the League, I cannot identify myself with such proceedings. Had you arranged for the views of Mr Balfour and the Unionist Party to be explained at the same time, I should have been very glad to have attended the meeting. But, under existing circumstances, I must reluctantly decline.

> Believe me, Yours Faithfully,
> [signed]   Jennie Cornwallis-West.[60]

While Winston was travelling, Jennie looked after his political chores: 'It was very kind of you to open the Bazaar & I am sure those people were vy pleased at your going. I don't know what I should have done if you had failed me. They were already put out at my absence. . . .'[61] And now he kept her informed of his political activities:

I send you another crop of newspaper cuttings. I daresay they will amuse you.

I have had eight small meetings in Oldham, of 200 apiece, and have been extremely well received, as you will see from the papers. . . . There are of course a lot of Protectionists and Fair Traders in the party there, and there is no doubt that everything will have to be handled very carefully; but they are all quite agreed in recognizing that I am the only person that has got the slightest chance of winning the Election for the Tory Party there, and in consequence, they are prepared to give me very wide liberty. In addition to this, there is a great deal of personal enthusiasm, and I find that the working classes are very much attracted by the idea of a representative whose name they read frequently in the newspapers, and who as they think, confers distinction on the town. . . . We must try to see something of each other in Scotland. . . . I hope your cure has been satisfactory. I find myself in very good health, but I shall be glad to lead a quiet, regular, temperate life, for a month. I shall do my exercises every day.[62]

When they later missed each other in Scotland, he wrote:

I am indeed sorry to miss you here: but we shall see each other often in the autumn & I may need you often in Oldham, if you have time & inclination.

The situation is most interesting & I fancy a smash must come in a few days. Mr Balfour is coming to Balmoral on Saturday. Is he going to resign or reconstruct? If he resigns, will the King send for Spencer or Devonshire? If for either, will he succeed in forming a govt & what kind of government? If he reconstructs – will it be a Protectionist reconstruction of a cabinet who does not contain the Free Trade Ministers, or a Free Trade reconstruction of a cabinet? . . . All these things are possible.[63]

Bourke Cockran had strongly influenced Winston's thinking. The two men had originally disagreed on the Boer War, but Winston gradually grew more sympathetic toward the Boers.[64] On the Free Trade question Winston and Bourke were of like mind and exchanged many long letters on the subject. In 1896 Bourke had differed so strongly with his own Democratic Party leadership on this single issue that he had crossed over to the Republicans to campaign for William McKinley for President.[65]

Winston in England was now prepared to cross over to the Liberals on the same issue. At the end of May 1904, he entered the House of Commons, stared for a moment at the Government benches, then at the Opposition benches, and walked quickly to the Liberal side, taking a seat alongside Lloyd George. It was a place where his father had once sat.

Seymour Leslie remembered being with his Aunt Jennie that night in her library. She was glaringly angry and told him: 'Haven't you heard? The moment Winston crossed the floor to the Liberal benches and rose to speak, that detestable Arthur Balfour and his entire party got up and walked out of the House! What an insult from a Prime Minister. . . . I'll never speak to him again. . . .' [66]

19

Jennie was fifty years old in 1904. A British author considered this the time of life when the American woman '. . . is filled with unrealizable ideals . . . her life frustrated, [so] she turns to religion or bridge, becomes either a colourless individual or a fanatic. . . .'[1]

Jennie, however, had achieved much in her life and now wanted little. Her handsome young husband continued to be adoring and was doing surprisingly well in business. Her sons had accepted George more readily than she could have hoped. She had come to terms with most of her husband's family, and although there was little warmth, there was a grudging acceptance of her. George's father, however, still kept his distance, and Winston gave Jennie encouragement: 'I thought a good deal over all you said to me about yourself & I feel sure you are right to concentrate on and take pains with the few people you really care about. But I have no doubt that when papa G. [Cornwallis-West] is at length gathered to Abraham, you will be able to renew your youth like the eagle. . . .'[2]

Jennie otherwise felt a sense of fulfilment and peace. The marvellous thing about her, too, was that she was still a handsome woman. George's sister, Daisy, who had become outwardly cordial to Jennie confided to her diary that Jennie was 'wearing lovely clothes . . . looking very well, but so fat. . . .'[3] A lengthy magazine profile, however, said of Jennie that her figure

has an almost girlish slightness . . . that definite seductiveness of outline announced irresistibly by erectness of carriage, correctness of proportion from bust to waist and from waist to hip, and that serpentine slope of the neck into shoulder which has been referred to by sculptors as the most maddening line in art. The taper of no waist in the world has more roundness, the freshness of no complexion in London entices with such genuineness. . . .

. . . Mrs Cornwallis-West is neither slim nor plump, neither young nor old, but to quote the words of *Truth*, 'just herself'. She has neither that mincing accent which has become so common nor the weird almost simian antics – for example, the shoulder-high handshake – nor the falsetto voice which go with the character she is made to play. . . . She has been praised . . . for spreading the spirit of graciousness about her, and for giving to human intercourse at social functions a new reality. It is not that she cultivates what the English call 'charm', but that fate has bestowed upon her, in addition to her enduring beauty of face and figure and perfect elegance of deportment, an instinct for courtesy. She avoids giving offense. She is stately without stiffness. There is no condescension in her distinguished air, which compels respect by an unconscious dignity of its own. One never detects in Mrs Cornwallis-West that studied indifference, approaching insolence, which, according to the French, buries the good manners of the English at their great social functions. . . . Time has not robbed her of the American accent in which she carries on her conversations with brilliant Englishmen, or diminished the brightness of a pair of eyes of which the late Grand Duke Sergius once said that they were the most beautiful in all Europe.[4]

Capping its admiration, the article discussed Jennie's new home at Salisbury Hall and quoted a newspaper as saying of her, 'She is the only hostess of genius in the United Kingdom.'

Salisbury Hall was not a stately home. It was comfortable and quiet, and a haven for friends and family. It was a lovely old manor house near St Albans, on the site of a thirteenth-century castle, and there was still a moat surrounding it and an Elizabethan hall with carved stone plaques on the walls. The house had a beautifully carved staircase, superb fireplaces, wood-panelled rooms, several adjoining cottages, and an elaborate servants' wing. King Charles II had used it as 'a home away from home' for his mistress, Nell Gwyn.[5] It was said that her ghost still haunted the place.

George, who believed in spiritualism and reincarnation and claimed to be psychic, insisted that he had seen 'the figure of a youngish and beautiful woman with a blue *fichu* round her shoulders. She looked intently at me, and then turned and disappeared through a door into the passage. I followed and found nothing.'[6] He later identified the apparition as the ghost of Nell Gwyn.

Jennie was much more relaxed at Salisbury Hall than in London.

And she never before had had a home with enough land for a proper garden. She loved colour and she loved flowers. Winston helped her to decide which ones to have and where to plant them, and the two of them spent a day getting the duckweed out of the moat. The more practical Jack advised on the bathroom renovation, and George supervised the installation of electric lights. George now had his own place for pheasant shoots.

Jennie no longer rode horses as much as she once did, but she and George played a lot of golf together and she was getting good at it. Their marriage was now four years old, and life was sweet and serene for them.

'George and Jennie have made this little house delightful,' said Daisy Pless; 'it is full of pretty things, and the garden will be very nice.'[7] 'SH' as Jennie called it, was not really 'a little house'. However, it had one drawback which became apparent when King Edward made one of his frequent visits, forcing Jennie to demonstrate some of her 'genius' as a hostess. The King had become very stout, and it was not comfortable for him to climb stairs. Jennie, therefore, had to create a suite downstairs, where there were no bedrooms. She did this by hanging green silk in the panelled drawing room to make it more intimate and by converting the gentlemen's cloakroom into a private bathroom. Walden served meals on the refectory table in the Tudor Hall. How simple all this was compared, for example, to the King's reception at Chatsworth, where the Duke and Duchess of Devonshire posted two lines of torchbearers from the railway station to their mansion, the whole area lit with thousands of coloured lamps and the marble staircase lined with footmen in powdered wigs.[8]

Daisy envied Jennie's easy relationship with Edward VII, and was probably not pleased that, when Kaiser Wilhelm II of Germany visited her Prussian castle, he reminisced warmly about the beautiful, charming Lady Randolph Churchill.[9] Moreover, for Daisy, royalty had been a bad bargain. Her marriage with the Prince of Pless was cold and unhappy, and she remarked in her diary: 'Royalties are very nice to meet occasionally, but difficult to live with.'[10]

But Daisy was especially jealous of Jennie's relationship with the Marquis Luis de Soveral. As one of King Edward's three closest friends, Soveral was usually invited wherever His Majesty was invited. He was the Portuguese Ambassador to Great Britain, and few were better informed on European politics; indeed it was said that 'had he wished he could have become one of Europe's leading statesmen. . . .' But Soveral preferred to remain in England, 'where he made love to all the most beautiful women and where all the nicest men were his friends. . . .' [11]

Soveral had long been one of Jennie's most unfailing admirers. He was a genial, charming, and tactful bachelor, with a fund of *risqué* stories. Always dressed at the height of fashion, he usually wore immaculate white gloves and a white flower in his buttonhole. He had a swarthy complexion and wore a fashionable moustache, and the press often referred to him as 'The Adonis of Diplomacy'.[12] His collection of court ladies was referred to by one woman as a 'harem'.

Initially Daisy was contemptuous of Soveral, even virulent. She called him

the oddest character in English Society: he imagines himself to be a great intellectual and political force and the wise adviser of all the heads of the government and, of course, the greatest danger to women! He is so swarthy that he is nicknamed the 'Blue Monkey' and I imagine that even those stupid people who believe that every man who talks to a woman must be her lover, could not take his Don Juanesque pretensions seriously. Yet I am told that all women do not judge him so severely and some even find him *très séduisant*. How disgusting! [13]

As the following letter to the Marquis reveals, however, Daisy's disgust was only part of her complex attitude toward him:

It says in the Bible – 'Put not your trust in Princes.' I say put not your trust in foreign ministers – you knew I wanted to go home and you simply went home without me after telling me you did not want to go so soon, for like Jenny you wished to dance some more dances. . . . You are simply getting bored with me and that's the truth. . . . No my dear, I am not going to be taken up one moment & dropped the next. . . .

Now that I have said all that I feel better. Let me know tomorrow if you are coming for lunch or not.

Yours,
Daisy.[14]

Jennie's relationship with Soveral was much more secure. He seems to have destroyed any correspondence between them, but he did save one note that was signed 'forever Jennie'.[15]

Soveral also became a good friend of Winston's and occasionally acted as his friend at Court when Winston began to differ with the King on some issues. One such issue was Free Trade.

Towards the end of 1904 Jennie wrote to Winston from Sandringham:

My dearest Winston,

I read your speech at Glasgow with such interest – I did *not* discuss it with the King, you will be surprised to hear. I think it was rather a pity your Chairman attacked A. B. [Arthur Balfour] the way he did. I see the audience resented it – at least so the papers make out. Henri de Breteuil tells me that in France they look upon you as the coming man. Here I am in a hotbed of protectionists. You have probably seen the party in the papers. We have been asked to stay on till Monday. It has been most pleasant nice weather – pleasant people & excellent sport. George shot very well & [we] are both seen in good favour – so *that* is all right. Where shall you be next week? Salisbury Hall is at your disposal if you want to come. By the way, I have been so ill ever since I ate those oysters with you – I had to see the doctor here, & he told me I had been poisoned. I am all right now. – We are thinking of going to Paris for Xmas. Why don't you come? The Breteuils would put you up – Now good-bye.

Yr loving
mother.[16]

Winston stayed often at Salisbury Hall now. He had an 'aerial summerhouse' built in an old lime tree, and there he would practise his speeches to an audience of sky and leaves. He had also begun writing a biography of his father and he prodded Jennie constantly to remember things that she perhaps would rather have forgotten: '. . . how you first began in Charles Street . . . then the row, I suppose in 1877, then Ireland. . . .'[17]

Jennie still maintained relations with many members of her first husband's family. In the early years of her marriage to Randolph, Jennie and Randolph's sister Fanny (Lady Tweedmouth) had politely detested each other. But gradually their friendship grew so close and warm that Jennie called Fanny 'without exception the noblest character I have ever met. . . .'[18]

George and Jennie were guests at a ball given by Lady Tweedmouth, 'and when we came away,' George recalled, 'Jennie was terribly depressed, almost in tears. I asked her the reason, and she told me that her hostess had confided to her that she had received her death warrant from the doctor that afternoon, and she could not live more than three months. . . . She had been the life and soul of the evening, and nobody would have guessed that this terrible sentence was hanging over her. . . .'[19]

Jennie had lost other friends within the past few years: Cecil Rhodes, Baron Hirsch, Oscar Wilde. And now Mary Leiter Curzon was also seriously ill.[20]

When her husband was first made Viceroy of India, Mary told Jennie: '. . . I feel like a ship in full sail on the high seas of dignity! . . .' And on another occasion she added: 'There is no happiness so great to a woman as the admiration she can feel to the depths of her heart for her Belovedest.'

Most of her letters to Jennie, however, indicated a longing to return to England. And finally she and Lord Curzon did, in 1905 after Curzon clashed unsuccessfully with the Commander-in-Chief of the Indian Army, Horatio Kitchener. Unfortunately, Mary's health continued to fail, and a short time later Mary Leiter Curzon died. Jennie felt deeply the loss of her tall, stately friend with the soft voice and the radiant smile.[21]

There was further sadness for Jennie that year. Since her marriage to George, she had seen little of Pearl Craigie. Pearl was always somewhere else: a long stay in India with the Curzons, a spring visit to Spain, a long summer with her son on the Isle of Wight, and then a tour of the United States for a series of lectures on 'The Science of Life'. The tour proved too tiring for her and she found herself unable to complete it. In February 1906 she wrote: 'I don't believe I shall live much longer. There is nothing organically wrong with me, but I flag, the pulse stops.' And then she added, 'Please don't think I want a long illness and horrors. I want to die in harness and at work. . . .'[22]

Pearl's final request of Jennie was a strange one for her: she wanted to be presented at Court. In Queen Victoria's time she had been barred from Court by the stigma of her divorce. But she had been the innocent party and her former husband had now remarried.

Providing Jennie with family background for the presentation, Pearl observed that her cousin, Admiral Cowles, had married Theodore Roosevelt's sister. Since Jennie also had a distant family relationship with

President Roosevelt, she and Pearl could claim kinship. Their kinship, however, was far closer than that of cousins. Indeed, their relationship was all the more remarkable because Pearl had so few women friends. She often said that she never really understood women.

> My mother was at one time very fond of telling how, when I was a very little girl, she left me alone one day with my dolls, to whose mute companionship she commended me for a short hour. On her return, she found a long row of sawdust puppets hanging by their necks, and me contemplating their dangling bodies in silent pleasure, and they were all women dolls, too. . . .[23]

'Jennie', the heroine of Pearl Craigie's novel *The Vineyard*, was an idealistic, intelligent woman in love with a handsome but morally weak man. In the novel, the dying father tells Jennie, 'If I fall asleep, take care of the candle.'[24] Earlier Pearl had written of herself that doctors 'told me some years ago that I should go out like a candle: my heart was broken with grief long ago. . . .'[25] In August 1906 Pearl Mary-Teresa Craigie died in her sleep, her rosary in her hand.

If Pearl Craigie had intended the handsome, morally weak man in *The Vineyard* to represent George Cornwallis-West, that descriptive arrow seemed now to be wide of the mark. George had matured through the years. He still loved his hunting, fishing and motoring, and kept careful count of the results of the shoot, the weight of the fish, and the miles travelled per hour ('averaged 31 miles an hour the whole way'). But by now he had also spent four years with the British Electric Traction Company, earning a good income from directorships and various other fees.

The year 1906 had begun well for him. He and a friend had by then established their own brokerage firm, 'Wheater, Cornwallis-West & Co.' George had made use of many of Jennie's contacts, and the company's earnings in 1905 were £23,000. By 1906, they had expanded, holding large interests in steel companies and copper mines, and George was travelling more than ever. One of the men he met was a quiet, capable engineer – then not interested in politics – named Herbert Hoover.[26]

For Winston the beginning of that year had been even better. In 1904 his cross-over from the Conservatives to the Liberals on the Free Trade issue had brought a worried letter from Bourke Cockran, who had been disturbed by a cartoon in the *Pall Mall Gazette*.

It represented you as a mosquito or a fly or a wasp or some variety of winged irritant perched on the coach of Sir Henry Campbell-Bannerman whose repose you have evidently disturbed and are plainly striving to ruin. Under it is the paragraph to which I have referred and which states in substance that Mr Winston Churchill will not be given a place in the Liberal Cabinet if one should be formed after the next election. . . .

Now this conception of your attitude presents you in rather a sordid character. . . . Of course we must realise that where a man changes sides, however lofty the motives which actually govern him, he is very likely to be accused by those whom he has left of being actuated by the very basest desires and ambitions. . . . Why not confound the hostile and surprise the indifferent by declaring now that you won't seek or even accept membership in a Liberal Government if one is to be formed with the new parliament? Such a declaration would be in the nature of a bomb whose explosion would resound throughout the whole Empire but whose fragments would damage none but your critics. . . .[27]

Winston, however, clearly expected to be offered a Cabinet post in the new Liberal government, and he fully intended to accept it. Balfour had resigned in December 1905 and the Liberal leader Henry Campbell-Bannerman had become Prime Minister. A seventy-year-old man who had led the public fight against the Boer War,[28] 'C-B' was 'easygoing to the point of laziness', liked French novels, had few enemies and fewer intimate friends, but a core of fundamental honesty. He offered Winston the post of Under-Secretary of State for the Colonies.

Winston accepted, but a member of the government still had to represent a constituency. The election Winston had to fight for and win was at Manchester.[29] Jennie was there with him. One of the issues against the Conservative Party was their support of expensive coal, and Jennie told a crowd, 'The Conservatives give you dear coal, I give you dear Winston. . . .'

To Leonie, Jennie wrote: 'The election is most exciting – they say it will be a close thing. The female suffrage women are too odious. Every night they make a disturbance and shriek and rant. They damage their own cause hopelessly. . . .'[30] On another occasion, Jennie told a crowd of suffragettes that 'they ought to be forcibly fed with common sense.'[31]

Jennie was at the Town Hall while the votes were being counted and afterwards at the Reform Club 'where the scene', she said, 'was indescribable. . . . I have been to lots of elections, but I never saw such excitement. . . . Winston told me two days before that he thought there would be a clean sweep. . . .'[32]

Jennie also took advantage of this opportunity to chide Leonie who had been miffed by Winston's switch from the Conservatives:

> I am amused by what you say about turncoats – I suppose that is a dig at Winston for going to the other side. There is no doubt it takes a big man to change his mind. You might have quoted Dizzy, Gladstone, and last but not least, Chamberlain. As for Arthur Balfour, his mind is never made up, so he has none to change. . . .[33]

This had been an important time for Winston: his biography of his father had been published and was an enormous success;[34] the Cabinet post was just what he wanted; and now his overwhelming victory in Manchester crowned it all. Jennie immediately set herself to work on another job she loved: decorating a house she had rented for Winston in Bolton Street. 'It will be charming,' she confidently told Leonie.

Winston also hired a new private secretary, a young friend of Leonie's whom he had met at a party. His name was Edward Marsh, and Leonie strongly recommended him. Edward Marsh would become one of Winston's most intimate lifelong friends. Marsh wrote to Leonie:

> Such an excitement. I *must* tell you. Your nephew has asked me to be his private secretary for 6 months or so. It will be the most interesting thing I have ever done but I'm most terribly afraid of not being the right person and turning out a failure. I am sure it's your doing. When you come back in May I'll tell you whether I bless you or curse you! You'll find me a grey-haired skeleton in either case as he means to work me to death. It's funny that just after we were discussing the problem of what I should do to age myself, this easy solution should have dashed forth. I've just dined alone with Winston. He was most perfectly charming to me, but made it quite clear what he would expect in the way of help and I almost *know* I can't do it – its [sic] awful! . . .[35]

Through the years, Marsh also became very close to Jennie and wrote of her:

It was at Blenheim that I first met Lady Randolph Churchill, who soon became one of my dearest friends. She was an incredible and most delightful compound of flagrant worldliness and eternal childhood, in thrall to fashion and luxury (life didn't begin for her on the basis of less than 40 pairs of shoes) yet never sacrificing one human quality of warm-heartedness, humour, loyalty, sincerity, or steadfast and pugnacious courage.[36]

After their first meeting, Jennie said she thought Marsh 'very pleasant', but she could not refrain from adding, 'I think it is a pity he has such a squeaky voice. . . .' [37]

As much as Jennie came to like Marsh, she may have had some reservations about his being secretary to her son. This had nothing to do with Marsh's qualifications – he was loyal, sincere, warm-hearted, sensitive, and hardworking. But he was also homosexual. Indeed, as the year passed, Marsh – who became Sir Edward Marsh – was recognized as 'the centre of a large homosexual artistic colony' in England.[38] There was never any scandal about it, but Jennie could hardly forget how an alleged homosexual association had jeopardized Winston's military career. A similar smear might have had an even more crippling effect on the career of a young politician.

The year which had begun so brightly finally brought trouble. The worst of it was for George. The promising capitalist, booming in every direction, was suddenly in financial trouble. He had been swindled by a glib lawyer who left him £8,000 in debts. The Duke of Westminster wrote to Winston on August 19, 1906:

. . . I hear you & your brother Jack have between you come to his aid. I would have helped before I left if there hadn't been some misunderstanding between us. I send you enclosed cheque to be used on condition that George should not know of this transaction till I choose, if ever, to let him know. I think it very hard that you & Jack should bear the brunt, when it should have come on me, as his brother-in-law.[39]

Winston immediately sent a confidential letter to George:

My dear George,
    I send you herewith a cheque for £3,000 to be devoted to the re-

266

payment of the sums of wh you were robbed by your solicitor, & wh I understand you have now borrowed from Cox's Bank. The transaction is personal between us & the money is a loan to be repaid at any time at three months notice on my request. Meanwhile you should pay interest at $2\frac{1}{2}\%$ per annum into my account at Cox's. Perhaps you will write me a letter confirming this in precise detail.[40]

And George answered: '. . . I thank you also, my dear Winston, for your great kindness of heart. . . .'[41]

George was not the only one who had trouble. He mentioned to Winston that Consuelo, Duchess of Marlborough, had come to Salisbury Hall at Jennie's invitation:

Poor little Consuelo . . . I do pity her with all my heart, what a tragedy. The whole thing reminds me of Hogarth's series of satyr [sic], 'Marriage à la mode'. Take my advice & if ever you do marry, do it from motives of affection & none other. No riches in the world can compensate for anything else.

So come down here soon; I am sure you want a rest, or soon will.[42]

The week before, in a letter marked 'SECRET', Winston had written to his mother:

Sunny has definitely separated from Consuelo, who is in London at Sunderland House. Her father returns to Paris on Monday. I have suggested to her that you would be vy willing to go and stay with her for a while, as I cannot bear to think of her being all alone during these dark days. If she should send for you, I hope you will put aside other things & go to her. I know how you always are a prop to lean on in bad times.[43]

But Jennie now needed a prop for herself. George's financial disaster had caused him to become edgy, irritable, and increasingly argumentative. They quarrelled more, most often about George's wandering eye, which was perhaps partly his way of bolstering his ego. Both Jennie and George, however, were quick to regret their battles.

Jennie had gone to Cannes, and George wrote to her: 'I'm awfully worried as I find you thought I chased you away. You know I didn't and that I'd sooner see you than all the others. . . .'[44] And Jennie wrote to

Jack. 'Please tell Walden to send me by post George's photograph on my mantel-piece. He is to take it out of the frame....'[45]

Part of the time she was away, Jennie stayed with George's sister Daisy, who had rented a villa nearby. When Jennie arrived there on April 14,1907, Daisy, with her usual bite, commented in her diary: 'We are all going on a motor trip – Jennie, my sister-in-law – who married George and still loves him immensely poor dear; she is uncommonly nice and still very handsome, but of course the difference in age is a sad and terrible drawback (no babies possible); well, she is coming with us. The Duke of Marlborough, her cousin by marriage ... also comes....'[46]

Daisy also mentioned an attempt Sunny made to move the picnic table. It was loaded with food 'and down the whole thing went. . . . The Duke was miserable; by the way he looked at the debris one might have thought he was peering at his own life, which at the present moment is in much the same state....'[47]

While Daisy suffered the young Duke politely, she actively disliked Winston. When Jennie and George were married, Daisy had noted, 'It made Winston Churchill a connection of ours, a prospect we viewed with somewhat mixed feelings. I cannot honestly say I ever cared for him very much....'[48]

So closely intertwined was international society that it was perhaps not surprising for Jennie to discover that Daisy was related by marriage to Charles Kinsky. Daisy was also a close friend of Kinsky's wife Lily, which might have helped determine her attitude towards Jennie.

With the death of his father, Count Kinsky had become Prince Kinsky. He had left the diplomatic service and become Privy Counsellor and Chamberlain to the Emperor of Austria. He was also a Major in the Army Reserve, and a hereditary member of the Austrian House of Lords. When one of Jennie's young friends, the brilliant pianist-composer Ethel Smyth,[49] wanted to study and work in Vienna, Jennie wrote to Kinsky asking him to help her. Miss Smyth described the incident in her memoirs:

Dear Lady Randolph Churchill, who had the beautiful faculty of keeping the friendship of those who were said to have loved her in her youth, had written to one of these, a perfectly delightful man, and a great power in Vienna – who at once promised to do all he could to influence his friend Count Montenuovo in my behalf. Count Montenuovo was the son of Marie Louise, and the Emperor Francis

268

Joseph had created for him some very dignified post connected with the Opera. . . . Lady Randolph's friend had worked up the feeble Montenuovo to a pitch of zeal. . . .

'I wish she had married Kinsky,' Ethel Smyth later remarked, '. . . he was so delightful. . . .' [50]

Kinsky and his wife came to England at least once a year to see the Grand National, and he and Jennie might well have attended some of the same parties. It is unlikely, however, that they ever wrote to each other. But they had mutual friends and were not ignorant of each other's lives. How delighted the hypocritical Daisy Pless would have been to tell Jennie any happy news about the Kinskys – and how careful Jennie would have been not to give her the satisfaction of a reaction.

Jennie now received news of another former lover. Bourke Cockran had remarried. The headline in the *Sunday World* read:

She, Pretty and Popular; He Famous and Wealthy. [51]

She was Anne Ide, daughter of the Governor General of the Philippines. [52] She, Bourke, Alice Roosevelt and Nicholas Longworth had all travelled together to the Philippines on a government-sponsored inspection tour. The trip resulted in both couples marrying. And again, in the constant interweaving of upper-class society, Anne Ide's sister later married Jennie's nephew, Shane Leslie, with the ceremony taking place on Bourke Cockran's estate at Sands Point, New York. [53]

Shortly before her marriage, Alice Roosevelt had visited England, where she met Jennie. Jennie invited her to stay with her at Salisbury Hall. 'I got the feeling,' Alice Roosevelt Longworth remembered, 'that she was terribly lonely, and that she was grasping at me as if I were a sturdy straw.' [54]

It was a time when George was travelling a good deal, when Winston was kept busy by the Colonial Office, and Jack was preoccupied with a stock-market panic. Clara had moved to Brede Place in Sussex, and Leonie alternated between Ireland and London. 'The fact is when I go to London, there are only two people I ever try to see, one is Winston, the other you,' Jennie wrote to Leonie from Salisbury Hall. 'Both are aforesaid disappointments. One is on account of work, the other on account of pleasure. I may go away feeling sore at heart. I snatch a few minutes of Winston's society by driving him to the Colonial Office, and the most you can afford are a few words uncomfortably (for me) on the telephone.' But then she added, 'You know I love you and that when you want me, I am to be found.' [55]

It is hard to imagine Jennie being lonely. She was so vibrant, she had so many friends, so many interests. But this was a loneliness that only a husband or family could fill.

There was never any rift between the three sisters, but there was no longer the physical closeness provided by their clustered houses on Great Cumberland Place. Clara's husband, Moreton Frewen, travelled that year between Africa, where he planned to buy forest land, and Prince Rupert, Canada, where he planned to create a great port city. Both projects failed. Clara was often alone, and Jennie made frequent visits to Brede Place. Compared to the fine, logical minds of her sisters, Clara was almost a fey creature, easily abstracted. Her nephew, Seymour Leslie, recalled her greeting him at the end of his school term: 'Why you *Dear Thing!* how perfectly *lovely* to see you back from school! I can't *wait* to hear your news of it! Tell me *all* about it, sit on the sofa there and don't leave any thing out!'

'Whereupon,' said Seymour, 'she turned to continue her correspondence.' [56]

Yet this was a woman of penetrating passion, and her love letters to her husband reveal a woman few people ever knew.

Clara shared Jennie's disregard for money: she spent it, often when she didn't have it. The renovation of the beautiful, historic Brede Place was a drain of thousands of pounds.[57] She built dams and rose gardens and had outdoor sculpture done by the American Augustus Saint-Gaudens, while her artistic daughter Clare [58] modelled cement swans around the lily pond. Clara's most inexpensive innovation was to establish a tradition of having trees planted by visiting celebrities – King Edward, Rudyard Kipling, Clemenceau, Queen Marie of Rumania, and even her nephew Winston.

Winston and his lovely cousin Clare were good friends, and years later the two posed for each other – Clare sculpting while Winston painted. In 1907 Winston also agreed to find an administrative job in Nigeria for Hugh Frewen, Clare's brother, who wanted to spend some time there.

Late that year, Winston went on a four-month trip to Europe and Africa with Eddie Marsh; Jennie wrote to Marsh: 'Bless you, dear Eddie ... Look after my Winston – he is very precious to me.' [59]

Before leaving, Winston had asked his mother to sub-let his house, find work for his secretary, and take care of a number of other things. 'I do rely upon you dear Mamma to help me in arranging these affairs; for wh I am not at all suited by disposition or knowledge.' [60]

She was happy to oblige. She advised him of what she planned to do and told him, 'Don't worry about it. . . .' Then she went on to say:

. . . I have followed the H of C debates and Eddie wrote to me of your all-night sitting. You will be glad to get away from speeches – I thought the Govt wd have to practically drop the Scotch Bill – I hear nothing but abuse of it. I don't pretend to know anything about it – but that dual ownership business has been tried in Ireland and has been found more than wanting! I liked yr Transvaal speech, and quite agree with you. . . .

Do try and read my chapters at SH. The 3 will only take you an hour – if as much – I want you to add to the 5th chapt that story of yr father and Goschen and the Exchequer. If told at all it must be well told – and I feel diffident – also, make a little note in the 4th as to where I can get some Irish data – that chap is too short. . . .

. . . I hate to think of your going off for so long – and that I shall not see you again before your departure. But you will enjoy it, and it will be a great rest and change. . . . Mind you get Trevelyan's *Garibaldi* to read en route – also, *Memories and Impressions* of George Brodick. . . . [61]

The chapters Jennie wanted Winston to read were from her *Reminiscences*. 'I am struggling with this book,' she said. 'My feelings fluctuate about it. Sometimes I think it is going to be splendid, and then again I am most depressed. . . .' [62]

Winston tried to advise her: 'You have a great chance of making a charming woman's book about the last 30 years, & do, I beg you, lavish trouble upon it, & banish ruthlessly anything that will hurt other people's feelings. It is well worthwhile.' [63]

She did exactly that. She ended her reminiscences with the time just before her marriage to George West and refrained from including anything that might make anyone unhappy. The tone was not apologetic, but neither was the book very revealing. As she said in the Preface, '. . . there may be some to whom these Reminiscences will be interesting chiefly in virtue of what is left unsaid.' [64]

Although Winston himself was sensitive to criticism, his mother's response to some of his remarks indicates that he took a different attitude towards her work:

... We are still in Scotland, as you see. . . . It is very mild up here, but I like the outdoor life, & have taken to fishing, which I enjoy. I write all the mornings & have got on with the book. I received the chapters. You were a bit scathing about Chap. V, but I did not mind, as I ought to have told you that V was *quite* in the rough – merely a lot of notes put together which Miss Anning typed in order that you might see them. In any case, I shd never have sent the chapter to the *Century* as you saw it. I have added a lot to Chapt 4 & lead up to Ireland. The *Century* have now 4 chapters & I hope they will leave me in peace for a little. . . . In the memoirs of Mde de Boigne, she gives an account of a conversation she had with Napoleon. I have copied it out for you, as I know yr keen interest in him. Bless you, darling. Thank you so much for looking at my chapters & I forgive you for saying 'Fie!' to your loving

Mother.[65]

Faced with this reaction, Winston took a tactful approach: 'You must not regard my criticisms as personal. Literary judgments are not worth much – but they are worth nothing unless they are at once impartial & impersonal.'[66]

A few months later Winston received startling news from Jack:

I am writing to tell you that a very wonderful thing has happened. Goonie [Lady Gwendeline Bertie] loves me. I have loved her for a long time – but I have always attempted to put thoughts of that kind out of my mind – because I thought that I had nothing to give her – and also chiefly because I never for one moment imagined that she would ever care for me.

This is absolutely secret. Only my mother and George know about it. Her parents know nothing. Nor must they – *until I can come with some proposition. . . .*[67]

Winston may have wondered about Jack's reference to 'my mother'.

'You understand all this?' Jack continued.

272

I wish you were here. You were in love really once – and you know what that meant. But you had other things to think of. Your career and your future filled more than half your life. I love the same way you did – but I have no other thoughts. All dreams of the future – my career and everything else, are wrapped up in one person. Nothing else matters to me in the least. I suppose that sounds very silly – but the only people who think it so are those who have never been able to feel these things themselves.

Write to Goonie – but I impress on you, keep our *secret absolutely*. If her family suspected now – her life at Wytham would be unbearable. . . .

I am going through a mixture of happiness and fear, that is not enviable.[68]

Winston later wrote about the contrast between his brother and himself:

He is quite different from me, understanding women thoroughly, getting into touch with them at once, & absolutely dependent upon feminine influence of some kind for the peace & harmony of his soul. Whereas I am stupid & clumsy in that relation, and naturally quite self-reliant & self-contained. Yet by such different paths we both arrive at loneliness.[69]

Winston had known 'Goonie' well. Discussing Jack's news, Jennie commented to Winston, 'I sometimes thought you had designs in that quarter. . . .'[70] Indeed, Goonie's earlier letters to Winston had seemed edged with anticipation. Clearly, however, Winston had had other ideas. Now he only wanted to help his brother. 'Poor dear – We must manage to drive that through for him,' he wrote to his mother. 'How happy he must be & how glad he must be & how glad I am he had not married some beastly woman for money. . . .'[71]

Goonie told Winston about a lunch she had had with Jennie, '. . . a very wonderful woman & so philosophical. . . . In spite of everything her spirit and vitality are wonderful. She never gives in – not for a single moment. . . .'[72] A financial panic in New York in 1907 had compounded the losses George had suffered in the swindle. As Jennie told Winston, 'George hasn't been able to draw one penny from his business this year – so we have no nest egg to fall back on. . . . It preys dreadfully on poor George, who is getting quite ill over it all. . . .'[73]

Jennie could bear the crisis, but George couldn't. A few months later Jack reported to his brother that 'things seem to be going pretty badly in the home ménage. Poor George who has little stamina, has knuckled under to bad times and is in a bad way. I am trying to make him "buck up" against the bad times – but it is hard work.' [74]

Jennie described their situation: 'George has been so seedy these last 4 weeks with a cold that the doctors have ordered him off to St Moritz to recoup. Unfortunately owing to the expense I have not been able to go with him – which is depressing for both – as he feels ill & lonely – & I hate being away from him as you know. However, there it is!' [75]

She was so short of money that she apologized to Winston for not sending him a cable on his birthday. She didn't have his address, she said, but she also 'thought it might be expensive. "Strange fit of economy", you will say. . . .' [76]

However, anxiety about money did not prevent her from keeping active and from keeping Winston posted on some of the latest news. The Prime Minister was seriously ill, and a change in Government was expected soon; she had dined with Cassel, who sent regards; Leonie had met the German Emperor who 'asked a great deal after me';[77] Consuelo was looking very well '& quite fat for her . . .'; she had opened an Exhibition of Books in Bond Street: 'All the publishers and authors were there – & I made a speech & Mr John Murray proposed a vote of thanks to me. He is very deaf & made a "fuddly" speech – said, "Mrs Cornwallis – who is an authoress & the mother of an authoress!" Shrieks from the Audience. . . .' [78] *The Times* recorded that in her speech Jennie had described herself as 'neither bookish nor literary', and added, 'Publishers are as important to authors as Cabinet Ministers to suffragettes.' [79]

In an effort to economize, Jennie and George decided to move back to London. The good thing about their return, she wrote to Winston, 'is that I shall see more of you. . . .' [80] But after referring to Jack's engagement, in another note to Winston, she remarked, wistfully, 'I suppose you will be next to "pop off"; it is always so in a family. . . .' [81]

Goonie also wrote to Winston. She told him that Jennie had read her parts of a recent letter from him, and she chided him – 'how cruel you are' – about his criticism of his mother's 'little "potions & histories". – A forbidding-looking "no!" on the margin.' [82]

Jennie still had another duty to perform on behalf of Winston, this

274

one particularly difficult. His long-time servant Scrivings had died, and Winston asked Jennie to break the news to Scrivings's wife. Then she had to find another servant for Winston, as he would soon be returning from his four-month trip. Winston gave Jack the details:

. . . On my return I think I shall go to the Ritz Hotel, & please ask Mamma to engage me a bedroom, a bathroom, & a comfortable sitting room, & to make the vy best terms she can with the Manager. She should tell them that if they make me comfortable & do not charge me too much I will in all probability stay a month, but if they overcharge me I will clear out at once & tell everybody what robbers they are. . . .

P.S. Show this to Mamma with my best love.[83]

Jennie answered: 'I came here on Sat, Jack being here & George still abroad. . . . How I wish you cd have taken George with you. He needs an open-air life. This City grind is very hard for him. . . . I am longing to get you back – but it is cold & grey here. Stay away as long as you can is my advice. . . .'[84]

George returned from St Moritz 'a little better', but he needed an operation on his nose. 'Poor fellow, he never seems to be out of the hospital,' Jennie wrote.[85] Jennie herself was not in the best of health. 'I feel like a boiled gooseberry,' she told Winston in January 1908. 'How I wish I could have gone to Paris to meet you!'[86] And, five days later: 'Do telegraph . . . the actual day & hour you arrive that your "Mommer" may be there. . . .'[87]

In the spring of 1908, not many months after Winston's return, Campbell-Bannerman had to resign because of ill health. His successor was Herbert Henry Asquith, a shrewd, unimaginative, stubborn Yorkshireman, who could also be genial and tactful when he wished. His wife was the brilliant Margot Asquith, a friend of Jennie and Winston. The new Asquith Cabinet included Winston as President of the Board of Trade. As a new Minister he was required by law to stand again in a by-election.

The weekend of his appointment, Winston attended a party his mother gave at Salisbury Hall. One of the guests was Clementine Hozier. Clementine's father had been Sir Henry Montague Hozier, a flamboyant, brilliant military man who had died the previous year. He had separated from his wife so many years before that he hadn't even listed his marriage in *Who's Who*. His wife, Lady Blanche, had known Jennie in earlier years,[88] and Jennie's brother-in-law John Leslie was Clementine's godfather.

Winston had first seen Clementine when she was nineteen. They were at a dance at Lady Crewe's in 1904, and Winston asked his mother if she knew the girl. Jennie said she didn't but would find out about her. It was then that she discovered Clementine was the daughter of her old friend, 'whom I haven't seen for years.'[89]

Jennie then introduced Winston to Clementine. 'Winston just stared,' Clementine later said. 'He never uttered one word, and was very gauche – He never asked me for a dance, he never asked me to have supper with him. I had of course heard a great deal about him – nothing but ill. I had been told he was stuck-up, objectionable, etc. And on this occasion he just stood and stared.'[90]

Two years before, Winston had demonstrated his gaucherie with another young woman, Violet Asquith. After a long silence, he suddenly asked her how old she was. She replied that she was nineteen. Almost despairingly, Winston said that he was already thirty-two – 'Younger than anyone else who *counts*, though.' And then he added, 'We are all worms, but I do believe I am a glow-worm.'[91]

The next time Winston met Clementine was in March 1908 at a party given by her great-aunt, Lady St Helier. On this occasion Winston did speak to her, asking if she had read his recent biography of his father. She had not. 'If I send you the book tomorrow, will you read it?' She said she would. But he never sent the book, and that, too, made a less than favourable impression.[92]

Now on April 12, at Salisbury Hall, here was Clementine again. Four days later he wrote to her:

I am back here for a night and a day in order to 'kiss hands' on appointment, & I seize this fleeting hour of leisure to write & tell you how much I liked our long talk on Sunday and what a comfort & pleasure it was to meet a girl with so much intellectual quality & such strong reserves of noble sentiment. I hope we shall meet again and come to know each other better and like each other more: and I see no reason why this should not be so. Time passes quickly and the six weeks you are to be abroad will soon be over. Write therefore and tell me what your plans are, how your days are occupied, & above all when you are coming home. Meanwhile I will let you know from time to time how I am getting on here in the storm; and we may lay the foundations of a frank and clear-eyed friendship which I certainly should value and cherish with many serious feelings of respect.

So far the Manchester contest has been quite Napoleonic in its openings & development. The three days I have been in the city have produced a most happy change in the spirits of my friends. . . .[93]

Despite his 'Napoleonic' campaign, Winston was defeated in the Manchester election[94] and had to run again for a safer seat, the working-class district of Dundee. He won overwhelmingly. He had openly attacked the Conservative Party, saying, 'It is filled with old, doddering peers, cute financial magnates, clever wire-pullers, big brewers with bulbous noses. All the enemies of progress are there – weaklings, sleek, smug, comfortable, self-important individuals.'[95] He also presented his views of the virtues of Liberalism in contrast with Socialism: 'Socialism wants to pull down wealth. Liberalism seeks to raise up poverty. Socialism would destroy private interests – Liberalism would preserve them in the only way they could justly be preserved, by reconciling them with public right. . . . Socialism attacks capital, Liberalism attacks monopoly.'[96]

Jack also had good news. His firm had guaranteed him a sufficient income to allow him to make marriage plans, and on August 7, 1908, Winston wrote to Clementine:

Jack has been married today – *civilly*. The service is tomorrow at Oxford; but we all swooped down in motor-cars upon the little town of Abingdon and did the deed before the Registrar – for all the world as if it was an elopement – with irate parents panting on the path. Afterwards we were shown over the Town Hall & its relics and treasures – quite considerable for so small a place – & then back go bride & bridegroom *to their respective homes* until tomorrow. Both were 'entirely composed' & the business was despatched with a celerity & ease that was almost appalling.[97]

On the next day, again from Abingdon, Winston wrote:

My Dear,

I have just come back from throwing an old slipper into Jack's departing motor car. It was a vy pretty wedding. No swarms of

London fly-catchers. No one came who did not really care, & the only spectators were tenants & country-folk. Only children for brides-maids & Yeomanry with crossed swords for pomp. The bride looked lovely & her father & mother were sad indeed to lose her. But the triumphant Jack bore her off amid showers of rice & pursuing cheers –let us pray – to happiness & honour all her life.[98]

As Jennie had predicted, Winston would be 'the next to pop off.' He lost little time in coming to his decision and planned to propose to Clementine at Blenheim Palace, his birthplace.

Let us all go to Blenheim for Monday & Tuesday & then go on Wed-nesday to Salisbury Hall. Sunny wants us all to come & my mother will look after you – and so will I. I want so much to show you that beautiful place & in its gardens we shall find lots of places to talk in, & lots of things to talk about. My mother will have already wired you. . . .[99]

At first Clementine was reluctant to go, but finally she did. Her mother did not accompany her, so Jennie was the chaperone. Winston took Clementine for a walk in the late afternoon. It started to rain and they took shelter in an ornamental temple overlooking the lake. There he proposed, and she accepted.

Jennie confided the secret to her friend Mary Crichton, saying, 'You see my Winston is not *easy*; he is very difficult indeed and she is just right.' [100]

A short time later Jennie received a letter from Clementine's grand-mother, Countess of Airlie, who said, 'I thank you for your loving wel-come to her. I hope she will be all you can desire as a wife for your son. . . . Blanche is an old friend of yours. So she will not be quite among strangers. . . .' [101] And to Winston, Countess Airlie wrote, '. . . Your mother has welcomed her so heartily, this will add to her happiness and she will learn much from her. . . .' And then she added a thoughtful note: '. . . A good son is a good husband. . . .' [102]

Winston later wrote: 'We were married on Sept. 12, 1908 – and lived happily ever afterwards.' [103]

The wedding took place at St Margaret's Church in London. The bride wore a lovely veil of *point de Venise* lace that Jennie had worn at her own wedding.[104]

Jennie herself was gowned in

golden beaver-colored satin charmeuse, made in the exacting princess style that is so merciless to the hips of middle-aged women. The
gown was finished with the widest of metal embroideries. The hat was
of satin antique of the same color, with large velvet and satin-petalled
lilies in metallesque coloring with bronze and silver centers around
the brim.[105]

As the widow of 'Randy' and the mother of 'Winny' swept up the aisle
on the arm of her strapping son John there was a murmur of admiration among the crowded pews which the appearance of the bride
herself quite failed to evoke.

It seems too cruel to say, [but] his mother seemed the junior of
the bride by at least two years....[106]

It was a gratifying compliment for the fifty-four-year-old Jennie.
The day after the wedding, she received another compliment, this one
from Winston at Blenheim:

Dearest Mamma,
Everything is vy comfortable & satisfactory in every way down here,
& Clemmie vy happy & beautiful. The weather a little austere, with
gleams of sunshine; we shall long for warm Italian suns. There is no
need for any anxiety. She tells me she is writing you a letter. Best of
love, my dearest Mamma. You were a great comfort & support to me
at a critical period in my emotional development.
We have never been so near together so often in a short time. God
bless you.
What a relief to have got that ceremony over! & so happily.
                                              Your loving son,
                                                        W.
P.S. I open this letter again to tell you that George said he could wish
    me no better wife or happier days than he had found in you.
                                                        W.[107]

20

Jennie became a grandmother twice in 1909: a boy for Jack and Goonie in May, and a girl for Winston and Clemmie six weeks later. But she neither felt nor looked like a grandmother.

For a while the quiet country life had agreed with her, but her energy and imagination could not long be confined to the peace of flowers and fireplaces. Soon she found herself again at the storm centre of international society. Mrs William Astor had expressed her views on New York Society for the press and Jennie's reply in the New York *World* was splashed on the front page:

> Modern society, and what is vulgarly dubbed the 'smart set', both in New York and in London, are constantly being arraigned, criticized and judged before tribunals which often are obliged to form opinions of their merits or demerits from the outside – perhaps, if the truth were known, secretly envying their '*joie de vivre*' and their so-called wicked ways. . . .
>
> The best society does not necessarily mean the 'smart set'. It certainly does not in London, and lately in an interview which has aroused much interest on both sides of the Atlantic, Mrs William Astor tells us that the women who have the greatest influence and who give New York Society its tone are almost unknown outside their own circle. Her views are expressed most freely as to the iniquities of certain would-be fashionable women whose empty lives and ostentatious, not to say vulgar, entertainments are naturally condemned by all sensible and right-thinking people. The glorified and detailed accounts of some of these senseless festivities, as given by the press, although probably exaggerated, have brought blushes to the cheeks of their compatriots abroad, who have been mercilessly chaffed on the 'strange doings' of their country people. We read of pink luncheons and violet teas, pale-blue dinners where the sauces match the hostess' gowns (shades of Lucullus!), and where everything is blue

except the conversation, red suppers and freak dinners where the guests are invited to sit on horses and imagine they are in the hunting field, or in a gondola and fancy themselves in Venice. . . .

. . . No one likes to have their shortcomings pointed out to them, and on social matters, we Americans are proverbially sensitive. If we are too proud to be led by anyone, our good sense ought to help us to know that we are not infallible, and that there is nothing derogatory in learning. Of all nationalities, Americans are the best in adapting themselves. With them, to see is to know – and to know is to conquer.

We are told that the most refined and cultured in New York Society find exclusiveness an absolute necessity. There is no doubt where there is no recognized authority – no 'fountainhead', so to speak – Society tends to break up into different sets, each a law unto itself, and looking down on the others as vastly inferior. This is the case in Paris, where since the Republic there has been no recognized head. New York Society is so small compared to the great numbers which comprise that of London, it seems incredible that those women, who, by their assured position and knowledge of the world would have the right to speak, should not be able to wield some authority on matters of taste.

Perhaps, if they opened their doors a little wider, their influence, not to say example, might be felt. In England, Society is easier of access than in any other place in the world, being built on broader and more solid foundations, and a long-established order of things has made people less apprehensive of having their privileges encroached upon or their position shaken, and can afford to receive whom they please, and, be it said to their credit, in the most exclusive of charmed circles, individual merit is more appreciated than rank or fortunes. Beauty and charm in a woman, and brains and good fellowship in a man will take them where dull duchesses and rich bores seek in vain to enter. You may be a princess or the richest woman in the world, but you cannot be more than a lady, and surely, this ought to be a passport all over the world.

In the interview already quoted, exception is taken to the manners of some of the United States Senators and Representatives who are so uncouth, it is averred, that they could not possibly be received in the best houses. Of these, I am not in a position to speak. In the older country, brains cover a multitude of sins, and those possessing them are received everywhere, in spite sometimes of their lack of manners. Nature's 'gentleman' is quite in the ascendant today, and people forgive want of knowledge of customs and usages, which, after all, are but conventionalities, if the man who has made his way is clever and has what the French so admirably described as a '*politesse du coeur*'. . . .

Taking modern society of the present day as a whole, . . . although undoubtedly in many ways deserving of criticism and even censure, is it really more pleasure-seeking and extravagant than that of other generations? I do not think so. One has but to study history to realize that in many respects this generation compares very favourably with the eccentricities and wild extravagances of past generations. It will not be denied that the majority of women are better educated than formerly, and that a larger view of life is open to them. In England, the most frivolous of social butterflies has her earnest and serious occupations, even if they be few and far between, and most are imbued with a certain desire to appear *au fait*, of the questions of the day. In this, she is better off than her cousin across the sea, to whom politics are a sealed letter, and who is restricted in rationally spending her money by having fewer outlets.

In concluding these remarks, which with diffidence I have ventured to make, I feel it may be said that my long absence from my own country incapacitated me from being a fair critic. But I have followed with the keenest interest any controversy affecting American women. I am sure that if, on this social question, some are making mistakes, it is only a passing phase which, with their good sense of the fitness of things and proverbial intelligence, can soon be put right.[1]

The *World* article aroused a rage of protest in America. New York Society matrons accused Jennie of 'talking through her millinery'. Mrs Oliver Hazard Perry Belmont, the mother of the Duchess of Marlborough, said she would give Jennie's comments 'the notice we would give some autumn leaf which tries, as it flutters to the earth, to attract attention.'[2] And Mr John B. Baker, an American millionaire who had spent forty years abroad, called Jennie's criticism 'distinctly un-American, not to say unpatriotic'.[3]

Jennie thoroughly enjoyed the fuss, but she was thankful that comments she received about her *Reminiscences* were less caustic. It was a pleasant, unpretentious book. She had written nothing about her love life, her frustrations, her relationship with her sons. But it was a successful book and went through several editions, both in England and the United States.

Her success spurred her on to playwriting. Her love of the theatre was an old love, and she had written and acted in a dozen amateur theatricals at her friends' country houses, from Sandringham to Blenheim.

She had started writing her first full-length play in August 1903. She was staying at Blenheim while George went shooting in Wales, and he wrote to her: 'I am glad you are working at your play. Stick to it.' But apparently she did not do much on it at that time, because, in July 1909, she told a reporter:

Whatever be the play's fault, and I am quite prepared to hear that they are many, it is, at any rate, my first dramatic effort. It was written in a single week, in the country, some two years ago. For one reason or another — partly because I was called away to write my book of reminiscences — it has been left lying idle in the meantime. But in that one week, it was undeniably written.[4]

Perhaps. However, Jennie had often complained that she wrote slowly, almost painfully. But regardless of the time it took, it was a venture that required courage. No less a literary lion than Henry James had met disaster with his first play [5] — it had been well acted, splendidly mounted, but a stupendous failure. When the leading man took his bow, he was hooted and jeered. He told the audience how pained he was at the rebuff, how hard the company had worked to do justice to the play. 'T'aint your fault, Guv'nor,' called a voice in the gallery, 'it's the rotten play.' [6]

The Victorian Age, generally, had been a stagnant period for English theatre. Although it had produced a score of great novelists and poets, it had not produced many playwrights of distinction until the early Shaw.[7] In contrast the Edwardian period produced the best work of Sir Arthur Wing Pinero, George Bernard Shaw, John Galsworthy; and the Irish theatre yielded many writers of talent, including J. M. Synge. Furthermore, repertory theatre in the provinces was in its full flower. '. . . Since the beginning of the century, a great number and a greater variety of plays have been produced in the English language than in any other,' wrote theatre historian William Archer.[8]

Despite the variety, it was generally an age of 'cup-and-saucer' plays, frivolous and witty. It usually took four acts for a gentleman, having triumphed over his rivals, to be accepted by the lady.

The theatres are abominable [wrote Daisy, Princess of Pless]. . . . No theatre is prosperous, or a play complete, unless there is a bedroom scene in the second act; the hero is always in bed with his wife or his *vieille amie*, his *ancienne cocotte*; and then they get out of bed and dress on the stage; he puts on his trousers, she her drawers and stockings; one cannot help laughing, but the 'tone' of the whole thing is horrible.[9]

Pearl Craigie had had a different view: 'The British public does not care about verbal wit, and must have emotion and intensity and action.'[10] But her own plays were successful,[11] and so were the serious plays of Shaw,[12] Galsworthy, Synge, and Maugham. Somerset Maugham's *Smith* was described by a critic as 'In many ways, the best of his plays, although the fact that his central character is a servant somewhat lowers the standard of his comedy.'[13] Clerks and greengrocers, artists and landladies could figure in farce, perhaps, and provide 'comic relief' in melodrama, but were not thought worthy to appear as main characters in drawing-room comedy. In *Smith*, Maugham allowed an honest, hardworking parlourmaid to win the love of a pioneer returned from Rhodesia.

The Edwardian period was exceptionally distinguished for its acting. Much of it, no doubt, was what we might now consider 'hammy'. An actor let himself go, spoke his words with a relish, and used all kinds of flourishing gestures.

'Mrs Pat' – Beatrice Stella Campbell – was one of the great theatrical stars of the Edwardian era, together with Sarah Bernhardt, Eleonora Duse[14] and Ellen Terry.[15] She was a sultry, striking beauty and an actress with perfect diction and dramatic intensity. She acquired sudden fame with her role in Pinero's *The Second Mrs. Tanqueray* in 1893, and throughout the rest of her career played every major part from Juliet to Lady Macbeth. A highly-strung woman herself, she preferred playing women who were highly-strung, complex, fascinating, magnificent, and she played them with 'a glorious flamboyance'. 'The rich drift of the black hair, the movements in the full-skirted costume, feline in their grace. And the husky voice . . . infinitely suggestive of nervous strain within, and yet soothing in its sheer beauty. . . .' [16]

She was known to startle her leading men on stage by sticking pins into them; she smoked long cigars, and George Bernard Shaw, along with a host of other men, was in love with her.[17]

Her husband, Patrick Campbell, had been killed in the Boer War, leaving Mrs Pat with two children. Her daughter was old enough to share the stage with her, and in 1908 they had a highly successful American tour together. They had also appeared with Dublin's renowned Abbey Theatre players in William Butler Yeats's *Deirdre*. Mrs Campbell admitted to being forty-four years old in 1909 – eleven years younger than Jennie. She and Jennie had much in common: their attitudes, their beauty, their aura of excitement, their way of life. And it may well have been George who recommended to Jennie that she engage Mrs Pat as actress-manager.

In his memoirs, George claims to have first met Mrs Patrick Campbell in the winter of 1909, when she 'became a constant visitor to the house.' 'Besides being a very beautiful woman,' he said, 'she was a brilliant conversationalist, and had a keen sense of humour and a ready wit.' [18] But in a letter to her husband several years earlier, Clara Frewen had written: '. . . Leonie says Jennie seems so happy and contented, so I do hope George's little flirt with Mrs Pat Campbell means nothing. . . .' [19]

Jennie told Mrs Pat about her play, *His Borrowed Plumes*, at a luncheon party.[20] 'She read the play to me,' Mrs Pat said. 'It had certain points of cleverness, and I considered that, with ingenious production and good actors, it could be pulled together, and perhaps made into a success. . . . Feeling it would be a friendly act and an amusing piece of work for me, I offered to produce it for her. . . . So it was eventually arranged.' [21]

There is a play within a play in *His Borrowed Plumes*. The heroine, Fabia Sumner (Mrs Campbell) has written the scenario of a novel. The 'other woman', Angela Cranfield, steals it and hopes to steal Fabia's husband, Major Percival Sumner, too. Angela gives Fabia's manuscript to the Major (he does not suspect its source), and he uses it as the basis of a play of his own. The last act takes place in the ante-room of the National Theatre. Through a door leading into a stage-box, we get a view of the auditorium, and hear the actors declaiming and the audience cheering and calling for the author. Before he faces the audience, the

Major makes his peace with his wife. Then he announces to the theatre audience that his wife, and not he, is the real author of the play, and that he has been masquerading 'in borrowed plumes'.

'My adventuress [Angela Cranfield] is not quite the cut-and-dried villainess that she seems to have appeared to some people,' Jennie told a reporter.

> She is not supposed to steal the manuscripts in cold blood. It was a sort of half-accidental deed, done without full intention, in a moment of outraged pride. She is just such a woman as is to be found again and again in London Society.[22]
>
> It is these little refinements of temperament that are so difficult to express unerringly, definitely, obviously, on the stage. But that, again, is what gives writing for the stage its fascination. It is so tempting to try the most difficult thing possible.
>
> As to sheer facts, perhaps, the best answer to anyone who disagrees with them is that the story, in its main details, happens to be a true one. Some of my scenes I know are more melodramatic than the vogue is, but I admit being old-fashioned in these matters. I myself have grown rather tired of plays that are all talk. Personally, I like something to happen, so I just did my best to be dramatic in the old-fashioned way.
>
> . . . In drama it is more difficult than in almost any other art to express exactly what one means to express. There are so many things in between one's own mind and that of the audience.[23]

Friends found it interesting to speculate how much of George was in Major Sumner, and how much of Jennie in Fabia.

> *Fabia:* . . . I'm always leaving my work to fly about after him. (*After a pause*): Better if I did it more often. He does love Society.
> *Basil:* I'm not surprised, he's so popular.
> *Fabia:* But you see, he doesn't realize how slowly I write, how easily I lose the thread of my ideas. It takes time to start the machine again.
> *Fabia (collecting notes):* Oh dear, I have intended writing such a lot this week, but these parties upset one's train of thought.
> *Basil:* You wonder you are handicapped, leading this ridiculous life, trying to write in a hotel, with people in and out all day, expedi-

286

tions, river parties, and near enough to London to have a crowd today ... How can you work? You ought never to have come.

Fabia: It amuses Percival. I couldn't let him come alone.

And then, later:

Fabia: But am I not the one to blame? I feel I don't enter into Percival's plans and amusements half enough.

Jane: But how can you, with your work? He has more time for frivolities. He doesn't write half as much as you do.

Fabia: Ah, that's just it! I believe my writing so much bores him. And if it does, what's it all worth to me?

Jane: I don't think he's bored – but jealous.

Fabia (impetuously): My dear Jane, what nonsense you talk! Percival jealous! Your affection for me makes you unjust. How could he be jealous? To begin with, our work is so different.

Jane (sulkily): The real difference in this case is that you are successful, and he isn't.

Discussing Fabia's husband, two men say:

Walter: ... He is gay and light-hearted.

Martin: Large-hearted, you mean.

Walter: And very generous to the fair sex, I am told. You must own, physically he is a fine type of a man.

Martin (shakes head): ... Insists on being the centre figure, wherever he is. Must have the first place, and the prettiest woman to talk to. Look at him now.

(Percival in the background, surrounded by several of the ladies.)

Mrs Cranfield (to Fabia): If I had your brains, I too would not indulge in frivolity. When you can command all the cleverest people in London to come to you, why should you seek them in a crowd? *(She goes on.)* How I envy your position. I mean, your supreme independence. You can do without Society. If you had half a dozen lovers, and tomorrow elected to run away with one of them, all your clever world would rally around you – They are tolerant, understanding and open-minded – 'Natural selection – affinity of souls,' they would say. You'd find no difference.

Mrs Cranfield: I take my happiness where I find it – stolen or otherwise.

Basil tells Fabia that Mrs Cranfield is just a passing fancy for Percival.

> *Fabia:* Perhaps so, but he may think he cares, which comes to the same thing. She is clever and unscrupulous, and her influence is already altering him.
>
> *Basil:* Altering him? How?
>
> *Fabia:* He has become restless and anxious, and what is worse, to ease his conscience, I suppose, he likes to dwell on my short-comings. . . .
>
> *Basil:* But remember, a man ends by hating the woman who he thinks has found him out.

Somebody asks Martin how Percival and Fabia get on.

> *Martin:* I fancy as well as most married couples who have lived to-gether for ten years. If you can stand that strain, it ought to last forever. . . .
>
> *Alma:* I rather suspect her of being in love with him.
>
> *Martin:* Her own husband? Monstrous! What a selfish woman!
>
> *Fabia (discussing a visiting actress):* You think that she and my hus-band are too much together?
>
> *Jane:* You're so occupied you don't see what all your world does. Among snakes, that woman is a puff-adder.
>
> *Fabia (with a bitter laugh):* Are you so sure that I do not see – that I don't know? [24]

If Jennie did know, she didn't show it. '. . . The rehearsals are getting on,' she wrote to Leonie,

and this week there are to be two daily. Mrs Pat has really been an angel, and the Play would not exist without her. . . . I can't under-stand why I feel so calmly about the Play. Bernstein tells me he's *dans les trances* for weeks beforehand. Perhaps I do not know the horrors before me! I gave a supper party at the Ritz last Friday, too success-ful for words. . . . Kitty, Ann, Consuelo, Juliette, Violet Rutland, and Mrs Pat, Stella [her daughter], Muriel Wilson, Henry Ainley, Yates, Hugh Cecil, Bernstein, Martha Bibesco, Maurice Baring, . . . Clare [Frewen], Winston and Jack, etc. We kept it up till 2.30 AM. A hun-dred wild dances and fandangos . . . everyone taking the floor. . . . [25]

However much Mrs Pat may have enjoyed the party and Jennie's appreciation of her, she afterwards expressed a colder view of the situation:

An exaggerated importance gradually grew around the production, owing to Royalty and many distinguished people being interested in it.

Serious work became difficult – but was most mandatory to hold the play together – some of the actors started calling the play, 'Sorrowing Blooms' – a dangerous sign.

Jennie, I fancy, imagined producing her own play would be of some social advantage to all of us: I was intolerant of what I thought nonsense, and showed it quickly.[26]

Nonetheless, Mrs Pat let Jennie design one of the scenes in the play – the ante-room behind the Royal Box at the National Theatre. It was a room Jennie knew well. She herself supplied the Elizabethan furniture and decorations.

The opening matinée at Hicks' Theatre in London on July 6, 1909 was in the old tradition of splendour, 'one of the most brilliant audiences of the season.' Winston Churchill, President of the Board of Trade, 'looking profoundly nervous', sat in a box with his mother and his stepfather, Mr George Cornwallis-West.[27] There was no mention of Jack, but he surely was there.

In the opposite box was the Dowager Duchess of Manchester, and among the audience were Prince Francis of Teck, Grand Duke Michael of Russia, the Duchesses of Marlborough, Rutland, and Roxburghe, Earl Howe, Lord Elcho, Lord Charles Beresford, Mrs Asquith, and a score of other celebrities and well-known peeresses – complete with their tall wide-brimmed hats and their Directoire gowns. Mr Walkley wrote in *The Times* amusingly about the hats:

When mundane ladies – if the Gallicism may pass – when mundane ladies produce original, modern comedies out of their own original, modern, and quite charming heads, all of the other mundane ladies who have written original, modern comedies themselves, or might have done so if they had chosen, or are intending to do so the very next wet afternoon, come and look on. These are the occasions that reconcile one to the theatre. For a sudden feminine glory invades it

289

and transfigures it, so that it becomes an exhibition of beauty and elegance; the very latest dialogue on the stage is accompanied by a *frou-frou* of the very latest Paris fashions in the stalls. An especially pleasing detail is the air of sweet resignation – Is it the firm composure of the martyr or the serene smile of the seraph? – with which the ladies remove the wide-brimmed and very high-crowned hats of the present fashion from their heads and pose them very delicately upon their knees. It is with an effort you avert your gaze from this fascinating spectacle to the proceedings on the stage. But this is only to exchange one pleasure for another of the same sort. On the stage you have a bevy of ladies supporting – beautiful caryatides that they are! – the same remarkable hats, with the privilege of not having to remove them. In the presence of so many, and so beautifully complicated hats, it is, of course, impossible to think of them as mere coverings for the head. They really fulfil the really important office of creating an illusion about life, like the poetry of Shelley or the music of Debussy. With their exaggerated brims and monstrous crowns they completely shut out the dull, the workaday, and the disagreeable. Everything you feel is for the best, and looking its best, and wearing its best in the best of all Directoire worlds.

And yet, by a sort of paradox, what was perhaps the most beautiful thing, but was certainly the most suave and distinguished thing in the Hicks' Theatre yesterday afternoon – we mean, of course, Mrs Patrick Campbell – wore no hat. . . .

Some of the performers had not properly adjusted their voices to the theatre's acoustics, and several times they were loudly commanded by the audience to 'speak up'. The actor in the role of an amateur dramatist had to make a derogatory remark concerning his actors. 'They speak so naturally,' he said, 'that not a word gets over the footlights.' The audience roared with laughter. But at the end, they called 'author, author' and Jennie took her bow 'amid much cheering'.

By and large, the critics also enjoyed themselves. One wrote: '. . . a new dramatist's first play is terribly like the curate's first sermon – very portentous and self-conscious, laden with long-bottled messages to mankind at large. "His Borrowed Plumes" has proved so entirely different, so free and light-hearted, that it seemed in some ways difficult to believe that it could be a first play at all.' [28]

He went on to praise 'the unburdened brightness of its dialogue and the undercurrent of cheery satire upon the foibles of either sex that lies beneath the dramatic scenes. . . .'

In *The Era* the reviewer wrote: 'Mrs Cornwallis-West's play opened badly, owing to an accident of acoustics; but it was soon evident that she has a real gift and instinct as a dramatist, and "His Borrowed Plumes" took a firm hold on the interest of the audience, and maintained it to the close of the performance.'[29]

Plays are meant to be seen, not read. Much of what Jennie wrote, and the manner in which she wrote it, seems dated, almost archaic, now. But one can sense the characters — they are not cardboard. And the parallel to Jennie's life gives the play an added dimension.

The most perceptive review came from the distinguished Max Beerbohm:

Now, from the standpoint of the average simple playgoer, 'His Borrowed Plumes' is a very good entertainment. From the standpoint of the purely technical critic, it is a very good piece of work: a story conceived and set forth clearly, without halting, with a thorough grasp of dramatic form. From the standpoint of a critic who desires an illusion of real life, it does not pass muster. The characters have been sacrificed to the story. Now and again, as in the scene between the two jealous women, the characters emerge and are natural, real and moving. There is much that rings true in the relations of Mrs Cranfield and the Major. But, for the rest, Mrs Cornwallis-West has let herself be led into the temptation that awaits everyone who essays dramaturgy for the first time — the temptation to write not as a seer of life, but as as a playgoer who knows all about the theatre. I conjure her not to bother, henceforth, about what she thinks is needed to make a good play, but rather to let her characters do just as they would in real life. Having, as she evidently has, an instinct for dramatic form, she need not fear for the result of this process. . . .[30]

Jennie seemed exhilarated by the reaction. 'Criticism is exactly what I want, and the more candid the better,' she told a reporter. 'Although this is my first play, I am not by any means determined that it shall be my last. . . .'[31]

In those days, even a good play often ran for only a couple of weeks. *Hedda Gabler* and *Electra*, and even *Deirdre*, with the splendid Mrs

Campbell, only lasted a few special matinées. *His Borrowed Plumes* lasted almost a fortnight.

Jennie's young nephew, Seymour Leslie, later admitted that he had seen the play five times, but the only line he remembered was: 'Mary has had a *fausse-couche*.' [32] There were, however, a number of trenchant lines that were given wide circulation:

We could all dress well if we could afford not to wear our failures.

Is there so much difference between politicians and actors? Both are equally eager for popular applause, both equally doubtful whether they will get it.

All natures are in nature.

What is love without passion? – A garden without flowers, a hat without feathers, tobogganing without snow.

Italians love – sun, sin and spaghetti.

Those sincere women are generally very sly.

She would remember some of those lines with pain. Her attitude now, though, was just short of smug. 'After all,' she wrote to Leonie, 'and I say this without conceit but as a fact, if I were to die tomorrow, of all the "Souls" lot, I am the only woman who should have a record behind her. The Primrose League, the Maine hospital ship, the Anglo-Saxon Review, my book, my play!' [33]

Her record would soon be longer than that.

21

In 1909, Colonel Louis Blériot had made the first aeroplane flight across the English Channel. The automobile was rapidly replacing the horse-drawn carriage. More homes and factories were being lit by electricity instead of gas. Increased industrialization had given trade unions pivotal political strength, maintaining the Liberals in power, and urging new social and tax reforms. When the House of Lords threatened to use its veto on the proposed budget the Liberals urged a reduction of the power of the Lords. 'The House of Lords is not the watchdog of the Constitution,' said Lloyd George, 'it is Mr Balfour's poodle.' 'The House of Lords represent nobody but themselves,' added Augustine Birrell.[1]

One of the loudest voices against the Lords was the new Home Secretary,[2] Winston S. Churchill, who had been appointed to the post in February 1910. Winston warned that 'the whole machinery of representative government had been brought to a standstill,' and that 'the Tory party regard themselves as the ruling class, exercising by right a Divine superiority over the whole nation.' He demanded 'a fair and equal Constitution', which could only be possible when 'the harsh and cruel veto', of the Upper House had been shattered into fragments 'so that they were dust upon the ground'.[3]

Conservatives bitterly attacked Churchill as 'a traitor to his class.' A new general election in 1910 – the second in twelve months – returned the Liberals to government control but by a greatly reduced majority. They were now dependent for political survival on the support of the Irish Nationalist vote in Parliament.

Jennie earlier had written to her nephew Shane Leslie, who was deeply involved in Irish politics: 'Two Sundays ago, Lord Crewe, Mr Lloyd George, Mr Birrell and Winston came down . . . quite a Cabinet council! In fact, they did hold an informal one on the Irish question. I wish you had been here. . . .'[4]

Besides the Lords, the Irish question, the threat of strikes, and the suffragettes, the political situation was also troubled by the spectre of a powerful Germany and the renewed threat of war. But the popular song said:

> There'll be no wo'ar
> As long as there's a King like Good King Edward.
> There'll be no wo'ar
> For 'e 'ates that sort of thing.
> Mothers need not worry,
> As long as we've a King like Good King Edward.
> Peace with 'onour
> Is his motter,
> So God Save the King.

Edward paid his usual spring visit to Biarritz that year, but a short while after his return, he became critically ill. He told his equerry, Frederick Ponsonby, 'I can't sleep. I can't eat. They really must do something for me.' Then as Ponsonby left, the King said, 'In case I don't see you again, good-bye.'[5] By the next day he had died.

When the King was dying, Queen Alexandra sent a brougham to fetch Mrs Alice Keppel, and Alexandra herself waited to take her up to Edward's bedroom. She left her alone with him for a long time.[6]

Jennie grieved for him, too. King Edward had been her supporter, an early love, and one of her oldest friends. His approval had eased Jennie's entry into British Society when she was one of the first of the American brides of prominent Englishmen. And although he had strongly opposed it, it was he who had hastened the acceptance of Jennie's marriage to George. Even when Winston embittered the King by denouncing the House of Lords, Edward kept his friendship with Jennie intact. Moreover, Jennie's relationship with the King was responsible for her lifelong closeness with Sir Ernest Cassel – and it was Cassel who was instrumental in furthering Jack's career, who helped George get started in business, and who acted as financial adviser to Winston.

Circulating among the people in the streets were broadsheets announcing King Edward's death:

> Greatest Sorrow England Ever Had
> When Death Took Away Our Dear Dad;
> A King Was He from Head to Sole,
> Loved by his People, One and All.

'With King Edward's passing, we lost a lovable, wayward and human monarch,' Sir Frederick Ponsonby wrote.

He was one who came to decisions by instinct and not by logic, and rarely made a mistake in his judgment of men. On the whole, he preferred the society of the female sex, and was never happier than in the company of pretty women. He always thought a men's dinner party was tiresome and dull. I remember one Ascot Week, after the death of the King of Denmark, when it was decided to have a men's party, as Queen Alexandra was in mourning, and I happened to be with him when the list of guests was sent in to him on his arrival at Windsor. He looked at it and said with a sigh, 'What tiresome evenings we shall have!' [7]

For three days the body of Edward VII lay on a raised catafalque in Westminster Hall, and at times the queue stretched unbroken for six miles. Every class of people was represented among the 250,000 mourners who filed past. The King's women friends made their final curtsies, the young Kings of Portugal and Spain knelt for a long time. Kaiser Wilhelm II came, preceded by an enormous wreath.[8]

In the funeral procession the King's saddle-horse was led behind the gun-carriage, and his dog Caesar was led by a valet.[9] At the head of the procession rode the new King, George V, in a field marshal's uniform, baton in hand.[10] Then came the King of Norway, the King of Greece, the King of Spain, followed by the Tsar of Bulgaria, the King of Denmark, the King of Portugal. The King of the Belgians rode behind the King of Denmark and between Archduke Ferdinand and the heir-apparent of the Ottoman Empire. Former President Theodore Roosevelt arrived just in time to represent the United States. (There had been some concern, because the American Ambassador was afraid that Roosevelt might wish to ride in the uniform of Colonel of the Rough Riders alongside the nine Kings who were to follow the coffin.)

The tribute that Edward VII would have appreciated most occurred at Ascot Week in July 1910, afterwards referred to as the 'Black Ascot'.

All the ladies admitted to the Royal Enclosure wore black feathers and ribbons in place of the usual flowers and gauzes. Their tall and slender figures, surmounted by enormous hats, were like weird blooms springing from the bright green lawns. It was on this race-course that the peace-loving King had won some of his greatest victories and passed the happiest hours. . . . The grandees of the Edwardian Era exchanged the latest items of news: 'Mrs Keppel had gone to China . . .', 'Queen Alexandra refuses to leave the palace . . .', 'Soveral has gone back to Portugal . . .'. 'Lillie Langtry has been ruined by racing debts. . . .' [11]

They might also have mentioned that Jennie Cornwallis-West had bought, redecorated, and sold another house.[12] It was her one sure way of making money. Her last venture along these lines had been so profitable that it drew high praise from Winston:

I am so glad to hear of your excellent stroke of business. The utility of most things can be measured in terms of money. I do not believe in writing books which do not sell, or plays which do not play. The only exceptions to the rule are productions which can really claim to be high art, appreciated only by the very few. Apart from that, money value is a great test. And I think it very creditable indeed that you should be able after two or three months' work, which you greatly enjoyed, to turn over as large a sum of money as a Cabinet Minister can earn in a year. There is no reason why the experiment should not be repeated. There are lots of other houses in London, and you will have learned a great deal more than you knew before of the latest methods of furnishing. I really think it would be well worth your while to look about for another venture of the same kind. Your knowledge and taste are so good and your eye for comfort and elegance so well trained, that with a little capital you ought to be able to make a lot of money, and if you sell a few more houses, you will be able, very nearly, to afford to produce another play. I am sure George admires your great cleverness over this house as much as I do.[13]

Through her interest in the theatre Jennie was able to help Winston in an unexpected way. As Home Secretary, he was profoundly concerned with prison reform. Having seen John Galsworthy's play *Justice*, he told his mother how much he admired it, and Jennie arranged a small dinner party for Galsworthy and Winston, at which the two men could meet informally and talk at leisure. Churchill later said that Galsworthy's views deeply influenced his own action on prison reform.

Whether she could afford it or not, Jennie was thinking seriously about her second play. A newspaper announced that she planned to go to America to arrange for the production of a new play which dealt with 'the uplifting of humanity' at the expense of personal domesticity. It added: 'There is a possibility that Mrs West may be induced to appear on a lecture platform in America, dealing with her own experiences in Society.'

The announcement, it turned out, was premature. Jennie had a larger theatrical project in mind – the creation of a national theatre. 'As things are in London,' she said, 'the establishment even of a permanent repertory theatre is really next-door to impossible without official and national status. . . . The more I see of our theatres, the more I am convinced of the need for the National School of Acting. . . .' [14]

Jennie helped organize a National Theatre Committee, co-authored a detailed report, 'The National Theatre, Scheme and Estimate', and was largely responsible for raising most of the £30,000 to buy a site opposite the Victoria and Albert Museum. Then, when the National Theatre Committee merged with the Committee for a Shakespeare Memorial Theatre, the combined group turned to Jennie to act as Chairman of the new Executive Committee. She held their first meeting at Leonie's house. [15]

Quickly immersing herself in the cause, Jennie realized that the greatest and most immediate need was for funds, and her imagination conceived an idea: a Shakespeare Memorial–National Theatre Ball at which all six hundred guests would be dressed in either Shakespearean or Tudor costume. Jennie decided to be Olivia from *Twelfth Night*.

The place: Royal Albert Hall. The date: June 20, 1911.

'It will rank with the Eglinton Tournament and the most famous masques of earlier ages,' wrote H. Hamilton Fyfe.

Those who were fortunate enough to see it have something to recollect all their lives. . . . For a few all-too-brief hours the magnificence of Tudor England was revived. Here were no tawdry stage costumes, no mere imitations of reality. Here was the real thing.

Real satins and ermines, real silks and brocades, real gold and silver embroideries, real lace of the finest periods, were cunningly employed to set off the beauty of the fairest women in England. They made the Albert Hall glow with rich colour; they lent the scene a beauty which defied description. And among the sheen of wonderful stuffs, there was the sparkle of jewels, real jewels, priceless heirlooms, glittering in the hair of fair possessors, rising and falling on their bosoms, clasping them with glittering girdles, or flashing from Elizabethan 'stomachers' of a value beyond belief. . . .

. . . In 48 hours the Albert Hall was transformed from its habitual sombre Early Victorianism into an Italian garden. . . .

. . . The blue sky which had the roof was a positive inspiration. It struck the note at once of gaiety and freedom from care. It made everyone light-hearted and sunny tempered. People came in looking doubtful about enjoying themselves, worried about their costumes perhaps, uncertain whether late hours (dancing was from 11.00 to 5.30 a.m.) were not a mistake. When they had recovered from the pleasant shock of finding themselves in such a delightful place, they had forgotten all their doubts and anxieties. They caught the spirit of their surroundings. They dropped their self-consciousness. They were infected with the Southern atmosphere. . . .

. . . The first tier of boxes . . . resembled bowers in the tall hedge of clipped yew, with quaintly-fashioned birds topping them, after the manner of old-world gardens.

Over the next tier there appeared to be growing a noble grapevine, above that the boxes were made to look as if they formed part of a marble terrace. Then came slopes of green turf, and on top of all a balcony, where supper was laid.

All round the hall, at the height of the balcony, a very fine impression was made by tall, dark cypresses, standing erect and dignified. . . .

The guests arrived with more than usual punctuality. By a quarter to eleven, there was a string of carriages half a mile long. . . .

. . . While the throng that covered the floor moved slowly round and about between the dances, as if stirred by some gigantic, invisible spoon, the colour effects were delicious. . . .

. . . Then, when a dreamy waltz began, or a lively two-step, the whole arena broke into movement at once. The kaleidoscope, which had been revolving slowly, slowly, was given a brisker turn. The scene became more and more fascinating. The whirl of colours kept one simply breathless with delight.

And then, when the pageant of the Court of Queen Elizabeth began! The signal for clearing the hall was given by bugles. Upon a platform in front of the hidden organ, the Tudor Queen and her courtiers took up their places. Applause greeted Mrs Arthur James [as Queen Elizabeth] as she bowed with infinite dignity and condescension. Nearly all her Court were either direct descendants or the wives of direct descendants of the historical characters they played. They made a very splendid show as they ranged themselves round their Sovereign and settled down to watch the quadrilles and the procession of all the dancers, each group taking parts from one particular play, with additional companies of Amazons and Lovers, and a special quadrille of the famous people of Tudor times.

This is the period of the ball which will linger longest in the memory. It was like a dream of fair women. With graceful swayings and rhythmical steps, they went through the figures of their dance. There was a hush of admiration and delight. Alas! It was over too soon.

. . . It never could happen again. . . . Such a company of masqueraders could not be assembled twice. Such an array of spectators – boxes filled with royal persons, with the aristocracies of birth and brains and wealth; rows of great ladies glittering with diamonds of priceless worth – could not be twice drawn together in an age . . . this age has shot its bolt. And whatever the future may conceal of splendour and beauty, it will certainly not outdo this.[16]

The date of the Ball had been synchronized with the Coronation of George V, which took place on June 22. Clementine Churchill was a guest in the Royal Box, but Jennie was not. London was ablaze with flares and fireworks, and the next night Jennie dined with F. E. Smith, later Earl of Birkenhead, 'and walked out into the dark streets to see the gushing flares outside the clubs in Pall Mall.'[17] Then Jennie and some friends motored down to Exbury for the Naval Review the following day.

During that summer of 1911, there were more rumbles of possible war with Germany, and in September Asquith easily persuaded Winston to switch Cabinet posts and become First Lord of the Admiralty.

Jennie meanwhile conceived another spectacular idea that would make her Shakespeare Ball seem just a prelude. The limitations of the Ball were that it had been evanescent – it had lived only for a single night – and it had been necessarily restricted to a small segment of the people, the titled and the rich. Why not create something more lasting and universal?

Her idea, simply, was to convert a section of London into an Elizabethan town. People would walk straight out of the twentieth century into the sixteenth. Jennie enlisted the help of Sir Edwin Lutyens, who had designed the interior of the Albert Hall for the Ball, to ensure that the Elizabethan buildings would be authentic. Many of them would be reproductions of houses, churches, and town halls which were still in existence.

But the exposition would be more than buildings. There was to be the same kind of street life and street incidents that Shakespeare might have seen and from which he got so many ideas for incidents in his plays. Every trade was to be represented at work, as it might have been then. A model of the Globe Theatre would be built. A company of players would give performances daily, as in Shakespeare's time, except that the women's parts would be played by women, not by boys. There would even be 'gallants' on the stage of the Globe and 'groundlings' making comments from the pit. There was also to be a Fortune Playhouse for concerts of sixteenth-century music with sixteenth-century instruments. There would be open spaces for country dancing, and halls for the more formal Assembly Balls. And there would be sideshows, pageants, singing and games. It would be called 'Shakespeare's England'.

The site selected was Earl's Court where there were some buildings fit for her purpose. Jennie's plan was to redecorate those existing buildings still usable and then build whatever else was needed.

To finance the vast project she wheedled an initial £40,000 from Cox's Bank, which was augmented by contributions wangled from her wealthy friends. 'Another fifteen thousand pounds was necessary,' George West later wrote, 'and Jennie asked me to approach Mrs W. B. Leeds, a great friend of mine and the widow of an American millionaire, who had left her everything he possessed. . . . I was loath to do so . . . however, I thought it over, studied the figures carefully, and came to the conclusion that, although there was an undoubted risk, if it were good enough for the bank . . . she might be justified in assisting my wife. . . .' [18]

George went to see Mrs Leeds in Paris, and returned with the money. Mrs Leeds's scarcely-concealed love for George was generally recognized in London Society.

The London *Daily Mail* referred to Jennie now as 'the busiest woman in London. . . . She has always been energetic. It is in her American blood. When she first came to England, as Lady Randolph Churchill, she gave London Society a fillip. Never has she been content to travel in a groove. But just now, she has in hand a scheme which is by far the biggest she has ever evolved.' [19]

A few months later the *Daily Express* wrote:

A handsome, fashionably-dressed lady, with striking dark eyes and a notably strong chin, is standing in a hall the size of a railway station with half a dozen men. The lady is talking. The men are listening. She asks them questions, terse, straight to the point, and the answers are given equally directly.

She is Mrs Cornwallis-West, the originator and tireless director of the 'Shakespeare's England' Exhibition at Earl's Court. There is nothing amateurish about Mrs West's management of this great Exhibition. There is nothing casual. Her staff are all experts, but she directs.

The features of the exhibition – the Globe Theatre, the 'Revenge' and the rest – were her ideas. . . . She knows exactly what she wants, and she has a very shrewd idea of how it is to be done. The big . . . hall, where an 'Express' representative found her was the old Empress Theatre, the scene of 'Savage South Africa' and many other famous shows, and Mrs West was intent on arranging for a series of six-penny popular dances, which are to combine the staid joys of Elizabethan Morris dances with the wilder thrills of the 20th century 'Turkey Hug'. The floor, the sitting-out accommodations, the refreshments, were all discussed. Mrs West is nothing if not thorough.

How tireless she is may be gathered from the fact that she is at Earl's Court every morning at eleven, and that she stays there until late in the evening. She has a charming Tudor house in the grounds, and, for the moment, Earl's Court is her home.

As one talked with her and realized the enthusiasm with which she has approached her work and the complete grasp that she has of all of the details, one began to understand how very much Mr Winston Churchill is the son of his mother. He may have inherited his political genius from his father, but he certainly owes to his American mother the superb energy and thoroughness with which he astounded the Board of Trade, appalled the Home Office and is delighting the best elements at the Admiralty. . . .

. . . Dances and tournaments in the Empress Hall do not monopolize Mrs West's attention. There is the Globe Theatre to be considered, and here, among the 'coming events' is an amateur performance of 'The Midsummer Night's Dream', with Lady Lytton as Titania.

There is not a detail of the show that escapes her notice. The signs outside the Tudor shops are a particular hobby of hers. . . .

Mrs West is an admirable example of the 'idle rich'. Earl's Court was particularly derelict. She has revivified it, and, incidentally, is not only giving London a distinctive pleasure ground, but is finding employment for hundreds of workers. All this is done, not for profit or for popularity (Mrs West's position is far too assured and distinguished for that), but from interest in a fine scheme, and also from the pure love of getting about and doing things.

Mrs West is the friend of queens and empresses. She has been on intimate terms with most of the famous men and women of her generation. Her reminiscences are a sort of inside history of our own times. And she is spending her days walking about Earl's Court Exhibition, concerned with pleasure-planning and the proper observance of trifles.

It is all very wonderful, and, in a way, very inspiring.

How this masterful lady succeeds in looking after everything, in approaching just the right people, in carrying through all her thousand-and-one plans, is a little difficult to understand. But her chin is very strong, and she has the cool 'nothing-will-flutter-me 'aspect of the born organizer. Moreover, no time is wasted in unnecessary discussion and chatter.

She herself is the committee — assisted by subcommittees.

Mrs West is not the least anxious to talk about her work. She is just keen to make the thing a memorable success, and success without work is impossible — and there is no more to be said. It is a new Earl's Court that she has called into being, and there is a new spirit in the place.[20]

The *Revenge* mentioned in the article was a full-size reproduction of one of the prize galleons in Sir Francis Drake's fleet, which defeated the Spanish Armada in 1588. To prevent the *Revenge* from looking like a stage prop, Jennie enlisted an historian who made sure that the ship's armour was copied from existing pieces, that sailors' breeches were fastened to their coats by hooks, and that the ship's interior was as accurate as its exterior — an expert had to be sent to Amsterdam and Nuremberg to copy drawings of the interior.[21] To add further reality, the ship basin smelled of tar and there were fish stalls where real fish could be bought.

Jennie's idea of a jousting tourney, although not historically related to Elizabethan England, turned out to be the most fascinating of them all. Such a tourney was something that the English had not seen since

302

the sixteenth century. The great Empress Hall was transformed into a replica of the courtyard of Warwick Castle, and Jennie persuaded a variety of dukes and other nobility to squeeze into their family armour – or rent some – and play the parts of knights of old in jousts of combat.[22] They were to charge at each other with fourteen-foot-long wooden lances, and points were to be awarded according to where opponents were hit and whether they were unhorsed. Then there was to be a mêlée in which a dozen knights with swords would attempt to slice the plumes from each other's helmets.

To celebrate the opening of Shakespeare's England, Jennie gave a series of parties at the Mermaid Tavern for groups of friends and European royalty.

Her guest book one night contained a surprise. The signature read simply 'C. Kinsky'. His wife had died the year before. Not only was Kinsky a guest, but he had also agreed to be part of the entourage for the Princess Errant pageant. The Princess Errant was Daisy of Pless, George's sister. George, of course, was also at the party, and it must have been a most interesting evening for Jennie. It is easy to imagine her sparkling in the company; it is not so easy to conjure up her thoughts as her eyes wandered from George to Kinsky.

For the past few years George had not been a model husband. The affair with the ardent Mrs Leeds had been but one among many. Much more serious was his persistent attention to Mrs Campbell. As 'Mrs Pat' put it, 'Then, in the unexpected way things sometimes happen in the world, George Cornwallis-West was seriously attracted to me. . . . I believed his life was unhappy, and warmly gave him my friendship and affection. . . . This caused gossip, misjudgment, and pain that cannot be gone into here. . . .'[23]

Shane Leslie had quoted from Stendhal, saying 'in France women watch each other, in Italy they watch the men.' And, he might have added, in England they do both. Jennie herself said cynically to a friend, afterwards, 'No woman ever loved a good man.'

Mrs Pat may have been 'a troubling enchanting enigma', as one theatre critic said,[24] but she made George feel enormously important. Jennie was so immersed in her Shakespeare's England Exhibition that George found himself filling only the odd corners of her life. There is little question that he resented her pre-eminence. In his novel *Two Wives*, one of the women is described:

Everyone knew Lady Carsteen by name; as one of the few remaining Edwardian beauties, her photograph was often in the weekly illustrated press – Lady Carsteen at Newmarket; as chairman of the committee of some charity ball; or even selling flags in the foyer of the Cosmopolitan Hotel. . . . Like most silly people who arrive in a position in life which they have always hoped for but never expected, she had an exaggerated idea of her own importance. If she happened to find herself thwarted in some petty way by persons in an inferior position to her own, who were unacquainted with her, she had a habit of saying, 'You don't appear to know who I am.' [25]

Jennie and George often quarrelled bitterly now.

'He had fallen, in the first instance, to her physical charms,' *Two Wives* explained, 'and, when these became stale, had come positively to dislike his wife. He loathed rows and she loved them. Now, in middle age, he tolerated her. All he wanted was peace and quiet, and to be allowed to collect stamps without hindrance.' [26]

George's stamps were guns, fishing equipment, and women, and for these he travelled far and often.[27] His and Jennie's absences from each other had become more frequent and prolonged. The Shakespeare exposition was the breaking point. In Jennie's guest book at the Mermaid Tavern someone had written, 'Oh, lady Fortune, stand you auspicious . . .', but it was, unfortunately, a fanciful hope. Shakespeare's England was a historical success but a financial failure. The pageant was splendid, the tournament was stirring, but the costs were too heavy to be recouped. C. B. Cochran, a successful theatrical producer who had worked with Jennie, said: 'Her ideas were wonderful. It was money that perplexed her. She threw it around like water.' [28] Cochran brought in more sideshows, a scenic railway, an international circus, and Jennie gave a harpsichord recital, but at the end the venture still lost money.[29]

George West often remarked that his major arguments with Jennie were about money. In his novel, the hero tells his wife:

We hadn't been in this house six months before I told you that we could not possibly afford to entertain on the scale you appeared to think necessary! and not the slightest notice has been taken, or ever is taken, of anything I say, and now I find myself in a very serious position.

. . . Lady Carsteen was aghast. Her husband was actually standing

304

up to her and displaying a trait of sarcasm which she had finally imagined she had long ago successfully suppressed, if not entirely obliterated. . . .[30]

The marriage was over. For George, the love was gone. Envy had replaced it. He now felt he could never be a man in Jennie's house. He could never be as important as she was. Cassel was right about him: he was not meant for money-making, and yet money was his measure of success. Jack Churchill was also right about him: he couldn't stand the strain.

George now had his own ideas – fostered by Mrs Campbell – of becoming a famous playwright and novelist. But they were illusions without substance. Jennie was fifty-eight and he was thirty-seven, but she was younger than he was. Not only did he not have her fire of youth, but he had little of her talent and almost none of her quality.

Nor did he have her sense of dignity, of grace, of style. On December 24, 1912, Jennie wrote:

Dearest George,
  I am glad that I was prepared for your letter – the blow falls hard enough as it is – But if this thing is to take place, it can't be done too quickly now – and we shall both be happier when it is over – Thank God I have the physical and mental strength and courage enough to fight my own battle in life.

George answered on January 2, 1913:

Dearest Jennie,
  Thanks for your nice letter. I have been on the verge of ringing you up once or twice but honestly don't think I could bear the sound of your dear old voice just now. . . .

The petition for divorce was filed by Jennie on January 20, 1913. The next legal step was an order against her husband for restitution of conjugal rights. This was handed down on March 3, 1913. The case was noted on the Court calendar as 'West *vs*. West'.

'What is the nature of the desertion?' asked the President of the Court, Sir Samuel Evans.

'The Respondent [George Cornwallis-West]', said Lord Tiverton, 'left the house where they had been living in Norfolk-street. Certain correspondence took place at the end of December and the beginning of January, in which the Respondent, after having been requested to do so, refused to come back.'

'Mrs West,' called the usher, and Jennie, who had only at that moment entered the court, went into the box.

She looked strikingly handsome. There was something stately about her figure, dressed in black velvet, in exquisite taste. Magnificent sables drooped from her shoulders; a black toque crowned her rich black hair, and a large sable muff hid one hand, from which a dainty purse of chain-gold dangled. She took the oath.

She was evidently suffering from a severe cold. She answered the questions that were put to her in a quiet, low voice that had a trace of huskiness in it.

'Are you the Petitioner in this case?' asked Lord Tiverton.

'I am,' replied Mrs West.

'Were you married to your husband on July 28, 1900?'

'I was.'

'After which you cohabited with him in various places, and latterly in Norfolk-street?'

Mrs West signified an affirmative with a nod of her head.

'On December 23rd last, did the Respondent leave Norfolk-street?'

'He did.'

'On December 29th, did you get a letter which was exposed in your affidavit before Milord?'

'I did,' said Mrs West in a businesslike voice.

'Did you reply on December 31st?'

'Yes.'

'Did you further reply to him on January 3rd last?'

'That is so.'

'Has he come back to you since?'

'No.'

There was a slight pause, while the judge looked at the correspondence that had passed between the husband and wife. The letters were not read.

'Is the Respondent in this country?' asked Sir Samuel Evans.

'I am not sure,' replied Mr Harvey Murphy [the counsel].

The usual order of restitution of conjugal rights was made, and Mrs Cornwallis-West left the court as quietly as she had entered it.[31]

The British correspondent of *The North American* magazine noted: 'Mrs Cornwallis-West is extremely anxious that the court proceedings should be kept as quiet as possible, and that there should be no scandal. She has no desire to drag in anybody unless it is absolutely unavoidable. . . . Mrs West's two sons, Winston and John, are anxious that their mother should get the divorce. . . .'[32]

The divorce had several further stages to go through, and the legal process would taken another year. In the interim, Jennie had another project to consume her time and attention – her second play. She had written a synopsis of it three years before and had been working on it intermittently for almost a year. Alfred Wareing now felt that it was ready for production at his Glasgow Repertory Theatre.

The Bill was a political play. Jennie described it to a reporter as 'a play about politicians . . . neither a propagandist play nor a controversial play. It is just a comedy with a political situation, a certain amount of lovemaking, the necessary dash of intrigue, a contrast in temperament between a father and his son, and just a little touch of villainy.'[33]

The critics gave it a rousing reception:

'An outstanding feature of Mr Wareing's season. . . .'

'. . . excellently written throughout. . . .'

'. . . Many of the speeches are brilliant, while the shrewd incisive hits at all political parties and many of our social conventions are delightful. . . .'

'. . . Mrs Cornwallis-West has succeeded perfectly . . . the characters of modern politicians are real flesh-and-blood people. . . .'

'. . . one of the most powerful comedies ever written. . . .'

Jennie was not swept away by the favourable reception. She was seen in the prompter's wings the first few nights, taking notes of the production and the audiences' reaction to it.[34]

The Bill concerns universal suffrage and the political manœuvring by women to help gain power for their husbands or lovers. 'So cleverly and naturally did the discussion seem last night that many members of the audience forgot their surroundings and gave vent to a chorus of "Hear! Hear!" and other evidences of approval or dissent.'[35]

One of the wives in the play reminds her husband: 'You had no ambition. I persuaded you to take office.' Then there is this exchange:

Sir George: You must allow for the fact that, taking her all around, she is the stronger animal of the two.
Vernon: 'Pon my soul, I believe you're right and she has the advantage of being utterly unscrupulous.
John: Men have made women unscrupulous.[36]

Later the leading lady remarks to 'Sir George', 'We don't elope nowadays, and we don't divorce, except out of kindness.'

The divorce action against George West was proceeding without complication. He and Mrs Pat were now together more openly. Jennie's comment on the two of them: 'Well, George evidently has a penchant for brunettes. I'm always taken for a gypsy, but as for Mrs Pat — why she's nothing more or less than an ink bottle!'

Mrs Campbell was still in the midst of her love affair in letters with George Bernard Shaw. Shaw, who was married but had never consummated his marriage, was fifty-seven years old and convinced that he was passionately in love with Mrs Pat. But she had written to him that 'George is more precious to me than my bones.'

Shaw answered her, calling her, 'Ever blessedest darling', and saying:

I want to implore you not to arouse the family solicitor by talking of marrying George. . . . No sooner do you mention George than I see with a frightful lucidity all the worldly reasons why you should marry him. . . . Therefore, though I like George (we have the same taste) I say he is young and I am old; so let him wait until I am tired of you. . . . And about you, I am a mass of illusions. It is impossible that I should not tire soon; nothing so wonderful could last. You cannot really be what you are to me; you are a figure from the dreams of my boyhood — all romance. . . . I promise to tire of you as soon as I can leave you free. . . .[37]

Shaw was writing *Pygmalion* at the time, primarily for Mrs Pat, and she continued to cultivate him. But when he planned a visit with the intention of making love to her, she told him not to come. He answered:

Very well, go; the loss of a woman is not the end of the world. The sun shines: It is pleasant to swim: it is good to work: my soul can stand alone. But I am deeply wounded. . . . I have treated you far too well, idolized, thrown my heart and mind to you (as I throw them to all the world) to make what you could of: and what you make of them is to run away. Go then: the Shavian oxygen burns up your little lungs: seek some stuffiness that suits you. You will not marry George! At the last moment, you will funk him, or be ousted by a bolder soul. You have wounded my vanity: an inconceivable audacity and an unpardonable crime. Farewell, wretch, that I love. G.B.S.[38]

Some years later Shaw was quoted as having said of Mrs Campbell, 'She was not a great actress, but she was a great enchantress, how or why I don't know; but if she wanted to capture you, you might as well go quietly; for she was irresistible.'[39]

Shortly after Jennie had filed her first claim in the divorce suit, Winston and Clemmie offered her a change of scene:

It wd do you a gt deal of good to get away from England, worry & expense for three weeks & to bask a little in Mediterranean & Adriatic sunshine. Why will you not come with us on the 8th & be delivered safely . . . back on the first or second of June. We start from Venice & go round by the Dalmatian coast to Malta, Sicily, Ajaccio & Marseilles (perhaps Athens). The Asquiths are coming; so that you wd have to make up your mind to get on with Margot & the PM. But again, why not?

Otherwise we are only Admiralty and Admirable. It wd be so nice if you cd come, & Clemmie and I wd so greatly enjoy it.

It wd cost nothing, or next to nothing.

Answer please in the affirmative.

Always your loving son,
W.[40]

Jennie agreed to go, but before leaving she sent a telegram about her play to Alfred Wareing in Glasgow: 'Don't let them over-act when they get familiar with the roles.'

The next step in the divorce suit came on July 15, 1913. Jennie's lawyers had petitioned unsuccessfully for the case to be heard *in camera*. They were able, however, to arrange for the case to be placed near the top of the court calendar, although it had originally been last.

'As she stood in the witness-box yesterday,' the newspaper reported.

she was seen to be a woman of no ordinary appearance. . . . Her second son, Mr John Churchill, accompanied Mrs Cornwallis-West to court. They and their solicitor stood chatting in the thronged lobby for ten minutes, while the President finished off for the day the Moosbrugger suit. Then, at four o'clock, the men and women interested in the fortunes of the Moosbruggers, swarmed out of court, and a dozen husbands and wives with 'undefended' petitions to be heard, filed in and filled the vacated seats.

Mrs Cornwallis-West entered and took her seat near the witness-box.[41]

The background facts were repeated, this time with the addition 'that Mr George Cornwallis-West stayed, from March 28th to March 31st, at the Great Western Railway Hotel at Paddington, with "a woman unknown".'

Asked whether her husband had complied with the order of the court for restitution of conjugal rights, Jennie replied. 'He did not, My Lord.' The court testimony continued:

Mr Drew, Private-Inquiry Agent and Ex-Chief Inspector of Scotland Yard, whitehaired, a 'Sherlock', told the President of the inquiries he made at Paddington, and of the identification of a photograph of Mr Cornwallis-West by one of the chamber-maids. Louisa Mintern, the chamber-maid, gave evidence of the stay of 'Captain and Mrs West' at the Great Western Railway Hotel from March 28th to March 31st. She knew their name from the luggage, she said, with a smile, and she had seen Mr Cornwallis-West at Mrs Russell's office.

Miss Mintern was leaving the witness-box when Mr Smith stopped her.

'One more question,' he said. 'Was the lady you saw at the hotel, the lady sitting below you?'

The chamber-maid looked down. Mrs George Cornwallis-West looked up. They glanced in each other's faces, and the maid said, 'No.'

There ended the story, and the President granted decree.

Jennie had obtained a decree *nisi* for the dissolution of her marriage, but it would take nine months for the decree to be made absolute. George and his sister Daisy went on a trip to South America that summer. Jennie did some travelling, too, mostly in Europe.

That winter, Winston, as First Lord of the Admiralty, asked his mother to christen a new battleship, the *Benbow*.[42] She was told she would only have to name it and wish it 'Godspeed'.

'With a light heart, I went off to Glasgow,' she later wrote, 'where the launch was to take place. I beamed on the crowds at the docks, I accepted bouquets. . . .' She said her 'Godspeed' and her words were 'drowned by the crashing sound of the breaking of timbers and snapping of ropes as the giant ship glided slowly down the slips.'

'Now for the luncheon,' said the Chairman. 'We've got a splendid crowd – at least 500, and they are all looking forward to your speech.'

Jennie explained that she had been specifically told that she would not have to make a speech. But someone whispered to her that they were going to present her with a handsome gift, 'a Louis XVI gold chatelaine, I believe', and the Chairman added that as the mother of the First Lord of the Admiralty, she must know all about naval matters. 'Surely, your son tells you everything? No? Well, you can always fall back on "Our Cousins Across the Seas" for a topic.'

'Oh! That miserable, untasted luncheon!' Jennie confided afterward.

What should I say? My mind was blank, and the fatal moment was approaching. A brilliant thought struck me. I would draw a comparison between the delicate, antique beauty of the old Louis XVI chatelaine, which was to be given me, and the modern, awe-inspiring, formidable iron monster I had just christened and launched. I was comforted – that would be a beginning, and for the rest, I trusted to Providence.

I was on my feet, receiving with many smiles and grateful thanks a velvet box, which I proceeded to open for the expectant and admiring company to see – Lo! and behold, a very modern diamond brooch! [43]

Alas! For my opening remarks, where were they? My dismay was so great that I burst into speech and threw myself at their mercy. . . .[44]

The audience was kind and sympathetic and Jennie's brief informal talk was received much better than a more formal, well-prepared one might have been.

As the date of the final divorce decree approached, Daisy decided that Jennie was preferable to a notorious actress as a sister-in-law and she sent a telegram: 'Wired you twice. Don't make decree absolute.'

But on April 14, 1914, Jennie wrote:

My dear George,

Mr Wheeler brought me your message. The d.n. [decree *nisi*] will be made absolute on Monday, and I understand that you are going to be married on Tues. You need not fear what I may say, for I will not willingly speak of you. And we are not likely ever to meet. This is the *real* parting of the ways. But for the sake of some of the happy days we had together – should you ever be in trouble and wanted to knock at my door, it would not be shut to you. I am returning you my engagement and wedding rings – I say good-bye – a long, long good-bye.

                                                                            Jennie.[45]

Moreton Frewen was less gentle: 'So that beauty George West is to be married on Tuesday to Mrs Pat Campbell – the decree absolute is Monday. Full Fathom Five they dive to a joint folly.' [46]

On April 16, 1914, within an hour after the decree was made final, George West and Mrs Patrick Campbell were married. The ceremony was performed in a Registry Office, and only two friends were present as witnesses. 'Mrs Campbell's wedding dress was of black silk, and she was wearing a black hat. She gave her age in the register as 47, and Mr Cornwallis-West as eight years her junior.' [47]

Mrs Campbell had left her house in Kensington Square after lunch, and motored to the Registry Office; all that was known at the house was that she was going to be married and that she would be away for a couple of days. She was to appear in Shaw's *Pygmalion*, at His Majesty's Theatre on Saturday night, 'rehearsals for which are now proceeding'.

Very few people had been in on the secret. '. . . Immediately after the ceremony, Mr and Mrs Cornwallis-West drove away in the car; and it is understood that they are staying in the country.'

Mrs Pat was later quoted as saying, 'Ah, the peace of the double bed after the hurly-burly of the *chaise longue*.'

In the Classified Notices section of *The Times* on April 7, 1914 there appeared this notice:

I, Jennie Spencer-Churchill, commonly called Lady Randolph Churchill, hereinbefore called by the name of Jennie Cornwallis-West, of

20 George Cornwallis-West

21 Jennie at about the time of her second marriage

22 Salisbury Hall, the home of Jennie and George, bought soon after their marriage

23 Pearl Craigie
('John Oliver Hobbes')

24 Jennie's sister-in-law, Daisy,
Princess of Pless

25 Frances, Countess of Warwick

26 and 27 Jennie's daughters-in-law, Clementine Hozier
and Lady Gwendoline Bertie

28 Edward Marsh in 1900

THE GLOBE THEATRE
Shaftesbury Avenue, W.

Sole Lessee and Manager • • • • CHARLES FROHMAN.

Mrs. GEORGE CORNWALLIS-WEST'S
MATINEES.

TUESDAY, WEDNESDAY, THURSDAY and FRIDAY AFTERNOONS,

JULY 6th, 7th, 8th and 9th,

Commencing at Three o'clock.

HIS BORROWED PLUMES

An Original Modern Comedy in Three Acts.

By Mrs. GEORGE CORNWALLIS-WEST.

Major Percival Summer, V.C.	Mr. DAWSON MILWARD
John Waterbury, M.P.	Mr. F. DONOVAN
Basil Delaine, K.C.	Mr. HENRY AINLEY
Henry Martin	Mr. ALAN URQUHART
Mr. Mowser (Manager of the National Theatre)	Mr. STANLEY TURNBULL
Butler	Mr. CREGAN
Footman	Mr. RUSSELL
Lady Mary Trianon	Miss SARA ALLGOOD
Fabia Sumner	Mrs. PATRICK CAMPBELL
Angela Cranfield	Miss GERTRUDE KINGSTON
Rose Wispey	Miss ANNIE HUGHES
Alma Dorset	Miss STELLA PATRICK CAMPBELL
Jane Linneth	Miss WINIFRED FRASER
Blanche (Maid to Angela Cranfield)	Miss RENEE DE VAUX
Attendant at National Theatre	Miss MURIEL VARNA

ACT I.
Annexe to Hotel, Bray, Berks (E. G. Banks)

ACT II.
Library at the Sumner's House, London. Three Months Later

ACT III.
Scene 1 — Mrs. Cranfield's Boudoir. One Month Later.
Scene 2 — Ante-Room of Royal Box at the National Theatre.
Evening of the same Day. (E. G. Banks)

Dresses by Madame Angèle "PAQUIN," Messrs. LIBERTY & Co., and JAYS, Limited.
Ladies' Hats supplied by FRANCE MARIOT, 29 Rue Royale, Paris, and 30 Orington Street, S.W.
The Furniture in Acts I., II., and Scene 1 of Act III., supplied by Messrs. MAPLE & Co.
The Furniture in Scene 2, Act III., supplied by LENYGON & Co., Old Bullington Street.
The Court Cupboard in Scene 2, Act III., lent by Mr. LEONARD F. WYBURD,
of 57 Wigmore Street, W.

Programme of Music.

OVERTURE		"Oberon"		Weber
ENTR'ACTE I.		(a) Selection of Melodies		Grieg
		(b) Humoresque		Dvořák
ENTR'ACTE II.		Ballet Music from "Gioconda"		Ponchielli
INTERLUDE				Quasha Manzura

Business Manager	Mr. H. LANGLEY
Musical Director — for Mrs. George Cornwallis-West	Mr. ALEC MACLEAN
Stage Manager	Mr. H. W. VARNA

BOX OFFICE (G. CLARE) open 10 to 5. Prices: Private Boxes, £2 2s. and £1 1s. Orchestra Stalls, 10s. 6d.
Dress Circle, 7s. 6d. and 5s. Upper Circle, 3s. and 4s. Pit, 2s. 6d. Gallery, 1s.

General Manager — for CHARLES FROHMAN	W. LESTOCQ
Business Manager	OSCAR BARRETT, Jun

Extract from the Rules made by the Lord Chamberlain. 1.—The name of the actual and responsible Manager of the Theatre must be printed on every play bill. 2.—The Public can leave the Theatre at the end of the performance by all exit and entrance doors, which open upon corwards. 3.—Where there is a fireproof screen to the proscenium opening it must be lowered at least once during every performance, to ensure its being in proper working order. 4.—Smoking is not permitted in the Auditorium. 5.—All gangways, passages and staircases must be kept free from chairs or any other obstructions, whether permanent or temporary.

29 Playbill for Jennie's first pla

30 Mrs Pat Campbell
  (Malcolm L Keep)

Playbill for
ennie's second
ay

32 Winston (centre) and Jack (right) at Army manoeuvres,
September 1913

Lady Randolph Churchill

By the Simmering Samovar

Writing exclusively for Harper's Bazar Lady Randolph Churchill this month discusses the inherent human weakness of "Vanity." Her conclusion that a sense of humour is the natural antidote for conceit gives an added reason for cultivating to the utmost that invaluable social attribute

33   Jennie in 1914, from an article she wrote in *Harper's Bazaar*

34   Jennie in 1915, from an article entitled 'Discipline' written for *Harper's Bazaar*

LADY RANDOLPH CHURCHILL

35 Montagu Porch,
Jennie's third husband

36 Jennie in 1920, a few
years after her third marriage

37 Jennie with Jack's son Peregr

38 Jennie's funeral, July 3, 1921. Winston at left,
Jack next to him with Jack's son John

32, Dover-street, in the County of London, hereby give public notice that on the first day of April, One-thousand-nine-hundred-and-fourteen, I formally and absolutely RENOUNCED, relinquished, and abandoned the use of my said surname of CORNWALLIS-WEST, and then ASSUMED, adopted, and determined thenceforth on all occasions whatsoever to use and subscribe the name of SPENCER-CHURCHILL instead of the said name of Cornwallis-West.

22

The next chapter of Jennie's life was filled with surprises. Hers was not a life that could slowly unwind. She was constantly renewing herself, her energy, her love of life.

Leonie told of a visit her sister made to her on a bleak afternoon in early 1914. Still smarting from the divorce and George's swift remarriage, she let the hurt show that day. She also bemoaned her financial insecurity and the forever accumulating bills. And now her sons had their own lives with their families, and her friends were dying or scattering. Jennie herself was sixty years old. After unburdening her anxieties and distress, she left. The loving Leonie had planned to attend a ball that night, but Jennie's talk had so depressed her that she decided not to go. The next day a friend telephoned her to describe the splendid evening. And who had been the belle of the ball, looking absolutely wonderful? Why, Jennie, of course.

Clara's son, Hugh Frewen, was being married in Rome to the daughter of the Duke of Mignano, and Jennie decided to attend. She stayed with her young friend, Vittoria, Duchess of Sermoneta, at her *palazzo*. It was peaceful and lovely, with its avenue of tall plane trees, the entrance gate flanked by carved stone bears, the inner court garden with its seven splashing fountains, the formal patterns of flower beds, the delicious fragrance of tangerine trees.

The wedding party was held at the Grand Hotel. Hugh introduced Jennie to a friend of his, Montagu Porch, a young man serving with him in the Colonial Service in Nigeria. He was very handsome, gloriously moustached, had a slim figure and prematurely white hair.

'I can remember still the first moment I saw her. . . . She was sitting with some friends. She wore a green dress. Was it long or short? Don't remember. But she looked very beautiful.' Porch asked her to dance. Jennie smiled and said: 'I think you'd better go and dance with some of the younger girls.'[1] Porch was thirty-seven, three years younger than Winston.

314

Not many weeks before, Leonie had had a dinner party for Jennie's sixtieth birthday. After the party, Jennie went to Leonie's room, sat despondently on her bed, and reminisced. How intoxicating it always had been to sweep into a room and know that every man would turn his head to stare at her; how unhappy she was that it was no longer true. Yet here was this very young, very handsome man who obviously found her very attractive. Her nephew Shane Leslie later said of her: 'She could have married young men until she was a hundred. . . .'[2]

For a certain kind of young man, Jennie was not just a beautiful woman, she was an overwhelming adventure into a new world. It was true of George West and Montagu Porch and a dozen others. They must also have seen in her something of a surrogate mother. She had the drive, determination, and strength they did not have, and by comparison they were insecure and dependent.

But when she bared her soul to Leonie, her strength had ebbed:

I wish we could see more of each other. Life is so short and we are both so down the wrong side of the ladder! The fact is that we are both 'Marthas' instead of 'Marys' and allow things which do not really count to take up our time and to keep us apart. We pander to the world which is callous, and it only wants you if you can smile and be hypocritical. One is forever throwing away substance for shadows. To live for others sounds all right – you do, darling – but what is the result? You are a very unhappy woman all around! As for me every effort I make to get out of my selfishness meets with a rebuff. My sons love me from afar and give me no companionship even when it comes their way. The fault is undoubtedly with me. Every day I become more solitary and prone to introspection, which is fatal.[3]

Such self-indulgence for Jennie never lasted very long. She always found someone or something more important than her own problems. Most threatening now was the rapidly looming war in Europe. Jennie had spoken with Winston about it and wrote to Leonie: '. . . He seemed to think the worst of the European situation and thought war inevitable. . . . As I am writing, the fate of the Government is hanging in the balance. . . .' Later, at a lunch with Winston, they had discussed a political question and she had told him: 'If that happens you will have the other side saying they have won the day.'

'What would that matter,' answered Winston, 'if good came of it. . .' [4]
She again wrote to Leonie: 'Winston is really so "big!"'

And on August 1: 'Only a line to tell you that Winston tells us [the French President, Raymond] Poincaré has written an impassioned letter to the King imploring his aid. The fleet will be mobilized today probably. . . .' [5]

The following evening Winston was dining with a friend at Admiralty House when an aide brought in a dispatch box. Winston opened it with a key and found a single sentence: 'Germany has declared war against Russia. . . .'

'There is one thing they cannot take away from you,' Kitchener later told Winston. 'The fleet was ready.'

The assassination of the Archduke Francis Ferdinand, heir apparent to the crowns of Austria and Hungary, had activated a chain of treaties that soon divided Europe into two camps. The murder plot had been hatched in Serbia, and the German Kaiser supported the Austrian attack on its ancient enemy. Russia mobilized. Britain suggested a conference. Germany asked that Britain remain neutral if a conflict were to develop. Britain refused to make such a pledge. Germany declared war on Russia on August 2, and the next day declared war on France. Britain asked Germany and France if they would respect Belgian neutrality. France agreed. Germany refused, and German troops invaded Belgium.

Britain sent an ultimatum to Berlin that required Germany to agree to withdraw from Belgium by midnight of August 4. The day before, on August 3, the Foreign Minister, Sir Edward Grey, recorded: 'We were standing at a window of my room. . . . It was getting dark, and the lamps were being lit in the space below on which we were looking.' Grey said to his guest: 'The lamps are going out all over Europe; we shall not see them lit again in our lifetime.' [6] World War I had begun.

It was a time of drama and personal despair for Jennie and her sisters. Each soon had a son at the front: Jack Churchill, Hugh Frewen, Norman Leslie. Norman was killed early in the war.

Deep in grief over the loss of her son and determined to help the war effort in some way, Leonie took a a job washing dishes at a soldiers' canteen. One night she saw a familiar face. It was George Cornwallis-West, again an officer. 'The day of my divorce was the saddest of my life,' he told her. 'Perhaps the happiest in my sister's,' Leonie answered sharply. [7]

George West had found that he could not be the head of the household with his second wife either. When Mrs Pat toured in *Pygmalion*,

George played the dustman.[8] He discovered, too, that his second wife was no less extravagant than his first, and he soon faced bankruptcy.

Prince Charles Kinsky had come quietly back into Jennie's life. After his wife's death, he and Jennie had seen each other intermittently. He had taken part in her Shakespeare's England, and he always retained his apartment on Clarges Street, only a short distance from her home.[9] If they had any thought of marriage, the war made it impossible; as a Reserve Officer in the Austro-Hungarian Army, Kinsky was recalled to duty.

'I said good-bye to him at the end of Goodwood Week in July 1914,' remembered Kinsky's close friend, George Lambton, 'when he left to go and fight for his own country, on the side of the Germans, a nation he had always hated. He loved England and the English.'[10] Rumours had circulated that Kinsky had ordered that his English racing horses be destroyed rather than serve the British Army. But the truth was that Kinsky had asked Lambton to have his horses distributed among his many friends in the English Army, and Lambton had done so.[11]

In order to avoid fighting against his British friends, Kinsky requested assignment to the Russian front. His nephew, Prince Clary, told of meeting his uncle at the Russian front in 1915. 'I found him sitting on a bench in the garden, reading *The Times*. His first remark to me was — in English! — "How odd, old X is taking a very strong line against racing during the War. . . ." '

A Major in a regiment of Hussars, Kinsky was an aide to the commanding general of an Army corps. 'When the Russians retreated in October 1914,' Prince Clary wrote,

some cossack detachments were left behind to hide in the big forests. They were dressed in civilian clothes to do spy-work and sabotage and take prisoners whenever they could. As the roads were impracticable for cars, and the telephone did not exist or had often been interrupted, the message from any headquarters to another had to be carried by ADC's [aides-de-camp] on horseback. These aides usually took an escort with them. Not so Charles Kinsky. I remember seeing him arrive one day, quite alone, and when asked by the General why he had not taken an escort, he answered that he would be quite capable of dealing alone with a few cossacks. On his way back he was stopped by two of them, but, pulling out his revolver, he shouted at them in Russian that they were his prisoners. The cossacks were so taken aback by this reaction and the old major's language that they let themselves be taken to headquarters.[12]

Kinsky kept in occasional contact with his butler in England, who still took care of his Clarges Street flat. One note from the butler said: 'Yesterday I saw Lady R.C., she told me to let you know that I saw her, and that she is well. . . .'[13]

In fact, Jennie was not well; she was often depressed. Her nephew Oswald's diary noted, 'Lady Maud Warrender came over and took Pa and Ma and Aunt Jane (she's very much out of the picture) off to lunch.'[14] But she didn't stay out of the picture very long. She and Lady Maud toured the camps and the hospitals, Jennie playing the piano and Maud Warrender singing, with Jennie joining in. Lady Maud remembered that Jennie was 'always full of good stories . . . a staunch friend with a lively sense of humour, the best company. . . .' One story she recalled Jennie telling was about an American Senator she had entertained at dinner. The Senator arrived very late, without his wife, and blurted out: 'Please excuse me, Lady Churchill. I regret to say that my wife is unable to accompany me here tonight; she is suffering from womb worries.'[15]

Jennie soon found herself organizing buffets for thousands of soldiers at railway stations, helping her sister-in-law start a convalescent home in the country for wounded soldiers, and raising money and acquiring space and staff for an American Women's War Hospital at Paignton in South Devon, for which she was chairman of the Executive Committee.

Jennie wrote of the courage of the wounded: 'A man shot through the face will smile crookedly and wink his one eye . . .'; of the incredulous civilians who said when the first wounded arrived in their town on troop trains: '. . . then there really is a war going on . . .'; of the stories some of the men told about opposing trenches at the front so close together that the German and the English soldiers could hear each others' singing; and of the plea of the newly arrived wounded, 'Please, Sister, let us sleep. . . .'[16]

Few things angered Jennie more than the pseudo-benevolence of some of the society ladies who took wounded soldiers out for drives. They asked at the Paignton Hospital for 'those with the most conspicuous bandages please. The last lot of officers you gave us might not have been wounded at all, for all anyone could see. . . .'[17] In contrast, Jennie told of her young friend, Eleanor Warrender, youngest daughter

318

of Lady Maud Warrender, who had worked with her on the *Maine* and now served at French front-line hospitals, where she was '. . . shelled at Furnes and Dunkirk, sleeping all night in cellars full of rats. . . .'[18]

Jennie also became an 'Olympian head matron' of a hospital at Lancaster Gate, and Lady Maud Warrender recalled how hard Jennie worked and how she 'never spared herself'.[19] In fact, Jennie was genuinely grateful for the chance to serve: 'We might have been pottering out our little humdrum lives, eating our chickens and going through our daily routine in comfort and smug complacency. . . .'[20]

Jack's son Peregrine Churchill remembers the time his grandmother took him to the Lancaster Gate Hospital where she was then spending most of her time. Jennie wanted her young grandson to balance his heroic view of war by seeing some of the casualties. He remembered, too, that she continually corrected his pronunciation of 'Ypres', the town in Belgium where a number of bloody battles had taken place. And the only time Peregrine ever saw his grandmother angry enough to hit anyone was during their hospital visit. A Boy Scout who had been assigned to act as a watchman was instead lounging elsewhere eating oranges, and Jennie boxed his ears.[21]

Jennie was a devoted grandmother. She gave her grandchildren not only love, but an education and a heritage as well. The devotion to music that she had shared with her son Jack had been passed on to Jack's son Peregrine. He remembered an occasion when he was perhaps five years old. His grandmother was attending a luncheon, and Peregrine was in another room picking out a tune on the piano. Jennie left the luncheon party to sit alongside her grandson at the piano and tell him the story of the opera from which the tune he was playing came. It was *Siegfried*, and she played the main themes for him, including the music representing the warning of the bird. Then she told him about a performance she had seen in which the bird song was sung by 'a great big fat soprano', and Jennie puffed her cheeks to indicate how fat the soprano was.

She went on to tell him that since the soprano was too fat to climb into a tree on stage, she stood on a box behind the cardboard tree, just pretending. But all that didn't matter, Jennie told him, because the soprano had a beautiful voice. 'You mustn't mind singers being fat,' she said, 'just listen and use your imagination.'

Peregrine Churchill never forgot that incident. It wasn't only the story, it was the way his grandmother talked to him – as if he were not a child but a young man.[22]

319

The grandchildren called her 'Granny' or 'B.M.' ('*Bonne Mère*'), and they were always delighted to see her 'because she always brought us presents. . . .'[23] They enjoyed her because she obviously enjoyed them. When her sons were young, she was the wife of an important political figure who demanded her constant attention; now her time was her own. She took her grandchildren on visits, picnics, automobile rides, to the theatre, to concerts, parties.[24]

Once she took Winston's and Clemmie's son Randolph to the birthday party of another child. A magician formed part of the entertainment and young Randolph was obviously not enjoying this. Suddenly he jumped onto his chair and exclaimed: 'Man, stop! Band, play!' And the man did stop and the band did play. How like Winston, Jennie must have thought.[25]

Jennie was also very attentive to her large numbers of nieces and nephews. 'She was always leading; we all followed,' said Shane Leslie.[26]

The diary of Oswald Frewen recorded: 'Lunch at Aunt Jane's . . . took us to the war pictures at the Sculos . . . very large-hearted of Aunt Jane. . . .' Later he added that she 'bore me off to the Admiralty to see Winston. He, however, was at a Cabinet meeting. . . .'[27]

In 1915 Winston suffered a major defeat over the Dardanelles. Earlier, he had gone to Antwerp, and had volunteered to resign from the Admiralty if Asquith would allow him to command the defence of that city. Asquith refused. Next Winston proffered a grand plan to end the war more swiftly: an intricate scheme to invade and open the Dardanelles, detaching Turkey from the Central powers. This would win control over the Balkan states and prepare the way for a sweeping British victory in the East. It would be a back-door attack on the enemy. Winston's friend and ally, Lord Fisher,[28] at first supported the plan, then opposed it, but Winston forced the plan through.

The official British Government history of the war records, 'The Turkish gun crews were demoralized and even the German officers present had, apparently, little hope of successful resistance if the Fleet attacked next day.' However, three British ships were blown up in a minefield and the admiral in charge broke off the action. Lord Fisher refused to overrule him.

After the war, the German General at the Dardanelles, Liman von Sanders, said, 'If the orders at that moment had been carried out, the course of the world war would have changed after the spring of 1915, and Germany and Austria would have been constrained to continue the fight alone.'[29]

Instead, when the British infantry did attack nearby Gallipoli several months later, they found a refreshed enemy, more deeply entrenched and better prepared. The result was a disaster in which British casualties reached over 200,000. The defeat caused a political crisis in England and the formation of a new coalition government – without Winston Churchill.

On June 10, 1915, war correspondent E. Ashmead Bartlett noted in his diary:

This evening I dined with Lady Randolph Churchill to meet Winston. . . . I am much surprised at the change in Winston Churchill. He looks years older, his face is pale, he seems very depressed and he feels keenly his retirement from the Admiralty. . . . He has no one but himself to blame for his misfortunes. He held the most important post in the Cabinet at the outbreak of the war, and he had only to curb his impetuosity and direct its labours, guided by his advisers, and he would still be First Lord. But his nature rebelled at the prospect of sitting in an arm-chair directing naval strategy when others were actually fighting. He was torn between conflicting emotions, the demands of his great office, and his paramount desire to take an active part in the war itself. . . .

At dinner, the conversation was more or less general, nothing was said about the Dardanelles and Winston was very quiet. It was only towards the very end that he suddenly burst forth into a tremendous discourse on the Expedition and what might have been, addressed directly across the table in the form of a lecture to his mother, who listened most attentively. . . .[30]

'This slow and supine government are now beginning to realize what Winston has preached for the last six months,' Jennie wrote to Leonie. 'If they had made the Dardanelles policy a certainty, which they could have done in the beginning, Constantinople would have been in our hands ages ago. *In confidence*, it is astounding how Winston foresaw it all. . . .'[31]

Earlier Jennie had expressed her concern about Winston to Clara:

I'm afraid Winston is very sad at having nothing to do. When you have had your hand at the helm for four years it seems stagnation to take a back place, and for why? No fault can be found with his work at the Admiralty and they give him the sack whereas a gigantic mistake is made at the War Office [Kitchener at Gallipoli] and the man responsible for it is screened and given the Garter. It makes my blood boil. . . .[32]

Winston described this period of enforced inactivity:

The change from the intense executive activities of each day's work at the Admiralty to the narrowly measured duties of a counsellor left me gasping. Like a sea-beast fished up from the depths, or a diver too suddenly hoisted, my veins threatened to burst from the fall in pressure. . . . I had long hours of utterly unwonted leisure . . . at a moment when every fibre of my being was inflamed to action. . . .[33]

Winston and his mother were guests at a dinner party, whose host overheard a conversation between them that he recorded in his memoirs. Jennie suggested to her son that he should do some painting. 'It sounded like an innocent wife, offering to read to her husband, while he was vainly hacking a golf ball out of a bunker.'[34] But in the country the following Sunday Winston experimented with a children's paint-box, and the next morning he bought a complete set of oils and an easel. It was not a new activity for him. When he was a little boy, he had accompanied his mother to her painting lessons with Mrs E. M. Ward, and painting was one of the few subjects at school that he had really liked and excelled in. He had written to his mother from school about his 'drawing little landscapes and bridges', and had illustrated many of his letters with drawings.

Now his mother's suggestion seemed exactly the right thing for him. 'Just to paint is great fun,' he later wrote. 'The colours are lovely to look at and delicious to squeeze out. Matching them, however crudely, with what you see is fascinating and absolutely absorbing. . . . I know of nothing which, without exhausting the body, more entirely absorbs the mind. . . .'[35] Indeed, after watching Winston painting, Lady Violet Bonham Carter said, '. . . it was the only occupation I had ever seen him practise in silence. . . .'[36]

'His last paintings are very good,' Jennie later wrote to Leonie. 'Lavery says that if Winston cared to take painting up as a profession he could, but of course he uses it as an opiate.'[37]

The war had become the bloodiest one in history, involving some thirty countries. Casualty lists continually became longer and longer, and there seemed to be no end to it. A great many of Jennie's friends had suffered personal losses. Conversation was muted and often grim, parties were few. Jennie concentrated more and more on her family, especially after Clara's daughter Clare — who was married to Wilfred Sheridan and the mother of two children — learned that her husband was missing in action and presumed dead. Jennie, who had contacts in the War Department, was the first to receive the news.

It came as a shock to learn that Winston had asked to rejoin his old Regiment at the front in France. He was then staying in his brother's home in Cromwell Road. F. E. Smith recalled after a visit, that the house was soon 'upside down while the soldier statesman was buckling on his sword. Downstairs, Mr "Eddie" Marsh, his faithful secretary, was in tears. . . . Upstairs, Lady Randolph was in a state of despair at the thought of her brilliant son being relegated to the trenches. . . .'[38]

Many times before, Jennie had bid her sons good-bye as they had gone off to war, but this time everything seemed more ominous. She had seen so many wounded soldiers at the hospital; and she had personally known many of the dead and missing. She also knew Winston's fearlessness, his need to be in the front-line fighting. 'Please be sensible,' she warned him. 'I think you ought to take the trenches in small doses, after 10 years of more or less sedentary life — but I'm sure you won't "play the fool" — Remember you are destined for greater things. . . . I am a great believer in your star. . . .'[39] Beyond that, she could do little more than pray for him.

She saw more of her daughters-in-law now, with Clementine and Goonie sharing the house in Cromwell Road. Clementine went to work in a munitions factory and Jennie spent more time with her grandchildren. Her relationships with Clemmie and Goonie were what one might expect — close but not intimate. The young women sensed her overpowering presence and were naturally jealous about maintaining their own independent lives. They did not resist, however, when Jennie offered to contribute regularly toward their housekeeping expenses and pocket money while their husbands were away.

Jennie was able to help her daughters-in-law with money she was getting from *Pearson's Weekly* for a series of articles which would later be collected into a book entitled *Small Talks on Big Subjects*.

Her first article appeared in the September 1915 issue. Called 'Mars and Cupid', it concerned marriage in wartime. Jennie inserted her own thrust at marriage, recalling the cynic who said he didn't know that there was much difference between marriage and war. She also quoted the remark, 'Marriage is a field of battle, not a bed of roses. . . .' And she commented rather acidly, 'Your castle in Spain has no foundation, that is why it is so easily built. . . .'

Jennie was equally well qualified to write the next month's essay on 'Extravagance'. As much as she endorsed wartime thrift, she made the wistful point, '. . . we owe something to extravagance, for thrift and adventure seldom go hand in hand. . . .' She might also have said that had it not been for a lifetime of extravagance, she might never have been able to move in the social circles she did and accomplish as much as she had. And if she had not done that, she would not have been able to ease the entry of her sons Winston and Jack into the positions they held.

Jennie's other essays covered a variety of subjects. Her views on suffragettes had been modified through the years, and she now believed that their cause 'must ultimately lead to victory'. She applauded their strategic switch from fierce agitation to peaceful demonstration. She was delighted with the new model of the Englishwoman. 'The girl of today, in whatever class of society, is not content to emulate her American cousin, she wants to go "one better". . . .' Independence, however, can go too far, she wrote, because a man 'is not inclined to feel very tenderly towards a girl who has just beaten him severely on his own ground at lawn-tennis or golf. . . .'

But she refused to fall into the trap of comparing generations, 'for we live in such different conditions'. She sympathized with the girl who wanted to emancipate herself from a dull home, 'but when she got her freedom, she often found bachelordom very dull without a bachelor boy to play with. . . .'

Jennie defined sins as 'exaggerated inclinations'.

All of her essays were enriched by her memories. What does success owe to failure? 'Everything,' an artist had told her. 'I am built on the failures of others. If their paintings were not so bad, mine would not be thought so good.'

'Another friend of mine,' she wrote, 'attributed all the disasters of his life to the fact of having had, at his first venture, the luck to buy a horse that won everything. . . . Thinking he could at any time buy more winners of the same type, [he] became too confident and was ultimately ruined. . . .'

She wrote about friendship: 'Treat your friends as you do your pictures, and place them in their best light.' And she tried to describe the perfect friend: warm, glowing, sensitive. 'I had such a friend once,' she wrote, thinking of Pearl Craigie.

It was impossible to know her and not love her. She was so human, so sympathetic and her brilliant and delicious mind so deep a well to draw from.

I remember a day we spent together in the country. We went for a walk. It was one of those days the English climate never wearies of giving – grey, raw, damp, odious. But we became so interested in our talk that it was some time before we noticed that we had wandered into a ploughed field. To me, it seemed, listening to her, that the field was enamelled with flowers, and that a warm sun beamed on us. She had the rare faculty of making you feel at peace with yourself, and inspiring you with unfailing hope. Her own life lacked much of the brightness she gave others, but she was happy in her work and overflowing interests, and notwithstanding her rather frail physique, her enthusiasm made her a true optimist.

The year 1916 began badly for Jennie. She had always had a special vanity about her lovely legs and dainty feet, but one toe had become badly infected and had to be amputated. To add to her miseries, her home was burgled.

LADY RANDOLPH CHURCHILL ROBBED
ROYAL GIFTS STOLEN

Early yesterday morning, at 72 Brook Street, Hanover Square, West, the residence of Lady Randolph Churchill was entered by burglars. Jewelry and articles of great personal value were stolen. Among them were a gold seal, with jade and ruby top, and a gold papercutter, both bearing an inscription, 'From King Edward to Lady Randolph Churchill'; a large shagreen box, inscribed 'Presented by Queen Alexandra', a heart-shaped gold box with cat's head, with emerald eyes, 'From George to Pussie', engraved underneath; a yellow enamel frame, ivory box, portrait of Col. Winston Churchill as a child, wearing a bead

325

necklace; gold metal [locket] bearing faces of Winston and John Churchill, at 17 and 20 years of age; and a small round, gold box, with blue-enamel round edges, and the portraits of King Edward and Queen Alexandra in the centre.

Of the store of trinkets carried off by the thieves, one, a flat, gold box, dated back to the Queen Anne period, and bore a bust of the First Duke of Marlborough in the centre, supported by Hercules and Mars. Also missing is an oval miniature, at least a hundred years old, mounted with seed pearls, showing the bust of a middle-aged woman, with hair dressed and powdered. The thieves appear to have forced one of the windows of the drawing-room.[40]

There was more unpleasantness to come. In her *Diaries*, Lady Cynthia Asquith described a dinner party held on August 8, 1916:

Conversation was mainly general and very agreeable. I felt in good form. Cowans [General Sir John Cowans, Quartermaster General of the Army] came on the block. There is an Enquiry Commission sitting on him, on account of the following ugly story: Lady Randolph Churchill (Black Jane[41]) fell in love with a private and, at her instance, General Cowans gave the man a commission. Either another woman entered the lists and captured this man, or in any case he did not respond to Jane's passion, and spleen and pique made her induce Cowans to degrade the man to the ranks again. . . . Cowans, poor man, has the reputation of jobbery, owing to his susceptibility to 'ladies', but this story sounds quite incredible. . . .[42]

It was. It was not incredible that Jennie might take a liking to some handsome soldier and try to help him, as she had many times before. When Winston was First Lord of the Admiralty she had asked him to help a young man named Crundal, but Winston was unable to oblige. 'I am very sorry about Crundal (whom I know). But the promotion of lieutenants is merciless. . . . It is cruel. The only thing that would make it crueller would be favouritism. . . .'[43]

The unlikely part of the Asquith story was the suggestion that Jennie would turn on the man and try to have him stripped of the commission. That would have been out of character. She might have thrown something, laughed bitterly, cursed her folly, but there was no meanness in her. Revenge was not her style.

The truth of the story was quite different. An article in *The Times* was headlined:

Army Inquiry

YOUNG OFFICER'S ORDEAL

A WOMAN CENSURED

The article named a sergeant in the Royal Welch Fusiliers who had been made a second lieutenant and described his attempted removal, which 'followed a letter of remonstrance to Mrs Cornwallis-West'. It seemed that the newly appointed lieutenant had 'consistently failed to respond' to 'a more than ordinary interest' which she had taken in him. At the Court of Inquiry, the officer was vindicated and Mrs West 'was found to have acted in a highly discreditable manner and have given untruthful evidence.' She was also accused of 'injudicious boasting of power she wielded at the War Office. . . . The lady's conduct [was] highly discreditable in her vindictive attempts to injure him.' [44]

The catch was that the woman was not Jennie. Mrs Cornwallis-West was identified as the wife of Colonel William Cornwallis-West of Ruthin Castle – Jennie's former mother-in-law!

The public confusion was not surprising. Not only had their names been similar, but both were beautiful women and both had had a similar reputation for favouring young men.

This reputation made Jennie particularly fascinating to her young niece.

'She was my heroine,' said Baroness Cedestrom, the daughter of Lord Randolph's sister.

She was the only person I ever knew who could physically light up a room by entering it. It wasn't just her beauty, it was her charm, it was her voice. I knew she was 'naughty', I overheard my family talk about her being 'free and easy with the gentlemen', and I was naive enough to ask them what they meant. I asked Jennie one day how it felt to be run after by all these young men, and she said quietly, 'I love people. I love the world. I love life.' [45]

We used to talk music all the time [the Baroness continued]. We both loved Wagner. We used to play piano duets. I wanted to be a concert pianist – I had all the training and teaching. But my parents thought it was common to play in public, and Aunt Jennie took my side and told them how cruel it was of them to prevent me. She would always ask for me when she came for a visit.

If it was a short visit, I'd wait until she finished talking to my parents, then I'd run to her and she would say, 'Let's walk around the block and talk.' . . . How I wished she was my mother. . . .[46]

Lady Betty Cartwright, whose sister was married to Jack, remembered: 'I was a young girl when Jennie took me to the opera and parties. I hadn't had my coming-out yet, and so it was my only chance to go. She was so fascinating to talk to because she knew everybody and had been everywhere.'[47]

She had, indeed. But now a new Jennie was gradually emerging. She had decided that she would not try to keep her youth by fighting Time. Her youth was within her. Oswald Frewen had noted in his diary the first trace of white in his aunt's hair. Edward Marsh, who visited her often, wrote: '. . . She suddenly decided to let hair, waist and complexion, and everything go, and became, in a day, one of the most beautiful human beings I have ever seen. . . .'[48]

But she was still lonely. 'When I go to the theatre, I often have to go with my maid, because no one else will go with me,' she told Oswald.[49] It was an exaggeration, but there were fewer men knocking at her door.

One who came calling late that year was Montagu Porch, the attractive young man she had met in Rome. Montagu Phippen Porch resembled George Cornwallis-West only in that they were both very handsome. But Porch was a much less forceful man, and he did not have George's talent for aggressive gallantry with women. His background was that of a country squire in Glastonbury. His neighbours there described him as 'nature's own gentleman', 'a quiet man and a kind man', 'a man of old-fashioned courtesy'. 'You never knew what he was really thinking and he seldom told you. . . .' '. . . At a meeting he would always agree with the majority.' 'He was a very dapper man – the kind of a man you would expect to wear spats, although he never did.'[50]

Porch was a member of the landed gentry, and his family represented the most solid social substance. Their wealth had originally come from Australian sheep. The family had a general reputation for being 'tight and meanfisted' with money, but no family was more active in community affairs. A Porch-Porch was the first Mayor of Glastonbury.[51]

Montagu Porch loved Glastonbury and eventually returned, but he was away for a long time. There had been a family scandal in which one of his sisters had been convicted of poisoning her husband in China. Her life sentence was later commuted and she returned to live in nearby Bath, where her mother joined her.

Porch was a graduate of Oxford and had served in the Boer War. After the war he went on an archaeological expedition, crossing the Sinai Desert by camel, to collect ancient stone implements.[52] He was a young man at loose end, still not wanting to go home. In the British Colonial Service it was said that traditionally the first-class young men went to India (as Montagu's father had done), and the second-class men settled for Africa.

When his period of service was over, Porch returned to London, 'and it was Winston, oddly enough, who gave me my next job.' That was in 1906, when Winston was Under Secretary for the Colonies. It was his secretary, Edward Marsh, who interviewed Porch, and he was assigned to Nigeria as a Third-Class Resident. 'I remember him [Marsh] asking me: "Do you ride?" I had done quite a bit with the Taunton Vale Foxhounds. That's how I came to get a job in Northern Nigeria. I built the first town of Kaduna there – a few mud and straw huts for the engineers building the railroad to Kano.'[53]

While he was in Nigeria, the Lagos *Standard* reported: 'The Third-Class Resident had two clerks tied and flogged because they did not prostrate themselves to the ground before him. All clerks must prostrate on the ground when meeting him.'[54] The name of the Resident was not mentioned, but since there were only a few British officials in Nigeria, some may have thought it was Porch. The man must have been another Third-Class Resident, as such actions do not fit in with the mild manner and character of Montagu Porch. Porch was concerned with introducing peanuts and cotton into the agricultural economy and keeping pet leopards off the streets.[55]

As a friend of Hugh Frewen's, he had taken time off to attend Hugh's wedding in Rome. When Jennie refused to dance with him, he did not persist. But the following day, the Duchess of Sermoneta invited him to lunch at her *palazzo*, and Jennie, of course, was there.

'We met again,' he remembered. 'We met a lot, though she was only there a fortnight. We looked at monuments a lot, talked a lot.'

They both loved music, and both played the piano.

'You look as though you've got snow on your hair,' she told him.

'It was true,' Porch recalled, smiling. 'It's a family thing.'[56]

On the eve of World War I, Jennie had written what he said was 'a wonderful letter' to him. Since then he had become a lieutenant in the Nigerian Regiment of the Cameroons Expeditionary Force, and now he was back in England on leave. Jennie was not in the mood to discourage him, and they saw a great deal of each other in a short time. After Porch returned to his Regiment, Jennie wrote to Leonie: 'I've met a young man I shall probably marry.'[57]

But there were soon other young men on the scene, as well as people she cultivated in order to help further Winston's career while he was away at war. J. L. Garvin, a gaunt young man with 'intense eyes' and 'a lovable nature', was a frequent visitor. Garvin was the brilliant editor of *The Observer*, and Jennie persuaded him to promote Winston as a political figure whose talents were urgently needed. Garvin regretfully informed her later that William Waldorf Astor had vetoed the plan. Astor, 'tho personally friendly to Winston, does not want *The Observer* to run him politically just now. . . .'[58]

Jennie also dined with Lord Frazer, who 'writes nearly all the leaders in *The Times*. . . . I thought he was a good person to "hot up".' There was also a long evening with her good friend Herbert Asquith, and Jennie sent Winston an account of it.

During this period Jennie told a friend, Lieutenant-Colonel A'Court Repington, that she had had the pleasure of seeing both her husband and her son leading the House of Commons – 'Winston once did so for a fortnight – and the pain of hearing them both make speeches when they resigned.' Repington also remembered how energetically Jennie went about trying to convert Winston's enemies. At a luncheon she met 'Austin Harrison, who is one of Winston's most bitter opponents, and she took him away with her afterwards. . . .'[59] She also kept in close touch with Winston's political friends, always urging them to pull him out of the war and back into the government. Among them was Lloyd George, who had succeeded Kitchener as Minister of War.

In December 1916, Lloyd George became Prime Minister,[60] heading a Coalition Government. One of his early acts was to invite Winston to become Minister of Munitions, and Winston accepted.

Winston was back in England, but his job was demanding and he spent most of his free time with his wife and children. The same was true of Jack. Jennie complained to Clara 'that her children never come near her'.[61] But her nephew Oswald recalled that she seemed well supplied with other male escorts: Norman Forbes Robertson, a man named Simon, an Italian gentleman called Casati and a soldier named 'Taylor, who has sung in public', among others.

She also translated a French book into English for a relief fund of the French Parliamentary Committee. It was called *My Return to Paris* and contained contributions by some of the prominent authors of the time. In addition, she edited and wrote the preface for a book entitled *Women's War Work*, a collection of articles telling of work performed by women in different countries to aid the war effort. She also organized a series of luncheon conferences under the auspices of *Outlook* magazine, in which leading French statesmen, including Clemenceau, spoke about the French effort in the war. These luncheons were held at the Ritz ballroom, and the tickets were always quickly sold.[62]

In her free time she called upon society women in an effort to collect a chorus of singers to be featured in Mrs Lloyd George's Welsh Memorial Matinée in December 1917; she also spent more time with her sister Clara, whose husband Moreton was seriously ill; organized a small dinner party for Winston so that he could meet Ivor Novello, the composer of 'Keep The Home Fires Burning', a song he especially admired, and talked to theatrical producers about adapting some French plays.[63]

Jennie had sold her house in Brook Street, again making a handsome profit. Winston had complimented her on the sale of a previous house because she did not have a fixation about staying in any particular home. 'Not being a snail,' he told her, 'you can get on quite well without it.' She now bought 8 Westbourne Street near Hyde Park. Most of the houses she had bought and sold were in the same small area. This one was a four-storey house with two columns at the entrance and a small garden. Each large window on the upper floors opened onto a small balcony. Within sight was an old church with a beautiful stained-glass window in the tower. A few minutes' walk away was Kensington Gardens.

The interior of the house did not have much to recommend it when she moved in, but Jennie soon gave it life and colour. 'She was an original when it came to interior decorating,' recalled her niece excitedly, as if she were recreating the scene. 'She was the first to use yellow curtains to catch the sunlight. . . . It was lovely. She transformed that house.'[64]

She made door handles out of old silver watch cases; used tinted electric bulbs to provide a softer and more flattering light; papered the drawing room with an artificial wall panelling which 'you can sponge . . . after the fogs'; and often used table-mats instead of tablecloths on the gleaming mahogany tables. The furnishings and ornaments were English (Queen Anne), French, Italian, Chinese and Japanese.

But Jennie did not stop at renovating the house. Her long-time servant Walden had pleaded to be allowed to serve in the war in some way, and Winston found him a position at headquarters. Instead of replacing him with another man, Jennie created a sensation by using her maids as footmen and waiters. To make them look more impressive, she designed a hybrid uniform. They wore tight-fitting black cloth jackets with lapels, but cut off above the hips. Under the jackets the maids wore white starched collars, black bow-ties and waistcoats. Completing the uniform was a plain black skirt. Jennie classified her new servant as a 'foot-maid'.[65] Eddie Marsh remembered a dinner at Jennie's house during which Lord Rosebery spent much of the time examining the foot-maids.

Increasing Zeppelin raids made dinner parties unpredictable. Lady Diana Cooper described a house being hit, the kitchen-maids screaming, the wounded brought to the basement. 'Later . . . arrived Jennie Churchill and Maud Cunard, both a little tipsy, dancing and talking wildly. They had been walking and got scared, and had stopped for a drink.' They were going to the opera because 'it being raid-night, the public required example'.[66]

Maud Cunard was another of Jennie's old American friends and had helped raise money for the *Maine*.[67] A short, slight figure with a receding chin and a high, piercing voice, she always wore a profusion of jewels and rings and called herself 'Emerald'. Her Grosvenor Square house was always open to the amusing, the important, the attractive. Maud Cunard could be malicious, but she was never dull. Beneath her excitability and her jewels was a pathetic, disillusioned woman. Jennie was a good listener.

Jennie had also listened to Winston's complaints about the government's inability to share his enthusiasm for tanks as a weapon of war. He had first urged their development when he was at the Admiralty, and after a time as Minister of Munitions he was able to do something about it. Later he had the satisfaction of being proved a prophet. At the end of 1917, when there was a successful Allied tank attack, Jennie wrote to Leonie:

Do you see how successful Winston's caterpillars have been and how disgusting the *Daily Mail* is today? Winston worked at those things, scratching the money for them. . . . Two years ago he went to France to 'boom' them and Haig sent for him when he was at the Admiralty to explain them. Of course Winston did not invent them but they would not exist today . . . had it not been for his foresight and push, and now they want to take away from him the credit for them. It makes my blood boil – the injustice and meanness with which he is treated.[68]

Jennie often visited Leonie at her castle in Ireland, occasionally combining business with pleasure. The *Daily Chronicle* assigned her to write several political articles. She wrote with loving memory of Isaac Butt, 'that broad-minded and far-seeing man' who had 'invented Home Rule', and expressed hope for the recently-convened Irish Convention, 'fiercest of enemies . . . but there they all are, meeting under the same roof to discuss for once in amity, the problem of Ireland.'[69]

She detailed the political problems in Ireland, analysed the varied positions, and wrote of the general mood: the lighted streets, the absence of air-raids, the remoteness of war. 'These men evidently do not understand or realize that, if the war is lost, their benighted country, under the iron rule of the Prussian mailed-fist, will cease to exist. . . .' But the Irish problem would not be solved, she concluded, 'by trying to make good Irishmen into bad Englishmen'.[70]

It was about this time that Jennie heard of the death of two of her earliest admirers, the Marquis Henri de Breteuil and Harry Cust. She was sixty-four now, still a remarkably handsome woman, her face smooth and unwrinkled, her eyes bright and eager. But she must have felt very mortal, even though she told her friends that she planned to live to be ninety. With her energy almost undiminished, they did not doubt her. Yet projects and social life could not satisfy her restlessness.

'She had been very lonely in her new house in Westbourne Street,' her nephew Seymour Leslie remembered. She often telephoned to ask him to come over to dine and play the piano with her. 'I would find her in tears,' he said.[71]

She had her moments of cynicism, too. She and some friends were listening to one man in their group praising his 'adored one' effusively. Her virtue, he said, was 'above rubies'.[72]

'Try diamonds,' Jennie retorted.

Montagu Porch was home on leave again in 1918. He had had two more years to think about Jennie and to decide that he still wanted to marry her. 'I don't think I remember proposing,' Porch said. He and Jennie had been invited to visit Leonie at her castle in Ireland, and 'by the time we got to the castle, there was an understanding.' [73] Jennie later confessed to him, 'You know I could never marry a man of my own age.' They stayed there two weeks, deep in the peace of the Monaghan forests, overlooking the silent lake, and Leonie told them, 'You look like a very happy and comfortable couple.' [74]

Winston, according to Porch, was 'very surprised'. His reaction must have certainly been stronger than that – he was then forty-four years old and Porch was only forty-one.

There were other questions: Would Winston be politically embarrassed? What was the likelihood of success for a marriage based on equal proportions of loneliness and love?

A'Court Repington lunched with them, and recorded in his diary: 'Lady R. charming about her future. Mr Porch quite good-looking and intelligent. They get married tomorrow and go to Windsor for the weekend. Winston says that he hopes marriage won't become the vogue among ladies of his mother's age. . . .' [75]

The wedding on June 1, 1918, was unheralded and simple. They arrived at the Registry Office in Harrow Road quite unnoticed. Porch remembered exactly what Jennie wore: 'A grey coat and skirt and a light-green toque. She looked very beautiful.' [76]

Winston was the first to sign the register as a witness, and then he told Montagu, 'I know you'll never regret you married her.'

'I never did,' Porch said many years later.[77]

23

'He has a future and I have a past,' Jennie told her friend Lady Essex, 'so we should be all right.' [1]

At dinner on the night of Jennie's wedding, Lady Cynthia Asquith recalled that the novelist George Moore

> . . . was rather funny about Lady Randolph. I suggested that perhaps she liked the idea of being known as the 'one white woman in Nigeria' instead of the one black one in London. He said he could only account for how they would spend the evenings by a re-application of the principle of the Arabian Nights, she regaling him with the recital of one of her amours (Moore claimed 200 lovers for her) nightly — and the collection would be known as the Nigerian Nights.[2]

Such acrid remarks soon spread all over the London dinner party circuit, and even Jennie joked to Porch about it: 'I think people are saying that Miss Jerome went up the Church Hill, to the West, into the Porch. . . .' But Jennie's favourite motto was: 'They say. What *do* they say? *Let* them say!'

At one dinner she attended, a woman was mentioned in conversation, and another of the guests, a waspish lady, completely dissected her character, 'practically casting her fragments on the dinner table.' The room quieted for an awkward moment, because everyone else there knew that the woman in question was a good friend of Jennie's. Leaning across the table 'with that curiously quick uplift of her flashing eyes which never lost its charm,' Jennie retorted, 'It's a wise virgin who looks after her own lamp.' [3]

When asked long afterwards, 'Didn't you care about the social censure?' Montagu Porch looked somewhat astonished. 'Care?' he said, 'I was in love.' [4]

Porch wrote to Winston that he found it incredible that he should be allowed so much happiness when the world was in anguish. He regarded this marriage as the most important step in his life and it 'is not taken in the dark'.

'I love your mother,' he said. 'I can make her happy – Her difficulties and obligations from henceforth will be shared by me – so willingly.' [5]

Before returning to Nigeria, Porch took Jennie to Bath to meet his mother, who had not attended the wedding. Her son was the last of his line, and now she could expect no heir. The meeting was polite and brief.

Jennie was not allowed to accompany her husband to Africa. Civilian travel was restricted for the duration of the war, and the government did not even permit Porch to make an official request to have Jennie go with him. A West African newspaper urged that Jennie be permitted a passport, saying that Nigeria needed Jennie's 'brains and push' to help right some of the country's injustices. [6]

'Poor Porchey is very lonely,' Jennie wrote to her sister, and Clara read to Jennie part of a letter from her son Oswald saying that Jennie ought to join 'Montie' that fall 'as it was the custom in England for married people to live together as much as possible.' Jennie was not amused. [7]

Reporters observed that Jennie spent 'many hours trying to persuade authorities to give her a passport,' although an influential friend had told her that it was hopeless. 'I feel so powerless to do anything,' she wrote to Leonie, 'but I must try.' But then she added, 'Life is so short, and I have had a good share already. . . .' [8]

There were those who felt that Jennie was not really making the greatest effort to get permission to go. 'She kept promising she would come to Nigeria, but she never came,' said Mrs Hadley Hucker, who became Porch's closest companion and friend in his later years. 'She was too old to stand the heat probably.' [9] Heat or no heat, the suspicion lingers that if it had been Kinsky or George in Nigeria, Jennie would have found a way to get there.

'My marriage will not in any way interfere with my war work,' Jennie told the press. 'I shall go on just as before, but I do not want to say what my plans are.' [10] In truth, she really didn't know what her plans were. One thing about which she was certain was that she did not want to be known as Mrs Montagu Porch. Her change of name to Mrs George Cornwallis-West had ended in a battered pride, and she did not want that to happen again. On a visit to Blenheim after her new marriage, she signed her name, 'Lady Randolph Churchill'. She had 'no snobbish

336

feeling about it,' she said, but she did want that name restored to her legally. 'My boys asked me to,' she added.[11]

London was a sombre city: few cars in sight, people grim and worried, Lancaster Gate Hospital where Jennie worked filled with 'poor gassed soldiers'. There had been four long years of casualty lists, rationing, and small hope. Then the military tide turned. There was a series of big battles and major victories. Suddenly – unbelievably – it was all over.

The Armistice of November 1918 allowed all the pent-up frustration and fear to explode into delirium. In London strangers marched down the streets arm-in-arm singing at the top of their voices; girls climbed on top of taxis and waved flags; people in automobiles kept up a steady blare of horns. That night Eddie Marsh collected playwright John Drinkwater and poet Siegfried Sassoon (who had been a patient at Lancaster Gate Hospital) and took them to a party at Jennie's house. 'The riotous celebrations were still in full swing . . .', Sassoon wrote later.

King Edward's death had brought one era to a close for Jennie; now with the end of World War I another was rounded. Jennie was sixty-four years old and most of her contemporaries had slipped into social retirement. They had neither the inclination nor the servants for any more entertaining in the grand style. There was a new tone to the times. Graciousness was being supplanted by speed. Cars were being driven faster and faster. Dinners had fewer courses. More entertaining was being done in restaurants. Younger people danced the Turkey Trot, migrated in an evening from one nightclub to another, laughed louder and more easily. Jennie was one of the younger people.

She was, in fact, much younger-spirited than her old-fashioned husband. He had come from the quiet countryside, and was accustomed to a more fixed and orderly world. At the end of the war he resigned from the Nigerian Civil Service, returned to London and decided that he wanted more of Jennie's life. He sold some of his Glastonbury land, and Jennie bought a house in Berkeley Square as an investment. She redecorated it and then sold it for £17,000, making an excellent profit. 'But she went through it like that,' said Mrs Huckler, snapping her fingers.[12]

Of course she did. She was not likely to change the style of a lifetime, nor did Porch want her to. Years afterwards, he said, 'we had a very happy life together. There was never a dull moment. . . .' [13]

They travelled through France. Jennie's friends there were still flourishing, and there were new and exciting people at the parties — Stravinsky, Picasso, Ravel, Proust, James Joyce. Some of them later visited Jennie and Montie in London. Jennie still invited old friends such as Queen Alexandra, too — when the Queen came, Porch had to 'telephone for a constable to be outside' [14] — but now she entertained younger people. It was at her house that Zelda and F. Scott Fitzgerald met Winston, whom they found at first 'so hard to talk to', until he later 'turned out to be so pleasant'.[15]

Shane Leslie remembered how exhilarated Porch was, as if he had come out of a cocoon into a new world. 'Oh, Porchey, Porchey,' said Leslie, with warmth and affection, as if he could still visualize the young man's wide-eyed wonder.[16]

In the midst of all this, Jennie was sharply recalled to old memories. Prince Charles Rudolf Andreas Kinsky died in Austria on December 11, 1919. His friend George Lambton wrote, 'If ever a man died of a broken heart, Charles Kinsky did. . . .' [17]

It was not a shock that Jennie could share with Porch, but never was she more grateful to have him. More than ever now she needed a man who needed her. She still arranged small dinners for Winston to meet certain people, but Clementine did most of the entertaining his career required. And she still wrote frequent notes to Jack about business contacts, but Jack now had his own contacts. Porch, however, depended on her completely.

After a year of fun and interesting people, he now wanted to take on some work of his own. Moreover, he and Jennie needed money. Jennie sought Jack's advice, as she did more often now. Winston was still in the Government, and in 1919 he was made Secretary of State for War as well as Air Minister, so he was usually inaccessible. Jack advised his mother on investments, listened to her complaints, adored her as always.

Porch's qualifications for a career were few. His only real knowledge was of Nigeria. But for a man who had knowledge of it, Nigeria was full of potentially profitable investment opportunities. Jack and Winston decided to finance his exploratory trip there.

Porch left for Nigeria early in 1921. He had become increasingly resentful of the snubs and sneers. 'I prefer the bullets of the Boer War or the flies of the Gold Coast,' he said, 'to the stings of the snobs in a London drawing room.' [18]

Shortly after he left Jennie wrote him a note that he always treasured:

My darling,

Bless you and *au revoir* and I love you better than anything in the world and shall try to do all those things you want me to in your absence.

Your loving wife,
J

PS Love me and think of me.[19]

'My second marriage was romantic, but not successful,' Jennie later said. 'My third marriage was successful, but not romantic.'

She was now sixty-seven years old and again alone. What could she do with herself?

She could try flying. At a party she met a jovial monocled man who was in the Royal Air Force, and soon she found herself sitting in a small wicker chair in his aeroplane flying at ninety miles an hour. 'An extraordinary experience. Right above the clouds in a little coupé.' [20]

She could act in a 'movie'. During a dinner party with a group of young people, a film director suggested they all go out to his set and improvise a film for charity. Everyone there was forty years younger than Jennie, '. . . but we never gave it a thought,' said Lady Altrincham. 'She was just one of us. Jennie *was* young.' [21]

She could take an interest in young people. A Welsh singer named Foster was making her début. Just before her appearance she was trembling with nervousness, but an older woman 'with extraordinary eyes' approached her without introduction and calmed her. That was Jennie.[22]

She could be controversial. 'LADY RANDOLPH CHURCHILL DESCRIBES AMERICAN EDICT AS ABSURD.' A Philadelphia clergyman had preached that for a gown to be 'moral' it must not be cut more than three inches below the neck or seven and a half inches above the ground. Jennie told the press: 'There is no such thing as a moral dress. . . . It's people who are moral or immoral. . . .' [23]

She could help her family. The American Embassy had mysteriously refused to permit her niece, Clare Sheridan, to enter the United States. Clare had been to Russia sculpting busts of Lenin and Trotsky, and Jennie discovered that there was a 'dossier' on her in England. Checking the dossier, she learned that detectives had observed a newspaper editor going into Clare's lodgings and often staying late. The newspaper was considered too friendly to Moscow, so the government suspected a plot.

Jennie called on the American Consul to explain that Clare had been sculpting a bust of the editor, and Clare got her visa.

Jennie accompanied Clare to the station, urging her to come back quickly if she wasn't happy there. 'She looked so beautiful that morning,' remembered Clare, 'and wistful. . . .'[24]

Her loveliness retained a contemporary quality. She wore her white hair 'not like an elderly lady but in the Marquis style of the Louis XV days, when white frothy curls were affected by sprightly belles. . . .'[25]

Her list of activities still included everything from the Shakespeare Union to the YWCA. There were no new dances which she did not dance expertly. There were few good contemporary books she did not read. 'I wept when I came to the end,' she said of one, 'and from such an emotionally hardened sinner, it meant a great deal. . . .' Her wit was still sharp. Describing an amorous gentleman, she observed that he had 'more buzz than biz'.

Her many friends pressed invitations on her, asking her to stay with them as long as she wished. In the spring of 1921 she accepted one from Vittoria, the Duchess of Sermoneta. From Florence, Jennie wrote to Leonie:

> I shall come home as good and sweet-tempered as a cherubim [sic]. How wonderful is this place! and what fun I am having! It seems positively selfish to be having such a good time and you in Ireland amidst a civil war.
>
> Winston, Clementine and I stayed with the Laverys at Cap d'Ail and he painted some delightful pictures. Vittoria met me in her car and I found Rome very gay, races, dances, *antiquaries*. Her palazzo charming but not grand like the Colonna palace where I lunched – such magnificence!
>
> They all play bridge *madly* and for very high stakes. I had to stop, you know how badly I play and the Romans are rapacious to a degree! . . . . I have bought some lovely things. . . .[26]

Jennie had bought 'some dainty slippers at the best Roman shoemakers'. The Duchess later observed that Jennie had the prettiest feet imaginable.[27]

'We did a good deal of sightseeing,' the Duchess also recalled.

> We ransacked all the old curiosity shops and Jennie bought profusely; her zest in spending money was one of her charms. She was still a

handsome woman, her dark eyes had lost none of their sparkle with the passing of years and the shape of her face was always admirable. Sargent's drawing of her was an excellent likeness; her beauty was of a dark southern type.[28]

The Duchess also remembered how much Jennie spoke of Winston and her 'unswerving faith in his capacities'. Jennie had said, 'Winston's shoulders are broad enough to bear any burden.' The Duchess also remarked that Jennie was 'absolutely certain' that everything Winston did 'was right'.[29]

After her lively trip to Rome, Jennie accepted an invitation from Lady Frances Horner to visit Mells Manor in Somerset, only a short distance from her husband's ancestral home in Glastonbury.[30] The home of 'little Jack Horner' stood high on a rock and had a broad terrace overlooking the lakes below. Mells Manor was a gay house, with light pouring in through its Georgian windows. Outside there were shimmering masses of primroses and bluebells; inside were old-fashioned furnishings, enormous and comfortable.

At teatime, Jennie put on her new Italian shoes and hurried down the well-worn stairway. Three steps from the landing, she fell.[31] 'I did not actually see what happened,' Lady Horner recalled, 'but I heard her fall and cry out . . . she could not rise. I propped her up with cushions under her back and feet and telephoned for the doctor from Frome. He came in a quarter of an hour and said it was a bad fracture of the left leg near the ankle.'[32]

The bones were set, and two days later she was taken in an ambulance with a doctor and nurse to her home in London. The doctor diagnosed the injury as a simple fracture of both bones directly above the ankle. There was very little displacement, but there was considerable swelling of the ankle and foot. Progress was satisfactory at first, but within two weeks a portion of the skin blackened and gangrene set in. When her fever became dangerously high, Winston was called.

'In spite of the late hour, and with a characteristic promptness, he called in a surgeon at once, with the result that an operation was decided upon without delay, and actually performed within two hours.'[33] When the doctor told her that her leg was to be amputated, Jennie calmly asked him to please make sure he cut high enough.[34] The amputation was done above the knee.

Oswald Frewen described the day in his diary on June 14, 1921:

She (Mom) habitually looks at the worst side of things, and if poor little Jane is suffering physically, its nervous reflection on Mumkin is intensified. And I long ago discovered it is fatal to sympathize with her over everything: she only uses the sympathy as fuel to add fire to her torments. Ma sits next to the hall at Westbourne Street, conjuring up a vision of an amputated leg all the time, and fearful lest she not be sufficiently miserable to prove her love for her sister. Aunt Leonie came in while I was there. If Ma was 75% distraught, Leonie was most certainly 95% prostrate.... She was grey, white, and far beyond scenes or hysterics, and like a spent wave on a level beach....

Jack (the only unperturbable sanity in the place) motioned me to escort him home, as he was manifestly distraught. As we set out, he said hollowly, 'I knew there was death in the house, I had a presentiment of it. I only did not know who it would be. I thought it was your father. And of course it has come.' [35]

But Jennie rallied wonderfully after the operation. She had good health, strength, and determination. When Eleanor Warrender came to visit, Jennie greeted her by saying, 'You see, I have put my best foot forward to meet you....' [36]

On June 28, two weeks after the operation, Oswald brought a bouquet of lilies to Westbourne Street.

I sent up to ask if she would see me, and she *did*!

Aunt Leonie there. She [Jennie] looked her old self, and asked of every individual member of my family, and was very sweet, but kept grimacing with pain. She said she never realized in her hospital what the men were suffering, and she said, 'The more it hurts, the more those devils of doctors like it. They say it's healing.'

Leonie said, quite low, 'You mustn't stay too long,' and Jennie overheard and said, 'Oh no, I like to hear you two pussies talking.' . . . [37]

The mail was arriving in a flood. Among the letters was a moving note from a legless soldier, wishing that Lady Randolph might be tended as she had once tended him.

Still in Nigeria, Porch finally received the news and immediately prepared to return to London.

On the morning of June 29, Jennie awakened feeling fine. Her spirits were high, and she inquired about Leonie's daughter-in-law, who was due to have a baby that very morning. Then she ate a good breakfast. Suddenly, without warning, the main artery in the thigh of the amputated leg haemorrhaged. 'Nurse, nurse,' she called. 'I'm pouring blood.' Before the nurse could rush in to apply a tourniquet there was a heavy loss of blood.

Quite by chance, Bourke Cockran and his wife were in London at the time.[38] Bourke drove Leonie to Jennie's house where they learned that she was in a coma. Jack had arrived and so had Winston still in his pyjamas.

Later in the day, Oswald Frewen telephoned Leonie's son Shane Leslie. Shane asked him, 'Have you heard the news?'

'No, what news?' asked Frewen.

'About Aunt Jennie. . . .'

'I just got a telegram from Ma, saying she's worse.'

'She's dead.'

Oswald was told to break the news to his mother Clara, but she had been in Trafalgar Square and had already seen the headline on news posters: 'DEATH OF LADY RANDOLPH CHURCHILL.' Another had a black border and simply said, 'LADY RANDY'.[39]

'They put Aunt Jennie in her coffin at three, and were to close it down at eight,' Frewen wrote in his diary on June 29, 1921.

Ma went up with me and Aunt Leonie. First time I had ever seen anyone laid out. . . . I didn't want to go up, but accompanied Ma. . . . I got no sort of psychic reaction from Jennie herself and her body, in death, was as unlike herself as Lord Jellicoe is from Evelyn Laye. I had never seen her before without puckers round her mouth, and powder on her nose and flashing eyes, full of vivacity. Here the mouth had set, not in a Cupid's bow, but in a crescent, corners dropping, grim as a warrior-chief, the nose emerged aquiline, the waxlike complexion was sallow, the brow noble. It might have been the body of a Roman emperor, or a red-skinned chief; the only woman it called to my mind was my formidable grandmother, who died in 1896. We all saw the likeness. Ma, Aunt Leonie, Winston. . . .[40]

On July 1 Winston wrote a perceptive letter to Lady Islington:

. . . But anyhow, she suffers no more pain; nor will she ever know old age, decrepitude, loneliness. Jack & I will miss her vy much: but for herself I do not know whether she has lost much. A long ordeal lay before her, at the end of wh there cd only be a partial & a limited respite.

... I wish you could have seen her as she lay at rest – after all the sunshine & storm of life was over. Very beautiful & splendid she looked. Since the morning with its pangs, thirty years have fallen from her brow.

She recalled to me the countenance I had admired as a child when she was in her heyday and the old brilliant world of the eighties & nineties seemed to come back. . . .

On July 2 the family travelled to Oxford in a reserved Victorian coach that had been attached to the train at Paddington Station. The blinds were half-drawn to keep out the blazing sun. It was a small but silent group: two sons, two sisters, three nephews, her butler Walden, a few friends, a representative of Queen Alexandra. Seymour Leslie remembered Winston saying to him, 'You, too, loved her very much. . . .'

At Oxford they went by car the last eight dusty miles over the parched landscape to the church at Bladon, where the funeral was held. It was a quiet, country church that seemed almost tucked away from the rest of the world. Simultaneously there was a Memorial Service in London at St Margaret's Church.[41]

'She was laid out amid a wealth of wonderful flowers,' Shane Leslie wrote.

I supplied two altar lights which burnt all night and Sir John Lavery painted the beautiful scene on canvas placing a crucifix between the lights to point the whole, and indeed the great suffering of her last days made her deathbed not unworthy of the crucifix. . . . Her sons and sisters were affected almost beyond the grief that is claimed by ties of flesh and blood. . . . Winston was bowed as under the greatest grief of his life. . . . We all threw roses into her grave. . . .[42]

Adjoining the small cemetery was a children's playground – Jennie would have liked that. She was buried in the Churchill family plot, alongside Lord Randolph. This was the cemetery where their two sons would one day join them.

There was a wreath of flowers from George West. Montagu Porch was still on a ship coming from Nigeria.[43]

344

Jennie's influence on Winston and the help she gave him would have justified her place in the history of our time. But the meaning of her life encompassed much more. More than the devotion of a King of England or of the many other men who had loved her. More than politics or an international literary review or a hospital ship or books and plays or war work.

Jennie was part of the action and passion of her world, and no woman of her era played a greater part in its history than she did. In doing so, she established her own frontiers and made her own rules. She had courage to match her beauty, an excitement to match her intelligence, energy to match her imagination.

Reminiscing with a friend, Jennie agreed that if they could begin again from the age of seventeen, they would do the same as they had done, only more so. 'Then we decided that we could not have done more so if we had tried.' [44]

The Prime Minister, Herbert Asquith, said of her: 'She lived every inch of her life up to the edge.' [45]

That could have been her epitaph.

Bibliography

of books referred to in the text and in the Critical References and Notes (see page 353).

Adam, Eve: *Mrs. J. Comyns Carr's Reminiscences* (Hutchinson, 1925).

Adams, James Truslow: *Empire on the Seven Seas* (New York, Scribner's, 1940).

Adler, Cyrus: *Jacob H. Schiff*, Volume II (Heinemann, 1929).

Andrews, Allen: *The Splendid Pauper* (Harrap, 1968).

Annual Register, Volume 137 (Longmans, 1896).

Anon: *Uncensored Recollections* (Philadelphia, Lippincott, 1924).

Archer, William: *The Old Drama and the New* (Heinemann, 1923).

Asquith, Lady Cynthia: *Diaries: 1915–1918* (Hutchinson, 1968).

Asquith, H. H.: *Some Aspects of the Victorian Age* (The Clarendon Press, Oxford, 1918).

  Letters of the Earl of Oxford & Asquith to a Friend, First Series, 1915–1922 (Geoffrey Bles, 1930).

Asquith, Margot [Oxford]: *Autobiography* (Thornton Butterworth, 1920).

  More Memories (Cassell, 1933).

Atherton, Gertrude: *Adventures of a Novelist* (Jonathan Cape, 1932).

Balsan, Consuelo Vanderbilt: *The Glitter and the Gold* (Heinemann, 1953).

Bartlett, E. Ashmead: *The Uncensored Dardanelles* (Hutchinson, 1928).

Beerbohm, Max: *Around Theatres* (Rupert Hart-Davis, 1953).

Benson, E. F.: *As We Were* (Longmans, 1930).

Frederick Edwin, Earl of Birkenhead, by his Son (Thornton Butterworth, 1933).

Blumenfeld, R. D.: *R.D.B.'s Diary* (Heinemann, 1930).

Bott, Allan, and Clephane, Irene: *Our Mothers* (Victor Gollancz, 1932).

Brittain, Vera: *Lady into Woman* (Andrew Dakers, 1953).

Brown, Malcolm: *George Moore: A Reconsideration* (Seattle, University of Washington Press, 1955).

Bryant, Arthur: *English Saga* (Collins, 1940).

Burdett-Coutts, W. L.: *The Sick and Wounded in South Africa* (Cassell, 1900).

The Intimate Letters of Archie Butt (New York, Doubleday, 1930).

Campbell, Mrs Patrick: *My Life & Some Letters* (Hutchinson, 1922).

Carey, Agnes: *Empress Eugénie in Exile* (New York, The Century Co., 1920).

Carter, Lady Violet Bonham: *Winston Churchill As I Knew Him* (Eyre & Spottiswoode and Collins, 1965).

Cecil, Lady G.: *Life of Robert, Marquis of Salisbury*, Volume III (Hodder & Stoughton, 1931).

Chapman-Huston, Major Desmond: *The Lost Historian* (Murray, 1936).

Churchill, Allen: *The Upper Crust* (Englewood Cliffs, N.J., Prentice-Hall, 1971).

Churchill, John Spencer: *Crowded Canvas* (Odhams, 1961).

Churchill, Lady Randolph (Mrs George Cornwallis-West): *The Reminiscences of Lady Randolph Churchill* (Edward Arnold, 1908).

 Small Talks on Big Subjects (Pearson, 1916).

Churchill, Randolph S.: *Winston S. Churchill, Youth, 1874–1900* (Heinemann, 1966).

 Young Statesman, 1901–1914 (Heinemann, 1967).

 Companion Volume I, Part 1, 1874–1896 (Heinemann, 1967).

 Part 2, 1896–1900 (Heinemann, 1967).

 Companion Volume II, Part 1, 1901–1907 (Heinemann, 1967).

 Part 2, 1907–1911 (Heinemann, 1969).

 Part 3, 1911–1914 (Heinemann, 1969).

Churchill, Winston S.: *Savrola* (Longmans, 1900).

 Thoughts and Adventures (Thornton Butterworth, 1932).

 My Early Life (Odhams, 1958).

 Painting as a Pastime (Odhams, 1965).

Churchill by his Contemporaries, ed. Charles Eade (Hutchinson, 1953).

Clark, Senator Champ: *My Quarter-Century of American Politics* (New York, Kraus Reprint Co., 1969).

Clarke, Isabel C.: *Six Portraits* (Hutchinson, 1935).

Cobbe, Francis Power: *The Duties of Women* (T. Fischer Unwin, 1894).

Cochran, Charles B.: *The Secrets of a Showman* (Heinemann, 1925).

Colby, Vineta: *The Singular Anomaly* (New York University Press, 1971).

Cooper, Lady Diana: *The Rainbow Comes and Goes* (Rupert Hart-Davis, 1958).

Cornwallis-West, George: *Edwardian Hey-Days* (London and New York, Putnam, 1930).

Two Wives (London and New York, Putnam, 1930).

Cowles, Virginia: *Edward VII and His Circle* (Hamish Hamilton, 1956).

Crewe, Quentin: *Frontiers of Privilege* (Stevens Press, 1961).

Curzon of Kedleston, Earl: *Subjects of the Day* (Allen & Unwin, 1915).

Davis, Richard Harding: *About Paris* (New York, Harper, 1895).

De Gramont, E.: *Pomp and Circumstance*, Jonathan Cape and Harrison Smith, 1929).

Dent, Alan: *Bernard Shaw and Mrs Patrick Campbell: Their Correspondence* (Victor Gollancz, 1952).

Dudley, Ernest: *The Gilded Lily* (Odhams, 1958).

Dunn, Arthur Wallace: *From Harrison to Harding* (New York and London, Putnam, 1922).

Edwards, Samuel: *The Divine Mistress* (Cassell, 1971).

Eliot, Elizabeth: *They All Married Well* (Cassell, 1960).

Emerson, Ralph Waldo: *English Traits* (Oxford University Press, 1967).

Ensor, R. C. K.: *England: 1870–1914* (Oxford University Press, 1936).

Falk, Bernard: *He Laughed in Fleet Street* (Hutchinson, 1933).

Fishman, Jack: *My Darling Clementine* (W. H. Allen, 1966).

Letters of F. Scott Fitzgerald, ed. Andrew Turnbull (Bodley Head, 1964).

Fortescue, Sir John: *The Post-Victorians* (Nicholson & Watson, 1933).

Fyfe, H. Hamilton: *Shakespeare Memorial Souvenir of the Shakespeare Ball*, ed. Mrs George Cornwallis-West (Frederick Warne, 1911).

Gardner, Brian: *Mafeking: A Victorian Legend* (Cassell, 1966).

Garvin, J. L.: *The Life of Joseph Chamberlain*, Volume II (Macmillan, 1933).

Glyn, Elinor: *The Reflections of Ambrosine* (Duckworth, 1902).

Grayson, Rupert: *Voyage Not Completed* (Macmillan, 1969).

Grey of Fallodon, Viscount: *Twenty-Five Years* (Hodder & Stoughton, 1925).

Hamilton, General Sir Ian: *Listening for the Drums* (Faber & Faber, 1944).

Harrap, George G.: *Some Memories* (Harrap, 1935).

Harrison, Michael: *Lord of London: A Biography of the Second Duke of Westminster* (W. H. Allen, 1966).

Hassall, Christopher: *Edward Marsh* (Longmans, 1959).

Hibben, Paxton: *The Peerless Leader* (New York, Russell & Russell, 1967).

The Life of John Oliver Hobbes, ed. J. M. Richards (Murray, 1911).

Jackson, Holbrook: *The Eighteen-Nineties* (Jonathan Cape, 1927).

The Notebooks of Henry James, ed. F. O. Mathiessen & K. B. Murdock (Oxford University Press, 1947).

Jennings, Ivor: *Parliament* (Cambridge, Macmillan, 1939).

    The British Constitution, 5th ed. (Cambridge University Press, 1966).

Jullian, Philippe: *Edward and the Edwardians* (Sidgwick and Jackson, 1967).

Kennedy, Ambrose: *Bourke Cockran, American Orator: His Life and Politics* (Boston, Bruce Humphreys, 1948).

Keppel, Sonia: *Edwardian Daughter* (Hamish Hamilton, 1958).

Lambton, George: *Men and Horses I Have Known* (Thornton Butterworth, 1924).

Lang, Theo: *My Darling Daisy* (Michael Joseph, 1966).

Laver, James: *Edwardian Promenade* (Edward Hulton, 1958).

Le Gallienne, Richard: *The Romantic '90s* (Putnam, 1952).

Lehmann, John: *I Am My Brother* (Longmans, 1960).

Leslie, Anita: *Mr Frewen of England* (Hutchinson, 1966).

    Jennie, The Life of Lady Randolph Churchill (Hutchinson, 1969).

Leslie, Seymour: *The Jerome Connexion* (Murray, 1964).

Leslie, Shane: *American Wonderland* (Michael Joseph, 1936).

    Men Were Different (Michael Joseph, 1937).

    Film of Memory (Michael Joseph, 1938).

    Long Shadows (Murray, 1966).

MacGurrin, James: *Bourke Cockran, A Free Lance in American Politics* (New York, Scribner's, 1948).

The Duke of Manchester: *My Candid Recollections* (Grayson & Grayson, 1932).

Manvell, Roger: *Ellen Terry* (Heinemann, 1968).

Martin, Ralph G.: *The Bosses* (New York, Putnam, 1964).

    Lady Randolph Churchill, A Biography, 1854–1895 (Cassell, 1969).

Martin, Ralph G., and Harrity, Richard: *Man of the Century: Churchill* (New York, Duell, Sloan & Pearce, 1962).

Mason, A. E. W.: *Sir George Alexander and St. James' Theatre* (Macmillan, 1935).

349

Massingham, H. J. and Hugh: *The Great Victorians* (Nicholson & Watson, 1932).

Maurois, André: *The Edwardian Era* (New York, Appleton Century-Crofts, 1933).

May, James Lewis: *John Lane & The Nineties* (John Lane, 1936).

The Milner Papers, Volume I, ed. Cecil Headlam (Cassell, 1931).

Minney, R. J.: *The Edwardian Age* (Cassell, 1964).

Lord Moran: *Winston Churchill: The Struggle for Survival, 1940–1965* (Constable, 1966).

Mowat, C. L. (ed.): *The New Cambridge Modern History*, 2nd ed., Volume XII (Cambridge University Press, 1968).

Myers, A. Wallais: *Memory's Parade* (Methuen, 1932).

Neilson, Francis: *The Churchill Legend* (Nelson, 1954).

O'Connor, Harvey: *The Astors* (New York, Knopf, 1941).

O'Connor, Mrs T. P.: *I, Myself* (Methuen, 1910).

Ormond, Richard, in *The Saturday Book—25*, ed. John Hadfield (Hutchinson, 1965).

Otis-Skinner, Cornelia: *Madame Sarah* (Michael Joseph, 1967).

Pearson, Hesketh: *The Pilgrim Daughters* (Heinemann, 1961).

Daisy, Princess of Pless, by Herself (New York, Dutton, 1929).

Daisy, Princess of Pless: *From My Private Diary*, ed. D. Chapman-Huston (Murray, 1931).

  What I Left Unsaid (Cassell, 1936).

  The Private Diaries of Daisy, Princess of Pless, ed. D. Chapman-Huston (Murray, 1950).

Plummer, Douglas: *Queer People* (W. H. Allen, 1963).

Ponsonby, Sir Frederick: *Recollections of Three Reigns* (Eyre & Spottiswoode, 1951).

Porter, Kenneth Wiggins: *John Jacob Astor* (Cambridge, Harvard University Press, 1931).

The Duke of Portland: *Men, Women and Things* (Faber & Faber, 1937).

Priestley, J. B.: *The Edwardians* (Heinemann, 1970).

Proust, Marcel: *Remembrance of Things Past* (Chatto & Windus, 1949).

Raglan, Ethel: *Memories of Three Reigns* (Nash & Grayson, 1928).

Raymond, E. T.: *Uncensored Celebrities* (T. Fischer Unwin, 1918).

  Portraits of the Nineties (T. Fischer Unwin, 1921).

  Portraits of the New Century (Ernest Benn, 1928).

Repington, Lieut.-Col. C. A'Court: *The First World War, 1914–1918*, Volume 2 (Constable, 1920).

Ridge, W. Pett: *I Like to Remember* (Hodder & Stoughton, 1925).

Roberts, Mary M.: *American Nursing: History and Interpretation* (New York, Macmillan, 1930).

Time Was: The Reminiscences of W. Graham Robertson (Hamish Hamilton, 1931).

Roe, F. C.: *Modern France* (Longmans, 1962).

Lord Rossmore: *Things I Can Tell* (Eveleigh Nash, 1912).

Sampson, Anthony: *Anatomy of Britain* (Hodder & Stoughton, 1962).

Scott, Sir Percy: *Fifty Years in the Royal Navy* (Murray, 1919).

The Duchess of Sermoneta: *Sparkle Distant Worlds* (Hutchinson, 1947).

Sheridan, Clare: *Nuda Veritas* [Naked Truth] (Thornton Butterworth, 1928).

To the Four Winds (André Deutsch, 1955).

Short, Ernest: *Sixty Years of Theatre* (Eyre & Spottiswoode, 1951).

Sichel, Pierre: *The Jersey Lily* (W. H. Allen, 1958).

Smalley, George: *Anglo-American Memories* (Duckworth, 1911).

Smyth, Ethel: *Streaks of Life* (Longmans, 1921).

What Happened Next? (Longmans, 1940).

Springfield, Lincoln: *Some Piquant People* (T. Fischer Unwin, 1924).

Titmuss, R. M.: *Essays of the Welfare State* (Allen & Unwin, 1958).

Tschuppik, Carl: *The Empress Elizabeth of Austria* (Constable, 1930).

Tuchman, Barbara: *The Proud Tower* (Hamish Hamilton, 1966).

Villiers, Frederic: *Peaceful Personalities and Warriors Bold* (London and New York, Harper, 1907).

Warrender, Lady Maud: *My First Sixty Years* (Cassell, 1933).

Frances, Countess of Warwick: *Life's Ebb and Flow* (Hutchinson, 1929).

Afterthoughts (Cassell, 1931).

Discretions (New York, Scribner's, 1931).

The Private Diaries of Sir Algernon West (Murray, 1922).

Wilson, A. E.: *Edwardian Theatre* (Arthur Baker, 1951).

Papers, official records, etc.

Bourke Cockran Papers, Manuscript Room, New York Public Library.

Peregrine Churchill Papers.

Moreton Frewen Papers, Manuscript Room, Library of Congress, Washington, D.C.

Oswald Frewen Papers.

Berg Collection, New York Public Library.
Marquis de Soveral Private Papers, Lisbon.
Blenheim Palace, Muniments Room.
Public Record Office, London.

Critical References and Notes

CHAPTER 1

Because this is the second volume of a two-volume biography, there is an obvious overlap in the use of some material. This particularly applies to the big black metal box of family archives in the Muniments Room of Blenheim Palace. The Duke of Marlborough graciously gave me access to the metal box, which is filled with a vast variety of correspondence, memoranda, diaries, etc. It is basic and invaluable to any biography of Lady Randolph.

Similarly invaluable are the private papers of Jennie's grandson Peregrine Churchill. These include a large file of correspondence between Jennie and her son Jack.

Another vital source of information are the Moreton Frewen Papers in the Manuscript Room of the Library of Congress in Washington, D.C. The range of documents is enormous, but a careful sifting reveals a variety of materials giving fresh insight into Jennie and her relationships with her family and her world. Moreton Frewen admired Jennie and was a good friend to her, and the correspondence between him and his wife Clara offers a source of information about Jennie that cannot be found elsewhere. There are also valuable clippings among the Frewen Papers as well as letters from Jennie and an interesting correspondence between Moreton and Winston.

Indispensable for a biography of any member of the Churchill family are the collected letters in the Companion Volumes to Randolph S. Churchill's *Winston S. Churchill* (Volumes I and II). Although many of these letters are elsewhere available, they are here compiled and copied with admirable accuracy.

My interviews with Sir Shane Leslie had an enormous value that is reflected throughout my book. This includes the material and letters he showed me, as well as the books and clippings he made available to me. My correspondence with Prince Clary, Count Kinsky's nephew, which was so important in my first volume, has a continued importance here. Countess Kinsky in London was similarly helpful. Lady Altrincham, the daughter of Jennie's close friend Lady Islington, was kind enough to tell me many things of great value that I had not heard elsewhere. She also made available to me some important material. I am grateful to her son John Grigg for finding a copy of a moving letter about Jennie.

There is, of course, a vast library of excellent books describing England at this time. *The New Cambridge Modern History*, ed. C. L. Mowat, Second Edition, is very good. So is *England, 1870–1914*, by R. C. K Ensor. There is also some specific information of value in Anthony Sampson's *Anatomy of Britain*; H. H. Asquith's

Some Aspects of the Victorian Age; and James Truslow Adams's *Empire on the Seven Seas*. But of particular importance is the *Annual Register*, Volume 137, which is excellent not only in recording the important facts of a given year, but in capturing the mood of it.

Holbrook Jackson, *The Eighteen-Nineties*, does a fine job of recreating the literary flavour of the time and Richard Le Gallienne ably abets him in *The Romantic Nineties*. Virginia Cowles, *Edward VII and His Circle*, is very good on the social life of the Prince of Wales. But most valuable are the memoirs of the major people on the scene: Margot Asquith, *Autobiography*; Frances, Countess of Warwick, *Discretions*; Duke of Portland, *Men, Women and Things*; among many others. I also found many sidelights in *Our Mothers* by Allan Bott and Irene Clephane that I found nowhere else.

Inevitably a major source is the daily press: *The Times* in London, *The New York Times* and the *Tribune* in New York. The weekly New York magazine *Town Topics* requires careful examination and checking because of its inaccuracies, but it does offer a surprising number of leads and pieces of information which do prove true and which may not be available elsewhere.

1 Ralph G. Martin, *Lady Randolph Churchill, A Biography, 1854–1895*.
2 Letter from Clara to her husband, Moreton Frewen, January 19, 1895, Moreton Frewen Papers.
3 *Ibid*.
4 The will was filed at Somerset House. Probate was given on February 28, 1895.
5 Letter from Clara, January 19, 1895.
6 Interview with Sir Shane Leslie.
7 Excerpt from letter dated February 27, 1895. Randolph S. Churchill, *Winston S. Churchill*, Companion Volume I, Part 1.
8 Correspondence with Prince Clary, a nephew of Count Kinsky, in Venice; interview with Countess Kinsky in London.
9 Letter of May 18, 1903, from the Viceroy's Camp. *The Reminiscences of Lady Randolph Churchill*.
10 Speech at Harrow, October 29, 1941.
11 The house was rented as a club, first the University Club and then the Manhattan Club. Jennie continued to get her annual payments until the time of her death. At that time, the New York *Tribune* of November 16, 1921, carried the story: '250,000-Dollar Churchill Trust Fund Goes to Two Sons. Court Signs Order Cancelling Mortgage on Manhattan Club Property.' For a fuller description of the house, see Martin, *op. cit.*
12 Interview with Lady Altrincham.
13 *Scots Pictorial*, July 16, 1921.
14 The phrase is Walter Bagehot's from an article written in 1872, quoted in Anthony Sampson, *Anatomy of Britain*.
15 Ivor Jennings, *Parliament*.
16 Sampson, *op. cit.*
17 Ralph Waldo Emerson, *English Traits*.

18 The Rt Hon. H. H. Asquith, *Some Aspects of the Victorian Age*. (This was part of the Romanes Lecture, delivered in the Sheldonian Theatre on June 8, 1918.)

19 James Truslow Adams, *Empire on the Seven Seas*.

20 Allan Bott and Irene Clephane, *Our Mothers*.

21 *Ibid.*; also, R. M. Titmuss, *Essays on the Welfare State*.

22 Excerpt from speech of Sir Henry Campbell-Bannerman at Perth, reported in *The Times*, June 6, 1903. Campbell-Bannerman was then leader of the Liberal Party, and later became Prime Minister.

23 Margot Asquith, *Autobiography*.

24 Depew had made a private railroad car available to Jennie and her sick husband, Lord Randolph, when they travelled across Canada and the United States on their trip around the world. Depew had been the first U.S. Minister to Japan (1866). He was President of the New York Central Railroad (1885–98) and a U.S. Senator from New York (1899–1911).

25 E. T. Raymond, *Portraits of the Nineties*.

26 Richard Le Gallienne, *The Romantic Nineties*.

27 Holbrook Jackson, *The Eighteen-Nineties*.

28 *Town Topics*, January 17, 1895.

29 By 1895 almost a hundred towns in England had their own electric supply stations.

30 George Bernard Shaw was a friend of Jennie's and later wrote for her magazine.

31 Interview with Sir Shane Leslie.

32 Margot Asquith, quoted in Virginia Cowles, *Edward VII*.

33 Frances, Countess of Warwick, *Discretions*.

34 Shane Leslie Papers. Letter from Queen Alexandra to Lady Leslie, July 3, 1921.

35 The Princess's eldest son, the Duke of Clarence, seems to have been smitten with Jennie. *Town Topics* reported that 'Young "Collars and Cuffs" has been dogging her [Lady Randolph] about for months. He haunted her at her house, he stuck to her like wax at other people's houses, and was by her side everywhere in public. He is a ridiculous young creature, and the American lady's evident enjoyment of his devotion was the occasion for many a laugh, it was so evident a worship of the shadow of greatness.' The same Duke of Clarence was mentioned in *The Sunday Times* in November 1970 as possibly having been the sensational Jack the Ripper. This allegation came in response to a hint from the eminent author and physician, Dr Thomas E. A. Stowell, who had been accumulating evidence for fifty years. Dr Stowell said that Jack the Ripper was a young man of royal blood who contracted syphilis during a world tour just after his sixteenth birthday, and had been treated by the royal doctor, Sir William Gull. The Duke of Clarence died of syphilis at the age of twenty-eight.

36 Winston S. Churchill, *My Early Life*.

37 *Ibid.*

38 *Ibid.*

39 *Ibid.*

40 *Vanity Fair*, May 29, 1886, p. 201.

41 The Duke of Portland, *Men, Women and Things*.

42 Randolph S. Churchill, *op. cit.*

43 *Ibid.*

44 Winston S. Churchill, *op. cit.*
45 *Ibid.*
46 Allan Bott and Irene Clephane, *Our Mothers.*
47 *Annual Register*, Volume 137.

CHAPTER 2

The best book of description of the Paris scene at this time is Richard Harding Davis's *About Paris*. It is wonderfully alive.

The major source of facts about the happenings and the people in Paris is the Paris edition of the New York *Herald*. It is not only well edited, but its pages are filled with humour and anecdote, and very little reticence.

Of the American newspapers, the one which seems to have had the largest number of feature articles about Americans in Paris is the *New York Journal*. It is gossipy but informative.

Seymour Leslie, *The Jerome Connexion*, has some interesting anecdotes about his great-aunt Jennie in Paris. And Jennie herself records some in her *Reminiscences of Lady Randolph Churchill*.

For the purpose of this chapter and its subject, there are only a few things of interest in *Empress Eugénie in Exile* by Agnes Carey, and *The Empress Elizabeth of Austria* by Carl Tschuppik.

Shane Leslie offers rich memories as well as insights in *Long Shadows*. There are some good stories in the anonymous *Uncensored Recollections*.

It is most interesting to read Marcel Proust's fictional description of the Marquis de Breteuil in *Remembrance of Things Past*, Volume I.

1 See Ralph G. Martin, *Lady Randolph Churchill, A Biography, 1854–1895.*
2 Richard Harding Davis, *About Paris.*
3 *Ibid.*
4 This was particularly true of the salon of Mrs Richard Haight in the Place Vendôme, directly opposite where the Ritz Hotel now stands. The drawing rooms of Mrs Ridgeway, in the Rue François I, were also as exclusive as any in Paris.
5 The New York *Herald*, Paris Edition, February 26, 1895.
6 *The New York Times*, December 6, 1964.
7 *Town Topics*, February 21, 1895.
8 Some sources (e.g., *The New York Times*, December 10, 1964) suggest that the total dowry might have reached $20,000,000 (nearly £8,000,000). At one time, Consuelo and her husband each received $100,000 (about £39,000) a year from her father. Consuelo was the eldest of the three children of William Kissam Vanderbilt and the former Alva Smith. Consuelo's grandfather, Commodore Cornelius Vanderbilt, was the founder of the New York Central Railroad.
9 See Martin, *op. cit.*
10 The New York *Herald*, Paris Edition, March 5, 1895.
11 *New York Journal Magazine*, undated clipping.
12 *Town Topics* also quoted Henry Labouchere, editor of *Truth*, saying, 'I confess to a contempt for Americans who come over here with apparently the sole object of working by means of their dollars into English fashionable society,

as though society in their own country was not good enough for them.' March 25, 1897.

The *New York Journal* on October 24, 1909, had a story entitled 'How Titled Foreigners Catch American Heiresses'. It listed forty marriages, itemizing the amount of the fortune and the final result of the marriage. Most of them had ended badly.

13 The New York *Herald*, Paris Edition, June 27, 1896.

14 Winston S. Churchill, *My Early Life*; interview with Sir Shane Leslie.

15 Interview with Sir Shane Leslie.

16 Seymour Leslie, *The Jerome Connexion*.

17 March 2, 1895. Randolph S. Churchill, *Winston S. Churchill*, Companion Volume I, Part 1.

Clara Frewen's daughter Clare gave this description of her aunt Leonie in *Nuda Veritas*:

'Alone with me, she was almost a sage, disguised; she gave me direction and saved me from drifting along the path of doubt and cynicism. Her advice was profound. I thought she might have been a very great woman, had she the chance, or had she trusted herself. The world had either buffeted her too much, or perhaps not enough. She had led a strangely repressed life, but she was too proud to resent it, and had too much humour for self-pity. She hid behind her wit as completely as any Oriental woman behind her yashmak. Few people have known the face of Leonie, and Providence even dimmed her eyes, so that they should not reveal the intensity of her soul.'

18 Shane Leslie, *Long Shadows*.

19 Anonymous, *Uncensored Recollections*.

20 See Martin, *op. cit.*

21 Jennie had asked her father to find out more about the finances of the Garner girls. Her father wrote, 'There is no doubt they are very rich girls, but as to the incomes, I can't get at it with any certainty as yet.' It was obviously more than enough. Mr Garner had been the largest producer of cotton prints in the world, and had inherited a fortune of some $20,000,000 (nearly £8,000,000). The three Garner girls became orphans when their parents' yacht overturned – it had been the largest sailing yacht in the world.

22 Marcel Proust, *Remembrance of Things Past*.

23 *The Notebooks of Henry James*.

24 See Martin, *op. cit.*

25 *New York World*, Paris Edition, March 20.

CHAPTER 3

The Manuscript Room of the New York Public Library has the most complete collection of the Bourke Cockran Papers. The Irish Historical Society has his personal library, but most of the other many papers, letters, and clippings are in the Manuscript Room. It is a valuable and revealing collection.

There are several biographies of him – *Bourke Cockran: A Free Lance in American Politics*, by James MacGurrin; *Bourke Cockran, American Orator: His Life and*

Politics by Ambrose Kennedy – but neither catches the full quality and drama of the man. He comes much more alive in his letters and interviews, and also in the various newspaper reports from political conventions where he was a star performer. Particularly well written were articles in the Philadelphia *Press* (May 7, 1893 and December 19, 1897), the New York *Sun* (June 26, 1892), the *Toledo Sunday Journal* (June 26, 1892). There are also some unidentified clippings among the Bourke Cockran Papers containing interviews of high calibre.

Shane Leslie in his *American Wonderland* has some of the most intimate material on Cockran. Senator Champ Clark, *My Quarter-Century of American Politics*, has an excellent anecdote about him too.

1 Randolph S. Churchill, *Winston S. Churchill, Youth, 1874–1900*.

2 Bourke Cockran Papers.

3 The passport is dated, 'This 19th Day of March, A.D. 1895, in the 119th year of the independence of the United States.'

4 Interview with Alice Roosevelt Longworth.

5 James MacGurrin, *Bourke Cockran, A Free Lance in American Politics*.

6 From a published interview in *T. P. O'Connor's Weekly*, 1903, cited in MacGurrin, *op. cit.*

7 Bourke Cockran would in later years become the defence attorney of his own celebrated case, defending Labour Leader Tom Mooney. Mooney was convicted as a participant in the bomb killing of the San Francisco Preparedness Day Parade of 1916 and condemned to death. The sentence was commuted to life imprisonment, and Mooney was finally pardoned in 1938.

8 Extract from a speech in New York given in honour of a visiting priest from the County of Sligo (Bourke Cockran Papers). Cockran's love of his home county was indicated by his gift of £10,000 to County Sligo for the benefit of helping local industry.

9 Cockran had been sent to Ireland by the New York *Herald* to report the events marking the celebration of the centenary of the birth of Daniel O'Connell. On his return to New York, he was offered a position on the *Herald*'s Foreign News desk, which he declined.

10 Cockran's clients represented railroads, banks, bus companies, tobacco companies, public utilities, and steamship lines. In later years, he also acted as special counsel for the Long Island Railroad. His net income in 1895 was estimated at $100,000 (about £39,000).

11 Bourke's father 'was a cultured gentleman, well-versed in the classics'. His mother's kin included a gifted poet and dramatist, and a former Chief Justice of the United States, Edward Douglas White. Ambrose Kennedy, *Bourke Cockran, American Orator: His Life & Politics*. Bourke Cockran, however, had little love for his father, who had often beaten him. Bourke's father was twenty-three years old when he married Bourke's mother, who was then thirty-six. His mother was a convert to Catholicism, and wanted young Bourke to become a priest.

12 See Martin, *Lady Randolph Churchill, A Biography, 1854–1895*.

13 *The Splendid Pauper* is the title of an excellent biography of Moreton Frewen by Allen Andrews.

14 Shane Leslie also added: 'It was impossible for a third party to speak while they were locked in conflicting phrase and paragraph, but it was equally impossible to eat or drink during the time, or to feel that anything could be more satisfying than the schemes of one, or more intoxicating than the critical eloquence of the other.' With regard to the silver question, Cockran's strong stand on this issue resulted in his political break with the Democratic presidential candidate William Jennings Bryan in the 1896 election. Shane Leslie, *American Wonderland*.

15 The quote is from a Boston newspaper, undated, quoted in a book by Mrs T. P. O'Connor, *I, Myself*. The other two women named in the article were the Baroness Burdett-Coutts and Mrs T. P. O'Connor. Like Jennie, Mrs O'Connor was an American, and the Baroness was married to an American.

16 William Travers Jerome was actually Jennie's cousin twofold: his father was the brother of Jennie's father, and his mother was the sister of Jennie's mother.

17 Despite his pious front, 'Honest John' Kelly still managed to leave an estate of $500,000 (nearly £200,000). Ralph G. Martin, *The Bosses*.

18 MacGurrin, *op. cit.*

19 Martin, *The Bosses*.

20 Unidentified clipping.

21 Cockran was also quoted as saying 'All bosses look alike to me. I do not believe that Bossism is an essential feature of democratic government. On the contrary, I have never known it to flourish except where democratic government has been abolished.' Kennedy, *op. cit.*

22 Amos Cummings, the New York *Sun*, June 26, 1892.

23 Quoted in Arthur Wallace Dunn, *From Harrison to Harding*.

24 The Governor's full name was Roswell Pettibone Flower.

25 Philadelphia *Press*, May 7, 1893.

26 *Toledo Sunday Journal*, Toledo, Ohio, June 26, 1892.

27 The New York *Herald*, undated clipping. Bourke Cockran Papers.

28 *Toledo Sunday Journal*, Toledo, Ohio, June 26, 1892.

29 *Ibid.*

30 Senator Champ Clark, *My Quarter-Century of American Politics*.

Paxton Hibben, in his biography of William Jennings Bryan, *The Peerless Leader*, told how a young William Jennings Bryan had been similarly impressed:

'He listened enraptured to the type of oratory he'd never heard before – a diction, a phrasing, an eloquence, a passion that might have belonged to Pitt or Fox, as distinct as day and night from the stodgy pedantism of Daniel Webster and Henry Clay, in which young Bryan had been steeped. . . .' Bryan, who later became a Democratic presidential candidate in three different elections, strongly disagreed with Cockran on the gold-versus-silver basis of United States currency. It was William Jennings Bryan who made the historic speech in which he said, 'You cannot crucify mankind on a cross of gold.'

Theodore Roosevelt, in introducing Cockran to a New York audience in 1910, said, 'I will introduce to you now a great orator, one of the greatest of all time. . . .' And later, Roosevelt told his friend, Archie Butt, 'Archie, . . . I believe Cockran is the greatest orator using the English language today . . .' (*The*

Intimate Letters of Archie Butt). (Quoted in Letter to the Editor, *The New York Times*, January 3, 1953, by James MacGurrin.)

31 Shane Leslie, *Long Shadows*.
32 Bourke Cockran Papers.
33 Lincoln Springfield, in *Some Piquant People*, wrote this verse about Sir John Hibbert's opinion of the divided skirt:

> Let laws and commerce, wit and learning die;
> We'll even scrap our old nobility;
> Our Church may promptly disestablished be –
> But leave us still the ladies' *lingerie*.
> A disunited kingdom will not hurt –
> But do not, prithee, e'er divide the skirt.

34 Undated letter, Peregrine Churchill Papers.
35 *The New York Times*, March 4, 1895.
36 Cornelia Otis-Skinner, *Madame Sarah*.
37 Leslie, *Long Shadows*.
38 *Ibid*.
39 The Duke of Portland, *Men, Women and Things*.
40 The New York *Herald*, Paris Edition, March 11, 1895.
41 Richard Harding Davis, *About Paris*.
42 Mrs T. P. O'Connor, *op. cit*.
43 Davis, *op. cit*.
44 The New York *Herald*, Paris Edition, March 22, 1895.
45 E. De Gramont, *Pomp and Circumstance*.
46 Shane Leslie, *Film of Memory*.
47 March 1, 1895. The text of this letter, as of all letters quoted here unless otherwise noted, is to be found in Randolph S. Churchill, *Winston S. Churchill*, Companion Volume I, Part 1.
48 March 2, 1895.
49 March 1, 1895.
50 March 28, 1895.

CHAPTER 4

The prime source book on Moreton Frewen is *The Splendid Pauper* by Allen Andrews. It is excellent. Anita Leslie also has written a biography of him: *Mr Frewen of England*, but as a member of the family she is perhaps not as objective.

The Holbrook Jackson book has good background material for this chapter, as does E. T. Raymond, *Portraits of the New Century*. Lady Randolph's *Reminiscences* are also very useful here, and so is the book of memoirs by her niece, Clare Sheridan, *To the Four Winds*. A few relevant stories can be found in *Time Was: The Reminiscences of W. Graham Robertson*.

One of the best-written books of this period, and full of fascinating material, is *The Proud Tower* by Barbara Tuchman. Anybody writing about or interested in this period should read it.

Some Piquant People by Lincoln Springfield is worth referring to for anecdotal material.

The files of *Truth* magazine are also a necesary source of information.

1 Clare Sheridan, *To the Four Winds*.
2 Moreton Frewen Papers.
3 Letter dated April 16, 1895.
4 Electrozone was basically a deodorant obtained by the electrolysis of sea water, which freed chlorine with small quantities of iodine and bromine. However, it had a terrible smell. 'Just before that, Moreton Frewen was involved in something called the Ashcroft Process for treatment of sulphide ores, a process for separating zinc from lead and silver, and even from gold, by the electrolytic treatment of sulphide ores, whereby even the residue was saleable as crude sulphur. The exploration company, however, discovered Moreton Frewen's option was not entirely correct in its legal form, and disclaimed him and repudiated its agreement. The firm made a fortune in the next twenty years, dividends totalling 2,500 per cent per share – but not to Moreton Frewen.' Allen Andrews, *The Splendid Pauper*.
5 E. T. Raymond, *Portraits of the New Century*.
6 *Ibid.*
7 Holbrook Jackson, *The Eighteen-Nineties*.
8 *Time Was: The Reminiscences of W. Graham Robertson*.
9 Hesketh Pearson, *The Pilgrim Daughters*.
10 *The Reminiscences of Lady Randolph Churchill*.
11 Jackson, *op. cit.*
12 The New York *Herald*, Paris Edition, April 4, 1895.
13 Richard Le Gallienne, *The Romantic Nineties*.
14 Barbara Tuchman, *The Proud Tower*.
15 Lincoln Springfield, *Some Piquant People*.
16 E. F. Benson, *As We Were*.
17 Comment by Fannie Hurst, quoted in Springfield, *op. cit.*
18 E. T. Raymond, *Portraits of the Nineties*.
19 Springfield, *op. cit.*
20 The New York *Herald*, Paris Edition, April 4, 1895.
21 *Ibid.*
22 Tuchman, *op. cit.*
23 Raymond, *Portraits of the Nineties*.
24 Pearson, *op. cit.*
25 Randolph S. Churchill, *Winston S. Churchill*, Companion Volume I, Part 1. All letters, unless otherwise cited, are from this source.
26 *Ibid.*
27 March 9, 1896.
28 March 20, 1896.
29 Extract from *Truth*, June 25, 1896.
30 Letter dated November 12, 1896, from Randolph S. Churchill, *Winston S. Churchill, Youth, 1874–1900*.
31 *Ibid.*
32 *Truth*, October 8, 1896.
33 Interview with Sir Shane Leslie.

34 Winston S. Churchill, *Savrola*.

35 Lord Moran, *Winston Churchill: The Struggle for Survival, 1940–1965*.

CHAPTER 5

Here again, the files of the Paris *Herald* offer the most detailed picture of Paris at this time.

Shane Leslie's recollections and writings are of particular importance in this chapter. Peregrine Churchill also had some pertinent comments. His brother, John Spencer Churchill, provides further observations about their father Jack Churchill in his book, *Crowded Canvas*.

The letters between Jennie and her sons take on a growing importance in the book. The letters between Jennie and her son Jack come from the personal papers of Peregrine Churchill, and most of the Winston letters are in Randolph Churchill's Companion Volume of collected letters.

There is a fairly good summary of French politics in this era in *Modern France* by F. C. Roe.

The Duchess of Sermoneta in *Sparkle Distant Worlds* has an anecdote about Jennie worth telling. And Clare Sheridan, in another book, *Nuda Veritas*, has some excellent observations about her aunt Jennie.

A superb book on the social life of American brides in Europe, which was valuable to me in Volume I and again is valuable here, is Elizabeth Eliot's *They All Married Well*.

1 Undated letter signed, 'Your loving old Woom,' from 'St George's Vickerage, Barrow-in-Furness, Thursday'. Peregrine Churchill Papers.

2 Interview with Sir Shane Leslie.

3 Richard Harding Davis, *About Paris*.

4 *Ibid*.

5 The Liberal Government of Lord Rosebery was succeeded by a Coalition Government headed by the Conservative Lord Salisbury with a group of former members of the Liberal Party who had disapproved of Home Rule for Ireland.

6 Sir Edgar Vincent (1857–1941) was made the first Viscount D'Abernon in 1926. He had been Governor of the Imperial Ottoman Bank from 1889 to 1897. He would later serve as a Conservative M.P. for Exeter, 1899–1906, and British Ambassador in Berlin, 1920–26.

7 The New York *Herald*, July 7, 1895. The headline was 'THESE ARE THREE FAMOUS SISTERS'. The story added that it would be the first time that Clara had been back in the United States in fifteen years, and the first time in eight years for Leonie. Jennie, of course, had been in the States on her world tour with her husband the previous year. The story also noted that the Madison Avenue home of Leonard Jerome had become the Union Club, and in 1895 the University Club.

8 The *New York Journal*, undated article in 1895, quoted in Elizabeth Eliot, *They All Married Well*. The article is headed from London.

9 Letter dated May 2, 1895. Randolph S. Churchill, *Winston S. Churchill*, Com-

panion Volume I, Part 1. (Unless otherwise cited, all letters are from this source.) Among the 'many others' mentioned in the letter, Winston notes 'the Wolvertons'. Prior to his marriage that year, Lord Wolverton's name had often been coupled with Jennie's in the gossip columns. He was a prominent race-horse owner and all-round sportsman, especially interested in yachting and big-game hunting. It is interesting to note that Wolverton and Sir Edgar Vincent later joined together to buy the Stanley house stable. Wolverton was ten years younger than Jennie.

10 June 6, 1895. In this letter Winston also wrote that he had been selected to attend on and escort the Duke of Cambridge, a distinct honour for a young officer. However, it also meant seven hours on horseback without dismounting.

11 July 24, 1895.

12 July 3, 1895. Winston personally went to Harrow to tell Jack the news of Mrs Everest's death, 'as I did not want to telegraph the news. He was awfully shocked, but tried not to show it.'

13 August 31, 1895.

14 August 3, 1895.

15 For his part, Lord Randolph Churchill had detested Lord Salisbury, and confided to Margot Tennant that he wished he had never met him.

16 August 16, 1895.

17 Interview with Peregrine Churchill. Peregrine and John Churchill were the two sons of Jack Churchill. Jack Churchill also had a daughter who married Sir Anthony Eden, later Lord Avon.

18 John Spencer Churchill, *Crowded Canvas.*

19 *Ibid.*

20 November 27, 1894.

21 In one letter she pointed out to him that he had written 'I *here*', instead of 'hear'. Letter dated February 26, no year, Peregrine Churchill Papers.

22 Shane Leslie, *Long Shadows.*

23 Allan Bott and Irene Clephane, *Our Mothers.*

24 Leslie, *op. cit.*

25 Bott and Clephane, *op. cit.*

26 The Duchess of Sermoneta, *Sparkle Distant Worlds.*

27 On February 5, 1897, Jennie wrote to Winston: 'Both Jack and Warrender ... have written to you today. ... They can tell you more than I can, as I am in the throes of 24 to dinner tonight.'

28 August 31, 1895.

29 Leslie, *op. cit.*

30 October 4, 1895.

31 October 11, 1895.

32 *Ibid.*

33 October 8, 1895.

34 *Ibid.*

35 October 19, 1895.

36 October 21, 1895.

Chapter 6

Two of Winston S. Churchill's books of memoirs – *My Early Life* and *Thoughts and Adventures* – provide necessary facts and background for this chapter, as they do elsewhere in this book.

Bourke Cockran's speeches reveal much about the man, but there are few copies of his speeches among his Papers, because he spoke from notes and memory rather than from a written text. One must, therefore, go to the files of the newspapers in the cities where he spoke. Some of them, fortunately, are almost verbatim reports.

The Society conflicts in New York are reported in a number of books, but again, the local newspapers provide a fresh source of information. *The New York Times* then reported such social conflict on its front pages. The *New York World* was similarly thorough and descriptive. Allen Churchill has treated this aspect of New York Society in rich detail in his excellent book *The Upper Crust*. Harvey O'Connor has also done a creditable job in *The Astors*.

On the British side of Society, Frances, Countess of Warwick, *Life's Ebb and Flow*, goes into some fascinating detail. The Countess's frequently caustic approach comes from the fact that she became an avowed Socialist in her middle years. W. Pett Ridge, *I Like to Remember*, remembers his Society more warmly. So do *The Private Diaries of Sir Algernon West*.

1 Letters from Winston to his mother, November 10, 1895. All letters unless otherwise noted, are from Randolph S. Churchill, *Winston S. Churchill*, Companion Volume I, Part 1.

2 *Ibid*.

3 Winston S. Churchill, *Thoughts and Adventures*.

4 Bourke Cockran Papers.

5 *Ibid*.

6 Speech at the University of Rochester, New York, reported in *The Times*, April 10, 1954.

7 Speech at Westminster College in Fulton, Missouri, March 5, 1946. The title of the speech was 'The Sinews of Peace'.

8 In one of his speeches, Bourke Cockran said: 'I have a farm on Long Island. I require plows. I am told if I don't have protection against foreign plows, they'll be dumped on me. If that means I'll get plows cheaper than my country can produce them, cheaper even than the country of my origin can produce them, I say, "Dump on, dump on", and damned be he who first cries, "Hold, enough!" '

9 November 10, 1895.

10 November 12, 1895.

11 November 10, 1895.

12 November 15, 1895.

13 *Ibid*.

14 November 10, 1895.

15 Letter to Jack, November 15, 1895; letter dated November 10, 1895.

16 Letter to Jack, November 15, 1895. In this same letter, Winston also wrote of American journalism: 'Their best papers write for a class of snotty housemaids and footmen, & even the nicest people here have so much. . . .'

17 November 20, 1895.

18 The *New York Journal*, undated clipping. Quoted in Elizabeth Eliot, *They All Married Well*.

19 *Ibid*.

20 *Ibid*.

21 Interview in the New York *Herald*, December 19, 1895.

22 *Ibid*.

23 Winston S. Churchill, *My Early Life*.

24 December 25, 1895.

25 Issue dated February 15, 1896.

26 March 3, 1896.

27 February 29, 1896.

28 *Ibid*.

29 April 12, 1896.

30 *Ibid*.

31 April 27, 1896.

32 April 12, 1896.

33 May 1, 1896. At this time Chamberlain was Secretary of State for the Colonies; Viscount Wolseley, Commander-in-Chief of the Army; Henry Chaplin, President of the Local Government Board; Lord James of Hereford, Chancellor of the Duchy of Lancaster; Sir Francis Jeune, President of the Probate Divorce and Admiralty Division of the High Court and Judge Advocate General; and the 8th Duke of Devonshire was Lord President of the Council. Mrs Cornelia Adair was the sister of Mrs Arthur Post, who became Lady Barrymore. Mrs Adair was originally a Wadsworth from Rochester, New York. The wife of Senator Stuart Symington of Missouri was related to her.

34 John Morley had been an old friend of Lord Randolph Churchill's, and a close friend of Jennie's. He was a Liberal M.P. and a bitter critic of the Jameson Raid.

35 Winston S. Churchill, *My Early Life*.

36 Shane Leslie, *Long Shadows*.
   Clara Frewen did not move to Great Cumberland Place until about 1902. She did, however, live nearby in Chesham Place, and was a constant visitor at the homes of her two sisters.

37 Interview with Sir Shane Leslie.

38 May 1, 1896.

39 Cruikshank testified that he had spent most of the money on travel. He was sentenced to eight years in jail.

40 Undated letter. Frances, Countess of Warwick, *Life's Ebb and Flow*.

41 *Town Topics*, March 12, 1896.

42 'The family jar' had been a social war between William Waldorf Astor's wife and his aunt over which one was '*the*' Mrs Astor. It was a dispute so bitter that when William Waldorf Astor's wife died in 1894, and he brought her body back to America for burial, there was no member of the American Astor family

to receive the body at the pier. And on the night of the funeral, 'the' Mrs Astor had a large party.

43 *The New York Times*, February 21, 1896.

44 Quoted in Harvey O'Connor, *The Astors*.

45 When Astor later renounced his American citizenship in 1899 and became a British citizen, a hooting, jeering crowd burned his effigy in Times Square.

46 To improve his image, Astor invented his own genealogy and published it. In it, he connected himself with Spanish and French nobility. Recognized genealogists, however, soon discovered a variety of errors and there was no justification for most of his claims. Genealogist Lathrop Withington pointed out that John Jacob Astor probably had French Huguenot ancestors, but there was nothing which positively indicated noble descent, and certainly no authenticity in the account which found the family origin among the Spanish nobility (New York *Sun*, July 30, 1899, article entitled 'Astor Pedigree Upset'). From a two-volume biography by Kenneth Wiggins Porter, *John Jacob Astor*. The incident became an international joke, and some members of the press suggested that a more fitting family coat-of-arms for Astor should be 'a butcher's block with a cleaver', in memory of John Jacob Astor's humble origins in Germany.

47 George Smalley, *Anglo-American Memories*, however, said: 'The truth is, Mr William Waldorf Astor has remained, in spite of his British naturalization, an American. Nobody could take him for anything else: in appearance, in manner, in speech. He has the American abruptness, quickness, decision. He has been in close contact with three civilizations, American, British and Italian, but it is the American which has left its stamp on him; an ineffaceable hallmark.'

48 Undated letter, Peregrine Churchill Papers.

49 Conversation between William Waldorf Astor and the Countess of Warwick. 'My father was the hardest man I have ever known, and I strive to follow in his footsteps.' Astor told the Countess: 'He was a law unto himself, and a law unto me. He even chose my wife without asking me whether the lady was to my taste or not.' Frances, Countess of Warwick, *Discretions*.

50 Undated letter, Peregrine Churchill Papers, from 'The Deepdene, Dorking'.

51 Moreton Frewen Papers.

52 August 4, 1896.

53 Winston S. Churchill, *My Early Life*.

54 August 4, 1896.

55 July 3, 1896.

56 *Ibid*.

57 August 31, 1896.

58 October 1, 1896.

CHAPTER 7

Winston Churchill describes his youth best in *My Early Life* and in his regular flow of letters to his mother. The large number of biographies of Winston Churchill can be easily avoided here, because they add almost nothing to Winston's superb descriptions of this time of his life.

As for the fringe material, Frances Neilson makes a small contribution in *The*

Churchill Legend, but can otherwise be dispensed with. Consuelo Vanderbilt Balsan, *The Glitter and the Gold*, should be read for the personal sidelights she provides. Margot (Asquith) Oxford, *More Memories*, is, however, better written and more revealing. Lady Randolph's own *Reminiscences* are more discreet, but informative.

The best supplementary description of Winston at this time comes from a correspondent of the *Daily Mail*, reprinted in *Churchill by his Contemporaries*, edited by Charles Eade. This is a very good book of collected memories by those who knew him best.

1 October 14, 1896. Unless otherwise noted, all letters are from Randolph S. Churchill, *Winston S. Churchill*, Companion Volume I, Part 2.

2 December 24, 1896.

3 November 12, 1896.

4 December 8, 1896.

5 Winston S. Churchill, *My Early Life*.

6 January 21, 1897. Jennie had written to him earlier (October 1, 1896): 'You are like me in not minding heat – I simply loved it!'

7 Winston S. Churchill, *op. cit.*

8 October 15, 1896. Winston asked his mother to send his butterfly net and mounting equipment. He soon had a collection of sixty-five different butterflies, which was later 'destroyed by the malevolence of a rat who crawled into the cabinet and devoured all the specimens' (December 2, 1896).

9 December 24, 1896.

10 January 7, 1897.

11 Winston S. Churchill, *op. cit.*

12 *Ibid.*

13 January 21, 1897.

14 Winston S. Churchill, *op. cit.*

15 *Ibid.* The *Politics* of Aristotle was edited by James Welldon, Winston's former headmaster at Harrow.

16 March 31, 1897.

17 February 4, 1897.

18 Francis Neilson, *The Churchill Legend*.

19 Winston S. Churchill, *op. cit.*

20 July 24, 1895. Randolph S. Churchill, *Winston S. Churchill*, Companion Volume I, Part 1.

21 September 23, 1896.

22 *Ibid.*

23 October 14, 1896.

24 October 1, 1896.

25 October 21, 1896.

26 Undated letter, Peregrine Churchill Papers.

27 Winston S. Churchill, *op. cit.*

28 November 4, 1896. A 'godless land of snobs and bores', Winston had said of India (October 26, 1896).

29 October 14, 1896.

30 November 5, 1896. Winston had also written to his mother, 'Bourke Cockran writes me a long letter – describing his campaign against Bryan & is very pleased with himself indeed. He has had great audiences & much enthusiasm. He has received the volume I sent him, and is delighted. I shall endeavour to lure him out here; India to an American would be the most interesting experience possible to a human being' (October 26, 1896).

31 November 5, 1896.

32 February 25, 1897.

33 Letter to Jennie, November 18, 1896.

34 October 8, 1895.

35 Undated letter, Peregrine Churchill Papers.

36 Undated letter, Peregrine Churchill Papers.

37 December 11, 1896.

38 January 7, 1897. Winston also advised his brother: 'Find something *congenial* at all costs.'

39 January 14, 1897.

40 December 24, 1896.

41 Consuelo Vanderbilt Balsan, *The Glitter and the Gold.*

42 *Reminiscences of Lady Randolph Churchill.*

43 November 4, 1896.

44 November 19, 1896.

45 December 16, 1896.

46 November 27, 1896.

47 Margot Asquith, *More Memories.*

48 George Steevens was a correspondent for the *Daily Mail.* E. T. Raymond, *Portraits of the New Century.*

49 December 17, 1896.

50 December 24, 1896.

51 January 7, 1897.

52 December 30, 1896.

53 January 21, 1897.

54 February 18, 1897.

55 January 29, 1897.

56 December 24, 1896.

CHAPTER 8

Frances, Countess of Warwick, contributes still another book of memoirs, *Afterthoughts*, and R. D. Blumenfeld adds his *R. D. B.'s Diary* to supplement all the other books on London Society already mentioned. Because so many of these people knew each other, each book of memoirs seems to add another piece of mosaic to fill out the pictures. It is particularly interesting to get separate perspectives of some major social event from different memoirs. The best view of these affairs, from the royal side, is Sir Frederick Ponsonby's *Recollections of Three Reigns*. Ponsonby not only had an excellent vantage point but also an excellent memory. So did Lady Maud Warrender, *My First Sixty Years*. As for Jennie, her memory was always very good indeed, but in her *Reminiscences* she follows her son Winston's advice to try not to hurt anybody's feelings. She doesn't.

Apart from the previously mentioned books of Shane Leslie, his *Film of Memory* and his own interviewed memories have special meaning here. And, again, Barbara Tuchman's *The Proud Tower* is of particular value.

1 Undated letter from Mrs Pearl Craigie to Jennie, from 'Cliveden, Maidenhead, Monday'.

2 Letter to Winston dated February 12, 1897, from the Hotel Bristol in Paris. (Unless otherwise cited, all letters are from Randolph S. Churchill, *Winston S. Churchill*, Companion Volume I, Part 2.) Jennie had first met Cecil Rhodes in the early 1880s. She described him by saying, 'Although not a literary man, he could speak clearly and with great authority on his own particular subjects. He was then a handsome young man with a delicate chest, and was just starting for South Africa, where he hoped the wonderful air would cure him. This it did, for although he died at a comparatively early age, it was not from consumption. I remember once having a most interesting conversation with him over his aims and ambitions. His whole soul was bound up in the future and progress of South Africa, and although he was not a self-seeker in any way, he was justly proud of having the immense province of Rhodesia named after him. In his heart of hearts, he wanted his name to be handed down to posterity in this indelible manner, and he would have been bitterly disappointed had any other been chosen. When I questioned him as to this, he admitted it quite frankly. He was, I think, a very happy man, for he never allowed small things to worry him, and his mind was not encumbered with the subtleties with which so many are hampered. A man of big ideas, he knew what he wanted, and made for his goal. He was singularly outspoken. On one occasion, discussing a sculptor, he said, looking at me critically: "Why don't you let the fellow do you? You've got a good square face."' *Reminiscences of Lady Randolph Churchill*.

3 Undated letter, Peregrine Churchill Papers.

4 Undated letter, Peregrine Churchill Papers.

5 Letter to Winston, dated February 26, 1897. She wrote to Jack the same day, 'I have written him a very stiff letter which I fear hurt me more to write than it will him to receive.'

6 Letter dated March 5, 1897, to Winston.

7 *Ibid.*

8 Letter to Winston, dated March 18, 1897.

9 Letter to Winston, April 2, 1897.

10 Undated letter, Peregrine Churchill Papers.

11 Letter from Colonel J. P. Brabazon to Jennie on Saturday, February 6, 1897.

12 Letter to Winston, March 11, 1897.

13 April 21, 1897, from Bangalore.

14 *Ibid.*

15 Undated letter, Peregrine Churchill Papers.

16 Letter to Jennie from Winston, May 26, 1897, the S.S. *Caledonia* off Brindisi.

17 June 10, 1897.

18 Letter dated Monday, the 7th, 1897.

19 Letter dated Tuesday, 1897, Great Cumberland Place.

20 Ethel Raglan, *Memories of Three Reigns*.

21 R. D. Blumenfeld, *R.D.B.'s Diary*.

The latest style fad among lady cyclists was to wear gold and jewelled anklets showing beneath their knickers or short skirts. The new fashion for lady cyclists included a short Eton jacket, closing over the bosom with two buttons. Also popular was a coat buttoned high at the throat, single-breasted with short coat-tails. Bloomers were considered absolutely essential 'for sanitary reasons'

22 Letter to Jack from Halton, Tring, dated Monday the 7th, 1897.

23 Undated letter from Ness Castle, Inverness, Peregrine Churchill Papers.

24 *Town Topics*, August 13, 1896.

25 Shane Leslie, *Film of Memory*.

26 *Ibid*.

27 Sir Frederick Ponsonby, *Recollections of Three Reigns*.

28 Lady Randolph Churchill, *op. cit.*

29 *Town Topics*, July 22, 1897.

30 Lady Randolph Churchill, *op. cit.*

31 *Ibid*.

32 *Town Topics*, July 22, 1897.'

33 Lady Randolph Churchill, *op. cit.*

34 *Ibid*.

35 Lady Maud Warrender, *My First Sixty Years*.

36 Lady Randolph Churchill, *op. cit.*

37 Letter dated August 17, 1897.

38 Interview with Sir Shane Leslie.

39 Lady Randolph Churchill, *op. cit.*

40 Winston S. Churchill, *My Early Life*.

41 Barbara Tuchman, *The Proud Tower*. Tuchman quotes *Punch*'s parliamentary correspondent.

42 Margot Asquith, when she was still Margot Tennant, 'moved heaven and earth', according to Lady Jebb, to marry him. Queried on the rumour of this marriage, Balfour replied, 'No, that is not so. I rather think of having a career of my own.' Lady Jebb said of him, 'Arthur was the best in the family all of whom are best . . . a man that almost everyone loves.' However, she thought his nature was 'emotionally cold', and that his one attempt at love, with May Lyttleton, sister of a Cambridge friend and Gladstone's niece, had 'exhausted his powers in that direction'. May Lyttleton died when she was twenty-five (Balfour was then twenty-seven). Tuchman, *op. cit.* Mrs Tuchman believes it was not so much that Balfour was emotionally cold as that he was warmly attached to his freedom to do as he pleased.

43 Letter dated August 29, 1897.

44 Letter to Winston from Jennie, dated September 9, 1897.

45 September 5, 1897.

46 September 21, 1897, written from Langwell, Berriedale, R.S.O. Caithness.

47 Letter headed 'Friday, Great Cumberland Place'.

CHAPTER 9

In this chapter, probably more than any other in the book, excerpts from letters between Jennie and her sons provide the best possible description of their relationship. The regularity of their correspondence, their frankness with one another, and their mutual love and trust offer the most open view possible of what they meant to each other. Any interpolative material can only be redundant.

1 Letter dated October 2, 1897, from the 31st Punjab Infantry. Unless otherwise cited, all letters are from Randolph S. Churchill, *Winston S. Churchill*, Companion Volume I, Part 2.
2 Letter dated October 2, 1897.
3 Letter dated September 19, 1897.
4 Letter dated December 22, 1897.
5 Letter dated October 17, 1897.
6 September 12, 1897.
7 September 19, 1897.
8 October 7, 1897.
9 Undated letter, Tuesday, 1897, from King's Lynn.
10 October 25, 1897.
11 September 19, 1897.
12 *Ibid*.
13 December 22, 1897.
14 November 4, 1897.
15 November 2, 1897.
16 November 1, 1897.
17 November 3, 1897.
18 November 4, 1897.
19 December 2, 1897.
20 December 2, 1897.
21 December 24, 1897.
22 April 13, 1898.
23 May 16, 1898.
24 November 17, 1897. During the coming Christmas recess, and early in 1898, there were a number of by-elections, which suggests that the Government's popularity was declining. Lord Salisbury, however, fought and won another General Election, and did not retire until July 1902.
25 October 25, 1897.
26 December 9, 1897.
27 December 16, 1897.
28 Winston S. Churchill, *My Early Life*.
29 Letter to Winston, September 30, 1897.
30 Undated letter from Presles, Peregrine Churchill Papers.
31 Undated letter from Lambton Castle, Peregrine Churchill Papers.
32 Letter to Winston, December 10, 1897.
33 Undated letter from Great Cumberland Place, 'Saturday', Peregrine Churchill Papers.

34 Randolph S. Churchill, *op. cit.*

35 January 19, 1898.

36 January 10, 1898.

37 January 13, 1898.

38 January 19, 1898.

39 November 17, 1897.

40 January 23, 1898.

41 January 28, 1898.

42 January 30, 1898.

43 December 24, 1897.

44 January 20, 1898.

45 January 21, 1898.

46 January 26, 1898.

47 January 27, 1898.

48 January 27, 1898, from Sandringham.

49 January 6, 1898.

50 January 10, 1898.

51 January 21, 1898.

52 February 13, 1898.

53 February 9, 1898.

54 January 27, 1898. 'General Getacre' was William Forbes Getacre, who had gone to Egypt to command the newly formed brigade being sent from Cairo to take part in the advance on Khartoum.

55 Lord Rossmore, *Things I Can Tell*.

56 February 16, 1898.

57 Incident reported by Jennie's great-niece, Anita Leslie, *Jennie: The Life of Lady Randolph Churchill*.

58 *Ibid.*

59 *Ibid.*

60 *Ibid.*

61 *Ibid.*

62 April 22, 1898.

63 January 19, 1898.

64 January 27, 1898.

65 *Ibid.*

66 March 18, 1898.

67 In a letter dated April 13, 1898, in *The Athenaeum*.

68 April 13, 1898.

69 *Ibid.*

70 November 17, 1897. Winston's literary ambitions were almost unlimited at this time in his life. He mentioned at various times his interest in writing a short history of the American Civil War, a life of Garibaldi, a volume of short stories called 'The Correspondence of a New York Examiner', and later, a book on the Marlboroughs. About the Marlborough book, he said, 'I think it would do something that would ring like a trumpet call.'

71 April 18, 1898.

72 April 18, 1898, Bangalore.
73 April 19, 1898.
74 May 10, 1898.
75 Letter dated June, 1898, from the 4th Hussars, India.
76 May 22, 1898.
77 June (1898).
78 April 25, 1898.
79 March 27, 1898. Cyrus Adler, *Jacob H. Schiff*, Vol. II.
80 Margot Asquith saw him as 'dignified, autocratic and wise; with the power of loving those he cared for.' Cassel cared very much for Jennie. Whenever Jennie's finances became critical, she went to Cassel. But theirs was a close friendship, not a romance.
81 'A well-known physiognomist has formulated the axiom that full, blue eyes [such as the Prince had] are generally associated with a cheerful and happy disposition; that they evidence a candid and generous nature, and belong to those who make the best of unpleasant circumstances . . . and that they hint of strong feelings, love of children, and a general fondness for pleasure.' James Laver, *Edwardian Promenade*.
82 July 10, 1898.
83 July 10, 1898.
84 July 9, 1898.
85 Letter from Lord Salisbury to Winston, July 19, 1898.
86 June 1, 1898.
87 Undated letter.
88 July 15, 1898.
89 July 15, 1898.
90 Winston S. Churchill, *op. cit.*
91 *Ibid.*
92 *Ibid.*

CHAPTER 10

All the books of the Countess of Warwick are useful in this chapter. Theo Lang, *My Darling Daisy*, is of some slight value. Virginia Cowles's *Edward VII and his Circle* is better.

There are a great number of books about the Edwardian era. *The Edwardian Age* by R. J. Minney is interesting, but J. B. Priestley's *The Edwardians* is more crisply written. Michael Harrison has much to offer, for my purpose, in *Lord of London: A Biography of the Second Duke of Westminster*, more because of the content than the treatment.

George Cornwallis-West, *Edwardian Hey-Days*, is a basic book for this biography, however careful and controlled the author is about his feelings and his relationships. Apart from his letters, this is the only place where George West gives any inkling about himself. His sister Daisy, Princess of Pless, is not so reticent. In her series of memoirs, *Daisy, Princess of Pless, by Herself* and *From My Private Diary*, among others, she is revealing indeed about everybody, and even somewhat about herself. However, she is not always accurate.

1 Frances, Countess of Warwick, *Afterthoughts*. She also reported that Earl Fitzwilliam's house had about three hundred bedrooms. 'It is a very Vatican of country houses, ugly and uncomfortable, noteworthy only because of its useless size. . . . The labour of running country houses, where the light is made on the premises, and the water comes from your own wells – with no running water in the bedrooms, and one bathroom to each floor – makes the use of these old-time places out of the question.' Lady Warwick also observed that Welbeck Abbey, which belonged to the Duke of Portland, had a riding school in the grounds.

2 J. B. Priestley, *The Edwardians*.

3 Theo Lang, *My Darling Daisy*.

4 *Ibid*. Elinor Glyn used some of her Warwick Castle experience in a novel called, *The Reflections of Ambrosine*. She showed Lady Warwick the manuscript of another novel, *Three Weeks*, and Lady Warwick warned her not to publish it. If she did, said Lady Warwick, none of her noble friends would ever speak to her again; one might *do* such things, but one should not even talk – let alone write – about one's own or one's friends' love affairs.

5 Frances, Countess of Warwick, *Life's Ebb and Flow*.

6 *Ibid*. The Countess of Warwick wrote in her memoirs: 'Prince Charles Kinsky was a sharer of my horsey adventures!'

7 Lang, *op. cit.*

8 *Ibid*.

9 The Prince of Wales had signed the marriage register in 1881 when Frances married Lord Brooke, who later became the Earl of Warwick. Her love affair with the Prince began seven years after her marriage.

10 Frances, Countess of Warwick, *Afterthoughts*.

11 J. B. Priestley, *op. cit.* See Ralph G. Martin, *Lady Randolph Churchill, A Biography, 1854–1895*, pp. 138ff., for more details about country-house entertainment.

12 William Cornwallis Cornwallis-West, Honorary Colonel of the 1st Volunteer Battalion, Royal Welch Fusiliers, and holder of the Volunteer Decoration, was a grandson of the 2nd Earl de la Warr, Lord of the Bedchamber to George I, and Governor and Captain-General of New York. 'West', the additional surname of Cornwallis, was not 'officially' assumed by deed poll until 1895, though it had been in use for decades before that. George's mother, Mary Cornwallis-West, was a grand-daughter of the 2nd Marquess de Headfort, in the peerage of Ireland (Michael Harrison, *Lord of London: A Biography of the Second Duke of Westminster*). William Cornwallis-West was also the Lord-Lieutenant of Denbighshire, and Member of Parliament for that county from 1885 to 1892.

13 The music halls were full of skits and songs about the professional beauties. One of the most popular songs was:

> I have been photographed like this,
> I have been photographed like that,
> But I have never been photoed as a raving maniac.

Virginia Cowles, *Edward VII and His Circle*.

14 *Daisy, Princess of Pless, by Herself*.

15 Harrison, *op. cit.*

16 George Cornwallis-West, *Edwardian Hey-Days*.

17 Anita Leslie, *Jennie: The Life of Lady Randolph Churchill*.

18 Ethel Smyth, *What Happened Next?*

19 September 7, 1898. Unless otherwise cited, letters are from Randolph S. Churchill, *Winston S. Churchill*, Companion Volume I, Part 2.

20 Undated letter, Peregrine Churchill Papers.

21 Shane Leslie, *Long Shadows*.

22 *Ibid.*

23 Letter dated Tuesday, the 20th.

24 (September 19, 1898?) From the Bachelor's Club, Piccadilly, W.

25 Anita Leslie, *op. cit.*

CHAPTER 11

The Berg Collection has a large and important collection of letters of Mrs Pearl Craigie. The British Museum is also a good source of varied material by and about her. Aside from her own books and papers, she wrote considerably for magazines and some newspapers, and these can be consulted. *The North American Review* (October–December 1906) has a good article on her novels. Her father, John Morgan Richards, who idolized his daughter, has collected what is mainly a paean of praise in *The Life of John Oliver Hobbes*. Isabel C. Clarke has done a better job in a single chapter in *Six Portraits*. But by far the best source of information about Pearl Craigie – a portrait that really comes alive – is Vineta Colby's superb chapter in *The Singular Anomaly*. Earl Curzon of Kedleston, *Subjects of The Day*, has done a sensitive memorial to her.

Mrs T. P. O'Connor, *I, Myself*, also has recorded some vivid memories of Pearl Craigie.

Two other books of general use in this chapter should be mentioned: Vera Brittain, *Lady Into Woman* and Francis Power Cobbe, *The Duties of Women*.

1 September 3, 1898. All letters, unless otherwise cited, are from Randolph S. Churchill, *Winston S. Churchill*, Companion Volume I, Part 2.

2 September 5, 1898.

3 September 4, 1898.

4. *Ibid.*

5 Reprinted in *Churchill by His Contemporaries*, edited by Charles Eade. Steevens had represented the *Daily Mail* in the United States and also at the Dreyfus trial. He died of enteric fever in the Transvaal in 1900. Winston Churchill called him 'the most brilliant man in journalism I have ever met'.

6 Undated letter.

7 October 6, 1898.

8 Daisy, Princess of Pless, *What I Left Unsaid*.

9 *Reminiscences of Lady Randolph Churchill*.

10 *Ibid.*

11 Earl Curzon of Kedleston, *Subjects of The Day*.

12 Conversation with author George Moore. Moore later said of her: 'When a man

has collaborated with a woman it is the same as if he had slept with her. She has no secrets left to reveal.' Vineta Colby, *The Singular Anomaly*.

13 Unidentified clipping dated March 21, 1904.

14 Gertrude Atherton, *Adventures of a Novelist*.

15 Included among his products was Carter's Little Liver Pills.

16 Mrs T. P. O'Connor, *I, Myself*.

17 A verse circulated about her epigrams, *Bookbuyer* 127 (April 1894):

> John Oliver Hobbes, with your spasms and throbs,
> How does your novel grow?
> With cynical sneers at young Love and his tears,
> And epigrams all in a row.

18 Interview in the New York *Herald*, November 16, 1905.

19 Lady Randolph Churchill, *op. cit.*

20 Letter from 56, Lancaster Gate, W., dated July 19.

21 Letter from Guildford, dated Sunday.

22 Lady Randolph Churchill, *op. cit.*

23 Vera Brittain, *Lady into Woman*.

24 Francis Power Cobbe, *The Duties of Women*.

25 Richard Le Gallienne, *The Romantic Nineties*.

26 James Lewis May, *John Lane & The Nineties*.

27 Beardsley went to work for another new literary quarterly, *The Savoy*, which survived only for a year. The artist Whistler, who had been critical of Beardsley's work, told him, 'Aubrey, I have made a very great mistake – you are a very great artist . . . I mean it – I mean it – I mean it. . . .' May, *op. cit.*

28 *Ibid.*

29 Anna Eichberg was the daughter of a distinguished American musician, Julius Eichberg, who became Director of the Boston Conservatory of Music. At the age of sixteen she wrote the words to 'America'.

30 November 29, 1898.

31 December 1, 1898.

Chapter 12

One must of course read the ten volumes of the *Anglo-Saxon Review*. They tell better than anything else does the high quality of this literary quarterly. They also reveal much about Jennie's own interests. Invaluable here was the large file of correspondence between Jennie and John Lane, which describes not only the relationship between them, but Jennie's concern and effectiveness as a working editor.

Michael Rhodes in London, who has researched deeply into John Lane and this literary period, is an excellent fount of information and references. There is a book, *John Lane & The Nineties* by John Lewis May, but the full story still remains to be written.

Jennie's own *Reminiscences* are not very good on the story of the *Anglo-Saxon Review*. The biography of Sidney Low, *Lost Historian* by Major Desmond Chapman-Huston, has some references to Low's work on the *Review*, including an excellent short excerpt from his diary. Besides Jennie's letters to Lane, her correspondence with Winston about her project is perhaps the best source of information. But there is no full account of the development and demise of the *Review*. In fact, a book about literary magazines in England during this period would make intriguing reading.

1 January 1, 1899. (All letters, unless otherwise noted, are from Randolph S. Churchill, *Winston S. Churchill*, Companion Volume I, Part 2.) In that same letter, Winston told his mother that he did not think she should allow the full investment in the magazine to be made by outsiders, that she should guarantee some of her own money.

2 Frances, Countess of Warwick, *Life's Ebb and Flow*.

3 Undated letter from Blenheim Palace. In it she also said she would need about £1,500 for the first year.

4 *Ibid*.

5 Undated letter.

6 February 16, 1899. In his letter Winston dismissed other suggested titles such as *The Arena* and *The International Quarterly*.

7 Letter dated March 24, 1899.

8 *Reminiscences of Lady Randolph Churchill*.

9 March 2, 1899.

10 March 30, 1899. In the same letter Winston suggested that he and Jack should put £250 into the guarantee for the *Review*.

11 Undated letter from Great Cumberland Place.

12 Undated letter from Great Cumberland Place.

13 Undated letter from Great Cumberland Place.

14 Lady Randolph Churchill, *op. cit*.

15 March 22, 1899.

16 February 23, 1899.

17 January 1, 1899.

18 Undated letter.

19 A number of other people claimed to have 'discovered' Kipling, including Moreton Frewen.

20 Major Desmond Chapman-Huston, *Lost Historian*. Huston also quoted Low as saying, 'Journalism is the grave of genius.' Low was knighted in 1918.

21 *Ibid*.

22 *Ibid*.

23 April 19, 1899.

24 April 26, 1899.

25 George G. Harrap, *Some Memories*.

26 Undated letter from Great Cumberland Place.

27 Letter dated 'Saturday'.

28 Undated letter from Great Cumberland Place.

29 June 23, 1899.

30 Letter to 'Mr Chapman' dated May 26.

31 May 12, 1899.

32 Undated letter.

33 March 22, 1899.

34 Undated letter.

35 May 31, 1899.

36 February 13, 1899. In the same letter Pearl also wrote: 'I wish you could have heard Sir Evelyn's praise of your boy. He has the highest hopes for him.' (Sir Evelyn Wood was then Commander-in-Chief of the Army.)

37 Like Jennie, Pearl had studied music in Paris.

38 Sir Frederick Ponsonby, *Recollections of Three Reigns*.

39 Lady Randolph Churchill, *op. cit.*

40 Undated letters.

41 Her first play was produced in 1894, a one-act play called *Journey's End in Lovers Meeting*, with Ellen Terry in the lead. She had three other plays produced by Sir George Alexander between 1898 and 1900. The most successful of these was *The Ambassador*, produced in 1898. Jennie was publishing her most recent play, *Osbern*, in her *Anglo-Saxon Review* before its London production.

42 The poem was written by E. V. Lucas.

43 *Town Topics*, February 9, 1899. Whitelaw Reid had served as attorney on the Paris Treaty Commission. Reid had explained the action of the United States in giving Spain $20 million (nearly £8 million) for islands that were already theirs by force of arms. He said it was compensation 'solely in recognition of the principle that debts attaching to a territory, and incurred for its benefit, should be transferred with its sovereignty.'

44 *Ibid.*

45 March 22, 1899.

46 Letter to Dowager Duchess of Marlborough, March 26, 1899.

47 Winston had written earlier (March 30, 1899), 'The preface to the first number, I should like to write, but we can talk about this when I get home. . . .' The final product was signed by Jennie.

48 Quoted in Lady Randolph Churchill, *op. cit.*

49 Frances, Countess of Warwick, *op. cit.* The Countess had also written, 'Nobody, even the most literary, could have lived up to such a grand binding in a mere review.' Jennie had sent her a scribbled outline of the *Review*'s expected contents, including an article by the Prince of Wales about his childhood and youth – which she never received. She also asked her friend Daisy to send her 'the recipe for your Cumberland sauce for the Wench of my kitchen. . . .'

50 *Pall Mall Gazette*, undated clipping.

51 June 20, 1899.

52 Dated 'Sunday', from Great Cumberland Place.

CHAPTER 13

The newspapers, again, are important here for facts available nowhere else. The Oldham *Daily Standard* provides small pieces of description about Jennie's political campaigning for her son. There are other comments in other regional newspapers, the Manchester *Evening News*, for example, but they are not as worthwhile.

The letters to her key political friends, including the Prime Minister, indicate better than anything else does the range of Jennie's constant activity on behalf of her son. Other letters indicate clearly Winston's resentment and concern about Jennie's impending marriage to George West. George West's own memoirs are not very reliable on his romance with Jennie. Since they were written long after the fact, after resentment had set in, his views are more superficial than they should be, and less detailed. His letters at that time are a much better indication of his true feeling. Some of these are used in various places, including Anita Leslie's book, *Jennie: The Life of Lady Randolph Churchill*. The original file of George's letters in the Churchill archives is typified largely by the sameness of content: hunting, riding, fishing and romance, almost in equal proportion.

Jennie had never dealt with her romance with George in any book. Her *Reminiscences* end just before her marriage.

1 June 25, 1899. Unless otherwise cited, all letters are from Randolph S. Churchill, *Winston S. Churchill*, Companion Volume I, Part 2.
2 June 26, 1899. The letter was written by Winston's secretary apart from the words in italics. In the same letter he also asked his mother to bring some medicated spray for his inflamed tonsils.
3 June 28, 1899.
4 Sir Ivor Jennings, *The British Constitution*.
5 July 6, 1899. But earlier in the campaign, when Winston had denounced the Clerical Bill that Balfour had introduced, Balfour had said: 'I thought he was a young man of promise, but it appears he's a young man of promises.'
6 July 14, 1899.
7 July 20, 1899.
8 August 9, 1899.
9 July 23, 1899.
10 Winston S. Churchill, *My Early Life*.
11 On July 23, 1899. Winston, like his mother, enjoyed gambling – both at the races and at Monte Carlo.
12 E. F. Benson, *As We Were*.
13 Anita Leslie, *Jennie: The Life of Lady Randolph Churchill*.
14 October 6, 1899. The term 'dissenting' refers to Protestants who are not members of the Church of England. As used by George here, the term connotes low social class and a kind of grubby Puritanism.
15 Letter dated from Burlington Hotel. W. *Reminiscences of Lady Randolph Churchill*.
16 *Ibid*.
17 *Ibid*.
18 *Ibid*.
19 August 17, 1899.
20 George Cornwallis-West, *Edwardian Hey-Days*. In his memoirs, George West also said of Jennie: 'Like many well-bred American women, she had the will and the power to adapt herself to her immediate surroundings. She was equally at home having a serious conversation with a distinguished statesman, or playing on a golf-course. A great reader, she remembered much of what she had read, and that made her a brilliant conversationalist, but although gifted

with extreme intelligence, she was not brilliant in the deepest sense of the word. She was not a genius.'

21 August 13, 1899.

22 August 4, 1899.

23 Cornwallis-West, *op. cit.*

24 *Ibid.*

25 August 5, 1899.

26 Undated letter.

27 Undated letter, Peregrine Churchill Papers.

28 August 13, 1899.

29 August 22, 1899.

30 September 3, 1899.

CHAPTER 14

There is an extensive literature in England on the Boer War, or The South African War. R. C. K. Ensor, *England, 1870–1914*, presents the facts clearly and objectively. Winston's letters and Bourke Cockran's speeches (clippings in his Papers) show greater emotion on the subject. The involvement generated such emotion that there are few memoirs of this period that are not strongly expressive on the subject. Even clearer evidence can be seen in the Letters to the Editor column in *The Times*.

Winston's own writing in his books and letters contain some of the best combat description of the war itself. Burdett-Coutts's report on the hospital conditions presents the grimmer side.

The early story of the *Maine* and Jennie's organization of the hospital ship can be found in the newspapers, both in England and the United States. Specific detail of the ship itself and its staff is to be found in the issues of *The Nursing Record and Hospital World*, in the last two months of 1899. Jennie's *Reminiscences* are also quite informative about this. *The British Medical Journal* is also of value. The most vivid description of the actual sailing comes from a reporter of *The New York Times*, December 24, 1899. There is also a most interesting letter from Clara to Leonie, reprinted in Randolph Churchill's Companion Volume.

1 Shane Leslie, *Men Were Different*.

2 The *Daily Mail* followed the style of the sensational American 'yellow press'. It used fewer words and bigger headlines than other newspapers in England. Harmsworth (later Viscount Northcliffe) used to say that other papers served their news raw, but the *Mail* served it cooked. Lord Salisbury derided the paper, saying it was 'written by office boys for office boys'. Its circulation at that time had jumped to 200,000 copies a day, twice as many as any other daily newspaper in England.

3 *The Milner Papers*, ed. Cecil Headlam, Vol. I.

4 Joseph Chamberlain was then sixty-three years old. His explanation for his vigour was: 'No exercise and smoke all day.' At fifty-one he had married Mary Endicott, a twenty-three-year-old American girl from Cleveland, Ohio. J. L. Garvin, *The Life of Joseph Chamberlain*, Vol. II.

5 *Reminiscences of Lady Randolph Churchill.*

6 Randolph S. Churchill, *Winston S. Churchill, Youth, 1874–1900.*

7 R. C. K. Ensor, *England: 1870–1914.*

8 This represented the combined forces of Transvaal and the Orange Free State. There were about a million Boers scattered throughout South Africa.

9 In a letter to the editor of *The Times*, a Boer wrote that the British were a decaying race with its children born weak, diseased, and deformed, that the major proportion of British people consisted of females, cripples, epileptics, consumptives, cancerous people, and lunatics of all kinds, who were carefully nourished and preserved. Quentin Crewe, *Frontiers of Privilege.*

10 Winston had written to his mother from the ship, 'Sir R. Buller is vy amiable, and I do not doubt that he is well disposed towards me. . . .'

11 George Cornwallis-West, *Edwardian Hey-Days.* The letter was dated October 15, 1899.

12 Michael Harrison, *Lord of London: A Biography of the Second Duke of Westminster.*

13 Cornwallis-West, *op. cit.*

14 *Town Topics*, January 25, 1900.

15 Lady Randolph Churchill, *op. cit.* Sir W. E. Garstin had been a senior British official in Egypt, responsible for several vital irrigation schemes. He would later (January 19, 1900) write to her: 'I often think of that evening at the Van Andres [M. and Mme Edouard von André, a stockbroker friend of Jennie's and his wife, who was a portrait painter] when you were talking over the scheme before it had definitely taken shape or form. You have done more than most people, towards drawing the bonds closer between the two countries. They must always be made of sympathy & what you & other American ladies have done makes every Englishman's heart beat a bit faster.'

16 *Ibid.*

17 H. J. and Hugh Massingham, *The Great Victorians.* Florence Nightingale, in that article, also wrote, 'And marriage being their only outlet in life, many women spend their lives in asking men to marry them, in their refined way. . . .' Florence Nightingale went into nursing at the age of thirty-four, and her first organizational activity was to set up a hospital for women in Harley Street.

18 Mrs Fanny Ronalds had been an old romance of Jennie's father, Leonard Jerome. She was then in love with Sir Arthur Sullivan (of Gilbert and Sullivan) who helped considerably in the fund-raising for the hospital ship. Mrs Cornelia Adair had been one of the reigning beauties of Newport Society when Jennie was a girl. Her husband was John Adair; he owned vast ranches in Texas and was a good friend of Jennie's brother-in-law Moreton Frewen.

19 Lady Randolph Churchill, *op. cit.*

20 *Ibid.*

21 *The Nursing Record and Hospital World*, November 4, 1899.

22 Winston S. Churchill, *My Early Life.*

23 The cattle boat had been engaged in transatlantic trade between London and Philadelphia. It was an iron-screw steamer of 2,228 tons, with a speed of $11\frac{1}{2}$ knots.

24 *The Nursing Record and Hospital World*, November 18, 1899.

25 November 5, 1899.

26 *The New York Times*, November 9, 1899. In the same article Jennie was also quoted as saying that 'It is especially the province of American women to promote this cause, but it is a woman's function to foster and nourish the suffering. American women are more adept at it, we believe, than any others.'

27 *Town Topics*, January 25, 1900.

28 Consuelo Vanderbilt Balsan, *The Glitter and the Gold*.

29 January 7, 1900.

30 Interview in London *Daily Mail*, as reported in Oldham *Daily Standard*, November 9, 1899.

31 Lady Randolph Churchill, *op. cit.*

32 For New York Society, she was 'Mrs Hugo de Bathe'.

33 The Prince had given her a silver turtle to be used as an inkstand.

34 She sold a ticket to John Pierpont Morgan, Sr, by walking directly into his office.

35 Pierre Sichel, *The Jersey Lily*.

36 *The New York Times*, undated clipping.

37 Kipling himself donated £20 and some books for the *Maine* fund-raising. Kipling's wife was an American, Carolyn Belestier, and they lived for a while in Brattleboro, Vermont. His 'Absent-Minded Beggar' was set to music by Sir Arthur Sullivan and played on barrel-organs all over England. Kipling donated the income from it to a variety of charities, which resulted in the offer of a knighthood to Kipling – which he declined.

38 November 19, 1899.

39 Letter from Walden to Lady Randolph, dated November 17, 1899, printed in the Oldham *Daily Standard*, December 14, 1899.

40 Lady Randolph Churchill, *op. cit.*

41 Telegram, November 17, 1899.

42 November 18, 1899.

43 November 30, 1899.

44 December 3, 1899. Anita Leslie, *Jennie: The Life of Lady Randolph Churchill.*

45 November 18, 1899. *The British Medical Journal* of the same date also described the ship's facilities: 'The ship has four large wards and one small isolation ward, providing accommodation altogether for 218 patients on two decks. . . . The operating room has been fitted up on the saloon deck, and is provided with an enamelled iron operating table with plate-glass top, instrument cupboards, sterilizers etc., and also an X-Ray installation.' The operating room was described as 'the most remarkable yet designed for South African service'.

46 Lady Randolph Churchill, *op. cit.*

47 Winston S. Churchill, *op. cit.*

48 *Ibid.*

49 *Ibid.*

50 Lady Randolph Churchill, *op. cit.* Discussing the legal question of a ship sailing under two flags, *Truth* (December 21, 1899) wrote: 'The ladies in command possibly are not aware that a ship sailing under the flags of any two nations, is, by international law, a pirate.' *The United Services Gazette* (December 9, 1899)

had noted the rules for hospital ships: 'They are to afford relief and assistance to all wounded belligerents, irrespective of nationality. During and after an engagement, they run at their own risk – though by International Law, they are absolutely neutralized. The belligerents have the right to visit them and control their movements.'

51 The Army & Navy Stores was at the time a unique British institution. The stores itself was almost a club. Members were usually recognized by name by the sales staff and doormen, and there were writing and reading rooms where members often arranged to meet. The stores had their own factories to produce groceries, confectionery, cigars, shirts, watches, guns, golf clubs, perfume. They offered all kinds of special services, from home repairs, decoration and re-movals, to auction rooms and catering. They bottled and shipped their own wine, and their catalogue included everything from elephants' feet (made into liqueur sets) to big game trophy-stuffing. A catalogue of 1907 offered fifty-six different designs of bedroom-toilet services, as well as 'sculpture by corsetry' that promised a swan silhouette. There were also leather dress protectors for hems which swept the pavements. And there were two whole pages on dinner gongs. The store also had a listing of entertainers for hire for parties, from Mystery Men in Native Costume to a White Viennese Band. The catering department offered everything from a wedding breakfast to a thirteen-course dinner. (*The Very Best English Goods*, 1969. Introduction by Alison Adburgham. Army & Navy Stores' Catalogue of 1907.)

52 There had been a large party at the Carlton Hotel that night before the *Maine* sailed. The woman who organized the party was Mrs Arthur Paget. Her hus-band was Colonel Arthur Paget, George West's commanding officer, who decided to send George home. The doctors believed that his severe case of sun-stroke might have affected his heart.

53 *The New York Times*, December 24, 1899, reported: 'As the *Maine* moved into the river, three cheers were given for the ship, then for Lady Churchill, and finally, for the United States.'

CHAPTER 15

Jennie has done her finest writing in her description of the *Maine*'s voyage to help the wounded in the Boer War. She wrote it in rich detail as the final section of her *Reminiscences*, and also did it as an article for her own *Anglo-Saxon Review*. She also wrote constantly to her sisters and friends, and did a full report on the trip for the British government.

Mary Hibbard, the Chief Nurse, also wrote a series of articles about the hospital ship for *The Nursing Record*, but they do not have the quality of impact of Jennie's writings. Winston, in his letters and books, wrote about the combat most dramatic-ally indeed. Jack's letters are also very vivid.

E. T. Raymond, *Portraits of the Nineties*, has some excellent profiles of the important personalities, particularly Kitchener. Sir John Fortescue, *The Post-Victorians*, is also good.

A most interesting anecdote comes from Frederic Villiers, *Peaceful Personalities and Warriors Bold*. Michael Harrison's *Lord of London*, mentioned earlier, also has some relevant material on this subject.

1 Jennie told a reporter, 'I know of no better way to spend Christmas than on an American hospital ship bound for South Africa. . . . Wherever the ship goes, I go. . . .' *The New York Times*, December 24, 1899.

2 Jennie wrote to her sister Clara that 'the ship is not built for the big seas'. January 3, 1900.

3 *Reminiscences of Lady Randolph Churchill. The Times* (December 18, 1899) had written that the *Maine* 'is the first vessel which any nation has ever dispatched to succour the wounded forces of another state.'

4 Letter from Las Palmas, January 2, 1900. (Unless otherwise noted, all letters are from Randolph S. Churchill, *Winston S. Churchill*, Companion Volume I, Part 2.) In the same letter Jennie noted that the gale was so strong that the ship had to 'lie to' for forty-eight hours.

5 January 6, 1900.

6 Lady Randolph Churchill, *op. cit.*

7 January 6, 1900.

8 Undated letter, Peregrine Churchill Papers.

9 January 6, 1900.

10 Lady Randolph Churchill, *op. cit.*

11 Undated letter, Peregrine Churchill Papers.

12 *Ibid.*

13 Miss Hibbard was Canadian-born, a member of the American Society of Superintendents of Training Schools for Nurses, and also a member of the Daughters of the American Revolution. Her great-grandfather was a chaplain in the Revolutionary Army and also one of the earliest graduates of Dartmouth College. Miss Hibbard later became a leader in the development of nursing in Cuba, where she established seven schools of nursing and became Inspector General of Nurses. She also spent four years in the Panama Canal Zone. At the Gorgas Hospital in Ancon there is a bronze plague which honours her as 'Nurse, patriot, gentlewoman, humanitarian, friend, who rendered outstanding service to the development of better health in the tropics'. Mary M. Roberts, *American Nursing: History and Interpretation.*

14 Undated letter, Peregrine Churchill Papers.

15 Lady Randolph Churchill, *op. cit.*

16 Jennie and Sir Alfred Milner had both been members of The Souls, the small social group of intellectuals who had become politically powerful in England. Two of them became Prime Ministers: Balfour and Asquith; Haldane became Lord Chancellor; Curzon, the Viceroy of India, and, later, Secretary of State for Foreign Affairs; Alfred Lyttleton became Secretary of State for War and George Wyndham Chief Secretary for Ireland. They had met mostly at George Wyndham's house near Salisbury, called 'The Clouds'. In July 1899, Wyndham had written to Milner, 'The country has settled down to a stolid view that we must vindicate our supremacy, and that you must guide us as to how to do it.' Wyndham regarded Milner as the coming man of the nineteenth century. Milner was the one man to whom Joseph Chamberlain had written a letter of

introduction for Winston Churchill when he first went to South Africa, and Chamberlain had told Winston, 'You will not need any other letter.' Milner had been in love with Margot Tennant, who then married Herbert Asquith. Michael Harrison, *Lord of London.*

17 Winston had written 'I cannot begin to criticize – for I should never stop. . . .' January 10, 1900.

18 When the Boer War broke out Lord Roberts returned to England after forty-one years in India. The Marquess of Lansdowne, who had been Viceroy of India when Roberts was there, appointed Roberts Commander-in-Chief in South Africa. Roberts, who had been one-eyed since infancy and was of considerably less than average height, was often called 'Little Bobs'. An orphan of Irish descent, he had made his way on sheer ability. He was a neat, precise man, quick and nervous in his movements, direct in his conversation. He was amiable, able, courageous, and devoted to duty. In contrast, Kitchener was complex and secretive. E. T. Raymond, *Portraits of the Nineties*; Sir John Fortescue, *The Post-Victorians.*

19 Lady G. Cecil, *Life of Robert, Marquis of Salisbury*, Volume III.

20 Undated letter, Peregrine Churchill Papers.

21 Letter to Leonie, January 5, 1900. In that letter he had also written, 'I trust Winston and he would never make me go 7,000 miles on a wild goose chase. . . . I look too beautiful in my big sombrero hat . . . I have becoming tummy bands and revolvers and belts and bayonettes and rifles and all the necessary implements of war, including a chain round my neck and a few charms. . . .'

22 March 27, 1898.

23 Lady Randolph Churchill, *op. cit.*

24 Undated letter, Peregrine Churchill Papers.

25 Lady Randolph Churchill, *op. cit.*

26 Frederic Villiers, *Peaceful Personalities and Warriors Bold.*

27 *Ibid.*

28 February 10, 1900.

29 Lady Randolph Churchill, *op. cit.*

30 *Ibid.*

31 February 13, 1900.

32 Winston S. Churchill, *My Early Life.*

33 March 27, 1900.

34 February 18, 1900.

35 Captain Percy Moreton Scott (who later became an Admiral) was a year younger than Jennie. His ship was diverted from a trip to China so that Scott could bring his heavy 4.7 naval guns to the defence of Ladysmith. He afterwards went on to China, where he was active in putting down the Boxer Rebellion. By 1910 Scott had received £10,000 as reward for his various inventions. At the beginning of World War I, he was responsible for the creation of the anti-aircraft corps, and the anti-aircraft defence of London.

36 Lady Randolph Churchill, *op. cit.*

37 *Ibid.*

38 W. L. Burdett-Coutts, *The Sick and Wounded in South Africa.*

39 Lady Randolph Churchill, *op. cit.*

40 *Ibid.*

41 *Ibid.* Sir Percy Scott, *Fifty Years In The Royal Navy.* In his book of memoirs, Scott wrote, 'I ordered the main brace to be spliced (for which I subsequently got hauled over the coals by the Admiralty). Every one in the town who could get a firework, let it off. . . .'

42 W. Pett Ridge, *I Like To Remember.*

43 Lady Randolph Churchill, *op. cit.*

44 *Ibid.*

45 Anita Leslie, *Jennie: The Life of Lady Randolph Churchill.*

46 Undated clipping.

47 Undated letter, Peregrine Churchill Papers.

48 To Jennie, the elegant clothing and the babble of both the men and the women in Cape Town were 'bewildering, and seemed under the circumstances rather out of place. . . .' Lady Randolph Churchill, *op. cit.*

49 *Ibid.*

50 March 10, 1900. The Prince of Wales had been critical to the Countess of Warwick 'of some of the silly Society women who went to South Africa in the Boer War ostensibly to nurse the wounded, but actually to have as good a time as they could.' His main reference was to the women who 'walk the streets of Cape Town, dressed as though they were at Ascot or Monte Carlo. One would suppose that, if they were not prevented by a sense of fitness of things, at least they would be deterred by a sense of humour.' Frances, Countess of Warwick, *Afterthoughts.*

51 *Daily Mail*, April 24, 1900. The reporter quoted Jennie as saying, 'I have never had an idle moment all the time I've been away.' She also owned a chameleon which she called 'George'. 'It hates a chilly day,' she said.

CHAPTER 16

George Cornwallis-West is very expressive about his Boer War experiences in *Edwardian Hey-Days*, but he is very reluctant to dwell on the family opposition to his marriage to Jennie. For this conflict, we must go to Cornwallis-West's letters to Winston in the Companion Volume of Randolph Churchill's biography. Jennie herself barely mentions the bitterness, but there are no such qualms in the London and American press, or in the memoirs of her friends, already mentioned. *The Diaries* of Daisy, Princess of Pless, are more revealing for what they don't say; much of what she does say simply is not true.

George West does detail the opposition of the Prince of Wales and the military authorities to his planned marriage. Jennie's letters to her sons, reprinted in the Companion Volume, are particularly moving. So is the obvious opposition of her sons. *The New York Times* account of the wedding is better than anything else I found, which is why I reprinted it in full.

For other background, there is some interesting information in Hesketh Pearson, *The Pilgrim Daughters*, as well as other books already mentioned, such as Lady Maud Warrender's *My First Sixty Years*, Lincoln Springfield's *Some Piquant People*, Clare Sheridan's *Nuda Veritas*, and Seymour Leslie's *The Jerome Connexion*.

The Berg Collection also had a letter from Sidney Low about the *Anglo-Saxon Review*, which explained some of his work.

1 Anita Leslie, *Jennie: The Life of Lady Randolph Churchill.*
2 Samuel Edwards, *The Divine Mistress.* Madame Emilie du Châtelet also said she saw no virtue in repentance, 'for despair only destroys one's appetite for life; besides, if the purpose of repentance is to avoid making the same mistake again, the precaution is useless, for nothing in life happens the same way twice. If a woman finds herself depressed, let her get herself a new gown or some new furniture.' Voltaire said of Madame du Châtelet, 'She was a great man whose only fault was in being a woman. . . .'
3 Letter dated April 17, 1900.
4 Undated letter, Peregrine Churchill Papers.
5 Leslie, *op. cit.*
6 George Cornwallis-West, *Edwardian Hey-Days.*
7 Hesketh Pearson, *The Pilgrim Daughters.* Consuelo's eldest child, Kim, became the 9th Duke of Manchester and married Helena Zimmerman, daughter of a Cincinnati millionaire. Before he died, Consuelo's husband had led 'a disgraceful career – which included a shameful appearance in the police court and eventually sank absolutely into the gutter.' *New York Journal*, quoted in Elizabeth Eliot, *They All Married Well.*
8 Cornwallis-West, *op. cit.*
9 *Reminiscences of Lady Randolph Churchill.*
10 Undated clippings.
11 Quoted in Pearson, *op. cit.*
12 Undated letter to Jack, Peregrine Churchill Papers.
13 Undated letter from the Isle of Mull, Duart Castle, Peregrine Churchill Papers.
14 Cornwallis-West, *op. cit.*
15 Letter to Clement King Shorter, January 27, 1900. Berg Collection.
16 June 9, 1900.
17 May 1, 1900.
18 June 9, 1900.
19 May 12, 1900.
20 *Ibid.* Jennie also wrote in that letter that she was finishing an article about the hospital ship, was consulting Cassel about some investments, and had seen the Queen, who 'was most gracious'.
21 Letter to Leonie Leslie, May 15, 1900. His aunt had asked him to be the godfather to her expected child.
22 Undated letter, Peregrine Churchill Papers.
23 Lincoln Springfield, *Some Piquant People.* W. Pett Ridge also wrote of the event: 'Anyone in uniform was cheered and honoured. I saw a railway porter near Charing Cross being carried along triumphantly, much as though he were Baden-Powell himself. Cordiality between the sexes was helped by the tickling of necks with feathers. There was the sale, too, at the curbs, of less agreeable articles – ladies' tormentors, which sprayed water in your face, and that ridiculous toy that was being drawn down the back of a coat or blouse, making the sound of a tearing garment. Illuminations appeared at nearly every shop, every

house, and any exception was resented. Hats went into the air, and nobody seemed to mind whether or not they came back to their owners.' *I Like to Remember*. But see Brian Gardner, *Mafeking: A Victorian Legend*.

24 May 26, 1900.

25 Leslie, *op. cit.*

26 Cornwallis-West, *op. cit.*

27 *Ibid.*

28 June 20, 1900.

29 Undated letter, Peregrine Churchill Papers.

30 June 23, 1900.

31 June 17, 1900.

32 July 10, 1900.

33 June 23, 1900.

34 June 30, 1900. In the same letter she also told him that Leonie had given birth to a son, and also asked him whether he was short of clothing.

35 July 28, 1900.

36 An undated clipping from a British newspaper (no source) noted: 'Though the name of the Prince of Wales did not appear in Lady Randolph Churchill's present list, lest he should seem to abet a marriage of which his judgment disapproved, the Prince did not forget his friend, but personally gave to the bride, the day before the wedding, a little gold pig, set in jewels.' Jennie collected replicas of pigs.

37 The *Northern Whig* (August 6, 1900) estimated the crowd outside the church at several thousand. The *Yorkshire Herald* (August 4, 1900) observed that Jennie, being a widow, 'had no bridesmaids'. And, an undated clipping (no source) reported that the bride's dress was designed by Madame Hayward of New Bond Street and that the groom looked 'splendidly tall and handsome, well-built, and with a charmingly good expression to boot'.

38 Lady Maud Warrender, *My First Sixty Years*.

39 *The Private Diaries of Daisy, Princess of Pless*.

40 July 31, 1900.

CHAPTER 17

In my interview with him, Sir Shane Leslie provided very full descriptions and memories of George Cornwallis-West. He also deals with him at length in several of his books. And there is a letter to the editor of *The Times* written by Sir Shane Leslie in George's defence years after this period.

George West's description of his frustrating business career and his early marriage is surprisingly good in his memoirs. This is amplified by the exchange of letters between Winston and Jack and between Jennie and Winston.

Jennie's letters to John Lane highlight the conflict at this time. None of the books, or magazine articles on John Lane deal with the subject in any way. The best verbal source on the subject, again, is Michael Rhodes, who is currently preparing a biography of John Lane.

Shane Leslie's account of the death of Queen Victoria and her funeral – in his *Film of Memory* – is the most moving I have read.

1 Randolph S. Churchill, *Winston S. Churchill*, Companion Volume I, Part 2. Unless otherwise indicated, all letters quoted in this chapter are from this source.

2 Interview with Sir Shane Leslie, and quoted in Anita Leslie, *Jennie: The Life of Lady Randolph Churchill*.

3 August 12, 1900.

4 Lord Rosebery had written to Winston earlier advising him to take elocution lessons. In a letter of July 31, 1900, Winston said he would take the advice 'though I fear I shall never learn to pronounce an "S" properly'.

5 September 18, 1900.

6 September 20, 1900.

7 September 21, 1900.

8 October 12, 1900.

9 October 7, 1900. Winston also told Bourke in that letter that he was particularly proud of having reversed the 1,500-vote loss recorded against him there a year before.

10 October 16, 1900.

11 November 2, 1900.

12 George Cornwallis-West, *Edwardian Hey-Days*.

13 *Ibid.*

14 *Ibid.*

15 December 25, 1900.

16 *The Private Diaries of Daisy, Princess of Pless.*

17 Cornwallis-West, *op. cit.* Some years later, George took Jennie's nephew Seymour Leslie for his first real ride in an automobile and told him, 'Go in for electricity or motor-cars. ... The coming thing, don't-you-know!' Seymour Leslie, *The Jerome Connexion.*

18 Letter from the Moreton Frewen Papers, written on notepaper from a hotel in Milan, and dated November 9, 1900.

19 Letter from the Moreton Frewen Papers, written from Torquay, December 14, 1900.

20 December 15, 1900.

21 Lady Cynthia Asquith, *Diaries: 1915–1918.* Whibley was very enamoured of Lady Asquith.

22 Lincoln Springfield, *Some Piquant People.*

23 December 12, 1900. In the same letter Pearl Craigie told Jennie she had given up trying to produce her play in Egypt because the actors were terrified by the 'gang' in the gallery. 'No English actor or actress can perform unless they have their "receptions".'

24 Stephen Crane spent most of his dying days at Brede Place. He had asked that he might be taken to die in the Black Forest, and this was done. His death came on June 5, 1900, and Moreton Frewen organized a fund to pay Crane's debts. Rudyard Kipling was asked to complete Crane's unfinished work, but he said, '... a man's work is personal to him and should remain as he made or left it.' Allen Andrews, *The Splendid Pauper.*

25 The ghost of Brede Place was supposed to be that of Sir Goddard Oxenbridge, whose family had lived there from 1395. It was said that he had had the habit of devouring babies. According to legend, the children of Sussex plied him

with beer until he was drunk, then laid an enormous wooden saw on him and see-sawed him to death, cutting him in half. 'Many people have reported ghostly manifestations at Brede Place.' *Ibid.*

26 W. Pett Ridge, *I Like to Remember*.

27 Eve Adam, *Mrs. J. Comyns Carr's Reminiscences*.

28 Randolph S. Churchill, *op. cit.*, p. 1222n.

29 December 21, 1900. Letter from Boston.

30 January 1, 1901. He also wrote, 'I am vy proud that there is not one person in a million who at my age [he was then twenty-five] could have earned £10,000 without any capital in less than two years.' Several months earlier Colonel Brabazon had told Jennie how pleased he was that Winston was not marrying Pamela. 'She ought to be a rich man's wife.'

31 Letter to George from Chicago, January 16, 1901.

32 January 1, 1901.

33 July 31, 1900.

34 Undated letter.

35 Letter from Chicago, January 16, 1901.

36 December 25, 1900.

37 January 9, 1901.

38 *Ibid.*

39 Mrs Alice Frederica Keppel, the Prince's mistress.

40 January 22, 1901.

41 Sir Frederick Ponsonby, *Recollections of Three Reigns*.

42 Shane Leslie, *Film of Memory*.

CHAPTER 18

The books previously mentioned dealing with the Prince of Wales are again most useful in this chapter. This is particularly true of J. B. Priestley's *The Edwardians*. For general background on the new era, there is *The New Cambridge Modern History* (Volume XII), and Arthur Bryant's *English Saga*.

Two highly interesting books of recollections of this time are E. De Gramont, *Pomp and Circumstance*, and the Duke of Manchester, *My Candid Recollections*. Not very well written, but very pertinent to the chapter, is *Edwardian Daughter* by Sonia Keppel. Much more interesting and valuable is *They All Married Well* by Elizabeth Eliot.

George Cornwallis-West is the second best source for a full account of his social life in the early part of his marriage. The primary source is still Jennie, mostly through her letters.

1 February 14, 1901. Randolph S. Churchill, *Winston S. Churchill*, Companion Volume II, Part 1. Unless otherwise noted, all letters quoted here are from this source.

2 Cecil Rhodes, whose promising career had been broken by the Boer War, also warned those British who talked only of revenge: 'You think you have beaten the Dutch; but it is not so. The Dutch are not beaten; what is beaten is

Krugerism, a corrupt and evil government no more Dutch in essence than English. No, the Dutch are as vigorous and unconquered today as they have ever been; the country is still as much theirs as it is yours, and you will have to live and work with them hereafter as in the past.' Arthur Bryant, *English Saga*.

3 February 1, 1901.

4 March 26, 1901.

5 February 20, 1901. General Sir Ian Hamilton was happy to do this for Winston and Jennie. Earlier Winston had asked Hamilton to visit Jennie. 'She would be very grateful for news of me, and to meet one who has shown me much kindness.' Hamilton also remembered in his memoirs that Winston had given him a copy of the completed manuscript of Winston's novel, *Savrola*, and that he had 'handed it over to his mother, Lady Randolph Churchill'. General Sir Ian Hamilton, *Listening for the Drums*.

6 December 17, 1901.

7 Undated letter.

8 Margot Asquith (later, Margot Oxford when her husband became Lord Oxford) wrote in her memoirs: 'Arthur Balfour was born with perfect equilibrium, and an admirable temper and iron nerves. I have often seen him masterful, cool, and collected in debates which aroused prolonged party fury in the House of Commons. I have sat by his side on several occasions when his motor skidded down dangerous slopes, and one day when it went with a crash against a lorry in the dark. He never moved in his seat, and we continued our conversation as if nothing had occurred.' *More Memories*.

9 'The King dearly loved a joke, indeed only a man or woman who could keep him amused or interested was sure of ready welcome.' Frances, Countess of Warwick, *Discretions*.

10 King Edward smoked cigars incessantly, against his doctor's advice. He ate what he pleased, but he was always temperate in his use of alcohol. *Ibid*.

11 The King was also very superstitious. His hostesses had to be certain that knives were not crossed on the table, mattresses were not turned on Fridays, and, of course, that they never sat thirteen down to dinner. Virginia Cowles, *Edward VII and His Circle*.

12 Poem by Rudyard Kipling.

13 Cowles, *op. cit.*

14 *The Private Diaries of Daisy, Princess of Pless*.

15 Undated letter.

16 George Cornwallis-West, *Edwardian Hey-Days*.

17 *Ibid*.

18 E. De Gramont, *Pomp and Circumstance*.

19 Cornwallis-West, *op. cit.*

20 *Ibid*.

21 *Ibid*. At one of these parties, Jennie sat next to the Ambassador from Japan. Jennie had been to Japan and loved it, and had brought back prints and antiques for her house. They discussed proverbs and Jennie wondered whether there was a Japanese equivalent for, 'Penny wise and pound foolish'. The Japanese Ambassador hesitated thoughtfully, then answered, 'The literal trans-

lation of the Japanese equivalent is "The man who goes to bed early to save candles gets twins".'

22 *Ibid.*

23 Both King Edward and Lord Rosebery owned horses which won the Derby.

24 December 13, 1901.

25 In his novel *Savrola*, published the previous year (1900), Winston had great difficulty portraying women. One reveiwer wrote, 'His love scenes are shirked as far as possible.'

26 People were so partisan about the Boer War that there were still riots when pro-Boer speakers held rallies. Some 40,000 people surrounded the Town Hall where Lloyd George was to make a pro-Boer speech. They broke all the windows of the Hall and Lloyd George had to be smuggled out disguised as a policeman. De Gramont, *op. cit.*

The coronation had originally been arranged for June 26, 1902, eighteen months after his accession, but recovery from the operation took almost a month.

27 J. B. Priestley, *The Edwardians.*

28 Anita Leslie, *Jennie: The Life of Lady Randolph Churchill.*

29 *Ibid.*

30 Daisy, Princess of Pless, *op. cit.*

31 Some years later, there was a popular ballad, which included the verses,

> There is peace within the palace
> At a little word from Alice.
> *Send for Mrs Keppel!*
>
> She alone can keep the King from dumps,
> Once she's shown him how to play his trumps.
> *Send for Mrs Keppel!*

Shane Leslie, *Long Shadows.*

32 Sonia Keppel, *Edwardian Daughter.*

33 *Ibid.*

34 Margot Asquith, *op. cit.*

35 'When some people, jealous at not being in such high favour themselves with King Edward as she was, made ill-natured remarks about her, she never retaliated; and although her influence with the King was so great that, had she chosen to exercise it, she could have gotten the scandal-mongers into serious hot water, she never attempted to make use of her power in the smallest degree. Her magnanimity, which, while commanding my deepest admiration, makes me regard her as a truly remarkable, if not unique, woman.' The Duke of Manchester, *My Candid Recollections.*

36 Jennie told in her article that when Catherine of Medici became a widow she had her bedroom hung with black velvet embroidered with pearls forming crescents and suns. She also described Madame de Lafayette's bed of crimson satin, but noted that her bedroom also had 'a chest of drawers, a small bookcase containing two hundred volumes, eight tapestry chairs, white cotton curtains, a spinet, a picture representing the demolition of the Bastille, a card

table and two maps.' Marie Antoinette's bedroom featured a domed Imperial bed, fourteen and a half feet high, draped with silver brocade, and two enormous chandeliers of rock crystal.

37 Anita Leslie, *op. cit.*
38 So intense was the feeling over the Boer War that the owner of the *Chronicle* forced his pro-Boer editor to resign and launched a pro-war policy. On the other hand, Lloyd George formed a syndicate to buy the *Daily News* and oust its anti-Boer editor in order to reverse its editorial policy.
39 August 19, 1901.
40 Undated letters, Peregrine Churchill Papers.
41 John Morgan Richards had lived for thirty years in London, had a keen interest in literary matters, wrote a book called *With John Bull and Jonathan*, and for a while even owned a magazine called *The Academy*. He was a rich, popular American with a soft, gentle voice.
42 Mr Michael Rhodes, who has deeply researched the turn-of-the-century English literary magazines, feels that the first four issues were the best written, the best edited, and the most interesting. Jennie's involvement with the hospital ship, the Boer War, and her marriage diverted much of her time thereafter. Rhodes also feels that the *Anglo-Saxon Review* was not fated to last much longer because although the reading audience for such things had broadened vastly, the *Review*'s price was prohibitive. But he added, 'The *Anglo-Saxon Review*, even now, is unique. There has never been any other journal quite like it, an international literary review of high quality that really was international and literary.' Interview by the author.
43 September 27, 1902.
44 December, 1902.
45 Clare Sheridan, *Nuda Veritas*.
46 *Ibid.*
47 *Ibid.* On a typical week of the débutante season, Clare's social calendar read:

Monday 29th	(Go to *castle* concert)
Tues., 1st	(Royal Hospital Ball)
Wed., 2d	(Castle Ball)
Thurs., 3	(Dance)
Fri., 4	(Royal H. Dinner and Dance)

She also had a list of necessary clothes:
   Court train for best ball gown
   3 evening or ball-gowns
   3 tidy *silk* shirts, to come down to
      breakfast in, with tweed skirts
   3 ordinary shirts, to wear with short skirt
   3 nice shooting caps
   1 smart feather hat
   1 hat to drive to meets, etc.
48 Undated letter to Jack, Peregrine Churchill Papers.
49 Undated letter, Peregrine Churchill Papers.
50 Cornwallis-West, *op. cit.*
51 *Ibid.*

52 *Ibid.*

53 Elizabeth Eliot, *They All Married Well.*

54 Undated letter, Peregrine Churchill Papers.

55 January 29, 1903.

56 March 9, 1903.

57 January 28, 1904. The novel with 'Jennie' in it was *The Vineyard.*

58 January 11, 1904. Jennie joined the Ladies Automobile Club.

59 Shane Leslie had also written that after the King's visit 'the English royal family had a spiritual home on the Seine.' Shane Leslie, *op. cit.*

60 *The Times*, November 30, 1903.

61 December 19, 1902.

62 August 12, 1903.

63 September 18, 1903.

64 During the Boer War, Bourke Cockran had addressed pro-Boer rallies in New York, Chicago and Boston, and called it 'one of the most barbarous wars in all the dreary annals of aggression.' He said Joseph Chamberlain had generously consented to give the Boers a choice between subjugation and conquest, 'which was very much the same as if a man should invite another to commit suicide, in order to save the trouble and risk of murder. . . . This is a war of the London Smart Set, the stock exchange gamblers and the street mobs. It has never been approved by the sober judgment of the English people; it is abhorrent to the conscience of the American people. It is a fashionable war on both sides of the Atlantic; it is a popular war on neither side.'

65 At Bourke Cockran's death in 1923, Winston Churchill said of him. 'All of his convictions were of one piece. To him, the brittle loyalties of party were unimportant, compared with fidelity to principles.'

66 Seymour Leslie, *The Jerome Connexion.*

Chapter 19

Reading the files of magazines and newspapers for general background can be unproductive in terms of results achieved for time spent, but there are some newspapers and magazines of this period that deserve careful attention. The files of *Punch* give a marvellous insight to the mood and foibles of the time. The *Illustrated London News* is excellent because it is so visual, and the highlights are all here. *The Times* (London) and *The New York Times* are best for the details of major events. The New York *Herald* and the *New York Journal* both give a lot of space to London Society news. There are other specialized magazines in England, such as *Bystander* and *Gentlewoman*, which are worth examining, and the London *Spectator* also deserves attention.

Descriptions of Jennie's tenure at Salisbury Hall come from a variety of her friends' memoirs, most of them already mentioned. George Cornwallis-West's book is good, but the best material comes from family letters.

The Marquis de Soveral Papers in Lisbon are of selective value – the Marquis apparently destroyed a large number of his more private letters. That seems to be the pattern of a great number of surviving private papers, including those of the Marquis Henri de Breteuil. However, enough papers are extant to help complete the mosaic of information.

Edward Marsh by Christopher Hassall is very valuable here, but the Marsh Letters at the New York Public Library are a necessary supplement. There are also some important letters in the superb Churchill Collection of the Marquess of Bath. Douglas Plummer's *Queer People* confirms some well-known facts, and a correspondence with the author reveals even more.

Two books by Ethel Smyth, *What Happened Next* and *Streaks of Life*, both have some interesting anecdotes about Jennie, as well as some fascinating general background material.

In relation to his own romance and marriage, it is worthwhile to read Winston Churchill's novel *Savrola*.

1 Mary Borden also wrote in the *Spectator* that the American woman 'lives at great speed with high intensity, acts quickly on her beliefs, dashes into every adventure.' She also regarded them as being 'very ignorant and very emotional. . . .' An article in *Review of Reviews*, April 1902, entitled 'Do Americans Live Too Fast?' said: '. . . Americans are developing their brains and nerves at expense of their bodies. This is especially the case with women.' It recommended more fresh air, dumb bells, Indian clubs, and chest weights. It also said that the morning newspaper 'devours a large part of the nervous force which ought to be derived from breakfast.'

2 August 22, 1904. Randolph S. Churchill, *Winston S. Churchill*, Companion Volume II, Part 1.

3 *The Private Diaries of Daisy, Princess of Pless*. Daisy, who was then thirty, admitted, 'I would be much plumper if I did not wear long and well-made French corsets.'

4 'The Most Influential Anglo-Saxon Woman in the World', *Current Literature*, December, 1908.

5 Nell Gwynne (or Gwyn), who had been an orange seller at the Theatre Royal, had made her début as an actress at Drury Lane in 1665. She was best in comic roles. She became the mistress of Charles II in 1669 and bore him two sons, one of whom became the Duke of St Albans.

6 George Cornwallis-West, *Edwardian Hey-Days*.

7 Daisy, Princess of Pless, *op. cit.*

8 The Duchess of Devonshire wore a formidable iron corset to keep her rigid, 'and although she took an hour to climb the stairs, she led in all respects the life of a very young woman. Balls, dinners, races, the Opera, the social gatherings, charity committees – she presided over and managed everything . . . her age vanished between the aids of art; a wig made up of little fair curls framed the petal-pinkest of faces. . . .' E. De Gramont, *Pomp and Circumstance*. Gramont added: 'Animal spirits in England are more impetuous than in France. It has been demonstrated that English legs move with greater velocity than ours. And this world carries even the ancient with it. Evening functions in London are a mass of venerable reliquaries, bewigged and covered in jewels. They go on showing themselves at an age when French women softly cling to the fireside and lock up their jewels in the vaults. . . .'

9 Kaiser Wilhelm had known Jennie since the time she had first visited Berlin with Lord Randolph. See Ralph G. Martin, *Lady Randolph Churchill, A Biography, 1854–1895.*

10 Daisy, Princess of Pless, *op. cit.*

11 Sir Frederick Ponsonby, *Recollections of Three Reigns.*

12 Sheffield *Daily Telegraph*, October 29, 1909.

13 Daisy, Princess of Pless, *op cit.*

14 Marquis de Soveral Private Papers, courtesy of Viscountess de Soveral. Undated letter from Vice Regal Lodge, Dublin.

15 *Ibid.*

16 November 12, 1904.

17 February 9, 1905.

18 *Reminiscences of Lady Randolph Churchill.*

19 Cornwallis-West, *op. cit.*

20 In India, Mary Leiter Curzon was called 'The Leiter of Asia'. She was a lovely woman with deep, dark eyes and black hair.

21 Lord Curzon, the man so many considered cold and stiff, wrote a poem about his wife which began:
  I would have torn the stars from the Heavens for your necklace,
  I would have stripped the rose-leaves for your couch from all the trees. . .,

22 Vineta Colby, *The Singular Anomaly.*

23 Untitled newspaper clipping dated February 3, 1903. Signed 'W. F. B.'

24 Colby, *op. cit.*

25 *Ibid.*

26 Cornwallis-West, *op. cit.*

27 June 12, 1905.

28 'C-B' once said of the Boer War: 'When is a war not a war? When it is carried on by the methods of barbarism in South Africa.' He received a letter from an indignant clergyman who called him 'a cad, a coward and a murderer'. E. T. Raymond, *Portraits of the New Century.*

29 The Duke of Devonshire appeared with Winston at a Free Trade meeting in Manchester and asked him whether he felt nervous before he made a speech. Winston said yes. 'I used to,' said the Duke, 'but now whenever I get up on a platform, I take a good look around, and as I sit down, I say, "I never saw such a lot of damned fools in my life," and then I feel better.' Barbara Tuchman, *The Proud Tower.*

30 Undated letter to Leonie, Moreton Frewen Papers.

31 Lord Riddell quoting Jennie in Jack Fishman's, *My Darling Clementine.*

32 Undated letter to Leonie, Moreton Frewen Papers.

33 *Ibid.*

34 Literary editor Frank Harris, a good friend of Lord Randolph's, served as Winston's literary agent for this book. Winston had asked Harris to do this, telling him, in a letter, that he thought Harris had written (in a book) the best short biography of Lord Randolph that he had ever read.

35 Undated letter in 1905, Shane Leslie papers. Randolph S. Churchill, *op. cit.* Marsh later quoted Pamela Plowden (who became Lady Lytton) as saying, 'The first time you meet Winston, you see all his faults, and the rest of your

life you spend discovering his virtues.' Christopher Hassall, *Edward Marsh*.

36 *Ibid.*
37 Letter to Leonie, January 6, 1906.
38 Douglas Plummer, *Queer People*.
39 Randolph S. Churchill, *op. cit.* The young Duke of Westminster had married George's sister Shelagh in 1901. He was one of the richest men in Britain Besides estates in Cheshire and Scotland, he owned 600 acres of rich property in London, and an estate in Flintshire that covered 30,000 acres. His home there was one of the great houses in England. When his bride first saw it, she said, 'It's not a house; it's a town.' Shelagh and the Duke were separated in 1910, but the Duke maintained a pension for the Cornwallis-West family. Michael Harrison, *Lord of London*.
40 October 18, 1906.
41 October 20, 1906.
42 *Ibid.*
43 October 13, 1906.
44 Anita Leslie, *Jennie: The Life of Lady Randolph Churchill*.
45 Undated letter. Jack, not Winston, acted as the peacemaker in Jennie's fights with George.
46 Daisy, Princess of Pless, *op. cit.*
47 *Ibid.*
48 *Ibid.* Jennie and George often visited Daisy at her palace in Furstenstein where George had every kind of hunting and fishing facility. Winston once asked George to get him an invitation to go there.
49 Ethel Smyth, *What Happened Next*. Ethel Smyth, *Streaks of Life*. Ethel Smyth's brother served in the same regiment as Winston at the Battle of Omdurman. Her brother wrote to her: 'Winston taught us a new game called bridge, which comes from Constantinople, and is like whist, but more of a gamble.' Her brother also said of Winston, 'If he lives, he'll be a big man some day.' Miss Smyth also became an ardent suffragist, and from a jail cell window she once used her toothbrush to direct the singing of a chorus of sympathizers.
50 Smyth, *What Happened Next*.
51 Undated clipping.
52 She was born on Christmas Day and received much publicity when Robert Louis Stevenson publicly offered her his birthday as her own. He gave his birthday (November 13) to her in the form of a legal document. The document stated that the birthday should be celebrated by feasting and singing, and, if this was not done, then the birthday would be taken away from Miss Ide and given to whoever was President of the United States at that time.
53 They were married in 1912.
54 Interview with Alice Roosevelt Longworth.
55 Leslie, *op. cit.*
56 Seymour Leslie, *The Jerome Connexion*.
57 Within a year the bailiffs moved into Brede Place and auctioned off all the furniture which Mrs Jerome had saved through the Paris Commune. Jennie was there to bid for and buy a few things that Clara really wanted to save. Clare wrote to her mother: 'Poor old Mumkin, she made a choice, she chose

her husband and sacrificed her children, she must abide by her choice.' Allen
Andrews, *The Splendid Pauper*.

58 Jennie and her niece Clare were so close that even as early as February 1904,
Clare wrote to her mother, 'Tell Auntie J. that the chief reason I want to come
to London is to see her.' Letter from Moreton Frewen Papers. And another
time, 'Give my tenderest love to Aunt Jennie. . . .' Andrews, *op. cit.*

59 Undated letter; Hassall, *op. cit.*

60 August 21, 1907.

61 August 22, 1907.

62 August 30, 1907.

63 September 26, 1907. Randolph S. Churchill, *Winston S. Churchill*, Companion
Volume II, Part 2.

64 Lady Randolph Churchill, *op. cit.*

65 September 17, 1907.

66 September 26, 1907.

67 November 14, 1907.

68 *Ibid.*

69 August 8, 1908.

70 November 21, 1907.

71 January 3, 1908.

72 November 26, 1907.

73 November 21, 1907.

74 January 2, 1908.

75 December 13, 1907.

76 December 5, 1907.

77 December 13, 1907.

78 November 21, 1907.

79 *The Times*, November 22, 1907.

80 November 21, 1907.

81 December 5, 1907.

82 December 16, 1907.

83 December 28, 1907.

84 December 30, 1907.

85 January 3, 1908. Letter on Ladies Automobile Club stationery from Claridge's
Hotel, Moreton Frewen Papers.

86 January 7, 1908.

87 January 12, 1908.

88 On January 4, 1882, Jennie had recorded, 'Went out and breakfasted with
Blanche Hozier.'

89 Randolph S. Churchill, *Winston S. Churchill, Young Statesman, 1901–14.*

90 *Ibid.*

91 *Ibid.*

92 *Ibid.*

93 April 16, 1908.

94 After the loss at Manchester, Austen Chamberlain, son of Joseph Chamberlain, wrote to his stepmother (Chamberlain's third wife): 'Have you heard the
stock exchange telegram to Winston on the morrow of his defeat? . . . It ran:

"To Winston Churchill, Manchester: 'What's the use of a W.C. without a seat?' " ' Randolph S. Churchill, *Winston S. Churchill, Young Statesman.*

95 *Ibid.*
96 *Ibid.*
97 August 7, 1908.
98 August 8, 1908.
99 August 7, 1908.
100 Anita Leslie, *op. cit.*
101 August 17, 1908.
102 August 20, 1908.
103 The wedding account in *The New York Times*, September 13, 1908, mentioned that '. . . the list of wedding presents fills two columns of small type.' The presents included some duplicates: twenty-five candlesticks, twenty-one inkstands, twenty silver bowls, fifteen vases, fourteen silver trays, eight sets of salt cellars, and ten cigarette cases. Ralph G. Martin and Richard Harrity, *Man of the Century: Churchill.*
104 *Ibid.*
105 *Current Literature*, December, 1908.
106 *Ibid.*
107 September 13, 1908. In his only novel, *Savrola*, Winston had this dialogue between his hero and heroine:
    'Do you despise me very much?' she asked.
    'No,' he replied, 'I would not marry a goddess.'
    'Nor I,' she said, 'a philosopher.'
    Then they kissed each other, and thenceforth their relationship was simple.

CHAPTER 20

The Victoria & Albert Museum has a comprehensive collection of research materials on the history of the British Theatre. This ranges from old playbills to clippings and photographs, much of it not readily available elsewhere. In addition to the library at the British Museum, there is also a very good collection of books on the subject at the University of London.

Some of the more useful books for the purpose of this chapter include: William Archer, *The Old Drama and The New*; A. E. Wilson, *Edwardian Theatre*; Ernest Short, *Sixty Years of Theatre*; Roger Manvell, *Ellen Terry.*

The most pertinent, and therefore the most necessary, to our subject is Mrs Patrick Campbell's autobiography, *My Life & Some Letters.*

Of much less value, but worth checking, is A. E. W. Mason, *Sir George Alexander and St. James' Theatre.* Max Beerbohm, *Around Theatres*, has a review of Jennie's play that should be read. Again, the richest material comes from the newspapers, both in London and Glasgow, where there are not only reviews and articles about the plays, but several excellent interviews with Jennie. This is particularly true of the London *Daily Chronicle.*

Copies of Jennie's plays can be found in the Lord Chamberlain's Office at St James's Palace. They cannot be removed, but they can be consulted.

1 October 13, 1908. Also on the front page was a three-column picture of Jennie. She signed the article 'Jennie Cornwallis-West'.

2 Mrs Belmont's comments were sent in a telegram to the Paris *Herald*.

3 Quoted in the *Express*, October 21, 1908.

4 *Daily Chronicle*, July 8, 1909.

5 The play was *Guy Dornville*, and had opened on January 6, 1895.

6 *The New York Times*, January 6, 1895.

7 George Bernard Shaw's first play, *Widowers' Houses*, opened in 1892. Shaw also had the experience at one of his early plays of hearing some booing. During a curtain call after an opening performance, in response to a solitary loud boo, he said, 'Personally, I agree with my friend in the gallery, but what can we two do against an audience of such a different opinion.'

8 William Archer, *The Old Drama and the New*.

9 Daisy, Princess of Pless, *From My Private Diary*, entry on April 28, 1904.

10 In conversation with Sidney Low, as reported by Major Desmond Chapman-Huston, *The Lost Historian*.

11 However, her last play, *The Flute of Pan*, was a financial failure and it cost her £1,000 a week to keep it going. It had also been booed on its opening night. 'When, on the first night, I heard that discordant note, I resolved to go on. It simply fired my resolve. I had no tears at that moment. But when I had finished, and the audience applauded; when the audience took it off my shoulders upon theirs – then I broke down.' Unidentified article, dated November 19, 1904.

12 *The Era*, July 3, 1909, reported that Shaw's new play, *The Showing Up of Blanco Posnet*, had been forbidden by the censor, probably because the leading character too closely imitated a living person. Shaw's letter of protest said that he himself was so successfully imitated on stage that a near relative actually believed the actor to be Mr Shaw himself. The reference was to John Tanner in *Man and Superman*, in which Shaw represented himslf as a Don Juan, with all the women running after him. But in his stage directions, he described the character as a megalomaniac. In July 1909 Shaw also wrote a skit called *Press Cuttings*, for a private performance, in which he had the Prime Minister disguised as a suffragette shrieking, 'Votes For Women!' – in order to get from Downing Street to the War Office.

13 A. E. Wilson, *Edwardian Theatre*.

14 Duse was a guest of Jennie's at Salisbury Hall one weekend. In his memoirs George Cornwallis-West recalled that Duse had just broken with her lover, the Italian writer and soldier Gabriele D'Annunzio, and she arrived in tears. Jennie took her into the drawing room 'where she remained the whole day, visited at intervals by the lady members of our party.' Neither George nor any of the male guests ever managed to speak to her.

15 Ellen Terry remembered a dinner at the Beef Steak Room where Jennie arrived 'wearing a dress embroidered with green beetles' wings'. That dress was the origin of the idea for Lady Macbeth's robe that Ellen Terry later wore. Roger Manvell, *Ellen Terry*.

16 Ernest Short, *Sixty Years of Theatre*.

17 Although their correspondence became a part of literary history, George Bernard Shaw never consummated his love affair with Mrs Pat.

18 George Cornwallis-West, *Edwardian Hey-Days*.

19 Anita Leslie, *Jennie: The Life of Lady Randolph Churchill*.

20 Winston also read his mother's play and wrote to her. '... The last half is the best. There are many criticisms I could make on detail and structure. But I will keep these until the business of production has actually been undertaken. Then I will give any assistance in my power....' May 14, 1909.

21 Mrs Patrick Campbell, *My Life & Some Letters*.

22 Jennie's play might well have been inspired by the legal ado of Mrs W. K. Clifford, a well-known author who had written a play called *The Likeness of the Night*, which Jennie had published in the *Anglo-Saxon Review*. The play was to be produced in London a year after its publication in the *Review*. However, at the same time another play was produced which had an astonishing resemblance to her own. The main difference between the two plays was that in one play the former mistress commits suicide by poison, and in the other play, the wife does so by drowning. Mrs Clifford, a woman of social distinction, refused to sue for plagiarism and still produced her own play. Both plays were successful. A. E. W. Mason, *Sir George Alexander and St. James' Theatre*.

23 Interview in the *Daily Chronicle*, July 8, 1909.

24 Play filed as No. 34 in Lord Chamberlain's Office; date of licence, July 12, 1909.

25 Letter to Leonie, June 27, 1909; Leslie, *op. cit.*

26 Patrick Campbell, *op. cit.*

27 Unidentified clipping, dated July 7, 1909.

28 Unidentified clipping, undated.

29 July 10, 1909.

30 Max Beerbohm, *Around Theatres*. Beerbohm was not only one of the foremost critics of his time, but he was also a noted essayist and caricaturist. He succeeded George Bernard Shaw as dramatic critic for the *Saturday Review*. His most famous book was *Zuleika Dobson*, a satiric fantasy about Oxford.

31 *Daily Chronicle*, July 8, 1909.

32 Seymour Leslie, *The Jerome Connexion*.

33 June 1910.

CHAPTER 21

All the books about the Edwardian era previously mentioned are necessary reading for the history of King Edward's final years. Of these, though, the best are Sir Frederick Ponsonby's *Recollections of Three Reigns* and J. B. Priestley's *The Edwardians*. Margot Oxford's *More Memories* has an intimate anecdote and André Maurois, *The Edwardian Era*, has a few sidelights of interest, as have the memoirs of Daisy, Princess of Pless. Philippe Julian, *Edward and the Edwardians*, also has some pertinent quotes. The Edwardian period is one of the few areas in this book where outside published material is better than personal letters.

The only copy of the *Shakespeare Memorial Souvenir of the Shakespeare Ball* that I could find was at the office of the publisher that printed it privately. It is not listed in the British Museum. It is, however, an indispensable source for information about the ball. Jennie edited the *Memorial Souvenir*, and the leading writers of the day, including George Bernard Shaw, contributed to it. Newspapers and magazines gave colourful descriptions of the ball, but they do not compare to the *Souvenir*.

About the Shakespeare's England Exhibition at Earl's Court, the biography of *Frederick Edwin, Earl of Birkenhead, by His Son*, has an amusing anecdote, and Charles B. Cochran, *The Secrets of a Showman*, has some interesting facts, as does George Cornwallis-West's book. The best material, however, comes from the London newspapers and magazines, which are rather full in their descriptions. A good American account can be found in *The Literary Digest* (July 6, 1912).

Neither George Cornwallis-West's nor Mrs Patrick Campbell's book deals very deeply with his divorce from Jennie. Jennie herself was most circumspect about it, even in her letters. The newspapers are the best sources, and their accounts are detailed. George Cornwallis-West's novel, *Two Wives*, is interesting indeed in its obvious parallels.

In this connection, a fascinating book to read is Alan Dent, *Bernard Shaw and Mrs Patrick Campbell: Their Correspondence*, and the Moreton Frewen Papers provide a great deal of tangential information.

1 Quoted in J. B. Priestley, *The Edwardians*.
2 The office of Home Secretary concerned itself with everything from strikes to prison reform.
3 E. T. Raymond, *Uncensored Celebrities*, wrote: 'The American strain in Winston might be traceable for his lack of simplicity, a taste for self-advertisement, uncommon in any English aristocrat, an unbridled tendency to naked "bossing" of any "show", and for any and other peculiarities which make Mr Churchill a difficult man for any plain Englishman to "get on with". It may also have imparted an extra touch of recklesness and speculation, while giving him also a doggedness which was not visible in his father. It may also have given him a certain impatience for what he once called "Tory claptrap".'
4 Undated letter, Peregrine Churchill Papers.
5 Sir Frederick Ponsonby, *Recollections of Three Reigns*.
6 'I say God bless her for it. Few women would have done it,' Daisy, Princess of Pless, wrote in her diary. *From My Private Diary*.
7 Ponsonby, *op. cit.*
8 The German Emperor had once said of Edward VII, 'A Satan — you cannot imagine what a Satan. . . .' André Maurois, *The Edwardian Era*.
9 Margot Asquith saw Queen Alexandra after King Edward's funeral and the two of them 'cried together'. Trying to divert the Queen's attention, Margot commented how touched everyone was at the sight of the King's dog Caesar at the funeral. 'Horrid little dog!' said the Queen. 'He never went near my poor husband when he was ill!' Margot said she remembered having seen the dog lying at the King's feet after his death. 'For warmth, my dear,' answered the Queen. But Margot added that the dog had put his paws on the coffin before they screwed the top down. 'Curiosity, my dear,' said the Queen. Margot Asquith, *More Memories*.
10 That evening Winston dined with the Asquiths, and proposed a toast to the

new King. 'Rather to the memory of the old,' replied Lord Crewe. Philippe Julian, *Edward and the Edwardians.*

11 Unidentified clipping.

12 Jennie had bought the lease of the house of her friend and former neighbour in Great Cumberland Place, Madame Melba. She then completely redecorated it and soon had a long list of friends wanting to rent it from her. The *Daily Chronicle*, January 11, 1910.

13 August 4, 1909, Randolph S. Churchill, *Winston S. Churchill*, Companion Volume II, Part 2.

14 Unidentified clipping.

15 Seymour Leslie, *The Jerome Connexion.*

16 H. Hamilton Fyfe, in *Shakespeare Memorial Souvenir of the Shakespeare Ball.* Among other contributors were George Bernard Shaw and G. K. Chesterton. Jennie edited the contributions and wrote the introduction.

17 *Frederick Edwin, Earl of Birkenhead, by His Son.*

18 George Cornwallis-West, *Edwardian Hey-Days.*

19 January 18, 1912.

20 May 27, 1912.

21 *The Literary Digest*, July 6, 1912.

22 F. E. Smith, later the Earl of Birkenhead, was to be one of the knights in the jousting. 'The armour was brought to him for his inspection. It looked very heavy and very hot; at the last moment, he decided to substitute his brother Harold.' *Frederick Edwin, Earl of Birkenhead, by His Son.*

23 Mrs Patrick Campbell, *My Life & Some Letters.*
    A much quoted line of the time came from an American dancer, Harry Pilcer: 'Every woman wants something another woman has got.' Ernest Dudley, *The Gilded Lily.*

24 *The Times*, October 25, 1922.

25 George Cornwallis-West, *Two Wives.*

26 *Ibid.*

27 He travelled as far as Canada for a big game hunt. On the journey home he was operated on for appendicitis in New York. *Daily Telegraph*, August 29, 1911.

28 Anita Leslie, *Jennie: The Life of Lady Randolph Churchill.*

29 Charles B. Cochran, *The Secrets of a Showman.*

30 Cornwallis-West, *Two Wives.*

31 Unidentified clipping, March 4, 1913.

32 February 23, 1913.

33 Unidentified clipping.

34 Jennie's friend Pearl Craigie had once told Sidney Low that she always tried to 'hear' her dialogue when writing it, almost as if she were writing for music. Major Desmond Chapman-Huston, *The Lost Historian.*

35 Unidentified clipping.

36 Filed as 1483 in Lord Chamberlain's Office. Date of licence: March 8, 1913.

37 Letter from Ayot St Lawrence, Welwyn, dated June 9, 1913. Alan Dent, *Bernard Shaw and Mrs Patrick Campbell: Their Correspondence.*

38 *Ibid.*, letter dated August 11, 1913.

39 Quoted in *The Sunday Express*, July 31, 1955.

40 April 24, 1913, Randolph S. Churchill, *op. cit.* Companion Volume II, Part 3.

41 Unidentified clipping, July 16, 1913.

42 *The Times*, November 13, 1913.

43 It was described by *The Times* as a Brazilian diamond necklet.

44 Lady Randolph Churchill, *Small Talks on Big Subjects*.

45 Anita Leslie, *op. cit.*

46 Moreton Frewen Papers.

47 *The Daily Mirror* (April 17, 1914) printed a photograph of the marriage certificate, on which it described George West as 'The divorced husband of Jennie Cornwallis-West, formerly Churchill (widow).

CHAPTER 22

I was fortunate enough to talk to Montagu Porch before he died, and his comments were vital to my description of his marriage to Jennie. There is also an excellent interview with Porch in the *Daily Express* (December 21, 1959). Other views of the marriage come from interviews with other members of the family: Lady Betty Cartwright, the Baroness Cedestrom, Peregrine Churchill, Sir Shane Leslie, among others, as well as from Mrs Hadley Hucker, Mr Porch's closest friend, who had invaluable comments. The Oswald Frewen Papers are very valuable, and there are also some relevant comments in the magazines and newspapers of the time and some books. Of course, Jennie's letters add a necessary dimension.

Absolutely necessary to this chapter are the essays in Jennie's book, *Small Talks on Big Subjects*. The essays are important for what they show of Jennie's ideas and for her illustration of them with specific incidents.

A key anecdote about Jennie's influence on Winston's painting can be found in A. Wallais Myers, *Memory's Parade*. Winston's own book, *Painting as a Pastime*, should also be read in this context.

World War I is treated well in C. L. Mowat, ed., *The New Cambridge Modern History*, Second Edition, among many other works. The dramatic story of the Dardanelles comes from E. Ashmead Bartlett, *The Uncensored Dardanelles*.

The information about Prince Kinsky during World War I is based primarily on correspondence with his nephew, Prince Clary, in Venice, and the books of George Lambton, one of Kinsky's close friends in England. Lambton's book, *Men and Horses I Have Known*, has an excellent account. There are also several interviews with Lambton about Kinsky in the London newspapers of the time, as well as a very good letter which Lambton wrote to the editor of the *Daily Dispatch* (December 16, 1919) dispelling some rumours about Kinsky. There are also a few references in Jennie's letters.

The Oswald Frewen Papers are of particular importance, as Oswald most conspicuously enjoyed his aunt's company at this time and faithfully recorded everything in his diary.

Of varying worth are a number of other books: Viscount Grey of Fallodon, *Twenty-Five Years*, Volume II; Lady Cynthia Asquith, *Diaries, 1915–1918*; Lady Violet Bonham Carter, *Winston Churchill As I Knew Him*; Bernard Falk, *He*

Laughed in Fleet Street; Lady Diana Cooper, *The Rainbow Comes and Goes*; John Lehmann, *I Am My Brother*.

It was very interesting and often amusing to read the issues of the Lagos *Standard* from the period when Montagu Porch was there.

1 *Daily Express* interview, undated clipping.
2 Interview with Sir Shane Leslie.
3 Anita Leslie, *Jennie: The Life of Lady Randolph Churchill*, letted dated July 24, 1914.
4 *Ibid.*, July 28, 1914.
5 *Ibid.*, August 1, 1914.
6 Viscount Grey of Fallodon, *Twenty-Five Years*.
7 Interview with Sir Shane Leslie. In a book review of Mrs Patrick Campbell's Letters, *The Times Literary Supplement* referred to George as a 'well-bred scalawag, whose taste was as bad as his debts'. Sir Shane defended George in a letter to the editor (May 5, 1961) saying, 'I don't think his *taste* was so bad, for he married on his own merits the two most remarkable women of the day, and as for the *debts* – he paid them up for both ladies.' After the death of Mrs Pat Campbell, in 1940, George married Mrs Georgette Hirsch, a close friend of the former Barbara Hutton. His business firm had gone bankrupt in 1917, with liabilities of £150,000. In 1920, George filed for personal bankruptcy. In 1951, after a lingering illness, he shot himself. He was seventy-six years old. He had called his years from 1895 to 1914 'a supreme vintage'.
8 This was during *Pygmalion*'s American tour. George played the part of Doolittle. He later also wrote an unsuccessful one-act play in which his wife starred.
9 Jennie mentioned to Leonie that 'Charles' had sent her a Cartier clock for Christmas (December 30, 1913).
10 George Lambton, *Men and Horses I Have Known*.
11 Letter to the editor, *Daily Dispatch*, December 16, 1919. Lambton also mentioned in this letter that 'it afforded him [Kinsky] great pleasure that 4 of his old favourites were carrying two generals. . . .'
12 Correspondence between author and Prince Clary.
13 *Ibid.*
14 May 17, 1914. Oswald Frewen Papers, courtesy of Mrs Oswald Frewen. During Jennie's divorce proceedings, Oswald had written in his diary, 'I wonder if he [George] will insult *her* if it appears in the press. It is strange, because in many ways he is chivalrous and charming too.' When Oswald was at sea on the H.M.S. *Plorus*, he recorded hearing somebody yell, 'Old Winston's got a nice old mug, like his Ma!'
15 Lady Maud Warrender, *My First Sixty Years*.
16 Lady Randolph Churchill, *Small Talks on Big Subjects*.
17 *Ibid.*
18 *Ibid.*
19 Warrender, *op. cit.* Rupert Grayson, in his autobiography, *Voyage Not Completed*, tells an anecdote about the hospital. 'This hospital happened to be conveniently next door to our London home at 100 Lancaster Gate. In spite of this, or because of it, Mother wanted to make a hole through the wall so I could

be passed through on a stretcher as soon as I was well enough to spend the day with her and the family. She even called on a builder to survey the job. Finally Lady Randolph Churchill, Winston's mother, who was in charge, persuaded her that it was a little impractical. . . .'

20 *Harper's Bazaar*, January, 1915.

21 Interview with Peregrine Churchill.

22 *Ibid.*

23 *Ibid.*

24 When Winston's daughter Diana was chistened in 1909, Jennie had sent an old coral rattle and Winston wrote to her, 'I remember it well.'

25 Warrender, *op. cit.*

26 Interview with Sir Shane Leslie.

27 October 20, 1914. Other earlier entries in the Oswald Frewen diary:
   'Lunched with Chicken [Clare] and Aunt Jane . . . then Clemmie came and Aunt Jane took her out. . . .'
   '. . . We went down to Winston's to have lunch with him and Clemmie. . . . Aunt Jane, Winston and Pa had a spirited argument on Free Trade and other topics. . . .'
   '. . . Went to Ladies Imperial Club, dined with Ma and Aunt Jennie, and went to first night of Strauss' "Salome" at Covent Garden. . . .'
   'Woke up Jack Churchill. We then brutally threw over poor Aunt Jane, and we got two stalls for the "Wall Stream". . . .'
   '. . . Aunt Jane lent us her car. . . .'
   '. . . Jennie gave me a lift to Buckingham Hotel where Ma smoked a cig. . . .'

28 This had been a most intimate friendship. Sir John Fisher often began his letters, 'Beloved Winston', and signed them, 'Yours till a cinder!'

29 Sir Basil Liddell Hart believed that the whole operation was 'a sound and far-sighted conception marred by a chain of errors in execution almost unrivalled even in British history.' C. L. Mowat, ed., *The New Cambridge Modern History*, Second Edition, Volume XII.

30 E. Ashmead Bartlett, *The Uncensored Dardanelles*.

31 Seymour Leslie, *The Jerome Connexion*; letter dated October 12, 1915.

32 July 4, 1915, Anita Leslie, *op. cit.*

33 Winston S. Churchill, *Painting as a Pastime*.

34 A. Wallais Myers, *Memory's Parade*.

35 Winston S. Churchill, *op. cit.*

36 Lady Violet Bonham Carter, *Winston Churchill As I Knew Him*.

37 August 27, 1916; Seymour Leslie, *op. cit.*

38 *Frederick Edwin, Earl of Birkenhead, by His Son*.

39 Undated letter. Shane Leslie records in his book *Long Shadows*, that in 1915 Jennie made a bet that Winston would become Prime Minister.

40 *The Times*, April 5, 1916.

41 She was so nicknamed in the press – presumably because of her dark complexion.

42 Lady Cynthia Asquith, *Diaries, 1915–1918*.

43 January 1913.

44 Article dated January 4, 1917.

45 Interview with the Baroness.
46 *Ibid.*
47 Interview with Lady Betty Cartwright.
48 Christopher Hassall, *Edward Marsh.*
49 Oswald Frewen Papers.
50 Interviews in Glastonbury with Mrs Hadley Hucker, Mr Scott-Stokes and several others who have requested to remain anonymous.
51 *Glastonbury and its Abbey* (Bristol, T. O. Elworthy n.d.).
52 Some of these implements are still in the British Museum.
53 Interview in the *Daily Express*, December 21, 1959.
54 Lagos *Standard*, March 13, 1912.
55 An article in the Lagos *Standard* (March 13, 1912) noted that a pet leopard was loose on Bishop Street in Olowogbowo. The article said: 'Must have belonged to a white man, for no native would keep such a brute.' It had injured several people.
56 *Daily Express* interview.
57 Anita Leslie, *op. cit.*
58 Undated letter, Peregrine Churchill Papers.
59 Lieut.-Col. C. A'Court Repington, *The First World War, 1914–1918*, Volume 2.
60 Bernard Falk, *He Laughed in Fleet Street*, tells of his visit to Downing Street to see the new Prime Minister, Lloyd George. 'I shared the coal-fire in the hall with Lady Randolph Churchill, a dainty and attractive figure in becoming furs.'
61 She said the same thing to Oswald Frewen, who recorded in his diary on February 9, 1917: 'Aunt Jane to tea, complaining that her children never come near her – "The fierce ingratitude of children's love," as Goethe used to say.'
62 She was also listed as one of the organizers of a Grand Bazaar at Claridge's Hotel for the 'Victims of the War'.
63 Hassall, *op. cit.*
64 Interview with Baroness Cedestrom.
65 'It is quite wrong if anyone has got the idea that I have put my maids into military uniform', she told a reporter for the *Daily Express*, March 15, 1915.
66 Lady Diana Cooper, *The Rainbow Comes and Goes.*
67 She was the daughter of George Burke of San Francisco, and the niece of a California millionaire whose money she inherited. Her husband was the grandson of the founder of Cunard Steamship Lines. He was most interested in fox-hunting and horses, and she was not. She once confided to a friend, 'No man has ever said to me, "I love you." ' John Lehmann, *I Am My Brother.*
68 Seymour Leslie, *op. cit.*; undated letter.
69 Article dated January 19, 1918.
70 *Ibid.*
71 Seymour Leslie, *op. cit.*
72 Repington, *op. cit.*
73 *Daily Express* interview.
74 Anita Leslie, *op. cit.*
75 Repington, *op. cit.*
76 *Daily Express* interview.
77 Conversation with author.

CHAPTER 23

All the material relating to Montagu Porch that was mentioned in the preceding chapter is also applicable here. There are some West African magazines that offer a little general background, but not much. The *West Africa* of July 2, 1921 did have some quotable comments.

The most intimate material about Jennie at the close of her life again comes from interviews with and memoirs of her family and her closest friends. There was also a massive amount of world-wide press comment at her death.

The Duchess of Sermoneta in *Sparkle Distant Worlds* provides a good description of Jennie's final visit to Rome. Lady Horner's testimony at the inquest of Jennie's death was most graphic and detailed and was fully reported in the London press. The best personal accounts come from Sir Shane Leslie, in interview, letters, and books, and from the diary of Oswald Frewen.

But the best summary of her life in a single sentence is the quotation at the end of this book, which is from H. H. Asquith, *Letters of the Earl of Oxford & Asquith to a Friend*, First Series, 1915–1922.

1 She was the former Adele Grant of New York who married the 7th Earl of Essex. Lady Cynthia Asquith, *Diaries, 1915–1918*.
2 *Ibid*. George Moore had had a frustrated love affair with Pearl Craigie. She had collaborated with him in writing two acts of a comedy, then abandoned it – but they had never been lovers. Susan L. Mitchell later described Moore as a lover who 'didn't kiss but told' (Malcom Brown, *George Moore: A Reconsideration*). Moore's caustic comments about Jennie may have been prompted by jealousy of Pearl Craigie's deep feeling for her. Vineta Colby, in her excellent chapter about Pearl Craigie in *The Singular Anomaly*, refers to George Moore's 'vicious scandal-mongering'.
3 *Bystander*, July 6, 1921.
4 *Daily Express* interview, December 21, 1952.
5 Undated letter, Peregrine Churchill Papers.
6 The correspondent for *West Africa*, July 2, 1921, also noted, 'She took steps to get a passport to Nigeria, but Downing Street refused because of the submarine peril. . . . She pleaded over and over again, but permission was withheld.'
7 Oswald Frewen Papers, Brede Place, Sussex.
8 Undated letter, Peregrine Churchill Papers.
9 Interview with Mrs Hadley Hucker in Glastonbury.
10 *Evening News*, May 31, 1918.
11 Jennie wanted her name changed by deed poll. She also felt it wouuld help if the King received her at Court as Lady Randolph Churchill, thereby giving the change of name his royal approval. 'I have made a name for myself,' she wrote. Letter to Leonie, January 20, 1919. Seymour Leslie, *The Jerome Connexion*.
12 Interview with Mrs Hucker.
13 Conversation with Mr Porch.
14 Interview in *Daily Express*.
15 *Letters of F. Scott-Fitzgerald*.

16 Interview with Sir Shane Leslie.

17 George Lambton, *Men and Horses I have Known.*

18 Interview in *Daily Express.*

19 March 8, 1921.

20 The pilot was Sir Sefton Brancker and the plane was a DH4.

21 Interview with Lady Altrincham, the daughter of Jennie's close friend, Lady Islington. She also remembered Jennie asking her, 'What beaux do you have?' She recalled that Jennie used a lot of American expressions. 'In a sense, she never grew up,' Lady Altrincham said. But then she added, 'Jennie smoothed the ruffled feathers of the friends whom Winston irritated. . . . If Jennie had been a man, she would have been a real power.'

22 Unidentified clipping. Jennie was an inveterate first-nighter. Her particular penchant was for grand opera and Russian ballet.

23 *Daily Chronicle,* February 16, 1921. In a magazine article she wrote called 'Art in Dress', she commented that the chief aims of art in dress should be 'either the artistic blending of colours, the clever effects that make beautiful the greatest simplicity, or the most gorgeous and sumptuous raiment.' And she added, 'The abominable practice of wearing long skirts for the street is dying out. . . . The sight of a woman dragging her gown in the street, sweeping up the filth and collecting millions of microbes, is a revolting spectacle; and yet with a long skirt the only alternative is to hold it up, a practice which induces cramp in the arm, as well as cold fingers in winter, and gives a decidedly un-graceful walk and attitude.' Jennie also wrote that 'Mme de Pompadour once, for a wager, wore radishes in her hair at a court festivity.' At the next, most of 'the court ladies made their heads into market gardens'. *Munsey's Magazine.*

24 Clare Sheridan, *Nuda Veritas.* Clare never saw Jennie again. In America, she did a bust of Charles Chaplin, and there were strong international rumours that the two planned to marry. Chaplin denied this to the press by saying, 'Why, she's old enough to be my mother.'

25 From an article by Caseur in *The Dispatch,* June 30, 1921.

26 April 20, 1921; Seymour Leslie, *The Jerome Connexion.*

27 The Duchess of Sermoneta, *Sparkle Distant Worlds.*

28 Duchess of Sermoneta, *op. cit.* John Singer Sargent, the noted American artist, had drawn a portrait of Jennie at the turn of the century. Winston much admired this portrait, not only because of the subject, but also because of the technique. Sargent was an excellent musican and he and Jennie played duets together. He became so much in demand as a portrait artist that he was quoted as saying, 'Ask me to paint your gates, your fences, your barns, which I would gladly do, but *not the human face!*' Article by Richard Ormond in John Hadfield, ed., *The Saturday Book – 25.*

29 Duchess of Sermoneta, *op. cit.*

30 Lady Horner's husband had been killed in World War I. She had a fluent know-ledge of Greek, did expert needlework, and had the reputation of having one of the most interesting literary salons in London.

31 She had always disliked stairs and once actually drew plans for a stairless villa. It had a circular ground floor area, off which all the rooms opened. *Irish Society,* July 30, 1921. She had also always felt that women should be escorted

to any dining room. In *Small Talks on Big Subjects* she wrote, 'Surely it is a time-honoured courtesy which is as graceful as it is convenient; I might slip on the stairs. . . .'

32 Belfast *Telegraph*, July 1, 1921.

33 *Evening News*, June 18, 1921.

34 *Ibid*.

35 Oswald Frewen Papers.

36 Correspondence with Violet Pym, Eleanor Warrender's niece.

37 Oswald Frewen Papers.

38 Bourke Cockran died two years later.

39 Oswald Frewen Papers.

40 *Ibid*.

41 The same church where Winston and Clementine were married.

42 Shane Leslie Papers.

43 Porch married again in 1926 and lived in Italy until his wife's death in 1938. He then returned to Glastonbury and rented a room from Mr and Mrs Hadley Hucker on Main Street. A neighbour quoted Porch as saying, 'I've had such a lot of trouble. My first wife died, my second wife died, and now my dog has died.' Porch himself died in November 1964.

44 Lieut.-Col. C. A'Court Repington, *The First World War, 1914–1918*, Volume 2.

45 H. H. Asquith, *Letters of the Earl of Oxford & Asquith to a Friend*, First Series, 1915–1922.

INDEX

and Switzerland with J, 67–8; his
indecisiveness and career, 94–6, 118;
Christmas at Blenheim, 96, 119; to
Versailles, 101; and Cockran (in
Paris), 104; gets a bicycle, 106; in a
duel, 110; and J and his future,
117–19; his eyesight, 121, 195; and
W, 118, 120; to Germany, 121; joins
Oxfordshire Yeomanry, 121; and a
place in the City, 129, 165, 236, 250;
and W's capture, 190; commissioned
in South African Light Horse, 195; in
Natal, 198–200; wounded, and on
Maine, 201–2; describes action at the
front, 202; still in South Africa, 211;
on General Carrington's staff, 213;
still dependent on J for moral
support, 214; and J's wedding,
217–19; and George C-W, 224, 305;
to live with J and George, 235, 236;
praised by his commanding officer,
235; and Salisbury Hall, 259; and
panic on stock exchange, 269; and
'Goonie', 277–8; and W's wedding,
279; his first child, 280; and J's
divorce, 307, 310; in World War I,
316; advises J on finance, 338; and
J's fatal illness, 342, 343; mentioned,
17, 18, 32, 41, 49, 51, 75, 76, 79, 82,
83, 89, 90, 93, 101–4 *passim*, 112,
113, 122, 133, 193, 197, 240, 242
Churchill, John (son of Jack, J's
grandson), 66
Churchill, Lady Norah, 221
Churchill, Peregrine (J's grandson), 280,
319
Churchill, Lady Randolph (Jennie, later
Mrs George Cornwallis-West):
personal details, 19–20, 23, 30–8
passim, 40–1, 47, 52, 86, 257–8,
301–2; and Lord Randolph's illness
and death, 17–18; life-long lover of
see Kinsky, Count; sons *see*
Churchill, Jack *and* Churchill,
Winston; her 'illusions', 17–18; and
legacy, 18; and Lord Rosebery, 22,
247; 'the new woman', 22–3; and

Prince of Wales *see* Prince of Wales;
Alexandra, Princess of Wales and,
24–5; and Colonel Brabazon, 25,
26–7; and W and a cavalry regiment,
25, 26–7; in mourning, 27–8; in
Paris, 28–50, 101; and Consuelo
Iznaga, 31; and Americans in Paris,
30–2; and Consuelo Vanderbilt, 32,
96; and Curzon, 32, 78, 94, 138–9,
142–3, 229, 236; and tributes to her
beauty, 33; an embarrassing episode,
33–4; her house in Paris, 34, 39, 44,
45, 62; and her sisters, 34–5; and
Paul Bourget, 36–8; and Marquis de
Breteuil, 36–7, 101; and W and
Bourke Cockran, 39; and Cockran
see Cockran, Bourke; and Ireland,
41; and New York, 42; and politics,
42–4; riding and cycling, 46; and
Paderewski, 47; and painters and
painting, 49; and her mother's
illness, 49–50; qualities inherited
from her father, 51; and her
mother's death and burial, 51–2, 63;
Oscar Wilde, and, 52, 53, 55; and
Edward Carson, 52; and the
Bruce-Pryce affair, 59; and
Labouchère and the racing scandal,
58–9; and her sons' need of
fatherliness, 59–60; and England and
America, 63; Aix-les-Bains, 64, 176;
and letters from her sons, 64–5; and
W and politics, 65; and Lord
Salisbury, 65; and her two sons,
65–7, 117–19; Switzerland, 67; Isle
of Wight (Cowes Week), 67; and
Kitty Mott, 67; and the future
Duchess of Sermoneta, *q.v.*, 68; and
Hugh Warrender, 68; in London
house-hunting, 68; her house in
London, 68–9, 71, 83, 89, 127; and
Nellie Melba, 69; and W's trip to
America and West Indies, 69–71, 72,
74, 75; on tact, 70; and Sir Henry
Drummond Wolff, 70–71; and
Primrose League, *q.v.*, 71; and W's
career, 71, 82, 88, 94, 98–100, 104,

Churchill Lady Randolph (*cont.*)

Lansdowne, 217; her second marriage and her sons, 217–19; wedding fixed, 218; reported in *New York Times*, 220–2; some guests named, 220–2; and the honeymoon, 222, 224–5; some wedding presents, 222; comments on the marriage, 223; C-W family absent, 223; seeks acceptance of her marriage to George, 224; finance of, on re-marriage, 225; social status and title, 229; weekend parties, 230; sacks Lane, 231–2; invites Jack to live with her and George, 235, 236; receives £300 from W, 239; hears W's maiden speech in House of Commons, 239; at Blenheim (as Mrs Cornwallis-West), 241; and Edward VII, 242, 245, 294, 325; back in royal society, 242–3; and the Tweedmouths, 244; wants W to marry, 245; at Edward's VII's Coronation, 245; and Alice Keppel, 246; on 'Decorative Domestic Art', 246–7; her royal honours, 249; and end of *Anglo-Saxon Review*, 249; and Clare Frewen, 250; social activities of, 250–1; and a motor car, 251; her second marriage begun well, 251–2, 257, 258–9; and a costume party, 252; and a social and professional women's club, 253; and Tariff Reform, 253–4; and W's political chores, 254; and his change of party, 255–6, 265; still handsome at fifty, 257–8; her new home at Salisbury Hall, 258–9, 261; and Marquis de Soverat, 260; and Lord Randolph's family, 261–2; deaths of her friends, 262; and W's victory at Manchester, 264–5; decorates W's house, 265; and Edward Marsh, 265–6; and Consuelo (Duchess of Marlborough), 267; and George's financial troubles, 267; Cannes, 267; and Daisy Pless, *q.v.*, 268; and Ethel Smyth, 268–9; and Alice Roosevelt,

269; lonely, 269–70, 328, 333, 339; reports to W (abroad) on home politics, 271, 274; and her *Reminiscences*, 271–2, 282–3, 302; and Jack and 'Goonie', 272–3; and George's financial crisis, 273–4; short of money and in ill health, 273–5; and John Murray, 274; economizing, 274; and W's servant, Scrivings (dead), 275; and W and Clementine, 275–6, 278; at W's wedding, 279; becomes a grandmother twice in 1909, 280; in international society again, 280; on society in New York and London, 280–2; play-writing, 283; and Mrs Patrick Campbell, *q.v.*, 284–5, 288–9, 308; her first play *His Borrowed Plumes*, 285–92; supper party at Ritz (guests named), 288; important activities, 292; and an informal Cabinet in her house, 293; and Edward VII's death, 294, 337; buys and sells houses profitably, 296, 331, 337; and W and prison reform, 296; her second play *The Bill*, 297, 307; and a National Theatre, 297–9; Shakespeare Memorial Ball, 297–9; and F. E. Smith, 299; at Naval Review (1911), 299; and exhibition 'Shakespeare's England', 299–303, 304; and a jousting tourney, 302–3, 304; her second marriage breaks up, 305; and divorce, 305–7, 309–12 *passim*; and a Mediterranean cruise with W and Clemmie, 309; travelling in Europe, 311; launches H.M.S. *Benbow*, 311; and speech afterwards, 311; abandons surname 'Cornwallis-West' and adopts 'Spencer-Churchill', 312–13; and Leonie Leslie, *q.v.*, 314, 315; depressed, 314, 315, 318, 333; and Hugh Frewen's wedding, 314; still attractive at sixty, 314–15; and Porch *q.v.*, 314, 328–30, 334, 335–6, 337–9; and World War I, 315, 316; entertains troops with Maud

Churchill Lady Randolph (cont.)
Warrender, 318; her good stories,
318; and hospital work for soldiers,
318, 319; and her grandchildren,
319–20, 323; and Peregrine's music,
319; and her nephews and nieces,
320; and W and Ashmead Bartlett,
321; and W and the Dardanelles,
321–2; painting lessons, 322; and W
going to the Front, 323; and her
daughters-in-law, 323; her Essays in
Pearson's Weekly (and later in book
form), 323–5; on marriage in
wartime, 324; on extravagance, 324;
on suffragettes, 324; on Pearl
Craigie, 325; loses a toe, and is
burgled, 325; and scandal at the War
Office, 326–7; and Baroness
Cedestrom, 327–8; and Lady Betty
Cartwright, 328; accepts her age,
328; but is still lonely, 328; and
Garvin, 330; and Lord Frazer, 330;
and Asquith, 330; and Repington,
330, 334; and Austin Harrison, 330;
and her sons, 330; and other male
escorts, 331; translates a French
book, 331; and edits *Women's War
Work*, 331; her 'Outlook' luncheons,
331; and Mrs Lloyd George's Welsh
Memorial Matinée, 331; and W and
Ivor Novello, 331; interior decorating,
331–2; her female footmen and
waiters, 332; and Maud Cunard, 332;
and W's 'caterpillars' (tanks,
A.F.V.s), 332–3; writes political
articles for *Daily Chronicle*, 333; and
deaths of Breteuil and Cust, 333;
becoming cynical, 333; her third
marriage to Porch, 334–6, 337–9;
meets Porch's mother, 336; tries to
get permission to join Porch in
Africa, 336; keeps her former name,
336–7; her Armistice Party, 337; in
France with Porch, 337–8; and
Kinsky's death, 338; consults Jack,
338; lonely again, 339; flying, 339;
and a film, 339; and a Welsh singer,
339; controversial, 339; and Clare
Sheridan, 339–40; her various
activities, 340; to Florence and Rome
with W and Clemmie, 340; still
beautiful at sixty-seven, 340–1;
her faith in W, 341; Mells Manor,
Somerset, 341; fractures and loses a
leg, 341–3; death of, 343; her coffin,
described by Oswald Frewen and
Winston, 343–4; her funeral, 344;
obituary, 345

Churchill, Lord Randolph Henry
Spencer: illness and death of, 17–18;
estate and will of, 17–18; and Prince
of Wales, 24; and Winston, 25, 26,
59–60 and his mother-in-law, 51;
and homosexuality, 59; and J and
his political campaigns, 166; a
gambler, 170; idolized by his
mother, 171; his engagement to
Jennie, 174, 176, 181; and J and a
revolver, 200; his barouche, 225; in
Parliament, 239; his grave at Bladon,
344

Churchill, Randolph (J's grandson), 320
Churchill, Winston Leonard Spencer-
(J's elder son, later Sir Winston
Churchill): needs J's support, 17; and
Count Kinsky, 18; qualities inherited
or acquired from J., 19, 39; his
affection, admiration and respect for
J., 25, 27, 33, 49–50, 60, 89, 115, 117;
and his father, 25, 26, 59–60; at
Sandhurst, 25; commissioned in 4th
Hussars, 27; on 'solitary trees', 27;
and Bourke Cockran, 39, 72–4, 75–6,
80–1, 88, 89, 94, 104, 190, 226, 234,
255, 263–4; and Clara Jerome's
illness, 49–50; Edward Carson, and
politics, 52; scandals concerning,
55–9; and Bruce-Pryce, 55–9; and the
racing scandal, 58–9; his memento of
his mother, 60; meets several royal
and prominent people, 64; and Mrs
Everest's death, 64–5; discusses
politics, with J., 65; on Lord
Salisbury's government, 65; and

meets Lord Salisbury, 65; and politics as a career, 65; 'tone deaf', 66; in Paris, 67; longs for home again, 68; proposes visiting America and West Indies (Cuba), 69–71; and Sir Henry Drummond Wolff, 70–1; on Bourke Cockran (later), 72, 73–4; reports a *cause-célèbre* in New York, 75; on America and Americans, 76; to Cuba *via* Florida, 77; on the Cuban War (1895), 79–80; back in New York, 79; returns to England, 80; and Spanish leaders, 80; writes about Cuba in *Saturday Review*, 80; on Irish Home Rule, 81; praised by Cockran, 81; at Aldershot on signalling course, 82; at Mrs Adair's party, 82; on Willoughby and Morley at J's house, 82–3; finances of, 84; at Deepdene, 87; and South Africa, 87–8; India, 88–94 *passim*, 113–15 *passim*; his demands on J, 89–90, 94, 97–100, 113, 115–17, 127, 213, 225, 240, 245, 271; his Indian letters to and from J, 89, 90, 92–3, 94, 95, 98–9, 113–16, 120–4; and polo, 90, 92–3; and butterflies, 90; his reading in India, 90–2; and a racing pony, 92–3; his daily life in India, 93–4; criticizes American and British politicians, 94; and Balfour, 94, 111–12; and Curzon, 94; and Jack's career, 95–6, 120–21; 'Duchess Fanny' on, 96; and Pamela Plowden, 97, 165–6, 213, 214, 215, 234–5, 245; and service in Egypt, 97–9, 116, 123, 130, 131–2, 140–1; reprimanded by J, 102–3; elected to Turf Club, 104; and Graeco-Turkish War, 104; asks for photo of J as 'Theodora', 110, 115; seconds Jack in duel, 110; first public address, 111; and Sir Bindon Blood, 112, 115; on war on North-West Frontier, 113; his reports to *Daily Telegraph*, 114; under fire at the front, 113, 114; and Kincaid-Smith, 115; and a political

career, 116; and his book, *The Malakand Field Force*, 116, 122–3, 126, 130; loves praise, 121; and his mother's finances and his own, 121–2, 128; and Prince of Wales, 123, 126, 141–2; short story by, 127; first novel of, 127; to Cairo and England, 127; and J's 'writings', 127; plans his stay in England, 128; to address public meetings, 128; and Prince of Wales' influence, 129–30; his magazine articles, 130; and Bradford meeting, 128, 130–1; his speech impediment, 131; on official resentment at J's efforts to get him to Egypt, 131; attached to 21st Lancers for Sudan Campaign, 132; with Kitchener's force in Sudan, 140–1; fights in and descibes battle of Omdurman, 140–1; G. W. Steevens on, 141; his friction with Kitchener, 141; and J's review, 148–9, 150, 151, 152, 153, 160–1, 212, 246; and John Lane, 148–9; and Sidney Low, 154; resigns Army commission and joins J on *Anglo-Saxon Review*, 160–1; and his book *The River War*, 165, 200; and political opportunity, 165; at Oldham, 165–8, 213, 225–6, 236, 254, 255; opposes Conservative Party on Clerical Tithes Bill, 167–8; defeated at Oldham, 168; comments by political leaders, 168; gives political dinner in London, 169; and Joseph Chamberlain, 169; and Labouchère, 169; and J's gambling, 169–70; and George C-W, 171–2, 176–7, 182, 224, 225, 226; and J's engagement to George, 174, 176–7; and war in South Africa, 179–80; war correspondent, 180, 195; captured by Boers, 189–90, 204; escapes, 191; Boers' description of, 191; and J's hospital ship, 194; and Jack's commission in S.A.L.H., 195; and *Maine* at Durban, 199; in Natal with J and Jack, 199–200; on Jack's wound

Churchill Winston (*cont.*)
and conduct under fire, 201–2; and a reconnaissance, 202; to Ladysmith, 206; at S.A.L.H. Brigade HQ, 206; on *Maine*'s departure from Durban, 206–7; still in South Africa, 211; and his book on Boer War, 213; and a lecture tour in USA, 213; and a play, 213; Bloemfontein and a narrow escape, 214; returning home, 217; and J's wedding, 217–19, 220, 221, 223; demands haberdashery, 225; wins Oldham election, 226; his first public lecture in London, 227; in America for lecture tour, and Mark Twain's introduction, 234; in Ottawa, 234; and Earl of Minto, 234; finances of, 235; and presents for South Africans who assisted his escape, 236; Queen Victoria's death and Edward VII's accession, 236–7; gives J £300, 239; his maiden speech in Parliament, 239; and J's finances, 240; seeing less of J, 244–5; and marriage, 245; at Balmoral, 249; and Free Trade and Protection, 253, 255, 261, 263; and his political interests, 254–5; joins Liberal Party, 255–6, 263–4; his Glasgow speech, 261; at Salisbury Hall, 261; his biography of Lord Randolph, 261, 265, 276; Under-Secretary of State for Colonies, 264, 269, 329; wins parliamentary seat at Manchester, 264–5; his house in London, 265, 271; his new private secretary, Edward Marsh, 265–6; and Duke of Westminster and George's finances, 266–7; and 'Sunny' and Consuelo separated, 267; Daisy Pless and, 268; and Aunt Clare Frewen, 270; his trip to East Africa, 270–1; and J's *Reminiscences*, 271–2; and Jack's love affair, 272; wants suite at Ritz, 275; President of Board of Trade, 275; and Clementine Hozier, 275–6, 277–8; his gaucherie with women,

276; defeated at Manchester, 277; stands for Dundee, 277; attacks Conservative Party, 277; on Socialism and Liberalism, 277; and Jack's wedding at Abingdon, 277–8; marries Clementine Hozier, 278–9; on honeymoon at Blenheim and in Italy, 279; his first child, 280; and J's first play, 289; and House of Lords, 293; Home Secretary, 293; his financial advisor, Cassel, *q.v.*, 294; and J's profitable dealings in house property, 296; and prison reform, 296; First Lord of the Admiralty, 299; 'the son of his mother', 301; and J's divorce, 307; invites J on trip to Mediterranean, 309; and J and H.M.S. *Benbow*, 311; and war in Europe, 315–16; mobilizes the fleet, 316; his son, Randolph, 320; and Dardanelles episode, 320–1; Ashmead Bartlett on, 321; on leaving the Admiralty, 321, 322; and painting, 322; and World War I, 323; and J and Porch, 329, 334; Minister of Munitions, 330; and Ivor Novello, 331; and tanks (A.F.V.S.) as weapons of war, 332–3; and Scott Fitzgerald, 338; Secretary of State for War and Air, 338; with J and Clemmie to Italy, 340; and J's amputation, 341; and J's haemmorhage and death, 343–4

Clara *see* Frewen, Clara

Clemenceau, Georges, 270, 331

Cleveland, President Grover (of USA), 44–5, 77

Cliveden (W. W. Astor's estate on the Thames), 85, 86

Cockran, Mrs Bourke (Anne, *née* Ide), 269, 343

Cockran, William Bourke: personal details, 39–40, 72; and Jennie, 39–50 *passim*, 61, 63–4, 72, 74, 75, 79, 80, 100, 101, 150–51, 212, 269, 343; and Winston, 39, 72–4, 80–81, 88, 89, 94, 104, 190, 226, 234, 255, 263–4; on Ireland, 41; and Tammany Hall,

Kreisler, Fritz, 244
Kruger, President Paul (of Transvaal), 169, 179–80

Labouchere, Henry du Pre, MP, 58–9, 169
Ladysmith (Natal), relief of (Feb. 1900), 199–200, 205, 206, 235
Lambton, George, 317, 338
Lancers, 9th: 87; 21st: 132, 140
Landowne, Marquess of, 58, 59, 88, 185, 207, 217, 222
Lane, John (publisher): personal details, 146–7, 154; and J's *Review*, 146–9 *passim*, 152–3, 155–7 *passim*, 164, 173, 211–12, 231–2
Langtry, Lillie, 187–8, 296
Lawson, Edward, 112, 122
Lavery, Sir John (artist), 322, 340, 344
Le Gallienne, Richard, 22, 53–4
Leeds, Mrs W. B., 300
Leiter, Mary *see* Curzon, Marchioness
Leonie *see* Leslie, Leonie
Leslie, John (J's brother-in-law), 35, 51, 139, 246, 276
Leslie, Leonie (*née* Jerome, J's younger sister): in Paris, 34; and J and Clara, 35; her legacy, 52; and the future Duchess of Sermoneta *q.v.*, 68; comfortably off, 83–4; at a costume ball, 111; and J's letter to Prince of Wales (not posted), 125; expecting another baby after 11 years, 211; and J's marriage to George C-W, 221; her advice (ethical), 250; and W's change of party, 265; and Edward Marsh, 265; alternating between Ireland and London, 269; and German Emperor, 274; and J's depression after divorce, 314, 315; and George C-W, 316; and her castle in Ireland, 333, 334; and J and Porch, 334; and J's last illness, 342; and J's death, 343; mentioned, 17, 50, 67, 69, 193, 194, 208, 213, 265, 285, 288, 297, 315, 316, 321, 330, 332, 336, 340

Leslie, Norman (J's nephew), 316
Leslie, Seymour (J's nephew), 35, 255–6, 270, 292, 333, 344
Leslie, Shane (J's nephew): on J, 33, 315; and Prince of Wales, 35–6; on Moreton Frewen, 42; on parties given by his mother and aunts, 83; on Queen Victoria's Diamond Jubilee, 107; on Queen Victoria's Death, 237–8; mentioned, 60, 139, 224, 253, 269, 293, 303, 338, 343, 344
Liberal Party, 255, 263–4, 277, 293
'Lily, Duchess' (widow of 8th Duke of Marlborough and later wife of Lord William Beresford), 92, 97, 222, 229
Lloyd George, David, 255, 293, 330
Lodge, Professor Sir Oliver, 156, 157
London: a sombre city, 337; Albert Hall, 297–9, 300; Berkeley Square, 337; Bolton Street, 265; Bond Street, 274; Brook Street, Hanover Square, 325, 331; Central London (tube) railway, 129, 228; Chesham Place, 68; Clarges Street, 317, 318; Claridges Hotel, 189; Connaught Place, 69; Cromwell Road, 323; Devonshire House, 107, 111; Dover Street, 313; Earl's Court, 300–3 *passim*; Empress Hall, 303; Great Cumberland Place, 68–9, 71, 82, 83, 89, 118, 127, 236, 250, 270; Grosvenor Square, 322; Hicks' Theatre, 289; His Majesty's Theatre, 312; influenza epidemic (1895), 49; Kensington Gardens, 331; Kensington Square, 312; Lancaster Gate War Hospital, 319, 337; Lansdowne House, 69; Mermaid Tavern, 303, 304; Norfolk Street, 305, 306; political élite (1896), 82; Ritz Hotel, 275, 288, 331; St Margaret's Church, Westminster, 278, 344; Soho, 24; Sunderland House, 267; Westbourne Street, 331–2, 333, 342
Longmans (publishers), 122, 123, 126, 213
Longworth, Nicholas, 269

423

MASADA
Herod's Fortress and the Zealots' Last Stand
Yigael Yadin

'Yigael Yadin's great book, whose splendour matches that of
the achievement which it records and that of the heroism it
commemorates'
Times Literary Supplement

£1·50 *Illustrated*

THE ARTS OF CHINA
A Short History
Michael Sullivan

A balanced picture of the meaning and beauty of the arts of
China from the Stone Age to the present day.

£1·75 *Illustrated*

1815
Ugo Pericoli
Supplementary text by Michael Glover

A spectacular display of the costumes worn by the armies at
the battle of Waterloo, accompanied by an exciting narrative
of the campaign.
A SPHERE BOOK £2·95 *Illustrated*

THE ENGLAND OF ELIZABETH
The Structure of Society
A. L. Rowse

Although in the second half of the sixteenth century England had a population of only five million, the achievements of Elizabethan society made the English the most creative of modern peoples, not only in the field of discovery, but also in commerce, literature, drama and the arts.

In this volume A. L. Rowse paints a portrait of this remarkable society, of the classes forming it, of its government and administration, law and religious organisation, education and the social order, resulting in one of the major historical works of our time. He has written a sequel entitled *Expansion of Elizabethan England* which depicts the extension of Elizabethan society at home and overseas.

'A *tour de force*. It is the work of one passionately in love with his subject, and endowed with the insight and imagination that enable him to recreate what he himself calls "a living age"'
English Historical Review

£1·50 *Illustrated*

THE LIFE AND DEATH OF MOZART
Michael Levey

An elegant biography of a musical genius who produced outstanding works while beset by poverty, ill-health and a constant battle for recognition. A perceptive, intelligent and poignant book, this scholarly biography contains splendid vignettes of the period and places in which the composer lived and worked, together with a readable non-technical appreciation of his music.

CARDINAL 90p *Illustrated*

POMPEII AND HERCULANEUM
Marcel Brion

This brilliant recreation of the bustling life of these famous cities, destroyed by the eruption of Vesuvius in A.D. 79, provides an unique insight into everyday life in a Roman province. And drawing on eye-witness accounts, M. Brion vividly portrays the disasters that overwhelmed the cities, as well as describing the fascinating story of their rediscovery and the still incomplete work of excavation.

CARDINAL £1·00 *Illustrated*

THE WORLD OF THE PHOENICIANS
Sabatino Moscati

A comprehensive survey of the culture, history and social life of the Phoenicians, one of the most enigmatic peoples of antiquity.

£1·00 *Illustrated*

THE CELTIC REALMS
Myles Dillon and Nora Chadwick

The definitive work on the history and culture of the Celtic peoples, from their prehistoric origins to the Norman invasion of Britain.

£1·25 *Illustrated*

THE WASHING OF THE SPEARS
Donald E. Morris

An enormously readable account of the rise and fall of the Zulu nation – Mr. Morris brings history to life in his description of the advance of the Boers into the vast interior of Africa and their confrontation in 1824 with the Zulus – then the most formidable nation in black Africa.

CARDINAL £1·00

THE EMERGENCE OF MAN
John E. Pfeiffer

An outstanding narrative of the science of prehistory – a dramatic exploration from the first primitive diggings to the latest computer and electro-implantation techniques of the evidence of human evolution.

CARDINAL £1·00 *Illustrated*

THE ENGLAND OF ELIZABETH
A. L. Rowse

A wonderful, panoramic view of the remarkable Elizabethans, whose achievements in literature, commerce, and discovery were equalled only by the forceful characters of their leading figures – Drake, Raleigh, Bacon, Shakespeare and, indeed, the Queen herself. How did this small, close-knit society achieve so much? This striking book is endowed with insight and imagination – a 'living age' recreated by a great historian.

CARDINAL £1·50 *Illustrated*

THE EXPANSION OF ELIZABETHAN ENGLAND
A. L. Rowse

What were the domestic and global impacts made by the Elizabethans? This acclaimed work traces the effects of the Elizabethans on the backward Celtic borderlands of Cornwall, Wales and Ireland; the oceanic voyages and the foundation of the first American colonies; and the long struggle with Spain at sea and on land. Famous events also fall into place in the story: the first trade with Russia; the defeat of the Armada; the search for the North-West passage and the first contacts with India and the Far East.

CARDINAL £1·50 *Illustrated*